MW00426623

AFTER PAUL LEFT CORINTH

AFTER PAUL LEFT CORINTH

*The Influence of Secular Ethics
and Social Change*

BRUCE W. WINTER

WILLIAM B. EERDMANS PUBLISHING COMPANY
GRAND RAPIDS, MICHIGAN / CAMBRIDGE, U.K.

© 2001 Wm. B. Eerdmans Publishing Co.
All rights reserved

Wm. B. Eerdmans Publishing Co.
255 Jefferson Ave. S.E., Grand Rapids, Michigan 49503 /
P.O. Box 163, Cambridge CB3 9PU U.K.

Printed in the United States of America

05 04 03 02 01   7 6 5 4 3 2 1

Library of Congress Cataloging-in-Publication Data

Winter, Bruce W.
After Paul left Corinth: the influence of secular ethics and
social change / Bruce W. Winter.
p.   cm.
Includes bibliographical references and index.
ISBN 0-8028-4898-2 (pbk.: alk. paper)
1. Bible. N.T. Corinthians, 1st — History of contemporary events.
2. Ethics — Greece — Corinth — History. 3. Ethics in the Bible.
4. Corinth (Greece) — Social conditions. 5. Corinth
(Greece) — Social life and customs.   I. Title
BS2675.5.W56 2001
227'.2067 — dc21

00-052150

www.eerdmans.com

Contents

CONTENTS

Contents

CONTENTS

Contents

Introduction

The aim of this book has been to gather for the first time all relevant extant material about life in the first century in the Roman colony of Corinth from literary, nonliterary, and archaeological sources. This has been done in order to understand what happened to its Christian community after Paul left Corinth, for the origin of many of the problems Paul dealt with in 1 Corinthians can be traced to culturally determined responses to aspects of life in Corinth.

It is self-evident that the Corinthian Christians had long been inhabitants of Corinth before they became Christians. After becoming followers of Christ they did not automatically abandon the culturally accepted ways of doing things in Corinth. They could only have contemplated responding differently if they had been specifically taught alternative ways to do so. The opening part of Chapter 1 argues that Paul appeared to have provided no apostolic traditions for the problems raised in 1 Corinthians while he was there, except for those he specifically cites in 1 Corinthians 11:17-34 and 15:3-4. He also commends them for observing all the traditions that he had delivered (11:2). The significance of the role that cultural conditioning continued to play in their lives as Christians after Paul left Corinth has been either ignored or underestimated in explaining the reason for their subsequent difficulties. Their problems are reflected in the questions they raised with Paul by letter and firsthand reports. The exploration of culturally determined responses to situations will be the focus of the Part I of this book.

Part II explores the social changes that occurred in the city of Corinth between Paul's departure and the time he received their letter of request and the verbal reports. These changes included severe grain short-ages, the shifting of the Isthmian Games back to their original site after almost a century in Corinth, and the introduction of a new federal impe-rial cult for the province of Achaea centred in Corinth. There was also pos-sibly a withdrawal of the provision of kosher meat in the official market. All these changes had a substantial impact on the life of the emerging Christian community.

The task involved in gathering this information is not as straightfor-ward as it might seem. A growing chasm has developed between the work of 'classical' ancient historians and that of papyrologists, epigraphists, and mainstream archaeologists.[1] The reason, in part, is the degree of specialisa-tion that epigraphists and papyrologists have developed and also the scien-tific sophistication of archaeology which has led its practitioners to define themselves in a negative way as 'not ancient historians'. If it is the case that there is a widening information gap because various subdisciplines of an-cient history have gone their own way and do not always communicate the fruits of their labours in readily understood terms to one another, then the problem has become all the more acute for those engaged in research in those parts of the New Testament which intersect most clearly with the first-century world.

Much of the evidence from inscriptions and archaeological discoveries has not been harvested for Corinthian studies in spite of over a century of excavations on the site. These first began with Dörpfeld in 1886[2] and have been continued by the American School of Archaeology since 1896. The last collection published by the American School was of those Corinthian in-scriptions discovered up to 1950, and was produced by J. H. Kent in 1966. Even though archaeologists have continued to inform scholars about further discoveries at Corinth in the journal *Hesperia,* with notable exceptions little new information has seeped through and the significance of the pre-1950s has not always been grasped for studies on 1 Corinthians.[3] It seems some-

---

1. See R. Lawrence and J. Berry, eds., *Cultural Identity in the Roman Empire* (London: Routledge, 1981), p. 1.

2. C. M. Cobern, *The New Archaeological Discoveries and Their Bearing upon the New Testament and upon the Life and Times of the Primitive Church,* 7th ed. (New York and Lon-don: Funk and Wagnalls, 1924), p. 497.

3. For the extensive use of inscriptions to drawn a profile of those who held public of-fice in Corinth see A. D. Clarke, *Secular and Christian Leadership in Corinth: A Socio-Historical and Exegetical Study of 1 Corinthians 1–6* (Leiden: E. J. Brill, 1993), Appendix A.

what ironic that one of the motivating factors for raising funds for the Corinthian excavations of this Roman colony was its early Christian connections.[4] The *TLG* on a CD-ROM has given access to most of the Greek corpus which has been largely unexploited for linguistic purposes, and 1 Corinthians has its own set of challenges. The Duke collection (*PHI* #7) for nonliterary sources has likewise been underutilised by New Testament scholars.

It is my hope that these studies will bring to life something of the first-century social and religious context of Corinth and help illuminate the text of 1 Corinthians for the reader. The explorations in both sections of the book have proved to be fruitful and have taken the author down paths of interpretation that certainly would not have occurred to him when he began his work. The book is not an exposition of the letter nor does it explore *how* Paul argued his response to the situation — a distinction only occasionally acknowledged and observed in the breach by some scholars and sometimes confused by others. This confusion has arisen partially because of the ambiguous use of the term 'background'. That the social, cultural, and religious background of Corinth was primarily Roman in Paul's day is argued from the evidence in Chapter 1. When Paul wrote he drew on his 'background' of the Old Testament, intertestamental Judaism, and early Christian traditions. 1 Corinthians bears witness to that background with a number of citations from the Old Testament, and even more allusions to it and to the traditions of Jesus. Therefore it may be helpful to observe the distinction by speaking broadly of the cultural background of the Corinthian Christians and the theological background of Paul which he drew on as he framed his answers to the Corinthians' letter and the reports he heard of their conduct. This book is about the cultural background of the Corinthians and not that of Paul. The author plans a sequel on Paul's resolution of the problems created by conflict, compromise, and change in the Corinthian church. That work will discuss the role of Paul's theological background and the nature of his rhetorical arguments in 1 Corinthians as he responded to their problems.

4. 'At a time when the Christian religion and Christian studies still played a central role in American cultural life, Corinth's association with St. Paul's mission and the development of early Christianity provided another major incentive for raising financial support for what the School hoped would be long-term excavations'; S. L. Dyson, *Ancient Marbles to American Shores: Classical Archaeology in the United States* (Philadelphia: University of Pennsylvania Press, 1998), p. 85. I am grateful to Dr. D. J. W. Gill for this reference and the one to Sir William Ramsay in n. 6.

Questions about hermeneutics are much to the fore in New Testament studies. It would seem that nothing could be more important as one of the critical first steps in interpretation than to seek to locate an ancient text such as 1 Corinthians in the first-century horizons of its religious, cultural, and social contexts. Only then does it seem appropriate to proceed with further questions of interpretation. One of the tendencies in hermeneutics has been to ignore what may be known of the cultural horizons of the writer and readers of the first century. This book should help to understand 1 Corinthians in its first-century social and religious settings.

D. Tidball made an important observation on the application of sociological models to the ancient world.

> Historical sociology is a branch of the discipline that has special difficulties all of its own. Sociologists can usually support their theories by devising some way of testing them such as through surveys, interviews or participant observation. But for obvious reasons the members of a bygone age are not available to be investigated in this way! The researcher therefore will inevitably be less assured than they would be in contemporary sociology.[5]

Just as modern sociological studies test their hypotheses with field trials, so too New Testament sociological studies must assemble all the available extant data that literary and nonliterary sources yield, along with archaeological evidence. Their 'field trials' must make sure that the same social conventions upon which such theories are built applied in first-century society in order to validate the use of a particular sociological theory. This will go some way to prevent New Testament sociological studies from falling into what E. A. Judge has aptly designated 'the sociological fallacy'. The research in this book should assist those who wish to see how appropriate a sociological model might be for illuminating an aspect or aspects of 1 Corinthians and other letters written to those cities which shared Corinth's dominant cultural setting.

The same applies to anthropology and the New Testament, for first-century Roman society in particular involved itself in sophisticated conventions and highly complex relationships. The Mediterranean was not culturally monochrome. Therefore anthropological insights brought to

---

5. D. Tidball, *An Introduction to the Sociology of the New Testament* (Exeter: Paternoster, 1983), p. 21.

bear on New Testament studies need to evaluate thoroughly the evidence we do possess about the nature of a particular society in which the early Christian message took root, lest they be guilty of a fallacy similar to that which sometimes occurs in the use of sociology.

The author, whose doctoral dissertation was undertaken in a department of ancient history after graduate studies in New Testament, has sought to make judicious use of the Book of Acts in this study on 1 Corinthians. While this is currently a very unfashionable approach among New Testament scholars, it is certainly not among ancient historians; they gladly adopt it where such a parallel exists with a corpus, and information about activities of its author is found elsewhere: the measured use by ancient historians of the letters of Cicero in dealing with the Catiline rebellion and the only slightly later history of it by Sallust; the corpus of Favorinus and the careful assessment of the comments about him by a contemporary, Gellius, and a later writer, Philostratus; and the much later case of the use of the letters of Julian and the history of Ammianus provide a paradigm for New Testament scholars. The approach of ancient historians must question the judgement of those who would dismiss outright as unscholarly any use at all of Acts in work on a letter in the Pauline corpus.[6] For those who would reject *a priori* this approach on the careful use of companion sources, the only chapters affected in this book are the last two, and then only partly.

I must express my appreciation to Dr. Frederick Finks, who kindly

---

6. For a discussion of these ancient authors and conclusions see T. Hillard, A. Nobbs and B. W. Winter, 'Acts and the Pauline Corpus I: Ancient Literary Parallels,' in A. D. Clarke and B. W. Winter, eds., *The Book of Acts in Its Ancient Literary Setting,* The Book of Acts in its First Century Setting (Grand Rapids and Carlisle: Eerdmans and Paternoster, 1993), I, ch. 8. See the famous Sarum Lectures of 1960-61 by A. N. Sherwin-White on *Roman Society and Roman Law in the New Testament* (Oxford: Clarendon Press, 1963), where he uses Acts in discussing matters related to his field of expertise in Roman law. His defence of this approach should commend itself to New Testament scholars, pp. 172-85. See also the work of a classicist turned New Testament scholar, C. J. Hemer, *The Book of Acts in the Setting of Hellenistic History,* WUNT 49 (Tübingen: J. C. B. Mohr [Paul Siebeck], 1989). Of Sir William Ramsay (1851-1939), J. G. C. Anderson said, 'The value of his New Testament studies is enhanced by the fact that he approached the subject, not as a theologian, but as a Roman historian first in the working of Roman institutions in the provinces and possessing an intimate knowledge of the country which figured so prominently in the early history of the church'; L. G. Wickham Legg, ed., *Dictionary of National Biography 1931-40* (Oxford: Oxford University Press, 1949), p. 728.

extended an invitation to deliver Fall lectures at Ashland Theological Seminary. It began this particular work on Corinth. The shape of the book was thus conceived and with expansions and additional chapters has finally come to fruition. A number of scholars have commented on particular chapters and have helped greatly in thinking through the issues. Dr. Richard Hayes made an important observation on an early version of Chapter 8, as did Professor Graham Stanton and Dr. Loveday Alexander at Dr. Philip Esler's anthropology group at a British New Testament Conference. Professor E. A. Judge kindly read through Chapter 5. Professor Stanton's graduate seminar in the Divinity Faculty of Cambridge University also provided an opportunity to discuss élitist ethics and 1 Corinthians 15:29-34. If I have failed to recognise the help of others, I sincerely apologise for that oversight.

It was not until I was appointed a Visiting Research Professor for two Spring semesters at Beeson Divinity School, Samford University, last year and this year that I was able to complete the book. I appreciated the invitations of Drs. Randy Todd, Paul Holloway, and Tom Berg to read in embryo Chapters 1 and 3 to faculty and members of Samford University at two joint seminars, that of the Classics and Religion Departments and Beeson Divinity School, and the University's Cumberland Law School at its seminar on Religion and Society in 1999. I record these invitations and teaching opportunities to share aspects of this book in order to express appropriately my appreciation to the participants and the forums they afforded me to refine my arguments. I do not shelter under the substantial expertise of any of those named above in order to shore up any deficiencies in my own research, but I do wish to express my thanks.

There can be no soloists in New Testament studies, for it is a collegial activity where we depend on the labours of scholars past and present. This is all the more so when seeking to make use of the work of ancient historians for New Testament studies. The bibliography indicates the indebtedness that I owe to epigraphists, archaeologists, and numismatists as well as to other ancient historians. The length of this book has precluded me from interacting in any detail with the vast body of literature on the text of 1 Corinthians by New Testament scholars. I trust that authors of the latter will not conclude that their interpretations are not known or that they have gone unappreciated on a New Testament book which has been the subject of my interest for a quarter of a century. What I have sought to do is to place before New Testament colleagues extant evidence of Roman

Corinth and its surroundings and thereby seek to make sense of the origins of the issues Paul deals with in 1 Corinthians.

In sending forth this work, I would also wish to acknowledge my indebtedness to Dr. Charles Williams II and Dr. Nancy Bookidis from the Corinthian archaeological site for their willingness to share the fruits of their research and their crucial insights into Roman Corinth. Dr. Ronald Stroud kindly made available his unpublished edition of curse inscriptions from the temple of Demeter and Kore, which was located on the slopes of the Acrocorinth, and invited comments on his translations.

This volume is another produced under the aegis of the Institute for Early Christianity in the Graeco-Roman World, Cambridge. This centre is committed to a study of the intersection of the New Testament with that world including Judea in order to understand the cultural settings of early Christianity.

Once again I have to thank my wife for her help with the manuscript, and also Professor Gerald Bray and Mrs. Judith Taylor for their willingness to read the final draft. This book is dedicated to our children, Elizabeth and Andrew, and their spouses, Orlando and Mary Lee. They have, by the grace of God, set themselves to serve in the Christian ministry in *imitatio Christi* (1 Cor. 11:1).

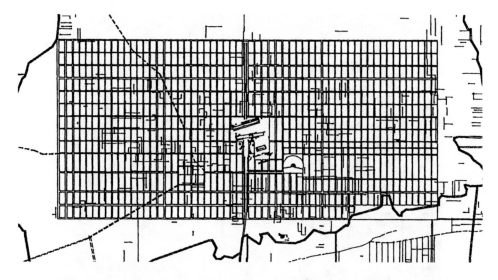

Plate 1 Corinth was laid out according to Roman town planning in 44 B.C. with 125 acres of urban land, with streets measuring 120′ × 120′, or 240′, or 360′, or 480′. It used the foundations of Greek Corinth's civic buildings, but its forum was built 3′ above the Greek agora. The reconstructed town plan is reproduced by courtesy of Professor D. G. Romano. (See pp. 8-9 on the Roman culture of Corinth.)

Plate 2 The longest inscription in first-century Corinth was erected in A.D. 43 to Junia Theodora, who was a civic patroness. On her role and that of Phoebe see pp. 199-200. (Reproduced by permission of the American School of Archaeology in Corinth.)

Plate 3 Augustus is portrayed as a priest offering a sacrifice with his toga covering his head. On Christian men covering their head to pray see p. 122. (Reproduced by permission of the American School of Archaeology in Corinth.)

Plate 4 The Roman statue tradition represented the Barbarian with medium-length hair. (Reproduced by courtesy of the Museum of Classical Archaeology, Cambridge University.) See p. 132.

Plate 5 In the Forum a prisoner in the great Facade of the Captives commemorating Roman's conquest of Corinth in 146 B.C. in Corinth's Forum were portrayed as weak, i.e., effeminate with a curly hairstyle. (Reproduced by permission of the American School of Archaeology in Corinth.) On the disgracing of men with long hair see p. 132.

Plate 6 A wife wearing the veil associated with marriage. (Reproduced by permission of the Museum of Classical Archaeology, Cambridge University.) See pp. 127-29.

Plate 7 The inscription of Tiberius Claudius Dinippus, who was in charge of the grain supply for famine relief on three separate occasions in Corinth during the early years of the Christian community. For inscriptions to him which mentioned his role three times as *curator annonae* see, e.g., Kent, *Corinth*, 8.3, nos. 158-63 (Reproduced by permission of the American School of Archaeology in Corinth.) See pp. 216-18.

CHAPTER 1

The Enigma and the Cultural Setting
of 1 Corinthians

I. Unresolved Issues for the Corinthian Church

This book seeks to answer the question, 'Why had Paul not dealt with some, if not all, of the problems he addressed in 1 Corinthians while he was in Corinth?' According to Acts 18:11, Paul had lived there for at least eighteen months. It is something of an enigma that he responded to many critical issues only when they were raised by letter or report from Corinth. From a reading of his letters a charge of apostolic neglect of duty while he was in residence could hardly be levelled against him, for he was assiduous in his instruction of Christian communities (15:10). Had his time with them been as short as that spent in Thessalonica, then a 'failure' to give substantial basic instruction on important and specific issues may be explicable. That he did not deal with such pressing matters cannot be attributed to the brevity of his stay in Corinth.

Paul had a reservoir of standard apostolic precedents for 'all the churches' under his jurisdiction (7:17). It cannot be argued that he adopted the policy of giving such instructions only after he had left Corinth, for he actually recorded that while he was there he had 'delivered traditions' (11:23; 15:1-4) and he warmly commended the Corinthians for diligently following them (11:2).

The Corinthians, however, had found it necessary to write to Paul about six matters on which they lacked clarity (7:1; 7:25; 8:1; 14:1; 16:1; 16:12).[1]

---

1. For an example of a περὶ δέ construction in responding to matters raised in a letter, see *BGU* 1141, ll. 31, 40; cf. l. 14, μοι τοῦτο ἔγραψας.

1

The last two could have arisen only after he had departed, i.e., the collection, which dealt basically with the logistics for gathering and sending money to Jerusalem (16:1); and the request for Apollos' return to Corinth (16:12). The Christian community as a whole was not certain about how to deal with four other pressing problems. Had they not been encountered before in the form in which they now presented themselves? It is puzzling that some of them give the impression of being very basic issues which a person would have faced soon after conversion to Christianity. For example, the issue of buying meat in the marketplace which had already been offered up in the pagan temple would surely have arisen for young converts while Paul was in Corinth. Paul, however, spent a good portion of the letter dealing with this matter and related issues (8:1–11:1). He cites no apostolic 'tradition' delivered when he resided there, although immediately after this lengthy discussion he refers to their adherence to all his traditions (11:2). Furthermore, Paul writes in 1 Corinthians on this and other concerns as if this Christian community had not encountered them while he was there.

The very fact that the Corinthian church wrote to Paul shows that not everyone was sure that the way some of the Christians reacted to these issues was appropriate (e.g., 8:10). If the letter from the church had the support of the Christian community as a whole (and there is nothing to suggest that it did not), then there must have been prior consultation among members before it was sent (7:1). Their divisions over former teachers, including Paul, did not prevent them as a body from writing to him on critical questions. At this stage there was a consensus about raising complex matters for Paul's apostolic ruling because they possessed no previously delivered tradition.

While it is true that some were not keen to have Paul back in residence because of their preference for Apollos (4:18, 16:12),[2] this must not blind us to the fact that the church felt the need to seek judgements on certain matters from their founding apostle *in absentia* and appeared to have done so readily. They had sought to observe his traditions (11:2), but now contacted him for help because they were in uncharted waters on crucial issues relating to their life and work.

Not only did the Corinthian church send an 'official letter', but members of Chloe's household — and possibly others (1:11; 16:17) — reported

---

2. 1 Cor. 16:12; cf. 4:6. For the cultural reasons why the presentation of Apollos in preaching was preferred to that of Paul, see Ch. 2.

different problems to Paul. Divisions in the church (1:12), the incestuous man (5:1-13), engaging in vexatious litigation against fellow Christians (6:1-8), indulging in the unholy trinity of eating, drinking, and sexual intercourse with prostitutes provided at private banquets (6:12-20), the veiling of men and the unveiling of wives (11:2-16), abuses at the Lord's Supper (11:17-34), and hedonistic conduct (15:33-34) were some of the problems they raised. On these matters the church as a whole seems to have felt no corporate desire to consult Paul by letter. Had not Paul taught them on such crucial issues as particular sexual improprieties, sharing at the Lord's Supper, and the nexus between ethics and the resurrection of the Christian's body (15:29-34)? Again in dealing with these matters in 1 Corinthians Paul makes no mention of any specific apostolic tradition delivered in Corinth except for the institution of the Lord's Supper and the content of the gospel.[3]

Why had he not mentioned the traditions aimed at resolving these problems in his letter? Perhaps Paul was happy to repeat teaching in 1 Corinthians on issues he had already dealt with but made no reference to the fact that he was doing so. But the opposite situation appears to have been the case. He did not hesitate to draw attention to those traditions which he had given them and to praise the Corinthians for holding fast to them — 'Now I commend (ἐπαινῶ)[4] you because you remember me in all things (ὅτι πάντα μου μέμνησθε), and hold fast to the traditions, even as I delivered them to you (καθὼς παρέδωκα ὑμῖν τὰς παραδόσεις κατέχετε)' (11:2). Most significantly they had maintained his tradition 'in all things' — a reference to his previous instructions. He later recalls a tradition he had delivered concerning the Lord's Supper which made their actions highly culpable, bringing upon them divine judgement by reason of it

---

3. Cf. A. Eriksson, 'Traditions as Corinthian *Premises*,' *Traditions as Rhetorical Proofs: Pauline Argumentation in 1 Corinthians* (Stockholm: Almqvist and Wiksell International, 1998), ch. 3. He suggests that there are eight Pauline traditions mentioned in 1 Cor., viz., 8:6; 8:11; 10:16; 11:23-5; 12:3; 12:13; 15:3-5 and 16:22. He locates what he sees as their *Sitz im Leben* in 'catechetical or baptism instruction', and concludes that Paul uses 'traditions as rhetorical proofs' (p. 304). This book is concerned to locate the *Sitz im Leben* of the issues raised by the Corinthians by way of their letter or reports and not how Paul answered them. That is the task of a sequel to this volume.

4. On the use of ἐπαινῶ as a formal and official recommendation see M. Borg, 'A New Context for Romans XIII,' *NTS* 19 (1973): 205-18; also my *Seek the Welfare of the City: Early Christians as Benefactors and Citizens* (Grand Rapids: Eerdmans; Carlisle: Paternoster, 1994), pp. 30-33.

3

(11:23-24, 30). He also referred to a letter he had written which they appeared to have misunderstood but which he then clarifies (5:9-10). It cannot therefore be argued that in 1 Corinthians Paul simply ignored previously delivered traditions whether oral or written.

Underlying this book is the view that Paul did not deal with many of the problems reflected in 1 Corinthians because either they had not arisen during his time in Corinth, or they had done so in a way different from that in which they were now encountering them.

II. Secular Ethics and Social Change in Corinth

Paul specifically charges the Christians with 'walking in a secular way' and behaving like other 'men' in Corinth (3:3, 5). Subsequent chapters will seek to show that, in 1 Corinthians, Paul was responding to problems which were created by the influence of secular ethics or social conventions on this nascent Christian community. They may have crept into the church imperceptibly and grown with the passage of time. Some were already there just below the surface (e.g., 3:1). Others were a rapid reaction to a problem which arose unexpectedly and were resolved almost unthinkingly on the basis of the cultural or legal mores of this Roman colony. These were sometimes judged to have required no specifically 'Christian' answer — hence the argument for cultural responses by the Christian community. We will explore what we know of 'accepted' Corinthian ways of doing things, for this had a preconditioning effect on everybody. These Christians had lived, possibly from childhood, in a Roman colony which was proud of its customs, and its inhabitants considered themselves to be culturally superior to those in Greek cities in Achaea.[5]

Part of the subtitle of this book, i.e., 'social change', suggests that life in the Roman colony of Corinth was neither static nor tranquil — something which is often wrongly assumed in Corinthian studies. As a Roman colony it was highly susceptible to changes or trends in Rome itself. It was governed by Roman law, and any changes in that or any other important

---

5. For the first-century criticism by the Argives that Corinth had 'abandoned' its Greek ways and that they now followed those of Rome, see 'On Behalf of the Argives': *Pseudo-Julian, Letters 198,* 409D, and A. J. S. Spawforth, 'Corinth, Argos and the Imperial Cult: *Pseudo-Julian, Letters 198,' Hesperia* 63.2 (1994): 211-32 for an important discussion of this text.

area of life in the imperial city could rapidly affect Corinth.[6] As the people of Argos noted, Corinth was proud of its status, having, in effect, turned its back on the Greek heritage of other cities in the federal league and thereby benefited greatly from its privileged position with Rome.[7]

As a colony it was always open to suggestions from Rome concerning demonstrations of loyalty to the emperor. During this particular period of the early church a provincial or federal imperial cult was created (c. A.D. 54) which from then on was celebrated annually in Corinth.[8] The reference to 'gods on the earth', which included the reigning emperor and, in some instances, members of the imperial family (8:5), suggests that here was a new, external factor which had a considerable impact on the Corinthian Christians.[9]

Another change which may well have disoriented the Christian community was the Isthmian Games. They were not moved from Corinth to the ancient, nearby site of Isthmia permanently until possibly the early twenties or fifties A.D.[10] when the then president of the Games, Lucius Castricius Regulus, hosted an inaugural dinner for all the citizens of Corinth.[11] At subsequent games the President gave multiple civic dinners to those who had Corinthian citizenship, i.e., Roman citizens.[12] 1 Corinthians 8:9 suggests that the 'right' (ἐξουσία) of some to eat in the idol temple may well have been connected with these games.[13] There was uncertainty on the part of 'weaker' brothers as to whether they should also avail themselves of this civic right. Unlike the 'stronger' brothers, they did not know

6. Cf. the expulsion of Jews from Rome and the anti-Semitism of the Corinthian crowd (Acts 18:2, 17).

7. *Pseudo-Julian, Letters 198,* 407.

8. *Pseudo-Julian, Letters 198,* 407Bff. For its dating and discussion of the federal imperial cult of Achaea centred in Corinth c. A.D. 54 see Spawforth, 'Corinth, Argos and the Imperial Cult: *Pseudo-Julian, Letters 198,*' 211-32 and his shorter version, 'The Achaean Federal Imperial Cult Part I: *Pseudo-Julian, Letters 198,*' *TynB* 46.1 (1995): 151-68.

9. See my 'The Achaean Federal Imperial Cult, Part II: The Corinthian Church,' *TynB* 46.1 (1995): 169-78. For further discussion see pp. 281-82.

10. E. R. Gebhard, 'The Isthmian Games and the Sanctuary of Poseidon in the Early Empire,' in T. E. Gregory, ed., *The Corinthia in the Roman Period,* Journal of Roman Archaeology Supp. 8 (Ann Arbor: University of Michigan, 1994), pp. 78-94.

11. J. H. Kent, *Corinth,* 8.3, no. 153; and the discussion on the re-dating of his inscription, in Gebhard, 'The Isthmian Games,' p. 87.

12. Plutarch, *Moralia* 723A.

13. See my 'Civic Rights,' *Seek the Welfare of the City,* ch. 9, esp. pp. 168-74.

that an idol was 'nothing' and felt somewhat apprehensive about feasting at the temple, possibly Poseidon's temple in Isthmia. The subsequent opportunity to join the 'strong' at these dinners may well be the clue that the Games were the *Sitz im Leben* that gave rise to conflicting views over an appropriate Christian response.

There is also evidence that three severe grain shortages occurred in Corinth during the early days of the church. Even a rumour of a famine was sufficient to cause social unrest — 'Thus it happens at time [of famine] that the populace is plunged into disorder and riots', an inscription from Ephesus records.[14] This compelled the city's élite to appoint an honorary superintendent of the grain supply, *curator annonae*. He might flood the market with cheap grain and thus force the grain merchants who speculated in this commodity to reduce their price as a matter of principle during a famine. Alternatively, he might collect money from the rich to import grain and make it affordable for everyone. Again, 'the present distress' (7:26) might have been caused by famine, for the term 'distress' (ἀνάγκη) is linked with the word for 'famine' in literary sources.[15] There are ten extant inscriptions in Corinth from this period honouring Tiberius Claudius Dinippus, who acted as superintendent of the grain supply during all three grain shortages.[16] Such, it will be argued, was another external change which had a disorienting effect on Christians, as it did on all the residents of Corinth (7:1bff.).

Did the Christian community have access to meat that was not offered to idols prior to being sold in the meat market *(macellum)* when Paul was in Corinth?[17] City authorities controlled the marketplaces, and there is evidence that they made special provisions for Jews on account of their religious scruples on this matter.[18] Given that Gallio perceived Christianity to be Jewish, Christians should have been able to buy specially slaughtered meat if a special civic provision had been made for them in the meat market. Was this particular concession to the Jews subsequently withdrawn by

---

14. *I Eph.* 215, ll. 1-4.

15. E.g., 'severe famine' (λιμὸς ἰσχυρός); Thucydides, 3.82:2; 85:2.

16. For evidence of the three severe famines from ten Corinthian inscriptions all produced at the same time and all recording these grain shortages see pp. 216-17.

17. D. W. J. Gill, 'The Meat Market at Corinth (1 Corinthians 10:25),' *TynB* 43.2 (1992): 389-93.

18. P. R. Trebilco, *Jewish Communities in Asia Minor*, SNTSMS 69 (Cambridge: Cambridge University Press, 1991), p. 17. For discussion see Ch. 13.

the Council of Corinth in concert with expressions of anti-Semitism in Rome (Acts 18:2)? Certainly some appear to have expressed their solidarity with Rome by assaulting the ruler of the synagogue immediately after the dismissal of the case unsuccessfully brought by the Jews to Gallio against Paul (Acts 18:12-17). Paul cited no tradition in 1 Corinthians 10 although idol meat was sold in Corinth when he was there.

These external changes occurred after Paul left Corinth, which explains why he could not possibly have dealt with them while he was there. The following chapters, then, explore the problem of Christians giving culturally determined responses to ethical issues and their reactions to social changes in Corinth. Given new developments in the study of Roman Greece, and significant work on Corinth in particular,[19] it is important that scholars and students of 1 Corinthians gather some of this rich evidence which throws new light on issues in this epistle and, along with older studies, provides explanations for the reactions of Christians after Paul left Corinth.

III. The Cultural and Social Background of Corinth

What dominant cultural ethos of this Roman colony impacted the behaviour patterns of its inhabitants when Paul wrote 1 Corinthians? The extant cultural evidence is fivefold, viz., archaeological, numismatic, epigraphic, literary, and, finally, a crucial first-century official source.

Archaeological Evidence

According to Pausanias, Greek Corinth was effectively dismantled as a *polis* and destroyed in 146 B.C. — 'Corinth was laid utterly waste'.[20] This meant that, after defeating an enemy, Rome had followed its custom of disman-

---

19. For the contribution to Roman Greece see S. E. Alcock, *Graecia Capta: The Landscapes of Roman Greece* (Cambridge: Cambridge University Press, 1993) and on Corinth the most recent composite volume T. E. Gregory, ed., *The Corinthia in the Roman Period.*

20. Pausanias 2.1.2. See also W. Willis, 'Corinthusne deletus est?' *BZ* 35 (1991): 233-41, and the reply by D. W. J. Gill, 'Corinth: A Roman Colony of Achaea,' *BZ* 37 (1993): 259-64, who assembled and interpreted the evidence showing that civic discontinuity was what was meant.

tling the city,[21] looting the treasures and taking them to Rome[22] — 'For 102 years Corinth remained a ruin, probably with squatters, but without a political life'.[23]

When the colony was founded in 44 B.C., the whole of the site was laid out afresh according to the Roman town-planning grid called centuriation.[24] Only the forum retained the alignment of the ancient *agora*. New buildings were constructed on the *stoa*, and the architectural design was clearly Roman. The amphitheatre was the only one of its kind in Roman Greece, and all of its three basilicas replicated the Roman West, something seldom found in Greece.[25] The bases and mouldings of the Ionic and Corinthian columns reflected the Italian design, again a style not reflected in any other city in Macedonia or Achaea.[26]

In Corinth ancient sanctuaries underwent Roman style 'modernisation' rather than restoration to Classical Greek 'authenticity'.[27] The ancient temple of Apollos was altered according to Roman temple conventions rather than to those of Greek origin. The reason for this was significant. Attributing his victory at Actium to Apollo, Augustus built a new temple

21. K. W. Arafat, *Pausanias' Greece: Ancient Artists and Roman Rulers* (Cambridge: Cambridge University Press, 1996), p. 110.

22. For the effect on the economy of Rome of the Corinthian plunder, see E. Badian, *Publicans and Sinners: Private Enterprise in the Service of the Roman Republic* (Oxford: Blackwell's, 1972), p. 53; and on the subsequent role of the conqueror, the Roman Consul Lucius Mummius, in Rome, including his building works apparently funded in part from the sacking of Corinth, see T. R. S. Broughton, *The Magistrates of the Roman Republic* (Atlanta: Scholars Press, 1986), I, 474.

23. C. K. Williams II, 'The Refounding of Corinth: Some Roman Religious Attitudes,' in S. Macready and F. S. Thompson, eds., *Roman Architecture in the Greek World* (London: The Society of Antiquaries, 1987), p. 26.

24. See D. G. Romano, 'Post-146 B.C. Land Use in Corinth, and Planning of the Roman Colony of 44 B.C.,' in T. E. Gregory, *The Corinthia in the Roman Period*, pp. 9-30 for a computer-based reconstruction of the centuriation of Roman Corinth aided by archaeological evidence and aerial photographs. On Roman town plans and buildings see E. J. Owens, 'Roman Town Planning,' in I. M. Barton, ed., *Roman Public Buildings*, Exeter Studies in History 20 (Exeter: University of Exeter, 1989), ch. 1; and E. J. Owens, *The City in the Greek and Roman World* (London and New York: Routledge, 1991).

25. D. Engels, *Roman Corinth: An Alternative Model for the Classical City* (Chicago: University of Chicago Press, 1990), p. 62.

26. Engels, *Roman Corinth*, p. 69, citing O. Broneer, 'Colonia Laus Iulia Corinthiensis,' *Hesperia* 10 (1941): 388-90.

27. Williams, 'The Refounding of Corinth: Some Roman Religious Attitudes,' p. 32.

to this god on the Palatine next to his own house in Rome early in his Principate.[28] The restructured Corinthian temple had particular significance because the colony was keen to imitate Rome, and Augustus in particular, in all things. An imperial cult temple looking down on the forum was built according to Roman design.[29] Its foundations were raised above ground level, making it higher than all the temples in the forum area, including that of Apollo. The colonists thereby made a telling statement, just as they did with the striking monument erected in the forum well over a century after the defeat and sacking of Corinth, viz., the Facade of the Captives. These were potent reminders of the subjugation of the East by Rome. In this regard the founders of Corinth acted no differently from those of Pompeii when the latter was made a colony c. 80 B.C. Both colonies consciously stressed discontinuity with the past, although Pompeii did not experience the sacking and dismantling of its city.

> The monuments of the early colony emphasised the defeat and destruction of the community that had opposed Sulla. The settlement of the Roman veterans demanded a new identity for the city, and to accompany that identity a new set of monuments that reflected the new situation. These monuments reflected the colonists' triumph and the original inhabitants' capitulation. . . . The inhabitants of Pompeii viewed with awe the shrines associated with the imperial cult. It should come as no surprise that the position of the emperor was so prominent in the locus of the city's power, the forum.[30]

Corinth did, in effect, begin *de novo* in that its heart had been removed at the time of its rape in 146 B.C. Some of the foundations of its buildings in the forum proved to be useful to the colonists, which explains the lack of symmetry of the forum in the Roman centuriation town plan of the city.[31]

---

28. J. B. Rives, *Religion and Authority in Roman Carthage from Augustus to Constantine* (Oxford: Clarendon Press, 1995), p. 54.

29. Temple E. C. K. Williams II, "A Re-evaluation of Temple E and the West End of the Forum of Corinth," in S. Walker and A. Cameron, eds., *The Greek Renaissance in the Roman Empire*, BICS Supp. 55 (1989), pp. 156-62; and R. M. Rothaus, *Corinth: The First City of Greece, An Urban History of Late Antique Cult and Religion* (Leiden: E. J. Brill, 2000), pp. 39-42.

30. R. Laurence, *Roman Pompeii: Space and Society* (London: Routledge, 1994), p. 137.

31. Romano, 'Post-146 B.C. Land Use in Corinth,' *The Corinthia in the Roman Period*, fig. 3.

However, the edifices built on it were deliberately Roman in design and construction. On the other hand, Pompeii retained its existing structures, while new buildings and alterations to the forum made important political statements of *Romanitas* to the inhabitants and to Rome itself. While there may have been some residents when the colonists arrived in Corinth, the raising of the level of the old *agora* for the Roman forum, as well as a new town plan, meant that all existing housing would have been demolished. Corinth was laid out and built as a new Roman city.

The reoccupation of the site of the Greek games at Isthmia indicates that Rome was not at this stage celebrating Greek classical traditions, for the restoration work and new housing for athletes was Roman. 'Corinth's control of the Isthmian games provided another means by which the city could act as a pro-Roman focal point in Achaean life.'[32] They were one of the three most important religious and athletic festivals in Greece and were held biennially. The Caesarean Games and the Imperial Contests took place every four years, having begun in the time of Tiberius to honour the imperial family. These contests provided opportunities to compete for the best encomium to the emperor and his family. Roman events were added to these ancient Games which had been transferred to Greek Sikyon during the desolation of Corinth. They were later returned to the colony.[33]

Those in Rome responsible for founding Corinth consciously named the colony *Colonia Laus Julia Corinthiensis,* and, as Engels notes, 'they avoided the more common *-ius* or *-us* ethnic, which implies that the Italian colonists wished to distinguish themselves from the original Greek inhabitants of the city.'[34]

More revealing was the way in which the colonists went about establishing divine patronage for Corinth. They had no 'intention in their action of evoking the Classical glories of Aphrodite Hoplismeni who had succoured the Greek city. . . . The Venus of the Forum is different. She is placed at the centre of the city as the Mother of the Roman Nation, and as such as Mother of the Roman colony'.[35]

According to Engels, 'The city reflects the Italian origins of many of

---

32. Alcock, *Graecia Capta: The Landscapes of Roman Greece,* p. 169.

33. Engels, *Roman Corinth,* pp. 51-52.

34. Engels, *Roman Corinth,* p. 69, citing *CIG* 1, no. 106.

35. C. K. Williams II, "A Re-evaluation of Temple E and the West End of the Forum of Corinth,' in S. Walker and A. Cameron, eds., *The Greek Renaissance in the Roman Empire,* BICS Supp. 55 (1989), pp. 155, 157.

its citizens in its architecture, from the Roman podium-style temples on the West Terrace down to details of the mouldings of its column bases.'[36] M. E. H. Walbank has also commented that cognisance is not always taken of the fact that 'in layout, organisation and religious practice, Corinth was a Roman colony and not simply a restoration of a Greek city'.[37] Dr. Charles Williams II, the former Director of the Corinth excavations of the American School of Classical Studies in Athens, expressed the view to the author that to see Roman Corinth as anything other than Roman in its structures and outlook would be to misread all the archaeological evidence of the period. In the second century A.D. Gellius wrote that Roman colonies were 'little reproductions, and seem to be images of Rome'.[38] His observation is confirmed by the archaeological evidence that has been uncovered in more than a century of digging by the American School in Athens.

Corinth, therefore, was not a Greek city with a Roman facade. It was conceived of, and deliberately laid out, as a thoroughly Roman colony. *Romanitas* describes the architectural style of first-century Corinth, and it reflected an ideological outlook which provides important evidence of Corinth's culture in Paul's day.[39]

Numismatic and Epigraphic Evidence

All coins issued by local magistrates were in Latin until the mint in Corinth was closed in A.D. 67.[40] While it is not absolutely certain that this Roman colony possessed the only provincial mint in Achaea, 'Corinthian coins are nonetheless remarkable for their early and strong preference for

36. Engels, *Roman Corinth,* p. 62. See L. Shoe, 'The Roman Ionic Base at Corinth,' in L. Freeman Sandler, ed., *Essays in Honor of Karl Lehmann* (New York: J. J. Augustin, 1964), pp. 300-304 for telltale evidence of this.

37. M. E. H. Walbank, 'Pausanias, Octavia and Temple E at Corinth,' *BSA* 84 (1989): 394.

38. *NA* 16.13.9.

39. The term *Romanitas* was a pejorative one. Its first recorded use was in the third century A.D. It has now become common currency among ancient historians to use this term to describe Roman values and culture.

40. For a detailed discussion of these coins see M. Amandry, *Le monnayage des duovirs corinthiens,* BCH Supplement 15 (Paris/Athens: Ecole Francaise d'Athenes, 1988).

Roman types, their fast response to imperial dynastic change, and their fidelity in conforming to Augustan monetary denominations'.[41]

What information does epigraphic evidence yield about Corinth's cultural setting? It has been well documented that the official inscriptions of the first century A.D. were in Latin, which is not surprising for a Roman colony of this era. Various assessments have been made of the significance of the evidence for the first one hundred and seventy years. G. Theissen believes 'that Latin was able to catch on and hold its own'.[42] His argument is based on the ratio of extant Latin to Greek inscriptions up to the time of, and during, Hadrian's reign with the radical changes brought about by his strong Hellenisation programme. The use of Greek in official inscriptions in the following century reflects the imperial promotion of the classical Greek revival especially from the time of the emperor Hadrian onwards.[43] W. A. Meeks suggests that the earlier Latin inscriptions were ordered by former freedmen who have telltale Greek-derived names. He wrongly cautions that 'the depth of this "Romanization" should not be exaggerated', and that the ratio of Greek to Latin inscriptions suggests 'that the fashion approved for public display may not have represented quite accurately the ordinary languages of the population'.[44] The use of Latin in official honorific inscriptions provides a clear picture, not so much of the languages used in the colony, but of the official cultural emphasis of Paul's Corinth as a centre of *Romanitas*. Corinth invariably took its cue from Roman and not Greek culture.

There is one composite public benefaction inscription in Greek erected in Corinth in A.D. 43. However, its language is explicable given the peculiar circumstances surrounding it. In contrast to the large lettering of the official Latin inscriptions of Corinth, this has very small lettering and records a number of official decrees detailing both the civic benefactions

41. Alcock, *Graecia Capta*, 168, citing Amandry, *Le monnayage des duovirs corinthiens*, p. 101.

42. G. Theissen, 'Social Stratification in the Corinthian Community: A Contribution to the Sociology of Early Hellenistic Christianity,' *Essays on Corinth: The Social Setting of Pauline Christianity* (Philadelphia: Fortress Press, 1982), p. 112, n. 20.

43. On Hadrian as the apostle of Greek Classical revival see F. E. Peters, *The Harvest of Hellenism: A History of the Near East from Alexander the Great* (New York: Simon and Schuster, 1970), pp. 530-31.

44. W. A. Meeks, *The First Urban Christians: The Social World of the Apostle Paul* (New Haven and London: Yale University Press, 1983), p. 47.

of a Corinthian lady, Iunia Theodora, and their official honouring of her.[45] The federal assembly of the Lycian cities of Patara and Telmessos, and not the Corinthians, were the recipients of her public beneficence. There were also official letters to Corinth from the Council and the People of Myra, which was another city in the same league and one from the same federal assembly in Asia Minor. All lauded her great generosity. As these official resolutions from Greek-speaking Lycia were naturally in Greek, it was highly apposite that this inscription in Corinth should be recorded in the original language.[46] It was, however, not an official inscription from Corinth's 'Council and People' honouring one of its own citizens for benefactions given to them. This adequately explains this exception in the first century B.C. or A.D. While in Athens, Epidaurus, and Sparta the official inscriptions were Greek, in first-century Corinth those authorised by 'the Council and the People' were in Latin.[47]

Valerius Maximus, writing in the time of Tiberius, recorded of the magistrates of old that they were 'never to make replies to Greeks except in Latin. Indeed they obliged the Greeks to . . . speak through an interpreter, not only in Rome but in Greece and Asia also, intending, no doubt, the dignity of Latin speech to be more widely venerated throughout all nations'.[48] Cicero drew criticism for addressing the Syracusan senate in Greek even though he was not a magistrate.[49] The epigraphic evidence of official Corinthian inscriptions, along with these observations, could well mean that the proceedings of the Council were conducted in Latin in Roman Corinth.

Engels believes that pottery provides important evidence of a change in ethnic composition after the first century. 'From the founding of the city to the mid-first century A.D., the potters had Latin names written in

45. The Romans dropped the elaborate genre of the Greek inscriptions. The latter normally recorded the liturgies held or simply the name of the civic benefactor on the actual benefaction. For a discussion of the Greek genre see my *Seek the Welfare of the City,* pp. 26-33, and for Corinthian benefactions see Kent, *Corinth,* 8.3, pp. 1-3.

46. See L. Robert, 'Inscriptions Lyciennes Trouvées à Solómos,' *BCH* 83 (1959): 498-503; and R. Kearsley, 'Women in Public Life in the Roman East: Iunia Theodora, Claudia Metrodora and Phoebe, Benefactress of Paul,' *TynB* 50.2 (1999): 189-211.

47. D. J. W. Gill, 'The Importance of Roman Portraiture for Head-coverings in 1 Corinthians 11:2-16,' *TynB* 41.2 (1990): 259, cited again in Gill, 'In Search of the Social Elite in the Corinthian Church,' *TynB* 44.2 (1993): 327.

48. *Memorable Deeds and Sayings,* 2.2.2.

49. *Verr.* 2.4.147.

the Latin alphabet; after that date, Greek names in the Greek alphabet are found, indicating a change in the makers and the market. Since these locally produced imitations were not exported in quantity, the change in names indicates a change in the ethnic composition.'[50] It should not be forgotten that one hundred years after the founding of Corinth, the city experienced a period of unprecedented economic prosperity.[51] It would be wrong to assume that there had been no economic mobility for its Roman founders' children's children or that potters had not been drawn from elsewhere in Achaea in the first century.

Ostraca have been found written in Greek.[52] Only one of the lead curse inscriptions located in the temple of Demeter was in Latin; all others found there and elsewhere in Corinth were in Greek.[53] This does not negate other evidence from nonliterary sources of the essential *Romanitas* of Corinth in our period.

The last piece of nonliterary evidence is from the middle of the first century A.D. Unlike the Augustan era, there was considerable 'enthusiasm of provincials' for Roman citizenship, which was acquired as a direct result of imperial encouragement.[54] Latin *cognomina* were given to the sons of freedmen who, as their offspring, were freeborn Roman citizens. Engels cites the case of the wealthy benefactor and freedman, Cn. Babbius Philinus, who named his son, Cn. Babbias Italicus.[55] It should not surprise us that Paul's Corinthian letters provide important literary confirmation. There are eight Latin names among the seventeen Corinthian Christians whom Paul mentions, i.e., Aquila, Fortunatus, Gaius, Lucius, Priscilla, Quartus, Titus Justus and Tertius.[56] While the fact that some Christians possessed Latin names does not *ipso facto* indicate Roman citizenship in

---

50. Alcock, *Graecia Capta*, p. 72.

51. C. K. Williams II, 'Roman Corinth as a Commercial Center,' *The* Corinthia *in the Roman Period*, p. 46.

52. Kent, *Corinth*, 8.3.

53. See pp. 168-69. These curses reveal the social status of the worshippers.

54. F. Millar, *The Emperor in the Roman World (31 B.C.–A.D. 337)* (London: Duckworth, 1977), p. 481. See A. N. Sherwin-White, 'The Claudian Problem and *Viritane* Grants', *The Roman Citizenship*, 2nd ed. (Oxford: Clarendon Press, 1973), ch. 9, cit. 249 on the change of policy under Claudius; see also A. Lintott, *Imperium Romanum: Politics and Administration* (London: Routledge, 1993), p. 167.

55. Engels, *Roman Corinth*, pp. 73, 218, n. 13. He wrongly cites Babbias' *praenomen* as Gn. rather than Cn. See Kent, *Corinth*, 8.3, p. 25.

56. Theissen, 'Social Stratification in the Corinthian Community,' p. 99.

every case, their presence at the very least provides important evidence of the influence of *Romanitas*.[57]

Literary Evidence

The following review of literary evidence indicates that the Roman ethos of Corinth in the early days of the Christian community was in contrast to a major shift of the cultural milieu of Corinth in the next century, a point that is often overlooked. We begin our exploration with significant evidence from the second century A.D.

Pausanias, who visited Corinth in c. A.D. 162, discusses its ethnic composition and also gives a particular perspective of the colony in the middle of the second century. He records 'the destruction of Corinth by the Romans and the extinction of its old inhabitants', and that 'the old population of Corinth is entirely gone: the present population is a colony sent out by the Romans'. Elsewhere he writes of 'a Corinthian, not one of the ancient Corinthians, but one of the modern population on whom the emperor has bestowed Corinth'.[58] While we know that in prosperous times rich families who were ethnically Greek settled in Corinth and played a significant role in its public life as major benefactors,[59] Pausanias' comments represent a particular *Tendenz* on his part and bring us to the heart of his concerns. Arafat in a recent work on this recorder of ancient religious sites in Greece observes, 'Second-century Rome's emphasis on the glorious past of Classical Greece . . . has formed a thread running through this book . . . the view of Greece then current at Rome'. He concludes his discussion by saying that for Pausanias 'Mummius represented the depths of decline, and that Hadrian represented the zenith of prosperity, material

57. See E. A. Judge, 'Greek Names of Latin Origin,' *New Docs.* 2 (1982): 106-8, who draws attention to the complexity of the issue because we do not possess the *praenomina*, *nomina*, and *cognomina*, although it is not possible to determine those who did, especially those whose *cognomina* are known.

58. Pausanias, 2.3.7, 2.1.2, 5.21.1.

59. E.g., Cn. Cornelius Pulcher came to Corinth and was appointed to senior public liturgies, i.e., *duovir quinquennalis* and President of the Games, and C. Julius Spartiaticus, who was formerly from Sparta, was the first high priest of the Achaean Federal Imperial Cult in Corinth; West, *Corinth* 8.2, no. 68, and P. Cartledge and A. Spawforth, *Hellenistic and Roman Sparta: A Tale of Two Cities* (London: Routledge, 1989), p. 104.

and cultural'.[60] While Pausanias provides important information on the topography and religious sites of Corinth from a later era, his rereading of Corinth from the fashionable perspective of the Greek Classical revival in the Rome of his day does not provide hard background evidence of the culture of the mid-first century.[61]

Apuleius' historical novel, *Metamorphosis* or *The Golden Ass*, refers in part to second-century Corinth and its Aegean port of Cenchreae c. A.D. 155. While Carthage, or more probably Rome, is considered to be the place of its writing,[62] the author was in Athens and appears to have had first-hand knowledge of the colony. Murphy-O'Connor's comment could be very misleading when he says that Apuleius 'offers a lower-class view of Greek provincial society, which has been brilliantly synthesised by Millar; this was the real world in which Paul moved'.[63] One of Murphy-O'Connor's extracts from *The Golden Ass* concerns Thiasus, who is from the élite of Corinth and records the liturgies he held, including the prestigious office of *quinquennial* magistrate. The election promises needed to secure that office were substantial and therefore indicate that he was an extremely wealthy person — he brought 'magnificent wild beasts and valiant gladiators' in from Thessaly for a three-day spectacle. The other two extracts deal with an Assyrian fortune-teller and a brief description of Cenchreae, the eastern port for Corinth.[64] The office of *quinquennial* magistrate which he mentions was very important and also existed in Paul's day. Like all liturgies, it was secured by promises of substantial benefactions to the city and/or its citizens. Cenchreae was then an important port. However, it is hard to see how these extracts concerning Roman Corinth present a 'lower class of view of Greek provincial society', especially when public offices required Roman citizenship.[65] Furthermore, how can it be

60. Arafat, *Pausanias' Greece*, p. 213.

61. J. Murphy-O'Connor, *St Paul's Corinth: Texts and Archaeology* (Wilmington, Del.: Glazier, 1983), p. 3, who cites his work, notes that this evidence could provide a misleading picture of the religious milieu of Paul's day as the city was extensively damaged by an earthquake in A.D. 77 and much rebuilding had to be undertaken.

62. K. Dowden, 'The Roman Audience of the Golden Ass,' in J. Tatum, ed., *The Search for the Ancient Novel* (Baltimore: Johns Hopkins University Press, 1994), ch. 23, pp. 421-22.

63. Murphy-O'Connor, *St. Paul's Corinth*, p. 123, citing F. Millar, 'The World of the Golden Ass,' *JRS* 71 (1981): 63-75.

64. Apuleius, *The Golden Ass* 2.12; 10.18, 35.

65. Millar's subject for his inaugural lecture for his chair in King's College, London,

said that these extracts represent the 'real' world of Paul's Corinth? Apuleius' evidence confirms what we know from epigraphic evidence of public liturgies in the first and second centuries. The conventions surrounding the appointments were unchanged from Paul's time to the next century when the imaginary events and personages of this historical novel were written.[66]

In A.D. 156 the famous orator Aelius Aristides delivered an oration at the Isthmian Games which makes substantial reference to the city of Corinth.[67] He surprisingly speaks of 'the Greeks' and the Isthmian Games being celebrated every two years by 'the Greek race'. He sees Corinth as a city that 'receives all cities and sends them off again . . . it is a common city for all the Greeks' (καὶ κοινὸν ἄστυ τῶν Ἑλλήνων), indeed, as it were, a kind of metropolis and mother in this respect'.[68] Clearly these public and effusive references to Greeks and Corinth were acceptable in the era of the neo-Classical Greek revival in Rome.[69] Corinth was still in Aristides' day 'the city of Aphrodite', which he describes as 'a pendant and a necklace of all of Greece' of the goddess, for she was seen as the Mother of the imperial family and patroness of Corinth.[70] Aristides is mindful of the fact that the Greeks were defeated by the Romans, for in this oration he comments to the audience that 'it is not appropriate to raise the memory of such things when the Greeks are celebrating a national festival'.[71] Given his oration on Rome delivered in the capital where he shows himself to be a strong advocate for the supremacy of Rome, he must have judged the cultural ethos correctly at the Isthmian Games to have sung the praises of 'the Greeks' and Corinth as he did.[72]

In the early second century Epictetus explains to a young Corinthian

---

shows how useful the historical novel, *The Golden Ass*, can be in providing evidence of legal and other aspects in the Roman world of the second century. See n. 63.

66. Kent, *Corinth* 8.3, pp. 24-26 for details of conventions.

67. C. A. Behr in his English translation of the orations of Aristides observes that he did not believe in the god even though the designation given the oration was 'The Isthmian Oration: regarding Poseidon'. The encomium is there regarded as one on the city itself, and he clearly devotes a particular section to the city including references to the market, 20-31; *Aelius Aristides* (Leiden: E. J. Brill, 1981), p. 422.

68. *Or.* 46.23-24.

69. See p. 15.

70. *Or.* 46.23.

71. *Or.* 46.31

72. See his 'Regarding Rome,' *Or.* 26.

student of oratory what 'career' path might be open to him by way of Corinthian liturgies as a Roman citizen if he were elected to them. He lists them in an ascending order of status which was unique to Corinth. The office of magistrate was the most senior in rank in a city or colony, except in Corinth where the President of the Games in Isthmia was more important. The President personally hosted these games. It was the most senior public liturgy because he paid for them. In other cities the Games were the responsibility of the 'administrator of the city' (ἀστυνόμος). Epictetus listed the correct order as 'administrator of the city, superintendent of the *ephebi*, magistrate, and president of the Games'.[73] However, these same liturgies operated in Paul's time as well as in the classical Greek revival of the following century, and provide no clues of the cultural ethos in the first century.

In an oration delivered in Corinth early in the second century, Favorinus shows that he was one of a new breed — the Roman Hellenophile speaking before a crowd in the Roman colony that had become Hellenised — 'though Roman, has become thoroughly Hellenised'.[74] From the way he spoke it is clear that the Corinthians were enchanted by Greek orators, as they had originally been with him — a Roman from the West in love with things Greek.[75] Favorinus was on his third visit to Corinth. He was engaged in an urgent polemic to have his statue reinstated after the Corinthians had overthrown it. They had done this to signify that he no longer enjoyed imperial favour and could not enjoy theirs because of allegations of sexual impropriety connected with the imperial household.[76] His evidence of a recent cultural change which now favoured Classical Greek culture after a century and a half of the promotion of

73. 3.1.34-36. Such a person could ultimately become a good citizen, i.e., a publicly honoured civic benefactor, a senator, and an orator, according to Epictetus. For a further discussion see my *Philo and Paul among the Sophists*, SNTSMS 96 (Cambridge: Cambridge University Press, 1997), pp. 119-21.

74. *Or.* 37.26.

75. For evidence see my 'Epictetus and the Corinthian Student of the Sophists' and 'Dio and Plutarch among the Corinthian Sophists,' in *Philo and Paul among the Sophists*, chs. 6 and 7.

76. On Favorinus see G. Anderson, *Philostratus: Biography and Belles Lettres in the Third Century* A.D. (London: Croom Helm, 1986), pp. 102-7 and *The Second Sophistic: A Cultural Phenomenon in the Roman Empire* (London/New York: Routledge, 1993), pp. 172ff.; see also M. W. Gleason, 'Favorinus and His Statue,' *Making Men: Sophists and Self-Presentation in Ancient Rome* (Princeton: Princeton University Press, 1995), ch. 1.

Romanitas is important. This early second-century cultural fashion originated not in Corinth but in Rome itself, and carried full imperial endorsement. His oration makes it clear that it was recent and therefore provides concrete evidence of the decade in which that change was officially and popularly embraced.

None of these literary sources provides evidence of the predominant cultural ethos of Corinth in the middle of the first century. There is information from a time earlier than that of Pausanias, Apuleius, Epictetus, Aristides, or Favorinus which confirms that these authors stand on the other side of a cultural watershed.

A Copy of a First-Century Official Petition

Recently evidence recovered from the Argive petition has been shown to be from the first century.[77] It provides important information which substantiates Corinth's adherence to Roman law and customs in the time of Paul, and indicates that neither the laws nor the customs of ancient Greece were those which Roman Corinth followed — they do not 'respect the high authority of the ancient laws and customs', but 'rather those which it seems they took over from the sovereign city' (409C). As a colony Corinth saw itself 'as a community that traditionally originated from Rome, could be regarded as an extension of Rome itself, . . . they could then exuberantly claim to form part of the grandeur and majesty of Rome'.[78] Had Roman Corinth valued the heritage of Greek Corinth, the payment of heavy tribute for extravagant entertainment for the federal imperial cult would not have been levied on Argos — so the latter city argued (409C). The petition suggests that this was not how the Corinthians saw the issue, for 'in reliance on the laws they now have, they claim that their city has gained the advantages since they received the colony from Rome' (409D). The reference to the expensive purchase of bears and panthers for its 'hunting shows' and not for gymnastic or musical contests indicates that Corinth's

---

77. *Pseudo-Julian* 198. For its first-century dating and discussion see Spawforth, 'Corinth, Argos and the Imperial Cult I: *Pseudo-Julian, Letters 198*,' 211-32 and 'The Achaean Federal Imperial Cult I: *Pseudo-Julian, Letters 198*,' 151-68.

78. E. T. Salmon, *Roman Colonisation under the Republic* (London: Thames and Hudson, 1969), p. 136.

preferences were for the former, which was a Roman innovation and not part of Greek culture (παιδεία) (409A).

It is clear that the Argive petition provides nonliterary confirmation of Corinth's loyalty, preference for, and adherence to Roman customs and laws at the end of the Julio-Claudian Principates. Its importance lies in the fact that this was not a religious travel guide, a salacious novel, an oration, or a philosophical dissertation of a student of rhetoric, but an official petition sent to the governor of the province following the city's unsuccessful legal challenge in the courts.[79] Therefore the comments Argos made about Corinth can be taken to be a correct reflection of its legal and cultural ethos. This first-century petition thus provides evidence that, in the very decade when the Christian church was being established in Corinth, it was consciously a colony that was Roman in its outlook and cultural emphasis, and was specifically criticised for being so by the city of Argos.

The archaeological evidence discussed previously confirms the cultural ethos reflected in the Argive petition.[80] This is decisive evidence for the dominant cultural setting of Paul's Corinth, for the Argive petition concerned the federal imperial cult which began in A.D. 54 and which was inaugurated around the time Paul wrote 1 Corinthians.

The implications of our findings have an important bearing on the selection of sources on which to base our subsequent explorations. It would be inappropriate to search for ethics, customs, etc. in ancient classical Greek or Hellenistic eras rather than the late Republic and early Roman period. This does not mean that sources written in Greek from the latter period may not be germane to our explorations, but that in dealing with Roman Corinth we must be aware of the Roman influences that had played *the* role in shaping life in Corinth for more than a century.

While the constitution setting up Corinth as a Roman colony is not extant, we are not unaware of how it was governed. The Latin epigraphic evidence confirms the nature of public offices such as magistrates in a Ro-

79. For a discussion of the importance of forensic petitions see my 'The Role of the *captatio benevolentia* in the Speeches of Tertullus and Paul in Acts 24,' *JTS* n.s. 42.2 (Nov. 1991): 505-31.

80. See the comments of R. Laurence on the importance of bridging the growing gap between archaeology and historical sources in R. Laurence and J. Berry, eds., *Cultural Identity in the Roman Empire* (London: Routledge, 1998), p. 1, and its significance for New Testament studies in my 'Editorial', *TynB* 50.2 (1999): 161-62.

man colony.[81] In addition, other elements can be pieced together from what remains of the constitution of another Roman colony founded by Julius Caesar c. 45 B.C., *Colonia Genetiva Julia*.[82] Here there are references to priests and augurs and 'all the conditions and . . . all the rights appertaining [to them] . . . in every colony.'[83] The reconstruction of parts of the constitution of Corinth would be possible on the basis of extant constitutions from other Roman colonies.

Corinth did not possess the *ius Italicum*. 'It was not given universally to colonial settlements, since the dispossessed Antonians of Italy whom Augustus settled in Macedonia held it, but the great Julian colonies of Corinth and Carthage did not'.[84] Its absence, however, does not detract from Corinth's tremendous importance in the East or its particular role as the spearhead for the penetration of *Romanitas* into the province of Achaea.[85] In stating this, it is not to be assumed that Corinth imposed cultural change upon cities in the province against their will. Rather it promoted Roman culture beyond its city limits. Its benefits to the élite in cities in Achaea were such that they stood to gain most depending on the degree of assimilation.[86] It was, however, different in Paul's Corinth itself, where its citizens had been Roman for one hundred years. They proudly fostered *Romanitas* in Rome's most important colony in the East in this era. Our investigation has shown that, in the time of Paul, Corinth's cultural emphasis was consciously Roman. Corinth was therefore 'the centre of *Romanitas*' in Achaea; and while there were other Roman colonies in Achaea, i.e., Dyme

---

81. Kent, *Corinth*, 8.3, pp. 24-31 for the offices and names of officeholders.

82. See E. G. Hardy, *Three Spanish Charters and Other Documents* (Oxford: Clarendon Press, 1912), pp. 7-60 for commentary and translation. Although the extant copy of this constitution dates from Flavian times, it preserves the original regulations of 45 B.C.; E. T. Salmon, *Roman Colonization under the Republic*, p. 135.

83. *Colonia Genetiva Julia*, LXVI.

84. Sherwin-White, *The Roman Citizenship*, p. 316.

85. Cartledge and Spawforth, *Hellenistic and Roman Sparta*, p. 104.

86. For the most recent discussion see P. A. Brunt, 'The Romanization of the Local Ruling Classes in the Roman Empire,' in D. M. Pippidi, ed., *Assimilation et résistance à culture gréco-romaine dans le monde ancien: Travaux du VIe Congrès International d'Etudes Classique* (Paris: 'Belles Lettres', 1976), pp. 161-73; Laurence and Berry, *Cultural Identity in the Roman Empire*; M. C. Hoff and S. I. Rotroff, *The Romanization of Athens: Proceedings of an International Conference*, Oxbow Monograph 94 (Oxford: Oxbow Books, 1997); and G. Woolf, *Becoming Roman: The Origins of Provincial Civilization in Gaul* (Cambridge: Cambridge University Press, 1998).

and Patrae, none had the 'strong gravitational pull' that Corinth had as the provincial and cultural capital.[87]

In stressing the *Romanitas* of Paul's Corinth, it would be wrong to assume that Corinth was populated only by Roman citizens in this or any other period. Spawforth suggests that 'the appearance of outside notables as office-holders from Claudius on marks a significant step in the integration of this enclave of *Romanitas* into the surrounding Greek world.'[88] Is his conclusion correct? The attraction of notables to the city and their integration into Roman civic life suggest that they, and not the colony, were undergoing a cultural metamorphosis. In his discussion of 'the seductions of [Roman] civilization', G. Woolf points out the attraction of Roman ways for wealthy Greeks, for Roman 'rich town houses offered sensual comforts, warmth in winter and the luxuries of bathing, to which we might add the softness of new fabrics, the glitter of Roman jewellery and the gastronomic splendours of the Roman table'.[89] Corinth possessed all these. The holding of main liturgies required the possession of wealth and resulted in the conferring of Roman citizenship on provincials.[90] The acquisition of citizenship had become the means of upward social mobility for provincials who could secure this much-prized possession, whether as freedmen through manumission after a period of service in a Roman household,[91] or as wealthy free men who promised civic benefactions and offered themselves for public service in the colony.

In conclusion, whether rich or poor, bond or free, the cultural milieu which impacted life in the city of Corinth was *Romanitas*. This does not mean that there were no ethnic minorities, but it does mean that the dominant and transforming cultural influence was Roman.

87. Salmon, *Roman Colonisation under the Republic*, p. 136, n. 300; and the citation from Cartledge and Spawforth, *Hellenistic and Roman Sparta*, p. 104.

88. A. J. S. Spawforth, 'Roman Corinth: The Formation of a Colonial Elite,' in A. D. Rizaki, ed., *Roman Onomastics in the Greek East Social and Political Aspects*, Μελετήματα 21 (Athens, 1996), p. 175.

89. Woolf, *Becoming Roman*, p. 68.

90. See *Lex Municipalis Salpensana*, xxi: 'All persons who become *duovirs, aediles,* or *quaestors* . . . shall be Roman citizens on laying down the magistracy at the end of the year [when the period of office expired]'.

91. See my 'Social Mobility,' *Seek the Welfare of the City*, ch. 8.

Pauline Ethnonyms and Language

In the light of the above discussion, it may seem incongruous that Paul himself used non-Roman ethnonyms when he wrote to the congregation in Corinth.[92] In 1 Corinthians 1:22-24 he used the terms Ἰουδαῖοι and Ἕλληνες (1:22) to refer to the ethnic dichotomy of the ancient world. Jews asked for signs, and the others pursued wisdom. The term Ἕλληνες is normally translated 'Greeks'. In the following verse, after declaring that the preaching of the crucified Messiah was a stumbling block to 'Jews' (Ἰουδαῖοι), Paul noted that the message seemed to be grossly stupid to the 'Gentiles' (ἔθνη). But to those who were called, both 'Jews' (Ἰουδαῖοι) and Ἕλληνες, the Messiah was the power and the wisdom of God (1:24). The term Ἕλληνες is an ambiguous one — it could refer to educational status, i.e., the students of the orators,[93] or to ethnicity. It might be argued that the term Ἕλληνες as used here was a play on words, given the context of this passage in which Paul reacted to issues relating to oratory and the virtuoso performances of 'the debater of this age'.[94] The alternative is that the term Ἕλληνες was a synonym for ἔθνη. This alone makes sense of how Paul applied it in these verses. Ἕλληνες was used of 'Gentiles', according to Liddell and Scott, who cite in support Isaiah 9:12 (LXX) and John 7:35, and the cognate Ἑλληνικός referred to 'pagan' citing 2 Maccabees 4:10. Paul also exhorts Christians not to give offence to outsiders, describing them with the dichotomous ethnonyms of Jews (Ἰουδαῖοι) and Ἕλληνες. He then added another group, 'the church of God' (10:32). He also indicated that all the Christians in Corinth were baptised into one body — 'Jews or Ἕλληνες, slaves or free' (12:13).[95] The term Ἕλληνες should be

92. For a discussion of this in relation to Roman Italy, see R. Lawrence, 'Territory, Ethnonyms and Geography', in Lawrence and Berry, eds., *Cultural Identity in the Roman Empire*, ch. 7.

93. See Philostratus, *Lives of the Sophists* 518, 571, 600. On the use of the term for the students of the orators and the discussion in the glossary of rhetorical terms see W. C. Wright, *Philostratus and Eunapius*, LCL, 569. Cf. Tertullian, *Apology* 46, 'What has Athens to do with Jerusalem or the Academy with the church? Where is there any likeness . . . between the disciples of Greece and heaven?'

94. See my *Philo and Paul among the Sophists*, pp. 186ff.

95. Cf. Gal. 3:28: 'there is neither Jew nor Ἕλλην, slave nor free, male nor female'. On male and female see R. Turton, 'Greek Racism? Observations on the Character and Limits of Greek Ethnic Prejudice,' in G. Tsetskhladze, ed., *Ancient Greeks East and West* (Leiden: E. J. Brill, 1999), p. 72.

translated consistently in 1 Corinthians as 'Gentiles', for that is to whom he was referring.

These designations are not out of character with Paul's other letters. For example, when he wrote to the Christians in Rome he cited them among the 'Gentiles' and admitted that he was under obligation to 'both Greeks and Barbarians' (Ἕλληνές τε καὶ βάρβαροι), affirming the gospel to be the power of God for salvation 'to the Jew first and also the Ἕλληνες (Rom. 1:13-16). The Greeks described the Romans as 'Barbarians' — as they did the rest of the world.[96] Paul never used the term 'Romans' (Ῥωμαῖοι) in his letters, and addressed those Christians who lived in the eternal city as 'all who are in Rome' (Rom. 1:7). Aristides in the second century said of those living in Rome, 'You do not "now" (νῦν) divide the races into Greeks and Barbarians . . . but you have divided the people into Romans and non-Romans (ἀλλ᾽ εἰς Ῥωμαίους καὶ οὐ Ῥωμαίους)' (*Or.* 25.63). The term Ἕλληνες was a common synonym for 'Gentiles'. In using it, Paul indicates neither the ethnic origin nor the citizenship of those early Christians living in Rome or Corinth, but he was repeating an all-embracing term.

Paul's use of these ethnonyms does not modify the conclusion that the cultural background of Corinth was Roman. Neither does the fact that he wrote his letters to the colony in Greek change the conclusions. The Greek language was of great interest to the Romans, and it was not uncommon for them to send their sons to Athens to learn the language to a standard where they could declaim in Greek.[97] We know from Philostratus that Greek was not unknown in Rome, for declamations delivered in Greek by visiting orators drew large crowds.[98] Paul was said to be at least bilingual (Acts 21:37, 40), and it should not surprise us that he was capable of conversing in Latin.[99] The multilingual character of Corinth, whose inhabitants included Romans, Greeks, Jews and others, meant that only some spoke Latin.[100] While bilingualism is well attested in the

96. Turton, 'Greek Racism? Observations on the Character and Limits of Greek Ethnic Prejudice,' ch. 2.

97. E.g., Cicero studied in Athens for this purpose (*Letters to Friends*, 16.21.5-6).

98. Philostratus, *Lives of the Sophists* 589.

99. The language in which the trial of Paul was conducted would have been either Latin or Greek. For evidence of the Roman policy on this matter see my 'The Role of the *captatio benevolentia* in the Speeches of Tertullus and Paul in Acts 24,' 526, n. 104.

100. A. Woolf, 'Romancing the Celts: A Segmentary Approach to Acculturation,' in

East (e.g., a number of bilingual inscriptions have been found in Asia Minor),[101] Greek was the *lingua franca* of the Roman empire in the first century and clearly a common language of the Corinthian congregation. Latin was the language of the élite. Had there been an option for the Corinthian church, it is unlikely that Paul would have selected the language of the élite, given the way in which the church appeared to have deferred to those few with social rank and status. Paul also comments on the class of 'the many', over against the 'not many' whom God had called into the kingdom in Corinth (1:26-29).

Paul's selection of ethnonyms and the language of his letters to the Corinthians is explicable and does not displace other evidence that the dominant cultural and social ethos which influenced the world of the Christian community was Roman.

IV. 'So Whatever Happened after Paul Left Corinth?'

This is an obvious question to ask after reading 1 Corinthians. A number of answers has already been suggested. Until the 1970s one explanation was the external influence of Gnosticism, although it was never an answer that accounted for all the issues raised in Paul's letter.[102] Later it was demonstrated that Gnosticism in Corinth was a construct using evidence from later centuries retrojected into the first century where there was no evidence for the movement at the time when 1 Corinthians was written.[103] The attempt to salvage it as a viable thesis by recourse to 'incipient gnosticism' generally failed to persuade New Testament scholars. It was replaced by the view that after Paul left the Corinthians embraced an overrealised eschatology.[104] That view has been subjected to scrutiny and found to be deficient, partly because of its misunderstanding of a text fundamental to its thesis,

---

R. Laurence and J. Berry, eds., *Cultural Identity in the Roman Empire* (London: Routledge, 1998), pp. 121-22.

101. See the forthcoming volume on this topic based on epigraphic evidence from I-III centuries A.D. by Dr. R. Kearsley, Macquarie University.

102. W. Schmithals, *Gnosticism in Corinth* (ET Nashville: Abingdon Press, 1971).

103. E. M. Yamauchi, *Pre-Christian Gnosticism: A Survey of the Proposed Evidence*, 2nd ed. (Grand Rapids: Baker, 1983), p. xiii indicates that 'we are dealing with a scholarly hypothesis rather than a phenomenon explicitly attested in first-century documents'.

104. A. C. Thiselton, 'Realized Eschatology at Corinth,' *NTS* 24 (1977-78): 510-26.

viz., 1 Corinthians 4:6ff. Paul skillfully used all the irony associated with the rhetorical device he actually cites, i.e., the covert allusion whose covertness he discloses.[105] There is an alternative explanation for certain assumptions concerning their belief about resurrection in chapter 15.[106]

It has also been argued that it was not the Corinthian Christians but Paul himself who created the problems that emerge. Had he modified his own teaching for strategic reasons? It was the 'younger, more vigorous Paul fired with enthusiasm in his new faith, less cautious in his theological statements than he later became' who with an unguarded emphasis taught on 'Christian freedom' during his eighteen-month ministry in Corinth. The reason for the change related to 'his understandable desire to strengthen the Gentile mission with the Jerusalem Church, about which he could not tell the Corinthians.' His original letter took a stronger line in conformity with the Jerusalem Council's emphasis (5:9). 'His sudden change in perspective and his demand for observance of a cautious list of prohibitions puzzled and angered them.' So 1 Corinthians is an ameliorating letter, where he returned to his former stance on most issues but cast them in a more cautious theological construct and modified the extremes of the 'younger' Paul's teaching when he was in Corinth.[107]

A more recent proposition has been defended that 'if we asked the Corinthian Christians how they could possibly have got into such a mess, they would have justified themselves by reference to teaching they had received'.[108] This reconstruction of the situation is given in greater detail where the traditions that the Corinthians followed were actually the teachings of Jesus. 'It seems that the Corinthians themselves were very familiar with the traditions of Jesus and were using them in ways that Paul strongly disagreed with (for example, justifying their immorality, on the one hand, and advocating Christian celibacy, on the other).'[109] 'How did the prob-

---

105. For a discussion of this point see my *Philo and Paul among the Sophists*, pp. 196-201.

106. J. Holleman, *Resurrection and Parousia: A Traditio-Historical Study of Paul's Eschatology in 1 Corinthians* 15 (Leiden: E. J. Brill, 1996), pp. 4-31. See also pp. 96-105.

107. J. C. Hurd Jr., 'Retrospect and Prospect,' *The Origin of 1 Corinthians*, 2nd ed. (Macon: Mercer University Press, 1983), p. 287 and ch. 9 for a summary presentation of what happened after Paul left.

108. D. Wenham, 'Whatever Went Wrong in Corinth?' *ET* 108.5 (Feb. 1997): 138.

109. D. Wenham, *Paul: Follower of Jesus or Founder of Christianity?* (Grand Rapids and Cambridge: Eerdmans, 1995), p. 392.

lems blow up so spectacularly in Corinth?'[110] In contrast to centuries of tradition in contemporary Christianity, the Corinthians 'were having to think through the teaching of Jesus and Paul in situations that were (in many cases) new'. Furthermore, while they had misapplied the same traditions, Paul in 1 Corinthians 'steered a remarkably fine course theologically, interpreting the tradition in a way that was balanced and (arguably) faithful to Jesus'.[111]

This book explores the thesis that the problems which arose subsequent to Paul's departure did so partly because the Christians were 'cosmopolitans', i.e., citizens of this world and, in particular, citizens or residents of Roman Corinth. They had grown up in, and imbibed that culture before they became Christians. They reacted to some issues that arose after Paul left on the basis of the learnt conventions and cultural mores of Corinthian *Romanitas*. One of these issues was the sexual conduct of some of the Christians, which reflected the defence made by the élite on these matters. This was among conduct reported verbally to Paul and not included in their letter, to which he refers (1:11; 5:1; cf. 7:1). Other concerns were the subject of that letter because there was no certainty or unanimity in the congregation as to an appropriate course of action. On most issues Paul did not specifically quote any dominical or apostolic traditions he had delivered to them while he was there when he responded to their letter in 1 Corinthians — the exceptions being the institution of the Lord's Supper and a summary of the content of the gospel (11:23-25; 15:3ff.).

How do we account for other problems discussed in the letter? In Corinthian studies it has normally been assumed that Paul wrote to a Christian community residing in a city which enjoyed the tranquil existence promised by the *Pax Romana*. While no external changes supposedly affected the inhabitants of the Roman colony as a whole, it will be argued that there were three from within the city. The first was warmly greeted by the Corinthians as a whole because of the prestige and prosperity it added to their prestigious Roman colony (Chapter 12). By contrast, the second was dreaded in any ancient city because of the personal misery, rioting, and social dislocation it could cause unless action was taken immediately to ameliorate its effects (Chapters 10 and 11). While there is significant extant evidence for these, the third suggested external change is based on evi-

---

110. Wenham, 'Whatever Went Wrong in Corinth?' 139.
111. Wenham, 'Whatever Went Wrong in Corinth?' 141.

dence beyond Corinth and is an attempt to search for a possible answer to a vexed question (Chapter 13). The Christian community, like the rest of the city, was not exempt from the effects of social change, even if some of their response proved to be somewhat different.

The social historian reading 1 Corinthians cannot but be struck by just how many of the issues Paul dealt with in that letter reflect aspects of first-century life generally. As a literary source it provides the best composite witness of its day to life in a Roman colony in the East. Its author, unlike any other who wrote on life in Corinth in that century, had actually resided in the colony. The following chapters seek to place 1 Corinthians in the context of Roman Corinth in the fifth decade of the first century.

The approach in this book has been to use external information to illuminate aspects of Corinthian life discussed in 1 Corinthians for the twenty-first century reader. The following chapters will show that in matters concerning the law, social conventions, and secular ethics, the primary influences on the responses of Christians were derived principally from *Romanitas*. These will help explain the origins of the conflicts and ethical dilemmas created for this early Christian community in the period after Paul left Corinth.

Methodologically, the approach has been the same as that of any ancient historian looking at any first-century literary or nonliterary document by examining it in its religious, cultural, and social settings.[112] The reader will need to make two judgements at the end of this book. Does the external evidence in the following chapters illuminate issues in 1 Corinthians, as it does for this author? Was it the influence of cultural conditioning and the impact of social changes, rather than one simple explanation such as Gnosticism, overrealised eschatology, misunderstanding of the teaching of Jesus by the Christians, or a theological change for political purposes by Paul that was responsible for the problems that arose in the Christian community after he left Corinth?

---

112. See, e.g., the treatment of late first-century and early second-century literary sources by C. P. Jones, *The Roman World of Dio Chrysostom* (Cambridge, Mass. and London: Harvard University Press, 1978) and *Plutarch and Rome* (Oxford: Clarendon Press, 1971).

PART I

THE INFLUENCE OF SECULAR ETHICS

CHAPTER 2

Secular Discipleship and Christian Competitiveness (1 Corinthians 1–4)

'Operating in a Secular Fashion' (3:3)

The pupils of secular teachers in the ancient world had long been called 'disciples' (μαθηταί). Christian disciples in Corinth applied to their own Christian 'teachers' such as Paul, Apollos, and possibly Peter, the same cultural mores that governed the relationship of secular pupils and their élitist teachers. After all, Paul did declare that what the members of the Christian community were doing with respect to their relationship to Apollos and himself was 'walking according to man' and behaving like the 'men' of Corinth (3:3-4). What did he mean?

There is important information from Corinthian sources which describes the secular conventions governing the disciple/teacher relationship. 1 Corinthians provides evidence that after Paul left Corinth, Christians shaped their responses with him, Apollos, and one another in the same way that secular disciples did with their teachers and fellow students.

In order to argue that this happened, it is proposed to explore (I) the nature of the secular pupil/teacher relationship; (II) the competitive spirit that existed between teachers; (III) the expected playing off of the merits of one teacher against another by their respective pupils; and (IV) the effects of importing these secular mores into the Christian community in Corinth and Paul's attempt to counter this by reshaping their perception of the role of Christian instructors who, along with the congregation, were disciples.

I. The Secular Pupil/Teacher Relationship

The term 'disciple' (μαθητής) was neither a Jewish nor Christian invention. There is substantial evidence that its use meant 'the pupil of a teacher' long before the first century. A survey of the *TLG* reveals that, with the rise of the First Sophistic movement in the fifth century B.C., the word is found in extant literature one hundred and ninety-eight times. The majority of occurrences are in Plato and Isocrates, some eighty-five examples are found in the following century, and the numbers fall sharply in the next three centuries to almost nil. In the first century A.D. with the rise of the Second Sophistic some one hundred and eighty-one occurrences are recorded apart from those in the New Testament. The first-century figure is significant given that there are fewer extant sources in that century compared with the preceding and following ones. Plutarch, who discusses the sophists, has some forty-eight examples, and Dio Chrysostom some twenty-eight. Statistical word counts are difficult to interpret, but the above evidence establishes at the very least that the term was used in connection with the sophistic movement both in its beginnings in the fifth century B.C. and in its 'renaissance' in the first century A.D.

Dio Chrysostom visited Corinth at the time of the Isthmian Games between A.D. 89-96 during his exile from Rome[1] and witnessed the activities of 'the disciples' of the sophists.[2] They provide important information on the nature of the disciple/sophist relationship. In his day the term 'sophist' was not a pejorative one but was used of those virtuoso orators who possessed a large public following and participated in the secular assembly (ἐκλλησία) of the city.[3] They were also the spokesmen for the city on embassies to the provincial governor or the emperor.[4] In addition to declaiming on topics at public performances

---

1. For dating see C. P. Jones, *The Roman World of Dio Chrysostom* (Cambridge, Mass.: Harvard University Press, 1978), p. 136.

2. *Or.* 8.9. While this oration purports to be by Diogenes, it is agreed that Dio used this ancient figure as a cover for himself, as did Socrates and Odysseus. Jones, *The Roman World of Dio Chrysostom*, pp. 47, 49; and P. Desideri, *Dione di Prusa: un intellettuale greco nell' Impero Romano* (Messina: Casa Editrice G. d'Anna, 1978), p. 201.

3. G. W. Bowersock, 'Professional Quarrels,' *Greek Sophists in the Roman Empire* (Oxford: Clarendon Press, 1969), ch. 7.

4. Bowersock, 'Sophists and Emperors,' *Greek Sophists in the Roman Empire*, ch. 4; and A. Bash, *Ambassadors for Christ* (Tübingen: J. C. B. Mohr [Paul Siebeck], 1997), p. 60.

for a fee,[5] they ran expensive schools. There they trained the next generation of the social élite to argue in the criminal and civil courts and debate in the secular assemblies as they did.[6] Paul himself refers to the 'debaters of this age' who were the virtuoso orators, i.e., the sophists.[7] Like their pupils, the sophists were drawn from the élite class and were seen as the custodians of the tertiary educational process of that time.[8]

The student who enrolled in the exclusive school of the sophist was called a 'disciple' (μαθητής), which implied that he was a learner who would model himself after his teacher. Dio Chrysostom was once asked of which wise man Socrates was a disciple, to which he replied, 'Homer'. A further question was plied, 'How would it be possible to be a zealous disciple of a person long since dead?' Dio responded, 'If [he was] a zealous person' (ζηλωτής), then he would also be a 'disciple' (μαθητής).[9] The discussion continued with this explanation. 'For whoever really follows anyone surely knows what the person was like, and by imitating his acts and his words he tries as best he can to make himself like him. But that is precisely, it seems, what the pupil (μαθητής) does — by imitating his teacher and paying heed to him he tries to acquire his art. . . . However, if you shrink from calling Socrates a μαθητής of Homer, but call him a ζηλωτής, it will make no difference to me.'[10] This further unpacks the significance of the term 'disciple' with respect to the concept of *imitatio*.[11]

Imitation was seen not only in terms of the oratorical style of the teacher but also in the way the disciple spoke, dressed, and even walked. According to Philostratus, the students of the sophist Hadrian not only imitated his rhetorical style and accent but also his walk, and 'the elegance of his attire'.[12]

A young Corinthian student of rhetoric who was a Roman citizen

5. See my *Philo and Paul among the Sophists*, SNTSMS 96 (Cambridge: Cambridge University Press, 1997), pp. 49-50.

6. On the élite status of sophists see E. L. Bowie, 'Greeks and Their Past in the Second Sophistic,' *Past and Present* 46 (1970): 3-41.

7. 1 Cor. 1:20. For a number of nineteenth- and twentieth-century scholars who have identified them as such, and for further evidence and arguments in support of this, see my *Philo and Paul among the Sophists*, pp. 187-94.

8. E. L. Bowie, 'The Importance of the Sophists,' *Yale Classical Studies* 27 (1982): 29-52.

9. *Or.* 55.4.

10. *Or.* 55.1, 3, 5.

11. K. H. Rengstorf, μαθητής, *TDNT*, IV, 417.

12. *Lives of the Sophists* 586-88.

came under the scrutiny of the critical eye of Epictetus,[13] the philosopher from Nicopolis and visitor, if not sometime resident, of Corinth. Epictetus' work was dedicated to the leading Corinthian citizen, L. Gellius Menander.[14] This early second-century discussion, 'On personal adornment', provides important evidence of a disciple imitating his Corinthian teacher, although Epictetus was careful not to openly attack him in his dialogue with the student of rhetoric.[15] The young man not only set his hair, wore jewellery, dressed elaborately in order to impress, but also removed all the hair from his body in order to appear 'godlike'.[16] He did this because 'bodily presence' had become immensely important in the Second Sophistic.[17] Philostratus recorded that when Alexander of Seleucia came to Athens, a murmur of approval went through the audience as he stood before them for the first time because of his appearance and 'perfect elegance'.[18]

Epictetus sought to shock the young student by contradicting the whole emphasis on the importance of striking the right image. He referred to this young man's 'paltry' body, hardly a compliment to a youth who, as part of his education, worked out regularly in the gymnasium in order to shape his body. Epictetus then inflicted a further insult by telling him to his face that he was ugly, a humiliation and loss of *dignitas* for any Roman citizen of Corinth.[19] This young Corinthian student was enjoined by Epictetus to give up this futile imitation of personal adornment since it would not prepare him for his public role in Corinth, and to go in search of that which could make him 'beautiful', i.e., the great cardinal civic virtues.[20] These alone would equip him for a life of public service.[21]

---

13. The indication of the public offices for which he might be appointed in days to come indicates that he possessed Roman citizenship, for without it he was not eligible to debate in the assembly, let alone be elected to these liturgies (Epictetus, 3.1.34-36). Epictetus' knowledge of the seniority of the public offices which were peculiar to Corinth further suggests that his knowledge of Corinth was firsthand.

14. G. W. Bowersock, 'A New Inscription of Arrian,' *GRBS* 8 (1967): 279-80.

15. The speeches, reconstructed from shorthand notes, were made by his pupil, Flavius Arrianus, c. 108. For discussion see F. Millar, 'Epictetus and the Imperial Court,' *JRS* 55 (1965): 142.

16. Epictetus, 3.1.1, 14, 26-27, 32.

17. Epictetus, 3.1.6.

18. *Lives of the Sophists* 536.

19. Epictetus, 3.1, 31, 41, 43.

20. Epictetus, 3.1, 6ff.

21. The philosophers poured scorn on the ways in which the educational process had

For more than two centuries 'rhetorical delivery' had encompassed both speech and 'bodily presence'; this included appearance and a stage presence. In fact, the incorporation of rhetorical delivery into the discipline of rhetoric owed its origins to the ancient profession of acting.[22] So critical was bodily presence and the timbre of the voice that there was a long history of able rhetoricians who never appeared in public to deliver orations simply because they lacked 'rhetorical delivery'.[23] It had become an essential requirement for a disciple if he was to have a successful career in oratory.[24] According to Paul's detractors, it was his telling deficiency, for his bodily presence was weak and his speech deficient (2 Cor. 10:10).[25] A disciple whose teacher failed in any aspect of rhetorical delivery had an uphill battle to defend him in the face of such an obvious defect, as it would quickly draw criticism from the disciples of other teachers. The interest in it dominated the first century as it witnessed the rise of the Second Sophistic.[26]

Parents were therefore particularly concerned to find the best sophist for their son. Because oratory was essential for any public career in the first century, it was important to have sons well trained in this sophisticated discipline.[27] It was primarily in the classroom that they heard their teacher produce demonstration pieces, called declamations, although he also would declaim in the theatre at public performances.[28] The disciples were given the opportunity to try their own hand at declaiming in front of their fellow students, and these were important practice runs before being launched into public life.[29]

Sophists were expected to have a profound influence on the young

---

developed under the sophists, yet the latter had won the young men into their schools at the expense of the philosophers.

22. For a detailed discussion of this point see my 'Philodemus and Paul on Rhetorical Delivery (ὑπόκρισις),' in J. T. Fitzgerald, G. Holland, and D. Obbink, eds., *Philodemus and the New Testament World* (Leiden: E. J. Brill, forthcoming).

23. Philodemus, 'On Rhetoric,' 1.195, xvi.

24. For the financial benefits for success such as exemption from taxes and liturgies, see 'Special Privileges,' in Bowersock, *Greek Sophists in the Roman Empire*, ch. 3.

25. 'Philodemus and Paul on Rhetorical Delivery (ὑπόκρισις)'.

26. For evidence on the rise of the movement in the first half of the first century see my *Philo and Paul among the Sophists*, pp. 233-34.

27. Quintilian, *Training of an Orator* 2.1.2; 8.1.

28. Winter, *Philo and Paul among the Sophists*, pp. 30-34.

29. Quintilian, *Training of an Orator* 2.7.5.

men in their school. It is clear that the relationship was an intimate one in which imitation at times went to extremes, as with the young man of Corinth in the time of Epictetus. He was not totally to blame because, as a disciple, he was merely imitating his teacher and conforming to what was expected of all young students of rhetoric. Their teacher was their exclusive paradigm; such was the student/teacher relationship.

II. Professional Competitiveness among Teachers

First-century teachers competed among themselves for students. If they secured good numbers of disciples to train in their schools, they had tapped a very lucrative market, for fees were exceedingly high.[30] If their services were needed in the secular assembly, they could secure public honours for faithful service, which normally included at least a public inscription, if not a crown of gold and sometimes a statue.[31] In Corinth there is ample evidence of orators being honoured by 'The Council and the People'.[32] Their skills as spokesmen in leading embassies to governors or emperors were regarded as invaluable, because by this means cities secured financial concessions, provincial honours, and imperial favours.[33]

There were established conventions by which a sophist secured a foothold in a city. On first arriving, the teacher advertised by sending out invitations indicating the time and place where he would present his credentials and declaim.[34] At the appointed hour he addressed the gathered assembly. Seated, he would engage in an encomium on the city and an oblique self-commendation, described technically as διάλεξις and ἀπολογία respectively, while the preliminary speeches were both regarded as προλαλιά.[35] The sophist then invited the audience to nominate any

---

30. G. B. Kerferd, *The Sophistic Movement* (Cambridge: Cambridge University Press, 1981), pp. 27-28.

31. For the conventions surrounding this see my 'Civic Honours for Christian Benefactors,' *Seek the Welfare of the City*, pp. 26-33.

32. Kent, *Corinth*, 8.3: Publius Aelius Sospinus, no. 226, (Lucius?) Maecius Faustinus, no. 264, Marcus Valerius Taurinus, no. 268, and Peducaeus Cestianus, no. 269.

33. Bowersock, *Greek Sophists in the Roman Empire*, pp. 44ff.

34. D. A. Russell, *Greek Declamations* (Cambridge: Cambridge University Press, 1983), pp. 76-77.

35. Russell, *Greek Declamations*, pp. 75-80. There are three full-length statues of ora-

topic on which he would declaim. Once that was known, the choice rested with him to rise from his seat and declaim immediately if he felt competent to speak to the subject, thereby displaying his great ability in extemporary rhetoric. He could delay the declamation for twenty-four hours in order to prepare for this 'make or break' situation.[36] Once he had completed his oration, it was up to the audience to either embrace him or reject the offer of his services. In the case of the former response, the élite were then willing to send their sons to his school, the city fathers were happy to reward him with citizenship so that he could debate in the public assemblies, and the citizens gladly welcomed him as a spokesman for an embassy.

The competition to gain a place in the city could be stiff. Aristides, when he arrived in Smyrna in A.D. 176, found himself in competition with an Egyptian sophist who had advertised his venue and time at the theatre. Aristides, with great presence of mind and at very short notice, packed the council chamber at the same hour and secured the approval of the élite, while the Egyptian retreated from the city in defeat,[37] for he had only managed to attract what was considered the derisory number, for only seventeen turned up.[38]

However, competition from other sophists within the city still existed once a newcomer had secured his following. Dio Chrysostom, during that visit to Corinth between A.D. 89-96, not only saw the disciples but also heard 'the many wretched sophists' around Poseidon's temple at the time of the Isthmian Games. These were the teachers of the disciples who were also present. He observed that the sophists were 'shouting and abusing one another',[39] engaging in invective against each other in order to demonstrate to the crowd and to their disciples just how inferior their competitors were. Some who acted as lawyers, for a branch of their discipline included forensic rhetoric, were clearly touting for business. They were

---

tors in the museum in Syrian Antioch, Turkey. Two of them have the orators seated with scrolls in their hands signalling that they were ready to rise and declaim, having passed through the first two stages. It was never a convention to read their speech, but to deliver it from memory.

36. Russell, *Greek Declamations*, pp. 76-77.
37. *Discourse* 51.29.
38. This number indicated failure according to Russell, *Greek Declamations*, p. 77, n. 16.
39. *Or.* 8.9.

aiming to attract clients whom they could represent in cases of vexatious litigation, for Corinth was a notoriously litigious society.[40] Claudius had abolished the 250-year-old law proscribing the taking of fees for representing clients in court, and fixed a maximum charge of ten thousand *sesterces.*[41] Competition for students and clients epitomised the sophists.

G. W. Bowersock devotes a whole chapter to 'professional quarrels' in his work on the sophists in the Roman empire,[42] citing some of the interesting evidence provided by Philostratus.[43] These struggles could be waged at a personal level, at a political one in a city, or even intercity. For example, it is known that Favorinus, who visited Corinth on three occasions, was locked in a struggle with Polemo, a struggle that had traditionally existed between their cities of origin, i.e., Ephesus and Smyrna.[44] So intense were some of the battles that they required provincial and even imperial intervention.[45] Philostratus epitomised the sophists in his spirit of rivalry, for he contended that 'when people called Favorinus "a sophist", the mere fact that he had quarrelled with a sophist was evidence enough',[46] for his life, like that of the sophists in general, was full of quarrels.[47] Their relationship with one another has been well documented, and the recurring term for describing it is 'strife' (ἔρις).[48] Philo of Alexandria, Paul's contemporary, like other first-century writers, including Plutarch, used it and a cognate, ἐριστικός, to describe the rivalry and contention among the sophists.[49]

III. Pupils' Loyalty to Their Teachers

Another noun used of the disciple of a teacher was 'zealot' (ζηλωτής). While New Testament scholarship has tended to associate this term with

---

40. *Or.* 8.9.

41. J. A. Crook, *Legal Advocacy in the Roman World* (London: Duckworth, 1995), pp. 129-31.

42. Bowersock, 'Professional Quarrels,' *Greek Sophists in the Roman Empire,* ch. 7.

43. *Lives of the Sophists* 559ff.

44. On Polemo see W. W. Reader, *The Severed Hand and the Upright Corpse: The Declamations of Marcus Antonius Polemo* (Atlanta: Scholars Press, 1996).

45. Bowersock, *Greek Sophists in the Roman Empire,* p. 100.

46. *Lives of the Sophists,* 491.

47. Bowersock, *Greek Sophists in the Roman Empire,* pp. 90-91.

48. For its use by ancient authors such as Plato, see Kerferd, 'Dialectic, Antilogic and Eristic,' *The Sophistic Movement,* ch. 6, esp. pp. 62-63.

the first-century movement of the anti-Roman tax party of the Palestinian Jews,[50] it had long been in currency in the academy. The term was coined because it described something of the exclusive loyalty that was expected of a pupil by his teacher, and expressed the zealousness with which the disciple both promoted and defended him before the disciples of others. Dio Chrysostom used the two terms of the ideal king when he wrote that one ought to be 'both a disciple and a zealot of this god', i.e., Zeus (μαθητής τε καὶ ζηλωτής τοῦ θεοῦ).[51] It was, however, more generally used of the attitude of pupils towards their teachers.

They were encouraged to be extremely zealous (ζῆλος) in demonstrating their loyalty to their teacher, promoting his professional attributes as an orator and his educative prowess. At the same time they created strife (ἔρις) by means of trenchant criticism of perceived deficiencies of other teachers.[52] It was not unknown for a student of one sophist to walk behind another teacher who was talking to his own students. If he heard some grammatical lapse or the use of non-Atticisms, he would then ridicule the deficiencies of that teacher.[53] Philostratus records an extreme case of a pupil who heaped such ridicule upon another teacher that the latter's disciples ordered their slaves to thrash him, and they did so with such force that they accidentally killed him.[54]

In Corinth Dio Chrysostom recorded that, at the same time that the sophists were shouting and abusing one another, their 'so-called disciples' (τῶν λεγομένων μαθητῶν) were fighting those of other's teachers.[55] Dio used the term 'so-called' to indicate that while they designated themselves 'disciples', in his opinion their conduct clearly belied their calling because

49. Philo, *Mut.* 10, *Her.* 246, *Flacc.* 41, *Det.* 45, *Congr.* 129; and Plutarch, *Lives, Caesar,* 33.

50. M. Hengel, *The Zealots: Investigations into the Jewish Freedom Movement in the Period from Herod I until 70 A.D.* (Edinburgh: T & T Clark, 1989).

51. *Or.* 1.38; cf. ζηλωτής τε καὶ ὑπηρέτης (*Or.* 4.122).

52. According to A. Stumpff, *TDNT,* II, 883, the cognate ζηλόω can mean 'to envy' when used in a hostile sense, but the use of the terms and cognates in the first century suggests that ἐρίζω and ζηλόω are not synonymous.

53. Philostratus, *Lives of the Sophists* 208. On barbarians, see G. Anderson, *Philostratus: Biography and Belles Lettres in the Third Century A.D.* (London: Croom Helm, 1986), p. 44.

54. Bowersock, *Greek Sophists in the Roman Empire,* pp. 91-92, citing Philostratus, *Lives of the Sophists* 588.

55. *Or.* 9.8.

THE INFLUENCE OF SECULAR ETHICS

of their antagonism towards other teachers and their disciples.[56] In this, however, they were being zealous on behalf of their teacher over against others. By engaging in verbal battles with other students they were simply following a long-established requirement of demonstrating their exclusive loyalty to their own sophist. Zealousness for one's teacher by promoting his attributes and at the same time openly criticising the deficiencies of another epitomised the behaviour of the disciples of first-century teachers.

IV. Secular Reverberations in 1 Corinthians

Paul told the Corinthian Christians that their perception of both Apollos and himself was wrong and stated categorically that their error arose from a secular judgement. They were thinking and acting like other Corinthians did, i.e., 'walking in a secular way' (κατὰ ἄνθρωπον περιπατεῖν) (3:3). The concept of walking was used as a metaphor for 'living' or 'acting',[57] and the phrase κατὰ ἄνθρωπον[58] refers to the fact that they were operating in the same way as the rest of Corinthian society.[59] Paul concluded that the Corinthian Christians were [behaving] like men [do]' (ἄνθρωποι), i.e., the other inhabitants of Corinth. The accusation was coupled with the complaint that their conduct was childish (σαρκικοί) and it was for that reason that he could not treat them other than what they were, i.e., babies needing milk (3:1-3).

56. For a discussion of the use of 'so-called' see J. L. Moles, 'The Career and Conversion of Dio Chrysostom,' *JRS* 68 (1978): 91, and further examples in Dio, *Or.* 77/78.34; cf. 49.3.

57. Eph. 2:2; 2 Cor. 10:2; Rom. 8:7. For a discussion of περιπατεῖν see R. Banks, '"Walking" as a Metaphor of the Christian Life: The Origins of a Significant Pauline Usage,' in E. W. Conrad and E. G. Newing, eds., *Perspectives on Language and Text: Essays and Poems in Honour of Francis I. Andersen on His Sixtieth Birthday, July 28, 1985* (Winona Lake: Eisenbrauns, 1987), pp. 303-13.

58. BAGD, κατά #5. J. B. Lightfoot, *Notes on the Epistles of Paul* (London, reprint 1985), p. 186.

59. Paul uses the phrase κατὰ ἄνθρωπον elsewhere and always in the singular to refer to agreed rules or conventions operating in society (1 Cor. 9:8); to illustrate a social convention (Gal. 3:15); to refer to a human way of speaking (Rom. 3:5); to indicate that a message had its origins in human reasoning (Gal. 1:11); and to remind his readers that the phrase he was using was to be taken as it was popularly or commonly understood (1 Cor. 15:32).

40

The evidence Paul produced was the verbal report he had received of divisions in the congregation (σχίσματα), witnessed by 'strife' (ἔρις) among them. He clearly explained the cause of it — 'and I am saying this because each one of you is saying, on the one hand, "I belong to Paul" and, on the other, "I belong to Apollos", and "I belong to Peter", and "I belong to Christ"' (1:10-12). Here was a situation where each Christian disciple declared his exclusive loyalty to an individual teacher. Paul later returns to their conduct, stating that 'where there is strife and zealousness (ζῆλος καὶ ἔρις) in your midst, are you not behaving in an immature way and operating in a secular fashion?' (3:3). He elaborates, 'For when any person says emphatically "I myself belong to Paul", and another says "I belong to Apollos", are you not behaving like '[other Corinthian] men' (3:4). Paul gives further details later in his discussion when he accuses them with respect to Apollos and himself of being 'puffed up on behalf of one over against the other' (εἷς ὑπὲρ τοῦ ἑνὸς φυσιοῦσθε κατὰ τοῦ ἑτέρου) (4:6).[60] The comparison was between a Jew of Alexandria whom Luke described as a 'man of education' (ἀνὴρ λόγιος) and an able speaker and debater (Acts 18:24, 28) and Paul, whose detractors in 2 Corinthians 10:10 conceded that his letters were 'weighty and strong' but his 'bodily presence was weak and his rhetoric [spoken] was contemptible'.[61] 1 Corinthians 1–4 provides important evidence of the inroads of secular perceptions of the Christian disciple's relationship to his teachers, Paul and Apollos. The preference for Apollos is seen in their request for him to return to the church in Corinth (16:12).

The conduct of the disciples of the sophists and the Christian disciples was identical. There were the same assertions of loyalty to one teacher, the same pride ('puffed up') with the same strife resulting as they denigrated other teachers while at the same time singing the praises of their own. The charge that Paul levelled at them — that they were conducting their relations with Apollos and himself in the same way the secular students of Corinth did with their sophists — was justified. The influence of secular conventions on the Christian disciples' relationships with their instructors is clear.

Further evidence of this inappropriate replication of the behaviour

---

60. For a discussion of Paul's use of the rhetorical device of the 'covert allusion' in 4:6 and its significance see my *Philo and Paul among the Sophists*, pp. 196-201.

61. See my 'Philodemus and Paul on Rhetorical Delivery (ὑπόκρισις).'

of the disciples of the élitist sophists in the Christian community can be deduced from the remedial steps which Paul took to counter it. First, he indicated that their relationship had been misconstrued. Contrary to their misconceived zealous 'oaths' of loyalty to either Apollos or others, including himself (1:12; 3:4), Apollos, Peter, and Paul all belonged to the body of the community. It was not the other way around, for all things belonged to them, including these instructors, and the community belonged exclusively to Christ (3:21-22a).

Second, he cast Apollos and himself in functional terms, not asking who they were in terms of their status and credentials, as the Corinthian Christians had done, but what was their task — 'What is Paul?' 'What is Apollos?' He did not invoke terms reflecting social status as the Corinthians did, but referred to both of them as servants who had different functions, i.e., planting and watering. These were labour much despised by the social élite, whose 'hands knew no labour' (3:5-7).[62] He concluded that servants were insignificant in the task because it was God alone who made the community increase in size (3:8).

Third, the image shifts as Paul indicates again precisely how the Corinthians should view their instructors. He declares them to be 'the employees of Christ and stewards of the mysteries of God'. The second term indicates that their task was to take from the resources God had revealed and, like good household stewards, to meet the needs and requirements of the members from the resources at their disposal (4:1).

Fourth, Paul rejected any possibility of identification of his entry to Corinth with that of a sophist entering a city in search of disciples. He specifically explained his own 'coming' to Corinth in terms that were consciously anti-sophistic, commenting that he did not come in 'the persuasiveness of rhetoric or wisdom', and that no topic was nominated from his hearers, for his message was fixed — 'Jesus Christ and him crucified'. He lacked 'rhetorical delivery', for he cut a sorry figure with 'his weakness, trembling, and much fear'. His oratory and the contents of his message lacked the persuasive tricks and sophisticated proofs of the sophists because he was not in search of disciples to follow him. He wanted their confidence to rest not in the wisdom of men but in the power of God (2:1-5).[63]

---

62. This comment was recorded by Philo, *Det.* 34.

63. For a full discussion of this passage and Paul's reference here to the three types of rhetorical devices used to persuade an audience and commended by the rhetorical hand-

Fifth, just as Dio Chrysostom claimed never to have had disciples,[64] Paul likewise never addressed the Corinthians or any other members of the congregations he founded as his disciples. He used other terms to describe his relationship with them such as familial terminology, addressing them as 'brothers' or 'beloved brothers' on twenty-nine occasions. His relationship with them was analogous to that of a father to his sons whom 'in Christ Jesus through the gospel, he himself had begotten' (4:15).

Paul's response to the problems in 1 Corinthians 1–4 aimed at further correcting the Christians' misunderstanding of their relationship to their instructors. It also provides evidence that secular educational mores had been highly influential in shaping their understanding. In part Paul's solution was framed in terms that made it clear that he chose antisophistic, non-discipleship, and familial categories to describe the Christians, Apollos, and himself.

The purpose of this chapter has been to establish that the Christian community was influenced by the secular educational mores of Corinth. It has also traced the effects of Christians embracing them, with their emphasis on the exclusive relationship of a student to his teacher, and the effect of zealousness in promoting loyalty to one and criticism of others. The same unhelpful effects that such activities had on the secular disciples from the Corinthian schools were debilitating the church after Paul had left Corinth. His charge, that they had replicated in the Christian community the secular élitist educational model which was promoted by the sophists, was justified.

---

books, i.e., *pathos, ethos,* and 'demonstrations', see my *Philo and Paul among the Sophists,* pp. 149-61; for a comparison with 1 Thess. 2, see my 'The Entry and Ethics of Orators and Paul,' *TynB* 44.1 (1993): 55-74.

64. On his disclaimer see *Or.* 12.13. However, Favorinus was a student of his.

CHAPTER 3

Criminal Law and Christian Partiality (1 Corinthians 5)

'Do You Not Judge Those Who Are Within?' (5:12)

In retrospect Roman law was a much admired system of jurisprudence,[1] and yet it had been consciously framed and administered to provide legal advantages for those with social status.[2] In the Julio-Claudian period, neither courts nor judges acted impartially in criminal cases towards the privileged or others in Rome, Roman colonies, and the provinces. Christians continued to exhibit the same partial attitudes towards the privileged with respect to breaches of criminal law as their compatriots did in Corinth. This chapter addresses the attitude towards criminal conduct of Christians in Corinth by examining (I) criminal prosecutions; (II) degrees of seriousness relating to incest under Roman law; (III) the guilty parties, and possible responses of the father of the incestuous son and the Christian community.

I. Criminal Prosecutions

The Romans distinguished between criminal and civil law. In Corinth, the capital of the province, the governor of Achaea was responsible for hearing criminal cases, while a local Corinthian magistrate or an *aedile* heard the

---

1. P. Stein, *Roman Law in European History* (Cambridge: Cambridge University Press, 1999).

2. For a detailed discussion of this extremely important issue see P. Garnsey, *Social Status and Legal Privilege in the Roman Empire* (Oxford: Clarendon Press, 1970).

civic and financial ones respectively. A first-century proconsul (ἀνθύπα-τος) of Achaea held the *imperium*. As with his predecessors of late Republican times, it gave him jurisdiction over criminal proceedings in Roman colonies as well as the province. While Provincials were only protected from his powers in the case of the law of extortion *(lex reputundarum)*, and Roman citizens from summary execution by the *lex Iulia* (or *vis publica*, in the case of incest), it was within the jurisdiction of the governor to try this case regardless of the status of the offender.[3]

Roman law allowed only private prosecutions. This right of prosecution was, however, not open to all the population. There were certain categories of people who could not institute legal proceedings. If the defendant was a parent, patron, magistrate, or a person of higher rank, then the plaintiff could not be a son, freedman, private citizen, or a person of lower rank respectively.[4] The magistrate (who served for one year) could not be prosecuted during his time in office, but, as in the case of the governor of a province, proceedings could be instituted after his term was completed.[5]

The initiation of proceedings in the case of incest, the issue discussed in 1 Corinthians 5:1ff., required a formal act of accusation in an official petition. As a criminal action it was heard by the governor assisted by his *consilium*. This included his legal advisors, who, as the governor's entourage *(cohors)*, would operate as the judicial court over which he presided.[6]

II. Incest — Degrees of Seriousness

Crimes covered by Roman criminal law were high treason, embezzlement of state property, bribery at elections, extortion in the provinces, murder

---

3. For a succinct but helpful discussion of the role and powers of the proconsul see A. N. Sherwin-White, "'Coercitio', 'cognitio', and 'imperium' in the first century A.D.,' *Roman Society and Roman Law in the New Testament* (Oxford: Clarendon Press, 1963), Lecture 1, although his primary interest is in establishing whether equestrian governors of Judaea had the same powers as proconsuls and imperial legates. See also A. W. Lintott, *Imperium Romanum: Politics and Administration* (London: Routledge, 1993), pp. 50-52; and D. Braund, ed., 'The *Cohors* and the Governor and His Entourage in the Self-image of the Roman Republic,' in *Cultural Identity in the Roman Empire* (London: Routledge, 1998), p. 12.

4. Garnsey, *Social Status and Legal Privilege*, p. 182.

5. Sherwin-White, *Roman Society and Roman Law*, p. 17.

6. Braund, 'The *Cohors* and the Governor and His Entourage', p. 12.

by violence, poisoning, endangering of public security, forgery of wills and coins, violent offences, adultery (where a husband divorced his wife and then brought a charge), the seduction of reputable unmarried women and incest, and the like.[7]

Two aspects of conduct mentioned in 1 Corinthians 5 could be prosecuted as possible criminal offences — adultery and incest. While adultery might result in a criminal action, the charge could be brought by a man against his wife only after he had divorced her.[8] It appears that adultery was committed in the church, not by women but by men (10:8). Incest is reported in 1 Corinthians 5:1. Those found guilty of the combined crime of adultery and incest could be banished from the city, possibly to a distant island. Permanent exile involved the loss of citizenship and all property.[9]

The categories of relationships which were deemed adulterous and incestuous under Roman law were specified in *The Digest* under the code title *'ad legem Iuliam de adulteriis et de stupro'* of 18 B.C. 'If adultery be committed along with incest as, for example, [by a man] with his step-daughter, daughter-in-law, or stepmother, the woman also will suffer a similar punishment.'[10] The charge of incest combined with adultery was so serious that it was excluded from a five-year statute of limitation.[11]

A man might be married and charged with incest because he breached one of the proscribed affinity relationships, i.e., he had married his stepmother who was widowed.[12] The alternative was the crime of adultery/incest in which a son or an adopted son[13] was having, or had had, intercourse with his stepmother while her husband was alive.

If the latter were the case in 1 Corinthians 5, there would have been no leniency under Roman law, which would have applied if the former was the case. 'Sometimes, however, even in the case of males, charges of incest,

---

7. W. Kunkel, *An Introduction to Roman Legal and Constitutional History,* 2nd ed. (Oxford: Clarendon Press, 1973), p. 66; and more recently the wide-ranging discussion of crimes in O. F. Robinson, *The Criminal Law of Ancient Rome* (London: Duckworth, 1995).

8. Robinson, *The Criminal Law of Ancient Rome,* pp. 61-62.

9. On the nature of exile see Garnsey, *Social Status and Legal Privilege,* pp. 111-21.

10. *The Digest* 48.39; Papinian, *Questions,* p. 36; and the discussion by T. A. J. McGinn, 'The *Lex Iulia de Adulteriis Coercendis,*' *Prostitution, Sexuality and the Law in Rome* (Oxford: Oxford University Press, 1998), ch. 5.

11. *The Digest* 48.40.2.

12. W. W. Buckland, revised by P. Stein, *A Text-book of Roman Law from the Time of Cicero to the Time of Ulpian* (Oxford: Clarendon Press, 1991), p. 281.

13. Robinson, *The Criminal Law of Ancient Rome,* p. 55, citing *The Digest* 23.2.14.

although they are naturally more serious, are by custom treated more leniently than [those of] adultery, provided only that incest was by way of an unlawful marriage' (*The Digest* 48.39.3).

Elsewhere *The Digest* declared that 'incest which was committed by way of an illicit marital union was customarily excused' (48.39.7). As Treggiari notes, 'A clear distinction needed to be made between extramarital incest and incestuous marriages. The former clearly fell under the law.'[14]

III. The Guilty, the Father, and the Christian Community

A number of issues need to be explored in the case of the son involved in this incestuous relationship. These concern the nature of his incest, the rights of the plaintiff, and the attitude of the community.

The Nature of the Incest

What is the meaning of Paul's statement 'the sort of immorality which [?] not among the Gentiles' (τοιαύτη πορνεία ἥτις οὐδὲ ἐν τοῖς ἔθνεσιν) (5:1)? He did not provide the actual verb. Those who translate the implied verb as 'is', understand Paul to be saying that even the pagan world did not know of incest by a son with his father's wife.[15] They cite Cicero in connection with the marriage of a woman to her son-in-law — 'Oh! to think of the woman's sin, unbelievable, unheard of in all experience save for this single instance'.[16] However, the laws cited in section II actually name and deal with incest. On this basis supplying the copula is factually incorrect as documents written in the early Empire discuss this form of incest. That these laws were on the statute books also rules out accepting a textual variant which has the word 'named' (ὀνομάζεται).[17]

The expression 'the sort of immorality' (τοιαύτη πορνεία) may refer

14. S. Treggiari, *Roman Marriage: Iusti Coniuges from the Time of Cicero to the Time of Ulpian* (Oxford: Clarendon Press, 1991), p. 281.

15. Cited by G. D. Fee, *The First Epistle to the Corinthians* (Grand Rapids: Eerdmans, 1987), p. 210, n. 24.

16. *Cluent.* 6.

17. For example, P[68] etc. have supplied ὀνομάζεται over against P[46], but this can be ruled out on factual grounds, i.e., incest is named in Roman law.

to incest that was not treated leniently by Roman law and therefore 'among the Gentiles'. Could Paul be alluding to the important distinction observed in Roman law on incest?[18] As already noted, the person who committed adultery and incest with a person who was in an existing marital relationship was distinguished from the person who was deemed to be in an illicit marital union.[19]

Does the text itself provide any clues which might confirm the former possibility? Paul explains the nature of the offence to which he has just referred — 'namely, one of you is having his father's wife' (ὥστε γυναῖκά τινα τοῦ πατρὸς ἔχειν) (5:1). What can be deduced from the construction of ὥστε with the present infinitive?[20] In other instances in Paul it means 'namely' (viz.) and therefore functions epexegetically.[21] The verb 'to have' (ἔχειν) means 'to have sexual intercourse' with another person.[22] It is used in 1 Corinthians 7:2 in the same way, this being an identical semantic field, i.e., sexuality.[23] The present infinitive means that the sexual liaison was continuing.

18. Like any normal Roman citizen Paul would possess a good knowledge of the law. See J. A. Crook, *Roman Life and Law, 90 b.c.–a.d. 212* (New York: Cornell University Press, 1967), pp. 7-8 for a discussion of the penchant of Roman citizens for a knowledge of legal matters.

19. This would rule out the possibility of the woman being a concubine. In an important survey of the discussion C. S. de Vos, 'Stepmothers, Concubines and the Case of ΠΟΡΝΕΙΑ in 1 Corinthians 5,' *NTS* 44 (1998): 104-14, admits that Paul did not use the term for concubine, suggesting that the distinction between a wife and a concubine would be lost on Paul because of his non-Roman background. This is a very tenuous conjecture (see n. 18), and this book generally argues that Paul is not ignorant of Roman culture or conventions.

20. In Attic Greek actual result was expressed by ὥστε and the indicative, while ὥστε with the infinitive 'denoted a result naturally and necessarily following the preceding cause'. Robinson proceeds to say 'that of the sixty-two instances of ὥστε with the infinitive they are nearly all consecutive, not final or even sub-final'. A. T. Robertson, *A Grammar of the Greek New Testament in the Light of Historical Research* (New York: Hodder & Stoughton, 1915), p. 1000.

21. For example, in 2 Cor. 1:8, 'viz., we despaired even of life'. Paul explains what he meant when he used the phrase 'the progress of the gospel', viz., 'my bonds became manifest . . . throughout the praetorian guard' (Phil. 1:13). See also 2 Thess. 2:4.

22. J. N. Adams, *The Latin Sexual Vocabulary* (London: Duckworth, 1982), p. 186: ἔχω and *habeo*. Contra Fee, *The First Epistle to the Corinthians*, p. 200, who sees this term as a euphemism for an enduring sexual relationship, citing its use in 7:2. It will be argued that it was used of actual intercourse. See p. 227.

23. See pp. 226-27.

Paul also refers to the report that a son was sexually involved with a woman who had, or had had, the status of being his 'father's wife'. Although the exact relationship of affinity between the woman and the father's son has been the subject of dispute, he was unlikely to have been the son's mother, given that the reference is to 'his father's wife', and not 'his mother'.[24] Commentators sometimes assume that the son is now married to his deceased father's wife, a situation which would have been treated more leniently by 'the Gentiles'. Paul's language suggests that the Gentiles treated this particular case as a serious criminal offence attracting punishment for both parties.

The reasons for exclusion from table fellowship and contact with the community include πορνεία, which is further defined as 'fornicators' and 'adulterers' (πόρνοι . . . μοιχοί) (6:9). Those who committed incest with adultery fell within the category of the adulterers (μοιχοί) in Roman law.

If this reading of the text is correct, his father was not deceased, and the young man's offence suggests that it was the form of incestuous liaison for which Roman law provided no leniency, but rather invoked the punishment of both parties.

The Plaintiff

Paul himself was in no doubt that what was reported to him was correct. He demanded that this man be banished forthwith or excommunicated from the Corinthian church with his full endorsement (5:3-5). It appears that criminal charges had not yet been instituted which, if proven at law, would have resulted in the exile of the son and his stepmother to an island together with the stripping of their assets and civil status.

What were the father's legal rights in such a situation?

> In early Rome the State interfered little within the family; the *paterfamilias,* as domestic judge, normally with a *consilium,* exercised supreme power and any restraint was indirect, through the Censor. In the Empire, the powers, though still great, were constantly diminishing. The chief el-

24. Valerius Maximus, *Memorable Deeds and Sayings* 5.9.1, notes that L. Gellius' son was guilty of adultery with his stepmother and plotted his father's murder, which would have cleared the way for him to marry her eventually.

ements of *potestas* were: 1. Power of life and death. . . . Classical law regarded the killing of a son, except under a formal domestic judgement, as criminal. Ulpian held it so in any case: the son should be handed over to the courts.[25]

All of this had changed by the time Paul was in Corinth.[26] The issue of adultery/incest became a matter for criminal adjudication early in the Empire. Augustus took the unprecedented step of legislating on divorce — which could become a criminal offence, as has been noted — and the remarriage of widows. It also made 'the condoning of adultery by an "injured" husband an offence open to criminal prosecution and punishable by expulsion from society.'[27] The possibility of incest was at the forefront of the emperor Claudius' thinking, for he himself desired to marry his niece, Agrippina. He ruled that marriage to a brother's (but not a sister's) daughter did not breach the laws governing affinity *(affinitas)* and so amended that law to exclude that relationship.[28] According to Buckland, 'The rule in the empire is simple. Ascendant and descendant could not intermarry. Other relatives could not, whether of the whole or half blood, if either was only a degree from the common ancestor.'[29]

Who should take criminal action against the son and his stepmother? Only the father could do so for the first two months, and thereafter 'anyone could exercise his citizen's rights, a third party's right, to make a criminal charge'.[30]

Why then, if this father was alive, had he not instituted legal proceedings at this point against his son and his wife and have them banished from Corinth? The law made special provision for a joint charge of incest to be

---

25. Buckland, *A Text-book of Roman Law,* p. 103.

26. W. V. Harris, 'The Roman Father's Power of Life and Death,' in R. S. Bagnall and W. V. Harris, eds., *Studies in Roman Law in Memory of A. Arthur Schiller* (Leiden: E. J. Brill, 1986), pp. 82-89, cites p. 92 after reviewing the Republican evidence and concludes, 'during the entire imperial period after Augustus not one instance is known in which the prerogative was employed against a son . . .'.

27. Buckland, *A Text-book of Roman Law,* p. 103; McGinn, *Prostitution, Sexuality and the Law in Rome,* p. 147; 'The *lex Iulia* defined the actions of the complaisant husband as *lenocinium* [enticement]' — he endorsed his wife's conduct.

28. Tacitus, *Annals* 12.6.

29. Buckland, *A Text-book of Roman Law,* p. 115, nn. 13, 14, where the legal sources are cited.

30. Robinson, *The Criminal Law of Ancient Rome,* p. 62.

brought.[31] If the father were to institute criminal proceedings against his wife for adultery of an incestuous nature, then he was required by Augustus' law first to divorce her. Only after this could the stepmother be punished, along with the son, for incest.

The 'sixty available days'[32] may not have expired, and the son's father might have been considering criminal action as the matter was being reported to Paul. 'Adultery was only one of numerous personal insults a Roman felt obliged to avenge. The Roman social structure was based on extremely cohesive families.'[33] If the family was one of high social status, as the next section suggests, a dissolution of a 'political' marriage may have been too complicated to undertake. Marriages from that rank would have had to take into account social networks among other considerations. The wife might have been of higher status than the husband, thereby inhibiting his power to act. The matter, if taken to court, might have involved public humiliation for the father as an incompetent *paterfamilias* who would suffer that which Romans most feared — shame which resulted in a complete loss of *dignitas*.[34]

Under Roman law the husband himself stood in danger of being exiled if he did not proceed against his wife. There were, however, husbands who turned a blind eye to the wife's adultery — if they did not they could be regarded as old-fashioned. Ovid writes, 'A man is really a bumpkin who takes her unfaithfulness seriously; he does not know enough about the morals of Rome',[35] as appears also to have been the case in this Roman colony. As we shall see in Chapter 6, a wife who did this was behaving in character with one of the 'new' Roman women. Their profligate lifestyle was the reason for Augustus' attempts to curb the moral laxity and legislate on adultery as a criminal offence. Illicit sexual liaisons by married women with younger men were among the concerns that prompted Augustus to act, and, in this case, it was with a younger man, her stepson.[36]

---

31. *The Digest* 48.7.8.

32. *The Digest* 48.7.8; and McGinn, *Prostitution, Sexuality and the Law in Rome*, pp. 145-46.

33. See D. F. Epstein, *Personal Enmity in Roman Politics 218-43 BC* (London: Routledge, 1989), pp. 34ff. and cited on p. 35.

34. R. A. Kaster, 'The Shame of the Romans,' *TAPA* 127 (1997): 1-19.

35. *Amores* 3.4.

36. For discussion see pp. 125-26.

Is there anything which indicates the religious status of either the woman involved or her husband? A clue is to be found in verses 9-13, i.e, that it was not the role of the church to judge 'the outsider' but 'the insider'. As the injunctions were directed against the son (5:2, 3, 5) and no judgement or excommunication passed on the woman, we can assume that the stepmother was 'an outsider' and not a Christian.[37]

Was the husband also in the same category, or was it only the son who professed the Christian faith? Wives were exhorted to hold to the religion of their husbands, as Plutarch reminded a young bride on her wedding night in the traditional speech given at the marriage bed before the consummation of the relationship — 'it is becoming of a wife to worship and know only the gods that her husband believed in, and to shut the front door tight upon all strange and outlandish superstition'.[38] Had Plutarch's dictum been followed in this case, then logically the husband would be 'an outsider'? Evidence from 1 Corinthians indicates that there were Christian husbands in Corinth who had non-Christian wives and *vice versa* (7:12). It is not possible to be certain of the religious status of the offended husband compared with that of his wife.

It is also difficult to determine whether, under Roman law, any citizen of equal or higher status could bring a charge of adultery/incest against the guilty parties. Both the son and the woman would have to be charged with this dual crime, given the nature of it. Could the charge of adultery/incest only proceed if the woman had been divorced by her husband? The husband could be penalised if he did not divorce his spouse if she was taken in adultery. 'His condonement countered as *lenocinium* [enticement] and rendered him liable to the penalties imposed for adultery. But he was bound to divorce when he had discovered the crime in commission.'[39] Augustus, however, attempted to stem the tide of the profligate conduct of wives with legislation which did not succeed.[40]

---

37. Fee, *The First Epistle to the Corinthians,* pp. 200-201.

38. Plutarch, 'Advice to the Bride and Groom,' *Moralia* 140D.

39. P. E. Corbett, *The Roman Law of Marriage* (Oxford: Clarendon Press, 1969), p. 142, citing *The Digest* 48.5.30, pr.

40. For further discussion of this point see pp. 125-26.

Christian Boasting

What was Paul referring to when he said that the Corinthian Christians were 'puffed up' and 'boasting' (5:2, 6)? The first censure against the Christian community in 1 Corinthians was that 'you yourselves are puffed up and are not rather mourning' (καὶ ὑμεῖς πεφυσιθμένοι ἐστὲ καὶ οὐχὶ μᾶλλον ἐπενθήσατε). It is sometimes suggested that the perfect periphrastic used in 5:2 could imply that they were proud of the incestuous man's conduct, but Paul states that their boastful attitude as a whole was totally inappropriate given such a case of incest in their midst. He had already accused them of having the same attitude, which he described as 'puffed up', in relation to Paul and Apollos, using the same verb in the present tense (4:6).

What else could they have been glorying in? Given the criminal nature of the act, it seems unlikely that church members flaunted or gloried in the son's activity as some misplaced example of Christian freedom that allowed even incest. The openness of the Christian meeting to the outsider to which Paul later referred (14:23-24) makes it extremely unlikely that they would have boasted or have been so blatant about endorsing such an activity as they were all too aware of its criminal nature and the severe penalties this crime attracted. Even pagan religious groups were concerned that certain inappropriate sexual activity by its members attracted censure or divine judgement.[41]

It has been suggested that the church was boasting about the social status of the son while ignoring his offence.[42] If this was the case, then it points to yet another example of the importance the church attached to social status and their deference to the rich. Paul had already pointed out the dichotomy that existed between the class of the wise, the powerful, and the well-born, and the 'underclass' of the foolish, the weak, and the despised (1:26-8). This possibility may be supported by his rebuke — 'your glorying' or 'boasting' (τὸ καύχημα ὑμῶν) (5:6). It would seem that their boasting was more than a general attitude and may have had a specific focus, i.e., the son's social status.

41. S. Barton and G. H. R. Horsley, 'A Hellenistic Cult Group and the New Testament Churches,' *JbAC* 24 (1981): 7-41.

42. A. D. Clarke, 'Secular Practices of Christian Leadership, II: Beyond Reproach,' in *Secular and Christian Leadership in Corinth: A Socio-historical and Exegetical Study of 1 Corinthians 1–6* (Leiden: E. J. Brill, 1993), ch. 6.

Further clues concerning the attitudes of the Corinthian Christians may be found in the summary injunctions which Paul gives to the church (5:8). Using the Passover preparation language of cleaning out leavened bread from the dwelling and having only unleavened bread there for its celebration, Paul commands the church 'to celebrate the feast' not with the leaven of 'evil' (κακία) and 'wickedness (πονηρία) but with the unleavened bread of 'sincerity' (εἰλικρινεία) and 'truth' (ἀληθεία). What the negative terms mean and whether it is possible to tie them down more specifically as indicators of the attitude of the church (which comes under the heading of 'boasting') has not been explored.

The first term, κακία, was traditionally the antonym for the concept of social or civic virtues which were central to education in the first century. The former was divided into four, i.e., 'folly' (ἀφροσύνη), 'excess' (ἀκολασία), 'cowardice' or 'timidity' (δειλία), and 'injustice' (ἀδικία), while their four antonyms epitomised 'virtue' (ἀρετή).[43] Paul naturally did not restrict Christian conduct to the categories of civic vices, and where he used this term he had a perspective which stretched well beyond the semantic field of civic conduct. Dio Chrysostom used 'virtue' and these words in the same way and is a helpful source for their use, especially in the area of life in a city or a private association.[44]

In an oration 'On Virtue' delivered in Corinth during the Isthmian Games Dio, under the guise of Diogenes, offered a solution for the disease of 'folly, wickedness and excess' (ἄγνοια, πονηρία καὶ ἀκολασία) (8.8).[45] Elsewhere he combines the term πονηρία with injustice and contrasts the former with 'virtue' (ἀρετή) (3.60) and again with 'excess' (ἀκολασία) (6.24). Dio uses the term πονηρία, along with 'vice' (κακία). He told the citizens of Alexandria, 'It is through man's folly and love of luxury and ambition that life comes to be vexatious and full of deceit, wickedness

43. Virtues were 'prudence' (φρόνησις), 'self-control' (σωφροσύνη), 'courage' (ἀνδρεία), and 'justice' (δικαιοσύνη). H. F. North, 'Canons and Hierarchies of the Classical Virtues in Greek and Latin Literature,' in L. Wallach, ed., *The Classical Tradition: Literary and Historical Studies in Honor of Harry Caplan* (New York: Cornell University Press, 1966), pp. 166-68.

44. C. P. Jones, *The Roman World of Dio Chrysostom* (Cambridge, Mass.: Harvard University Press, 1978), pp. 134-36 for the dating of these orations from the early seventies of the first century A.D. to its end.

45. C. P. Jones, *The Roman World*, pp. 47, 49 on the reasons for the use of the device of Diogenes.

(πονηρία), pain, and countless other ills'. He goes on to speak of 'opinions and wickedness' (πονηρία) and informs his audience that there are two ways to treat 'vice' (κακία). Those who allow him to be the city's saviour and guardian will discover how to control their civic 'wickedness (πονηρία) [i.e., rioting] before it reaches its final stage' (32.14-17).[46]

While the terms Paul uses had a broad range of meaning in the ancient world, the Corinthian context suggests that the church, by its toleration, acted with complicity in the son's incest, and had to cleanse itself from the 'vice and wickedness' by excommunicating the son. One might have expected Paul to use the specific term for 'immorality' (πορνεία) and not 'wickedness' (πονηρία). The κακός may be content to perish in his own corruption, but the πονηρός is not content unless he is corrupting others as well, and drawing them into the same destruction with himself.'[47]

Paul continues by exhorting the church to operate with 'sincerity' (εἰλικρινεία) and 'truth' (ἀλήθεία). The former term stands as a reprimand and a correction because of their disingenuous attitude influenced by status; the latter was used to describe the character of those who speak the truth, something that was sorely needed in this case. The discussion is concluded and summarised with a reprimand delivered by way of exhortations and helps illuminate the partiality of those Christians who were 'puffed up' and 'boasting'. It has been observed that 'the target of Paul's accusation is the Corinthian church rather than the individual man involved in transgression'.[48]

Further information concerning the attitude of the Christian community towards the son is found in 1 Corinthians 5:9-13. Some commentators wrongly assume that the discussion on incest was completed in verse 8,[49] and that Paul went on to deal with another issue in the remainder of

46. Cf. Josephus, *AJ* 1.75, 'God did not condemn them alone for their vice (κακία) but resolved . . . to create another race pure from wickedness (πονηρία).'

47. R. C. Trench, *Synonyms of the New Testament*, 8th ed. (London: James Clarke, 1876), p. 296.

48. J. A. Glancy, 'Obstacles to Slaves': Participation in the Corinthian Church,' *JBL* 117.3 (1998): 491, although it is difficult to see how 1 Cor. 5 impacts on her unsecured thesis concerning Paul's exclusion of slaves from full participation in the church in the light of 1 Cor. 7:21-3. See my discussion on this passage, 'St. Paul as a Critic of Roman Slavery in 1 Corinthians 7:21-23,' Proceedings of the International Conference on St. Paul and European Civilization, Παύλεια 3 (Varia, 1998): 339-54.

49. While it is true that Paul uses ὥστε on a number of occasions to complete and summarise his arguments, e.g., 11:33; 14:39; 15:58, there are other places where this con-

chapter 5. There is, however, no particle at the beginning of verse 9, which could indicate that Paul was moving to the next issue on his agenda of pastoral problems which had been reported verbally to him, before proceeding to issues raised by letter (7:1ff.).[50] While there are other offenders proscribed from the table fellowship of Christians in 5:11,[51] the previous verse repeats the term πόρνος ('not the πόρνος of this world nor . . .'). Chapter 5 should be treated as a discreet unit dealing with incest, the central theme of which was the son as a πόρνος (cf. 5:1, πορνεία). It concludes with a citation from Deuteronomy 17:7, 'Put away the wicked man (πονηρός) from among yourselves' (5:13). Here the term referring to 'wickedness' (πονηρία) was also used in 5:8.

Paul mentions the contents of his previous letter — 'I wrote to you not to have social intercourse with immoral people' (μὴ συναναμίγνυσθαι πόρνοις) (5:9). The same verb, repeated in 5:11, is translated as 'not to keep company with a brother'. The command is that they were 'not even to eat with' such people (5:11b). From Paul's comments it would seem that the Corinthian Christians had continued to conduct social relationships with this incestuous man, including eating with him. The development and maintenance of a network of social relationships was at the heart of Roman society. Invitations to dinner were an indication of the endorsement of a person. They were also a means of continuing friendships which was part of the Corinthian way of sustaining *societas*.[52] By 'keeping company' with this person and 'dining' with him, the Christians indicated their continuing desire to court his friendship. It would, then, have been a deliberate breach of Roman social etiquette to comment on his incestuous relationship. We do not know enough to determine whether this person had clients and if any from the Christian community had stood in that rela-

---

struction summarises a section but does not conclude the subject under discussion, e.g., 3:7, 21; 4:5.

50. See Fee, *The First Epistle to the Corinthians*, pp. 220-21 for convincing arguments that 5:9-13 is a continuation of the issue of incest.

51. This verse can read 'As it is, I wrote to you . . .' or 'And I then wrote to you' (νῦν δὲ ἔγραψα) with νῦν in enclitic form used to strengthen the command. Whatever misunderstanding Paul may be seeking to correct, it is not necessary to see the list of persons who practised certain sins being enlarged in 5:11, but rather an emphasis on the fact that any person who was a 'brother' was to be excluded from social interaction and table fellowship.

52. For a wide-ranging discussion see W. J. Slater, *Dining in a Classical Context* (Ann Arbor: University of Michigan Press, 1991).

tionship with him.[53] If they did, it would have been impossible to censure the son without breaking that relationship and creating one of lasting enmity with the former patron. In any case, the action Paul required would have created an enmity relationship with the Christian community. 1 Corinthians 5:9-13 is connected to the issue of incest and throws significant light on the courting of, and dining with, the son whose status may have enhanced the social standing of some of the Christians. This may have explained their inappropriate 'boasting', but not his conduct, given the severity of Roman law for this offence. Any legal or social *persona* played no part in Paul's demand that he be at least 'exiled' immediately from the Christian community.

Corinth like other cities in the empire had two standards in forensic matters, one for the élite and the other for the non-élite, as the next chapter will also demonstrate. The church, by replicating secular Corinth at this point, failed to show impartiality in dealing with the incestuous son. While they appear to have judged the outsider when they had no right to do so (5:12), they failed dismally to judge this insider when that was their task (5:13).

53. For a discussion of Christians and client/patron relationships, see pp. 190-91.

CHAPTER 4

Civil Law and Christian Litigiousness
(1 Corinthians 6:1-8)

'Brother Goes to Court against Brother' (6:6)

The previous chapter noted how Roman criminal law provided legal advantages for those of social status.[1] Roman jurisprudence was further devalued because of vexatious litigation in the civil courts which became a legitimate arena for the élite in their power struggles in *politeia* and private associations. This chapter gives information on civil litigation and how the Corinthian Christians resorted to the courts for vexatious purposes by examining (I) the role of civil litigation in Roman society; (II) the 'unrighteous' judges and juries who presided in civil courts; (III) enmity and vexatious litigation between Christians (1 Cor. 6:1-8); (IV) private arbitrators and conflict resolution; (V) those 'of no account' in the church; (VI) defrauding a 'brother'; and (VII) shaming others in Roman culture. Christians in Corinth took the same attitude towards competitors in the church as their compatriots took towards their competitors in associations and *politeia* generally.

I. Civil Litigation in Roman Society[2]

A civil case began in the court of the law officer. In Corinth he was either an *aedile* or one of two honorary magistrates *(duoviri)*, who were elected

---

1. For a detailed discussion of this extremely important issue see P. Garnsey, *Social Status and Legal Privilege in the Roman Empire* (Oxford: Clarendon Press, 1970).
2. My 'Civil Litigation in Corinth: The Forensic Background to 1 Cor. 6.1-8,' *NTS*

from among the élite by Roman citizens. These offices were undertaken for a year and, among other duties, administered civil law. The *aedile* presided over cases where there was a breach of Roman law covering commerce.

The plaintiff, when petitioning the magistrate or the *aedile*, explained the grounds for the charge, and if there was a case to answer, a private summons was issued requiring the other party to appear in court — 'when one is accused of committing a private wrong, one is made a defendant in a private suit before a jury of one's equals . . . they shall sit in judgement on one', according to Dio Cassius.[3] When the parties came to court, the preliminary pleadings were entered into, and the official declared the parameters within which the case was to be heard. It could then be tried by a single judge or argued before a jury.[4] A magistrate hearing a case in a Corinthian court had three tasks — to preside, to inform the court of the verdict, and to decide the penalties.

Jurors in the provinces were selected from the highest census group of men, whether Romans or Greeks, 'none having a census rating and property (if there is a sufficient number of men) of less than 7,500 *denarii*.[5] They also had to be over the age of twenty-five. In the time of Claudius one could be exempted if he had a large number of children. In Rome the emperor revised the list of jurors, and it was said of Claudius that he struck from the list a man of high birth who was a leading citizen of Greece.[6] In Roman colonies jurors were Roman citizens.

37.4 (Oct. 1991): 559-72 was subsequently questioned by A. J. Mitchell, 'Rich and Poor in the Courts of Corinth: Litigiousness and Status in 1 Corinthians 6:1-11,' *NTS* 39 (1993): 562-68 to which I provided a rejoinder in a reprint of the article in B. S. Rosner, ed., *Understanding Paul's Ethics: Twentieth Century Approaches* (Grand Rapids and Carlisle: Eerdmans and Paternoster, 1995), pp. 101-3. New Testament scholars seem not to have appreciated the extent to which social status determined legal privileges and the outcome of judgements in the Roman Empire. My original discussion has been expanded to emphasise this issue and to include new primary sources. It has a further section on the important issue of 'shaming' in Roman society and argues as well a new point, that Paul also rejected the use of officially appointed 'private' arbitrators by the magistrates for Christians.

3. *Roman Histories* 52.7.5.

4. Garnsey, *Social Status and Legal Privilege*, p. 6; J. A. Crook, *Roman Life and Law, 90 B.C.–A.D. 212* (New York: Cornell University Press, 1967), pp. 78-79; and on aspects of the civil trial before a single judge, see E. Metzger, *A New Outline of the Roman Civil Trial* (Oxford: Clarendon Press, 1997).

5. *SEG* 9.8, A l. 18. *Lex Irnitana,* ch. 86 specified 5,000 *sesterces.*

In civil litigation in Roman Corinth the right to prosecute was not granted to everyone. If the defendant was a parent, a patron, a magistrate, or a person of high rank, charges could not be brought by children, freedmen, private citizens, and men of low rank respectively.[7] Generally, lawsuits were conducted between social equals who were from the powerful (οἱ δυνατοί) of the city, or by a plaintiff of superior social status and power against an inferior.[8] The reason for these proscriptions was to avoid (i) insulting the good name of the person concerned or (ii) showing lack of respect for one's patron or superiors. 'Discriminatory rule or discriminatory practices, then, protected members of the higher orders from being taken to law in some circumstances' and 'the evidence shows that a humble prosecutor might be rejected merely because of the quality of his opponent'.[9]

Augustus had declared that 'except in capital cases the provincial governor must himself act and judge or appoint a panel of jurors (αὐτὸς διαγεινώσκειν καὶ ἱστάναι ἢ συμβούλιον κριτῶν παρέχειν ὀφείλει), but with the rest of such affairs it is my wish that Greek jurors be appointed'.[10] 'In Cyrene, a "province of the Roman people", under Augustus, iudices were normal for all civil suits'.[11] The governor left much of the minor litigation of a province to local municipal courts, for his concern was with matters which related to public order.[12] This was no less true in Corinth. Certainly in the early years of the empire, civil actions were left to local courts and were tried by judges or juries.[13]

II. 'Unrighteous' Judges and Juries

Who were 'the unrighteous' (οἱ ἄδικοι) Paul refers to in 1 Corinthians 6:1? One interpretation equates them with 'the unbelievers' (οἱ ἄπιστοι) in v. 6

6. Suetonius, *Claudius* 15.16.2.

7. Garnsey, *Social Status and Legal Privilege*, p. 182.

8. J. M. Kelly, *Roman Litigation* (Oxford: Clarendon Press, 1966), pp. 62ff.

9. Garnsey, *Social Status and Legal Privilege*, p. 187.

10. *SEG* 9.8, 4, ll. 67-69. For discussion see A. H. M. Jones, *The Criminal Courts of the Roman Republic and the Principate* (Oxford: Blackwell, 1972), pp. 98-100.

11. Crook, *Roman Life and Law*, p. 86.

12. Sherwin-White, *Roman Society and Roman Law*, p. 14.

13. Crook, *Roman Life and Law*, p. 79. See *Lex Irnitana*, chs. 86-89, on the *iudex*, *arbiter*, and *recuperatores*.

and does not regard the comment in v. 1 as 'a moral judgement'. Paul did not imply that 'the Corinthian courts were corrupt', nor did he 'intend to demean the Roman courts, to which he himself had recourse more than once, as if they were corrupt'.[14] Is that judgement correct or does it refer to 'judges whose judgement is unjust'?[15]

Judges and Juries

It is suggested that 'the unrighteous' referred to the character of the judges or the juries who pronounced verdicts in civil cases. Evidence warrants such an adverse evaluation of those engaged in resolving civil actions in the empire. The edict of Augustus of 7-6 B.C. clearly shows that injustices were being perpetrated by the jury-courts in Cyrene. Augustus refers to Roman 'jurors' (οἱ κριταί) who had formed certain 'cliques' (συνωμοσίαι) and who acted oppressively against Greeks on capital charges with the same people (i.e., the cliques) taking it in turns to act as prosecutors and witnesses. The emperor stated, 'I have learnt that innocent individuals have been oppressed in this way and have been consigned to the ultimate penalty'. Augustus' personal knowledge suggests the problem of corruption was not confined to Cyrene.[16]

Other nonliterary evidence confirms that juries could not be relied upon to administer justice impartially. In Egypt a former *exegetes* of the city of the Arsinoïtes was taken to court by a money lender who was charging forty-eight percent interest (double the current rate). A petition had originally been sent to the prefect of Egypt, who passed the case on to a judicial adviser so that it would be heard before a jury. The plaintiff then sent a further petition arguing that the jury would be open to the influence of a person of more senior status and therefore could not act impartially.[17]

14. E.g., H. Conzelmann, *A Commentary on the First Epistle to the Corinthians,* p. 104, n. 12 and G. D. Fee, *The First Epistle to the Corinthians* (Grand Rapids: Eerdmans, 1987), p. 232. 'Neither word ἄδικος nor ἅγιος is intended in a moralising sense'. R. H. Fuller, 'First Corinthians 6:1-11 — An Exegetical Paper,' *Ex Auditu* 2 (1986): 98. Paul's use of ἀδικέω in conjunction with ἀποστερέω in vv. 7-8 suggests the cognate has a moral sense. In v. 9 ἄδικοι was connected with moral conduct.

15. D. W. B. Robinson, 'To Submit to the Judgement of the Saints,' *TynB* 10 (1962): 3.

16. *SEG* 9.8, A, ll. 11-12.

17. *P.Fouad* 26 (A.D. 157-59).

It is important to note three witnesses who demonstrate that Corinth was no different. Dio Chrysostom records c. A.D. 89-96 that there were in Corinth 'lawyers innumerable twisting judgements'.[18] A decade later Favorinus refers to the unjust treatment which he had received at the hands of leading Corinthian citizens. He contrasts that with the actions of their forefathers in pre-Roman days who were themselves 'lovers of justice' (φιλοδίκαιοι) and shown to be 'pre-eminent among the Greeks for cultivating justice'.[19] Those in Roman Corinth were obviously not. Later, in the second century, Apuleius inveighs against the Corinthians, alleging that 'nowadays all juries sell their judgements for money'.[20]

The Powerful Elite and Unjust Judgements

The powerful in the city exercised a number of unfair advantages in the judicial system of the first century. These included financial qualifications for jury service, influence over honorary magistrates and judges, and the importance given to social status in weighing judgements.

In Nero's reign a complaint about the influence of a local power is recorded. 'We have therefore been robbed on every side by this man, against whom we made petitions and presented reports many in number, which he scorned in virtue of this superior local power'.[21] A prosecutor believed that his case could not succeed because the defendant 'possesses great local influence through his insolence and violence' and 'he will be unable to oppose him before a jury of this kind (i.e., local), for he is very influential'. In the original petition the prosecutor referred to the fact that the defendant, a former *exegetes*, was 'relying on the prestige of his position . . . possessing great local influence'. He was able to cite a case heard against the same defendant before a *strategos* in which the son of a *gymnasiarch* instigated proceedings against this defendant who 'behaved insolently, and the *strategos* made an entry about him in his memorandum-book'. The fact that, in a former case, the defendant cites a person of status, the son of a *gymnasiarch*, demonstrated that the jury could not be trusted to be impartial in

18. *Or.* 8.9; cf. *Or.* 7.123, where he calls them 'learned and clever pettifogging lawyers who pledge their services to all alike, even the greatest scroundels. . . .'
19. *Or.* 37.16-17.
20. *Metamorphoses or The Golden Ass* 9.33.
21. *P.Ryl.* 119 (A.D. 54-67).

the face of powerful people. This accounts for the attempt of the prosecutor to have the case heard by the prefect and not a jury.[22]

Seneca's case of a rich and powerful man daring a poor man to institute proceedings provides an apt illustration of the problem which the powerful created in the judicial processes. 'Why don't you accuse me, why don't you take me to court?' was his taunt, and Seneca comments, 'This rich man was powerful and influential, as not even he denies, and thought he never had anything to fear, even as a defendant'. The poor man's response epitomised the reality, 'Am I, a poor man, to accuse a rich man?' The rich man all but exclaimed, 'What would I not be ready to do to you if you impeached me, I who saw to the death of a man who merely engaged in litigation with me?'[23]

Even the veracity of a witness was determined by his status and wealth. Juvenal complained thus — 'At Rome you may produce a witness as unimpeachable as the host of the Isaean Goddess . . . the first question asked will be about his wealth, the last about his character: "how many slaves does he keep? how many acres does he own?" . . . A man's word is believed to be in exact proportion to the amount of cash he keeps in his strong-box'.[24]

Another unjust influence on the outcome of judicial decisions was the payment of bribes. The edict of A.D. 111, cited above, deals with judicial procedures of a *conventus* and adds further support to the view that there was substantial corruption in the judicial process. The prefect 'absolutely prohibits the receiving of bribes, not now for the first time forbidding this evil'.[25] The jury in civil litigation could be bribed to return a 'guilty' or a 'not guilty' verdict.[26] This may have been the reason why some had a passion for jury service.[27]

The relative importance of the social status of the prosecutor and the defendant was considered by the magistrate who determined the penalty.[28]

22. *P.Fouad* 26, ll. 21-24.

23. Seneca, *Controversiae* 10.1.2 and 7.

24. Juvenal, *Satire* 3.136-44.

25. *P.Oxy.* 2745, ll. 7-8. On the similar problem of bribing juries in Greece, see E. S. Staveley, *Greek and Roman Voting and Elections* (London: Thames and Hudson, 1972), pp. 108ff.

26. Garnsey, *Social Status and Legal Privilege*, pp. 4, 199ff.

27. Suetonius, *Claudius* 15.1.

28. Crook, *Roman Life and Law*, p. 74.

He fixed the fine and decided whether or not to carry out the sentence. Social status and legal privilege were clearly connected in the Roman empire.[29]

There were, of course, exceptions, and one such case in an unknown town near Sphinx, Egypt, proves the rule, for partiality was widespread in the empire and endorsed in Roman law. The city fathers expressed their gratitude for having been blessed with an honest *strategos* and mention that 'in his judgements he always dispenses justice correctly and without bribery' (τὸ δίκαιον καθαρῶς καὶ ἀδωροδοκήτως . . . ἀπονέμει).[30]

Cicero's observation also sums up many of the problems with litigation in the civic courts in the East. He declared that there were three hindrances in civil litigation: 'favour' *(gratia)*, 'power' *(potentia)*, and 'bribery' *(pecunia)*.[31] The first is defined as 'excessive favour' and is the favourable response in a judge or jury to *potentia*. The second he defined as 'the possession of resources sufficient for preserving one's own interests and weakening those of another'.[32] *Pecunia* refers to judicial bribery.[33] 'The unrighteous judges found all these pressures and partiality to the élite quite acceptable'.

III. Enmity and Vexatious Litigation

There was a legitimate role for civil litigation in trying cases connected with claims concerning legal possession, breach of contract, damages, fraud, and injury.[34] Roman society had also found the civil courts a useful instrument for pursuing enmity grievances. 'Personal insults or disagreements were entirely sufficient to start *inimicitiae*'.[35] Athenaeus recorded the outcome of inappropriate 'after dinner' conduct which resulted in the loss of *dignitas* and subsequent litigation. Epicharmus said, 'But after drinking comes mockery, after mockery filthy insults, after insult a lawsuit, after the lawsuit a verdict, after the verdict shackles, the stocks, and a

29. Garnsey, *Social Status and Legal Privilege*, p. 4.
30. *SEG* 8.527 (A.D. 22-23), ll. 9-10.
31. Cicero, *Pro Caecina* 73.
32. Cicero, *De inv.* 2.56.169.
33. Garnsey, *Social Status and Legal Privilege*, pp. 207-9.
34. Garnsey, *Social Status and Legal Privilege*, p. 181.
35. Epstein, *Personal Enmity in Roman Politics*, p. 34.

fine'.[36] The working out of enmity between the élite members of the community in the public forum was also perfectly acceptable in society. As C. P. Jones confirms, local politics 'were not conducted only in the council and the assembly, but spilled over into another area of public life, the courts'.[37]

Legitimate reasons for pursuing enmity relationships into the civil courts included: to settle scores with political opponents; retaliation for breaching relationships of trust and obligation; to take up the baton on behalf of offended relatives and friends; to compete for a rung on the ladder of the *cursus honorum* of political posts in the city; jealousy of a young rising star, to undercut the powerful because of their disproportionate influence in *politeia;* to retaliate against those who interfered with one's political aspirations; and to undermine a power base secured by one's clients by attacking them.[38] As Epstein observes, '*inimicitiae* were sufficient to mobilise the machinery of the Roman judicial system'.[39]

As the breach of the law in 1 Corinthians 6:2 surrounded 'the smallest cases' (κριτήριον ἐλάχιστον), it is suggested that the actions initiated by Christians against their fellow believers came within the scope of vexatious litigation. In Roman circles litigation caused personal enmity and was used to aggravate personal enmity.[40] Was the enmity which was evident in the Corinthian church (1 Cor. 6:1-8) caused by civil litigation, or was litigation being used to express publicly instances of personal or household enmity?[41] It is clear that it had developed because of personal loyalty to Christian teachers in the church.[42] This 'strife and jealousy' arising out of the issue of Christian leadership was also expressed in litigation, with one of the leading Christians taking another leading Christian to court. If in 1 Corinthians 3:1-

36. Athenaeus, *Deipnosophists* 2.36.

37. Jones, *The Roman World of Dio Chrysostom*, p. 99.

38. For an excellent discussion of this see Epstein, *Personal Enmity in Roman Politics,* ch. 3, and examples from the Republican period, pp. 104-26.

39. Epstein, *Personal Enmity in Roman Politics,* p. 102.

40. On 'Litigation as a Source of *inimicitia*,' and 'Litigation as a Manifestation of *inimicitia,*' see Epstein, *Personal Enmity in Roman Politics,* pp. 90-100.

41. P. Marshall, *Enmity in Corinth: Social Conventions in Paul's Relations with the Corinthians* (Tübingen: J. C. B. Mohr [Paul Siebeck], 1987) ignores 1 Cor. 6:1-8 although the passage fits his hubristic thesis extremely well, as does L. L. Welbourn, 'On the Discord in Corinth: 1 Corinthians 1–4 and Ancient Politics,' *JBL* 106 (1987): 85-111, where his discussion would be most relevant.

42. See Ch. 2.

4 'strife' (ἔρις) and 'jealousy' (ζῆλος) were signs of an 'immature person' (σαρκικός) and 'walking in a secular fashion' (κατὰ ἄνθρωπον περιπατεῖν) as the sophists and their 'disciples' (μαθηταί) did in Corinth, then the litigation of 1 Corinthians 6 was one expression of 'walking in a secular fashion' and behaving as men (ἄνθρωποι). The civil courts by convention provided another appropriate arena to conduct a power struggle within the church as it would in any association. The same struggle had moved from the meetings of the Christian community to a session of the civil court.

Dio Chrysostom in his Alexandrian Oration in the early seventies A.D. recorded the chaotic nature of the judicial scene with 'a multitude of quarrels and lawsuits, calumnies, writs, a hoard of professional pleaders'.[43] The proceedings were not conducted dispassionately but with great acrimony. 'What the Romans called *reprehensio vitae* or *vituperatio* — a personal attack on the character of one's opponents — was taken as normal; and manuals of rhetoric dealt in great detail with the most effective ways to construct a *vituperatio*. . . . [it] was the rule also in ordinary civil cases.'[44] Litigation in the Hellenistic period was accompanied by 'bitter wrangling' rather than calm judicial inquiry.[45]

The prosecutor, with his hostile speeches and damaging evidence of his witnesses, caused great personal resentment and loss of dignity for the defendant. No areas were immune from ferocious attacks. 'The advocate . . . was permitted to use the most unbridled language about his client's adversary, or even his friends or relations or witnesses.'[46] No rules of evidence guarded against this, and defendants were subjected to muckraking and fabrication. This lack of legal restraint helps to explain why prosecutor and defendant could so rarely avoid lasting animosity. 'In Quintilian's manual on rhetoric . . . we are expressly told that the beginning of a court speech should contain a consideration of the persons involved, and this must involve the blackening *(imfamandam)* of the person on the other side'.[47] It could also be the motivation for instituting legal proceedings.[48]

---

43. *Or.* 32.19.

44. J. M. Kelly, *Studies in the Civil Judicature of the Roman Republic* (Oxford: Clarendon Press, 1976), pp. 98-99.

45. J. W. Jones, *The Law and Legal Theory of the Greeks* (Oxford: Oxford University Press, 1956), p. 151.

46. Jones, *The Law and Legal Theory*, p. 98.

47. Epstein, *Personal Enmity in Roman Politics*, p. 102.

48. Epstein, *Personal Enmity in Roman Politics*, pp. 102-3.

This enmity was not restricted to the prosecutor, but included the presiding honorary magistrate, the witnesses, and even jury members. All could be objects of the defendant's fury.[49] Cicero notes that jurors 'consider the man they have condemned to be their *inimicus* [enemy]',[50] so a new set of enmity relationships had been created by civil action.

IV. The 'Private' Arbitrator and Conflict Resolution

An élite Roman citizen was concerned that disputes over legitimate causes for civil actions could develop into damaging vexatious cases. Provision existed in Roman as well as in Greek and Jewish legal systems for the use of arbitrators to act in a legal capacity with the agreement of the defendant and the plaintiff.[51] The Herculaneum Tablets made provision for a person to be an 'arbitrator by agreement' between X and Y — 'to give a decision'.[52] The city appointed an *arbiter* on an annual basis to hear 'private' cases.[53] Valerius Maximus records a number of what he describes as 'remarkable private trials' in which he notes an *arbiter* undertook the role of the judge.[54] As inhabitants of Corinth Christians could avail themselves of this facility, but some in the church opted for civil actions with judges and juries where damages were awarded to the successful litigant, hence Paul's reference to the 'defrauding' of a brother. (See section VI.) The former procedure meant that there were no punitive damages.

However, Paul did not suggest that Christians use this route of the officially appointed 'private' arbitrator. He wanted to know why those in the church had not used their gifts and training in a profitable way by acting in an extra-judicial capacity as arbitrators by mutual agreement, i.e.,

49. Epstein, *Personal Enmity in Roman Politics,* p. 90.

50. Cicero, *Pro Cluentio* 116.

51. See P. J. Rhodes, 'Political Activity in Classical Athens,' *JHS* 106 (1986): 137, for the Greek; Crook, *Roman Life and Law,* pp. 78-79, for the Roman era; and M. Delcor, 'The Courts of the Church in Corinth and the Courts of Qumran', in J. Murphy-O'Connor, ed., *Paul and Qumran: Studies in New Testament Exegesis* (London: Geoffrey Chapman, 1968), ch. 4; and for the Jewish world Fuller, 'First Corinthians 6:1-11,' Appendix: Judicial Practices in Judaism, pp. 103-4.

52. Cited by Crook, *Roman Life and Law,* p. 78.

53. *Lex Irnitana,* ch. 86.

54. Valerius Maximus, *Memorable Deeds and Sayings* 8.2.

arbiter ex compromisso, as did others in the city in general?[55] 'Is there no wise man among you who is able to judge?' (v. 5). Is Paul's question full of irony?[56] There were wise men 'according to this age' who were members of the congregation (1 Cor. 1:20, 26; 3:18). Their secular education consisted not only of intensive instruction in literature but also of training in oratory, including forensic skills. They engaged in declamation pieces before their fellow pupils and were taught to evaluate court cases.[57] Wise Christians were 'capable' (δύνασθαι) of actually applying the fruits of their secular education in disputes which would normally be settled by a civil action. Paul's question in v. 2, 'Are you not competent to judge a minor case?' may be a reference to such people. Those who boasted of their secular wisdom and who had clearly been the source of disaffection, particularly against Paul, had dissipated their energies in the wrong direction, creating havoc and disunity within the church.[58] He suggested that they could have employed their abilities in a more gainful activity, i.e., helping to settle minor legal disputes among Christians. Paul's preference is, of course, that they do not engage in such disputes among themselves,[59] but rather be prepared to suffer wrong (v. 7).

It should be remembered that if they had already successfully prosecuted fellow Christians (6:8), the person who won the action had been awarded financial compensation. This, together with the loss of *dignitas,* would have only aggravated the problem of strife within the Christian community as the contestants appeared in subsequent meetings of the church. If the jury took sides, would not the members of the church have been tempted to do the same? Whether one lost or won, the effect could only be harmful to relationships in the congregation. How could the Christian meetings achieve their purpose to edify, comfort, and console with such enmity and divisions among them (3:3; 12:25; 14:4)?

55. Crook, *Roman Life and Law,* pp. 78-79.

56. Fee, *The First Epistle to the Corinthians,* p. 237.

57. See my *Philo and Paul among the Sophists,* p. 31.

58. *Contra* Robinson, 'To Submit to the Judgement of the Saints,' pp. 4ff., where he suggests that the Jewish Christians had the right to act as judges in the congregation because they were 'the saints', i.e., the faithful Jews who had the Old Testament scriptures.

59. Paul was not setting up a quasi-official court comparable to the Jewish ones, *contra* Delcor, 'The Courts of the Church in Corinth and the Courts of Qumran,' p. 71, who is careful not to argue that similarity does not imply dependence.

V. Those 'of No Account' in the Church

Is the comment concerning those 'least esteemed' another case of Paul's use of irony? It has been suggested that it refers to Christian Jews as 'competent judges in the church who have been ignored and despised by those whom Paul is addressing'.[60] Paul draws attention to the way in which those 'least esteemed' in society (1 Cor. 1:28) had been chosen by God.[61] In the ensuing discussion (4:6ff.) he used with great irony the technique of 'covert allusion', deliberately applying the high-status terms to the Corinthian Christians, and the low-status term 'least esteemed' to himself and the other apostles. He refers to himself as an apostle of the crucified and humiliated Messiah who has been called to follow in Christ's steps. He summons the Corinthians not to imitate their teachers in the way secular followers of the sophists did, but to follow him in his nonstatus position.[62] The comment in 6:4 about those least esteemed in the ἐκκλησία may be a continuation of Paul's use of irony, and not a reference to Jewish Christian teachers.

It is possible that the reference to the 'least esteemed' in 6:1 reflected Paul's own judgement on the ethical conduct of the magistrates, juries, and the lawyers of his day. He would not have been alone in this, for Dio Chrysostom spoke of the lawyers in Corinth 'perverting justice'.[63] Favorinus, during his third visit to the same city, indicted the judicial process for their unjust ways, arguing 'would anyone have believed this to the discredit of the Corinthians whose forefathers were pre-eminent among the Greeks for cultivating justice?'[64] At least some, if not all, Corinthian Christians were conscious of the importance of secular status, which was expressed in the activities of the secular ἐκκλησία of Corinth and epitomised by facility in rhetoric. The boasting which Paul confronts in 1 Corinthians 1–5 also appears to have spilt over into the issue of the successful litigant scoring a victory. It does not seem that the Corinthian Christians felt a sense of disgust over the way in which the local legal system operated.

60. Robinson, 'To Submit to the Judgement of the Saints,' p. 6.
61. Paul uses the same verb, ἐξουθενεῖν in 1:28 and 6:4.
62. B. Fiori, '"Covert Allusion" in 1 Corinthians 1–4,' *CBQ* 47 (1985): 85-102. For Paul's deliberate negation of the covertness of the passage and the comparison of high status and low status in his argument, see my *Philo and Paul among the Sophists*, pp. 196-201.
63. *Or.* 8.9.
64. *Or.* 37.17.

On the contrary, they endorsed it by taking cases to it. In the Christian ἐκκλησία Paul excluded deference to those who possessed status by reason of their birth, wealth, and position. He had already stressed that people's status is derived by what they are in Christ (1:30). The social class from which secular Corinthian judges and juries were drawn had no status *per se* within the actual meeting of the Christian assembly (cf. 5:4). Christians needed to be reminded of that; hence Paul's description of judges and juries as 'those who are of no account in the [Christian] ἐκκλησία' (6:4) in contrast to what they are in gatherings of a legal or a political nature.

It would seem that the reference to those of no account in the Christian 'meeting' was to the outsider, i.e., the judge and the jury who presided over civil actions. They had no 'status' in the Christian family, even though there were Christians who were all too conscious of the importance and the deference that should be given to their civic status as annually elected magistrates and jurors.

VI. Defrauding a 'Brother'

It is easy to overlook the significance of the highly unusual way in which Paul used a familial term here and elsewhere (1:10, 26; 2:1; 3:1; 4:6; 5:11; 6:6). No Roman would have used the term 'brother' of another person except one who shared the same bloodline or a male who had been formally adopted into the family.[65] When Paul used this term he indicated that the Christian community is 'family' and,[66] as such, it would be unheard of for its members to engage in litigation. It was the role of the *paterfamilias* to rule in disagreements among blood or adopted brothers. 'But brother goes to law against brother, and that before unbelievers' (ἀλλ' ἀδελφὸς μετὰ ἀδελφοῦ κρίνεται καὶ τοῦτο ἐπὶ ἀπίστων).[67] Again Paul referred with astonishment to intra-family litigation as he concluded his argument — 'To have lawsuits at all is a

---

65. For a discussion see Buckland, *A Text-book of Roman Law*, pp. 121-27.

66. Cf. the words of Jesus in Matt. 23:8. The contrast is with the status demanded or accorded to scribes and Pharisees and the proscription was against the use of certain terms to which Jesus added a further reason, 'And all of you are brothers'. See my 'The Messiah as the Tutor: the Meaning of καθηγητής in Matthew 23:10,' *TynB* 42.1 (May 1991): 152-57.

67. The continuative use of the neuter demonstrative pronoun to denote undertaking litigation and to give emphasis to the astonishment Paul feels that family should operate thus. See p. 234.

defeat for you. . . . But (ἀλλά) you do wrong, you defraud and that [action against] brothers (καὶ τοῦτο ἀδελφούς)' (vv. 7-8).[68] Romans considered it highly inappropriate to engage in intrafamily litigation. Cicero wrote about a dispute relating to property, 'Do not allow brothers to engage in litigation and to settle their differences in a proceeding involving charges of scandalous conduct.'[69] As Epstein comments, 'The ideal of the family as a sanctuary from *inimicitiae* [enmity] explains the Roman horror of litigation, a certain cause or manifestation of *inimicitiae . . .* between brothers'.[70]

Paul sees the action, resulting in a successful prosecution, of taking a brother to court as a defeat. Why was this? The decision to institute proceedings was determined by the social status of the one against whom the initiator of litigation proposed to proceed. The plaintiff had to take into account the enmity which would arise from the actual court proceedings, or he might wish to express his existing personal enmity by means of civil litigation. The awarding of financial damages as an additional penalty may have been what Paul had in mind when he wrote of 'defrauding' a brother.

If initiating legal proceedings against a Christian brother was seen as a sign of defeat long before the case was heard by the magistrate and the jury, when the verdict was pronounced and the penalty imposed, it would have been better to be defrauded than to defraud another.[71] Paul writes of actual cases in which successful litigants have defrauded their brothers financially; they were also shamed before others because of the way in which such cases were conducted, resulting in the loss of *dignitas* or 'loss of face' (6:8).

VII. Shaming in Roman Culture

Paul's intention in this lengthy discussion on conflict over teachers in the Christian community had not been to shame but rather to admonish them as 'beloved children' (4:14). By way of contrast, on the issue of civil litiga-

---

68. The place of καὶ τοῦτο ἀδελφούς in the whole sentence lays stress on the Christian status of the defendant.

69. *Fam.* 9.25.3.

70. Epstein, *Personal Enmity in Roman Politics*, pp. 27-28.

71. Certain Christians in a later era resolved a claim and a counter-claim involving a large sum of money and garments by signing a *dialysis*, which was the legal contract recording the settlement between a bishop and two presbyters and a deacon; H. B. Dewing, 'A *Dialysis* of the Fifth century A.D. in the Princeton Collection of Papyri,' *AJP* 53 (1922): 113-27.

tion he declared that this was precisely what he had intended to do — 'I am saying [this] for shame' (6:5). He later repeated this intention in exactly the same words because their hedonism and drunkenness resulted in a lack of inclination to reach out to others with the gospel (15:34).[72] The impact of this statement was intended to powerfully humiliate the Christians in this Roman colony.

We can learn something of the peculiar nature of shame in Roman society in a recent article devoted to the topic by Kaster.[73] After surveying about two thousand examples of the use of the Latin term for 'shame' *(pudor)* and its cognates, he found that it 'primarily denotes a displeasure with oneself caused by vulnerability to just criticism of a socially diminishing sort'.[74] It expresses itself in a particular way among the élite — 'the richest sense of *pudor* [shame] belonged to the adult élite male, who had the widest range of relations. Bestowing favours and paying debts, conducting friendships and engaging in enmities . . . all the conventionally desirable occasions of Roman life were at the same time occasions that could cause *pudor*'.[75]

Martial records that one of the things that made life enjoyable was 'no lawsuits',[76] yet young men were keen to display their talents as orators by taking well-known citizens to court.[77] They were greatly admired for successful prosecutions because such success meant that they were undeterred by the enduring enmity which that created. In Corinth at the end of the century we find Dio Chrysostom complaining of lawyers touting for business at Poseidon's temple at the time of the Isthmian Games — 'lawyers innumerable twisting, like a wrestler, judgements' (μυρίων δὲ ῥητόρων δίκας στρεφόντων).[78]

How could a culturally conditioned response like this have resulted in any shame, at least for those who won? Paul wrote in order to secure a sense of shame 'with you' (ὑμῖν) — 'I speak with the intention of shaming you' (πρὸς ἐντροπὴν ὑμῖν λέγω) (6:5).[79] One would have expected the use

72. For discussion of this see p. 101, and with reference to 1 Cor. 7:36, see pp. 243-46.
73. R. A. Kaster, 'The Shame of the Romans,' *TAPA* 127 (1997): 1-19.
74. Kaster, 'The Shame of the Romans,' 4.
75. Kaster, 'The Shame of the Romans,' 10.
76. *Epigrams* 10.47.
77. Epstein, *Personal Enmity in Roman Politics*, p. 90.
78. Dio Chrysostom, *Or.* 8.9.
79. Liddell and Scott, IV.

of the neuter demonstrative pronoun 'this' (τοῦτο) with verbs of saying or speaking and ὅτι, or ὅτι understood, if the reference was to 6:5b, as happens elsewhere in 1 Corinthians.[80] The sentence following is a rhetorical question concerning one 'wise' person who could arbitrate, as he has noted that there were such in the congregation (3:18ff.). If the reference was to the previous verse, as it would seem (6:4), then Paul was shaming them for allowing the secular and unjust judges of Corinth to arbitrate on a case that was, in effect, a legal pretext by one Christian to humiliate another in a power struggle.[81]

They should be shamed because of their clear 'vulnerability to just criticism' by Paul.[82] Some Christians had already shamed their 'brothers' by engaging in vexatious litigation, but Paul shamed them because those who decided the case cannot have any esteem within the Christian community because of unjust judgements. They knew that a civil action was no place to secure a just outcome to the underlying issue, but simply raised the enmity relationship to a new level within the Christian community. A Roman *dictum* states, 'Reprove friends in private, praise them in public' *(Secreto admone amicos, palam lauda).*[83] Paul did the opposite in this instance, knowing how shamed-faced they should and would be as this letter was read to the Christian community.

It should be noted that the Corinthian church appeared to have judged the outsider when they had no right to do so (5:12) but failed dismally to judge the insider when that was their task (5:13). Paradoxically, they had allowed the unrighteous outsiders to judge the insiders (6:1) when they should have resorted to using a fellow Christian who, by reason of his legal training,[84] would have had the requisite qualifications to act as a private arbitrator.

In conclusion, these vexatious cases do not appear to have been disputes between citizens who were politically active in the city's formal 'gathering' (ἐκκλησία) or those in a local association but internal ones between members of the Christian 'gathering' (ἐκκλησία). The common

80. See p. 235.

81. Cf. 1 Cor. 15:34 where the reference is to his accusations concerning their immorality and drunken partying from which they needed to 'sober up'. See pp. 100-101.

82. Kaster, 'The Shame of the Romans,' 6.

83. Attributed to Publilius Syrus but wrongly so according to Kaster, 'The Shame of the Romans,' 16, n. 38.

84. See my *Philo and Paul among the Sophists*, pp. 23-24.

ground was the struggle between members of the élite who were social equals (or near equals) in the public arena. It is clear that the strife and jealousy aroused over teachers (1 Cor. 1:11ff.) had spilt over into the arena of civil courts. The power struggle in the church was not restricted to 1 Corinthians 1–4; a typical first-century contest for recognition and power among the élite themselves is reflected in 1 Corinthians 6:1-8. This was not about some injustice suffered by the poor Christians at the hands of their rich brothers.[85] Civil litigation in Corinth came within the purview of the local honorary magistrates who acted as judges and who, together with the juries, had been appointed by the citizens. They comprised the 'well-to-do' who could not be trusted to resolve matters solely on the grounds of civil law.[86] Those few in the 'church of God' (ἐκκλησία τοῦ θεοῦ) who belonged to the class of the wise, the powerful, and the well-born allowed the secular phenomenon of vexatious litigation to determine their dealings with one another in the Christian community.

This may help explain why certain Christians had seized 'the desirable occasion' for 'engaging in enmities' by going to court. The Corinthians were simply acting as the élite had always done in Corinth when a conflict situation arose. Epstein notes the rôle played by enmity in *politeia*. 'Roman society was unusual in allowing *inimicitiae* to compete along with other more conventional values such as patriotism and humanity in guiding a public figure's conduct. A reputation for successfully pursuing *inimicitiae* was a vital asset to a Roman politician seeking to establish and maintain an influential voice.'[87]

The nature of society was such that those who belonged to its upper echelons sought primacy in *politeia* by using vexatious litigation as an acceptable means of defeating one's adversaries. Again Epstein explains, 'The pursuit of *inimicitiae* [enmity] and the destruction of one's enemies were firmly entrenched among the virtues Romans thought necessary for the acquisition of *dignitas, virtus*, status and nobility' and were 'pursued from birth', i.e., they were culturally ingrained.[88]

Rajak and Noy have noted that in the proliferation of associations in

---

85. For a refutation of Mitchell, 'Rich and Poor in the Courts of Corinth', see my 'Civil Litigation in Secular Corinth and the Church: The Forensic Background to 1 Corinthians 6:1-8,' 101-3.

86. Cf. 1 Cor. 3:4, κατὰ ἄνθρωπον περιπατεῖν; for discussion see pp. 40-41.

87. Epstein, *Personal Enmity in Roman Politics*, p. 127.

88. Epstein, *Personal Enmity in Roman Politics*, p. 28.

Graeco-Roman cities there was 'a tendency to replicate in the synagogue in miniature the organization and government of the cities themselves. Not only names and methods are transferable, however, but, more importantly, an ethos'.[89] This was true in the Diaspora synagogues and certainly was the case among Corinthian Christians where the danger arose of further allowing the litigious spirit of the world of *politeia* into the Christian ἐκκλησία.[90] Some Christians appear to have had no qualms adopting the ethos of *politeia* at this point, for this was how citizens had long used the civil courts to pursue enmity relationships.

89. T. Rajak and D. Noy, '*Archisynagogos:* Office, Title and Status in the Graeco-Roman Synagogue,' *JRS* 83 (1993): 89.

90. 'It is remarkable that the Christians . . . did seize on the term [ἐκκλησία] that had been adopted by the Bible translators for the sacral assembly of Israel and applied it to themselves . . . [and] was the preferred self-designation of Christian groups in the cities of the Roman provinces'; W. A. Meeks, *The Origins of Christian Morality: The First Two Centuries* (New Haven: Yale University Press, 1994), p. 45, and my discussion of the ease of importing aspects of the secular assembly into the Christian gathering, 'The Problem of "Church" for the Early Church,' in D. Peterson and J. Pryor, eds., *In the Fulness of Time: Biblical Studies in Honour of Archbishop Robinson* (Sydney: Lancer, 1992), ch. 13.

CHAPTER 5

Elitist Ethics and Christian Permissiveness (1 Corinthians 6:12-20; 10:23; 15:29-34)

'All Things Are Permitted (for Me)' (6:12; 10:23)

How did philosophical discussion impact the daily ethical conduct of those who lived in the first century? It is one thing to understand the various schools of philosophy in the ancient world, but what inroads, if any, did their teaching make on the way people lived? This is a question raised by E. A. Judge, who suggests we search for 'the way in which a loose body of general principles for life develops amongst thoughtful people in a community. This common stock is not subject to the discipline of the philosophical schools, though it may draw from them and feed ideas into their systems'.[1]

Judge believes that 'there must have been some form of intellectual intercourse behind the closed doors of educated people'[2] and sees the value of pursuing Dihle's notion of *Vulgärethik*.[3]

Ancient extant aphoristic or pithy sayings were recorded on inscriptions and displayed publicly.[4] They contained, however, no argument or context supporting their affirmations and, in this way, are not dissimilar to

1. E. A. Judge, 'St. Paul and Classical Society,' *JbAC* 15 (1972): 32-33.

2. Judge, 'St Paul and Classical Society,' p. 32.

3. For a summary of Dihle's work in this field to 1973 see E. A. Judge, '"Antike und Christentum": Some Recent Work from Cologne,' *Prudentia* 5.1 (1973): 3-7.

4. For the Delphi Canon in English see E. A. Judge, 'Ancient Beginnings of the Modern World,' *Ancient History Resources for Teachers* 23.3 (1993): 125-48, and his discussion 'Ancient Beginnings of the Modern World,' in T. W. Hillard et al., eds., *Ancient History in a Modern University* (Grand Rapids: Eerdmans, 1998), II, 468-82.

sayings in the book of Proverbs. While papyrological evidence indicated how people created or handled crises, the aphoristic sayings demonstrated no clear nexus between ethical responses to situations and any underlying ethical or philosophical system.

One might expect that the Cynic philosophers would be the mediators of popular ethics since they operated on the streets; they did that not to teach, but to beg for money and thereby demonstrate the difference between themselves and other philosophers. Judge has suggested that Cynic preachers would have repelled people and so should not be seen as custodians of popular ethics. Our task may be made easier because the literary evidence we possess has been written by the educated élite. One crucial piece of first-century evidence comes from an unexpected source cited in Philo. It reveals how the élite argued from first-century Platonic anthropology to ethical norms in order to present a philosophical justification for their lifestyle.

This chapter suggests that the evidence may explain the philosophical basis on which some of the Corinthian Christians justified their behaviour and also determined the way in which Paul argued his case against them in various sections of 1 Corinthians. In order to test this, it is proposed (I) to examine the connection made in the first century between the Platonic view of the soul and the senses and its implication for ethical conduct; (II) to trace some of the evidence in the ancient world for the use and meaning of the aphoristic saying 'all things are permitted'; (III) to establish the nexus between banquets and sexual permissiveness; and (IV) to show to what purpose Christians put the aphorism in 1 Corinthians 6:12-20; 8:9; and 10:23ff. We will then establish the nexus between this élitist ethic and 15:31-34, where Paul attacks the hedonistic lifestyle of some of the Corinthian Christians. In the first century this lifestyle was seen as one implication of the pagan doctrine of the immortality of the soul.

I. The Soul, the Senses, and Elitist Ethics

Philo cites an account of the justification of élitist ethics based on the Platonic anthropology in 'The Worse Overcomes the Better', ##33-34. He says of its proponents,

> they [the sophists] leave no stone unturned, as the saying is, while they ply their questions 'Is not the body the soul's house?' 'Why, then, should

we not take care of a house, that it may not fall into ruin?' 'Are not eyes and ears and the band of other senses body-guards and courtiers, as it were, of the soul?' 'Must we not then value allies and friends equally with ourselves?' 'Did nature create pleasures and enjoyments and the delights that meet us all the way through life for the dead, or for those who have never come into existence, and not for the living?' 'And what is to induce us to forego the acquisition of wealth and fame and honours and offices and everything else of that sort, things which secure for us a life not merely of safety but of happiness?'

Here we have a summary of an important argument developed logically through a series of questions.[5] It begins with the premise that the body is the house of the immortal soul.[6] Philo argues that, if this is so, the house must not fall into a state of disrepair. The body was not to be despised but cared for. This represents a first-century adjustment to Plato's view that the body was 'the prison house of the soul'. Second, the senses are declared to be 'body-guards and courtiers' (δορυφόροι καὶ φίλοι) of the immortal soul and therefore are our 'allies and friends',[7] not enemies from whom one must escape, or against whom one must fight. Third, Nature, thought to determine custom in the first century, is here said to have given us our senses for 'pleasures and enjoyments and the delights' of life.[8] The discussion is taken a step further with a question which indicates that Nature did not give the bodily senses to the unborn or aborted, nor can they be used by those who are dead; clearly they were given for pleasure in this life. Here the ancient doctrine of hedonism is justified by means of a particular anthropology concerning the mortality of the body but not the soul.

If happiness is one of the blessings Nature has given, what should

5. LCL rightly places *Det.* 33-45 in quotation marks. #33 consists of a series of questions, as Philo himself notes. 'They leave no stone unturned, as the saying is, while they ply their questions', i.e., six questions sequential in thought and connected by particles. Then follows supporting evidence, #34a, where the lifestyle and status of the sophists are contrasted with those of their opponents, #34b.

6. On Philo's doctrine of the immortality of the soul, see D. T. Runia, *Philo of Alexandria and the Timaeus of Plato* (Leiden: E. J. Brill, 1986), pp. 334, 469-70.

7. Cicero, *Laws* 1.26-27, 'Nature . . . has also given man the senses, to be, as it were, his attendants and messengers . . . the special faculties and aptitudes of other parts of the body'.

8. On 'nature' as the determiner of customs see the first-century discussion in D. Jobling, '"And Have Dominion . . .": The Interpretation of Genesis 1:28 in Philo Judaeus,' *JSJ* 8 (1970): 50-82.

persuade a person to forego the things that make for pleasure as well as safety? These are secured through 'the acquisition of wealth and fame and honours and offices (πλοῦτος, δόξα, τιμή, ἀρχή) and everything else of that sort'. Those who undertook public offices did so in an honorary capacity. They had to be certified as being 'well-to-do'; and, as we have noted previously, those who proved to be major civic benefactors and holders of public offices were honoured by the civic authorities with crowns of gold, seats of honour, and inscriptions recording their public offices. In the following century Aristides outlined the benefits of being an orator, viz., 'wealth, reputation, honour, marriage, or any acquisition'.[9]

They further argued that the proof of their thesis concerning 'the good life' was evident from their lifestyle. They contrasted themselves with those who lived according to another view of life. 'The mode of life of these two classes is a witness (μάρτυς ὁ βίος τούτων) of the truth of what I say' (#33).[10] The élite looked down on those who pursued virtue and spoke of them in a very disparaging way. 'The so-called[11] lovers of virtue are almost without exception obscure people, looked down upon, of mean estate, destitute of the necessities of life, not enjoying the privileges of subject peoples or even of slaves, filthy, sallow, reduced to skeletons, with a hungry look from want of food, the prey of disease, in training for dying' (#34a).[12]

Philo called the first group 'the lovers of virtue', and the other 'lovers of self' (φίλαυτοι).[13] 'Those, on the other hand, who take care of themselves are men of mark and wealth, holding leading positions, praised on

9. Aristides, *Or.* 33.19.

10. Cf. Epictetus, 3.22, 88, 'I and my body are witnesses to the truth of my contention (ἰδοὺ καὶ τούτου μάρτυς εἰμὶ ἐγὼ καὶ τὸ σῶμα τὸ ἐμόν).

11. The term 'so-called' means popularly but erroneously. See, e.g., Dio Chrysostom, 13.11, 32.8, 34.3; and J. L. Moles, 'The Career and Conversion of Dio Chrysostom', *JRS* 68 (1978): 91.

12. This last reference to 'training for dying' has been seen as an equivalent statement for ἐπιτηδεύει ἀποθνῄσκειν used of the philosopher in Plato, *Phaedo*, 64a. See LCL II, 493-94, which also records Simmias' response that 'this is exactly what my unphilosophical countrymen would say of the philosophers.'

13. 'The focal point of his [Philo's] interest lies . . . in those aspects of psychology which are indispensable for his allegories, namely the struggle that takes place in the soul as the rational part strives to overcome the seductions of the senses and the tumult of the passions, while itself having to dispel the ignorance which may lead it to choose evil rather than good.' Runia, *Philo and the Timaeus,* pp. 266-67, cited on 389.

all hands, recipients of honours, wanton (πιόνες),[14] healthy (ὑγιεινοί) and robust (ἐρρωμένοι), revelling in luxurious (ἀβροδίαιτοι)[15] and "riotous" living (θρυπτόμενοι), knowing nothing of labour, conversant with pleasures which carry the sweets of life to the all-welcoming soul by every channel of the senses (ἡδοναῖς συζῶντες διὰ πασῶν τῶν αἰσθήσεων ἐπὶ τὴν πανδεχῆ ψυχὴν τὰ ἡδέα θερούσαις)' (#34b).

In the hands of the orators 'civic virtue' (ἀρετή), which they claimed to be the essence of what they taught, had effectively degenerated into 'a kind of amoral "art of success"'.[16] Their argument demonstrated how an anthropology associated with Plato's immortal soul was developed and interpreted in the first century A.D.[17] It allowed them to insist that ambition for status, privileges, and pleasures was legitimate, and their financial resources permitted them to engage in a hedonistic lifestyle in which everything was permitted to the full; their senses were, after all, 'friends and allies'. The 'success' which they acquired or inherited proved that they were right, while the philosophy of their opponents — the 'so-called' seekers after virtue — proved that their life was a witness to the fallacy of their beliefs.[18] This evidence shows clearly how the élite justified their hedonistic conduct.

14. 'to be fat', and metaphorically 'to be wanton'.

15. 'living delicately' or 'effeminately'.

16. J. C. Rowe, *Plato* (Brighton: Harvester, 1984), p. 158.

17. Runia, *Philo and the Timaeus of Plato*, pp. 306-8 shows that the sophists' rhetorical question 'Are not eyes and ears and the band of other senses guards and courtiers of the soul?' was an accepted canon of interpretation.

18. It is unclear whether in the latter quotation Philo was referring to Jews in general or the Therapeutai community in particular. See *Vit.* 13-17, where the Therapeutai gave away their possessions. Philo speaks of 'their longing for the deathless and blessed life'. That they were 'almost without exception' obscure people acknowledges that there were a few notables, and he may be referring to his own family who enjoyed wealth and influence in Alexandria; hence the reference was to Alexandrian Jews. On the question of the wealth and status of his wider family see J. Schwartz, 'Note sur la famille de Philon d'Alexandrie', *Mélanges Isidore Lévy. Annuaire de l'Institut de philologie et d'histoire orientales et slaves*, Université libre de Bruxelles 13 (1953): 591-602, and 'L'Egypte de Philon', *Philon d'Alexandre*, 35-45. But note also the reservations of S. Foster, 'A Note on the "Note" of J. Schwartz,' *SP* 4 (1976-77): 25-32.

II. 'All Things Are Permitted for Me'

It would seem that there was a long-established convention in the ancient world for people of status and power to articulate their actions on the basis that 'all things are permitted'. Polybius (200-118 B.C.) wrote of the privileges of a Roman citizen in Carthage, 'He may do and sell anything that is permitted for a citizen' (πάντα καὶ ποιείτω καὶ πωλείτω ὅσα καὶ τῷ πολίτῃ ἔξεστιν) (*Hist.* 3.24, 12). Dio Chrysostom, writing at the end of the first century A.D., suggested that the good ruler was one 'who needs more steadfast control than he to whom all things are permitted' (τίνι δὲ σωφροσύνης ἐγκρατεστέρας ἢ πάντα ἔξεστιν) (*Or.* 3.10). This contrasted with those rulers who misused their unlimited power to do as they wished — 'they are permitted to do anything' (ἔξεστι πάντα ποιεῖν) (62.2). Xenophon (428-354 B.C.) wrote of the ruler who used 'self-control' (σωφροσύνη), one of the four cardinal civic virtues. 'By making his own self-control an example, he disposed all to practise that virtue more diligently. For when the weaker members of society see that one who is permitted to indulge in excess (ᾧ μάλιστα ἔξεστιν ὑβρίζειν) is still under self-control, they naturally strive all the more not to be found guilty of any excessive indulgence' (*Cyr.* 8.30).

Dio Chrysostom's interlocutor asserted 'that whoever is permitted to do whatever he wishes is a free man, and that whoever is not is a slave' (ὅτῳ μὲν ἔξεστιν ὃ βούλεται πράττειν, ἐλεύθερός ἐστιν, ὅτῳ δὲ μὴ ἔξεστιν, δοῦλος) (14.13). Dio argued against this view that 'men in general are not permitted to do what they wish in part' (οὐ τοίνυν οὐδὲ τοῖς ἄλλοις ἔξεστιν ἃ ἐθέλουσι ποιεῖν), 'and if they violate the established law, they will be punished' (14.13). However, by implication, the free man and the élite in power did not have the restraints of those without social status who lived by the maxim 'all things are permitted'.

Dio sought to rectify this when he discussed 'intemperance' and its antonym, the cardinal virtue, 'prudence' (φρόνησις) — 'it is not permitted to do mean and unseemly and unprofitable things, but the things that are just and profitable and good we must say that it is both proper and permissible to do (ὅτι προσήκει τε καὶ ἔξεστιν)' (14.16).

It was not the powerful or the well-born but 'the wise persons' (οἱ φρόνιμοι), i.e., the person exhibiting the cardinal civic virtue of 'prudence' in government, φρόνησις: '. . . the wise are permitted to do anything whatsoever they wish' (οἱ φρόνιμοι ὅσα βούλονται πράττειν, ἔξεστιν αὐτοῖς), while the foolish attempt to do what they wish although it is not permissible (οὐκ ἐξόν)' (*Or.* 14.7). He argued that, of necessity, it followed that while the wise were free and were allowed to act as they wished, the ignorant were slaves and did that which was not permitted for them (14.17). As a result in his first oration on 'Slavery and Freedom', he concluded that, 'We are forced to define freedom as the knowledge of what is permitted and what is not' (ὧν τε ἔξεστι καὶ ὧν μή) (14:18). While philosophically he argued about the nature of freedom, it is remarkable that the persons who made this statement, or those to whom they were applied in daily life, were the élite.

Lists of aphoristic sayings were propagated across the Hellenistic world and were placed so that everyone could see them. They constituted evidence of the *Vulgärethik*. However, they contained no examples of the statement in 1 Corinthians 6:12; 10:23. Aphorisms such as 'look after your own things' (τὰ ἴδια φύλασσε), 'look after yourself' or 'do good to yourself' (σεαυτὸν εὖ ποίει), and 'look for advantage' (τὸ συμφέρον θηρῶ) provide interesting examples of somewhat self-centred ethical imperatives which were commonly accepted in the ancient world.[19] The closest we come to the sayings in 1 Corinthians 6:12; 10:23 is 'do good to yourself', but even then it cannot match the force or perception of the aphorism that 'everything is lawful'.

No pithy saying such as 'do whatever you wish' (ποίει ὅσα βούλονται), which is the imperatival equivalent of 1 Corinthians 6:12; 10:23, can be found in public lists. It was the prerogative of those who possessed power, whether they were privileged citizens or rulers, to live by that maxim with relative impunity. It was not a saying for ordinary members of a city nor was it one that the élite promoted for the non-élite.

III. Gluttony, Drunkenness, and Sexual Indulgence

In his 'Advice about Keeping Well', Plutarch discussed some of the hazards which the élite faced at feasts — the problem of social or civic obligations, 'the need to guard against excess in eating and drinking and against all self-indulgence especially when festivals and visits from friends are at hand' (123E). He also extrapolated on the problems of 'unavoidable social engagement' created 'in the midst of company and good cheer' associated

19. Judge, 'Ancient Beginnings of the Modern World', p. 9.

with entertaining kings and high officials. Plutarch's suggestion as to how one might refrain from overindulgence at such feasts (subterfuge so as not to cause offence) indicated the enormous social pressure to participate in eating and drinking at banquets, even when one 'is overloaded and in no condition to take part' (123F). Plutarch recorded the grand scale of Corinthian entertainment. 'During the Isthmian Games, the second time Sospis was president, I avoided the other banquets, at which he entertained a great many foreign visitors at once, and several times entertained all the citizens' (*Moralia* 723A).

'All the citizens' refers to those who were Roman citizens (*coloni*) rather than all who lived in Corinth (estimated to be about 100,000). A Corinthian inscription celebrating the moving of the Games to Isthmia notes that Lucius Castricius Regulus, the president of the Games, gave a banquet for 'all the citizens' (*omnibus colonis*). This custom of entertaining the élite at civic dinners continued at subsequent Games.[20]

Another issue, apart from the pressure of social and civic obligations, was unbridled gluttony. In 'Virtue and Vice' Plutarch noted that 'at dinner vice is an expensive companion because of gluttony' (466B). In 'The Eating of Flesh' he said that 'it is not so much our belly that drives us to the pollution of slaughter;[21] it is itself polluted by our incontinence.'[22] He believed that flesh could be eaten because of hunger, but in this case it was 'not for nourishment or need or necessity, but out of satiety and insolence and luxury' (996E-997A), and those who engaged in such indulgence 'were living the soft life' (ἀβροδίαιτοι ἦσαν) (225F). He discussed how one might avoid '"adding fire to fire", as the proverb has it, and gorging to gorging (μή πῦρ ἐπὶ πυρί, ὥς φασι, πλησμονή τις ἐπὶ πλησμονῇ), and strong drink to strong drink' (123F). Philo of Alexandria recorded that special tables were reserved for 'the drinking bouts which followed as part of but not the only event in "the after-dinners", as they call them (τὰς λεγομένας ἐπιδειπνίδας)' (*Vit.* 54).

Evidence from Plutarch's *Moralia* also shows that gluttony and sexual indulgence at dinners could be linked together. 'Just as with women who are insatiable in seeking pleasure, their lust tries everything, goes

20. Kent, *Corinth*, 8.3, no. 153. The term *colonus* and not *incolae*, 'inhabitants', preserves the distinction. See Engels, *Roman Corinth*, pp. 68, 70.
21. He discusses the terrible cruelty animals could suffer while being slaughtered for banquets in the belief that they could be made more tender to eat.
22. Athenaeus, *Deipnosophists* 3.97, 'You glutton, whose god is your belly, and with no whit for anything else.'

astray, and explores the gamut of profligacy until at last it ends in unspeakable practices; so intemperance in eating passes beyond the necessary ends of nature. . . . For it is in their own company that organs of sense are infected and won over and become licentious when they do not keep to natural standards. . . . From this our luxury and debauchery conceives a desire for shameful caresses and effeminate titillations' (997B).

'Is there any difference for a man who employs aphrodisiacs to stir and excite licentiousness for the purpose of pleasure, or stimulates his taste by odours and sauces?' asks Plutarch elsewhere (126B). He also notes that 'intemperate intercourse follows a lawless meal, inharmonious music follows a shameless debauch' (997C). Gowers also shows from Roman literature 'the common links between the two sensual pleasures of eating and sex' and how 'forms of greed, avaricious and sexual, are often expressed in terms of gluttony'.[23]

The nexus between insatiable greed, unrestrained drinking, and immorality is reflected in the well-attested saying, 'in well-gorged bodies love (or passion) resides' (ἐν πλησμοναῖς Κύπρις), which Plutarch cited elsewhere 'In surfeit love is found' (*Moralia*, 126C, 917B).[24] This saying is also found in Aristotle, *Prob.* 896A, where mating habits of animals are discussed. There he noted that man does this 'any time' and 'For sexual appetite accompanies satiety' (ἐν πλησμονῇ γὰρ Κύπρις).

Athenaeus in a second-century-A.D. work, *Deipnosophists* ('The Learned at Banquet') made a significant addition to the stock saying 'For love dwells where plenty is' when he wrote of those who were poor, 'but among those who are hard up Cypris (Aphrodite) will not stay'. Elsewhere he observed that 'in an empty belly no love of the beautiful can reside, since Cypris is a cruel goddess to them that hunger . . .'. He then cited Euripides, 'For love dwells where there is surfeit, but in a hungry man, no!' (ἐν πλησμονῇ τοὶ Κύπρις ἐν πεινῶντι δ' οὔ).[25] The identical citation is found twice in Menander of the fourth century B.C., who also boldly de-

23. E. Gowers, *The Loaded Table: Representations of Food in Roman Literature* (Oxford: Clarendon Press, 1993), pp. 101, 200, n. 319.

24. Cypris was a name for Aphrodite from the island of Cyprus and became an appellative for love or passion. Cited elsewhere; cf. A. Nauck, *Tragicorum Graecorum fragmenta* (Hildesheim: Olms, 1964); Euripides, *Fragments* 895.

25. *Deipnosophists* 1.28F, 6.270C. By contrast Philo, *Vit.* 56, says, 'one may well pray for what men most pray to escape, hunger and thirst, rather than for the lavish profusion of food and drink found in festivities of this kind'.

clared that 'love is at its greatest power where surfeit is (ἐν πλησμονῇ μέγιστον ἡ Κύπρις κράτος)'.[26] It is possible that by the early empire 'but in a hungry man, no!' had become a well-known addition to this stock saying. A well-gorged body and not a hungry one went hand in hand with sexual licence.[27] The context for these sayings was the banquet which wealthy guests attended. The pejorative comments about the hungry unashamedly asserted by the élite show that the former simply could not be part of that scene.

One of Athenaeus' fourteen volumes of extended 'table-talk' with a Roman knight is devoted to the role of women on banqueting occasions. 'Concerning Women' shows that their contribution was primarily at 'the after-dinners'. These prostitutes not only adorned the banquet but also provided sexual pleasures afterwards.[28]

The East of the empire had a long history of the unholy trinity of eating, drinking, and immorality at dinners.[29] Philo notes that the first century had changed in 'the method of banqueting now prevalent everywhere through hankering for the Italian expensiveness and luxury'. He referred to the extravagant dress which aimed 'to give pleasure to the eyes of the beholders', and which only heightened the anticipation of the sexual indulgence that would follow.[30] There are grounds for seeing such banquets as the possible *Sitz im Leben* for 1 Corinthians 6:12-20, 8:1–11:1, and 15:32-34 because what Philo calls 'Italian expensiveness' would certainly not have been absent from this Roman colony.

IV. Elitist Ethics and 1 Corinthians 6:12; 10:23; 15:29-34

Does the 'intellectual intercourse' by 'educated people' cited at the beginning of this chapter throw any light on the way some of the Corinthian Christians argued their case with the catch-cry, 'All things are permitted for me' (6:20) or 'all things are permitted' (10:23)? The above

26. A. Meinecke, *Fragmenta comicorum Graecorum* (Berlin: de Gruyter, 1970), 4.23 and 1.15.

27. Cf. 'the portly', which was the term reported by Philo, *Det.* 34.

28. Athenaeus, *Deipnosophists* 13.571ff. on their conduct at an actual banquet.

29. Plutarch, *Moralia* 705C, 'those whose shortcomings are in eating, drinking and sexual indulgence'; cf. 123E.

30. *Vit.* 48, 50, 57.

discussion forms a philosophical basis for this aphorism which the élite used.

To some this would immediately rule out the possibility that Christians could be involved as they were perceived to be among 'the poor' or 'the middle class'. It has been argued that both terms can be misleading as an adequate description of the social structures within a Roman colony. There are many examples of 'the élite.'[31]

Before we seek to establish the nexus between these ancient sources and 1 Corinthians, it is important to justify the use of a series of texts in that letter to support a particular thesis. There is a tendency in the study of 1 Corinthians to see various sections in the letter as dealing with a discreet issue after which Paul turns to another problem. The issues are judged to be quite independent of each other. That is not so in the divisions which were apparently dealt with in chapters 1–4. They appear again at the Lord's Supper (11:16) as well as in chapter 12:12-25, especially in the reference to 'no divisions' (12:25). Vexatious litigation (6:1-8) is yet another expression of internal divisions — a typical Roman convention for defeating one's opponents. A similar argument is reflected in 6:12 and 10:23 because the aphoristic saying is effectually the same. The problem Paul mentions (15:32-34) is the matter of 'eating and drinking' and the effect that bad company has on Christian conduct. He thus proscribes drunkenness. There are good grounds for suggesting that the issues arose from secular thinking which tolerated, and even endorsed, what we would term ethical 'permissiveness'.

1 Corinthians 6:12-20

Brothels and not banquets are the background which commentators normally associate with 1 Corinthians 6:12-20.[32] For example, Fee concludes

---

31. Meeks, *The First Urban Christians*, p. 73, where he sees the 'typical' Corinthian Christian as 'a free artisan and small trader'. For a response to Meeks and a critique of the use of terms in A. J. Mitchell, 'Rich and Poor in the Courts of Corinth: Litigiousness and Status in 1 Corinthians 6:1-11,' *NTS* 39 (1993): 562-86, see my comments on the use of 'rich' and 'poor' and its relevance for the social register of Corinthian Christians, 'Civil Litigation in Secular Corinth and the Church,' in B. S. Rosner, ed., *Understanding Paul's Ethics: Twentieth Century Approaches* (Grand Rapids: Eerdmans; Carlisle: Paternoster, 1995), pp. 101-3.

32. Others have sought to argue that the aphoristic statement, 'All things are lawful

that this section should be titled, 'On Going to the Prostitutes'. He reconstructs the situation thus: 'Apparently, some men within the Christian community are going to prostitutes and are arguing for the right to do so. Being people of the Spirit, they imply, has moved them to a higher plane, the realm of the Spirit, where they are unaffected by behaviour that has merely to do with the body'.[33]

Because Fee sees that Paul's argument is against the Corinthians' view of the human body and sexual immorality, he accounts for the abrupt change of direction in vv. 13-14 (where the topic of food and the stomach is introduced) by stating, 'The matter of food therefore is not the issue here at all; rather, it is intended to set up the issue of the body and sexual immorality'.[34] The nexus between the alleged notoriety of the Corinthians and sexual promiscuity allows commentators to conclude that some Christians were visiting brothels. This is sometimes based on a mistaken view of the outrageous religious promiscuity of Roman Corinth. In Greek Corinth the verb used in Greek to mean 'I practise prostitution' was literally 'I Corinthianise' (Κορινθιάζομαι), and the fourth-century-b.c. plays of Philetaerus and Poliochus carried the title 'The Whoremonger (ὁ Κορινθιαστής).[35] Strabo's comments about 1,000 religious prostitutes of Aphrodite and those of Athenaeus are unmistakably about Greek and not Roman Corinth. As temple prostitution was not a Greek phenomenon, the

---

to me', is really a Pauline statement but misapplied by the Corinthians. I find that not particularly plausible. Paul normally cites 'traditions' and corrects any misunderstanding (5:9-11). His previous discussion on who would be excluded from the kingdom of God makes the suggestion that gospel liberty and libertarianism could be connected very unlikely. Furthermore, Paul had already written to the Corinthians 'to have no relationships with immoral people' (5:9). They had misunderstood the contents of that letter, but it would have been clear by implication that Christians certainly could not engage in immoral conduct and, as Paul explains, they were not to keep company with Christians who were immoral, covetous, etc.

33. G. D. Fee, *The First Epistle to the Corinthians* (Grand Rapids: Eerdmans, 1987), pp. 250-51. See also T. Paige, "The Spirit at Corinth" (Ph.D. dissertation, University of Sheffield, 1993), p. 175, 'This section of the letter is directed against the problem of believers having concourse with prostitutes, and not with sexual immorality in general', as he begins his search for elements common to Graeco-Roman Hellenism in this period.

34. Fee, *1 Corinthians*, pp. 253-54. Cf. Plutarch, who, in 'Table-Talk,' *Moralia* 705C, warns in the context of the banquet to be 'alert not to be taken by surprise in the regions of belly, sex-organs, palate and nose'.

35. Aristophanes, *Fragments* 354; Philetaerus, 13.559a; and Poliochus, 7.31.3c. See Plato, *The Republic* 404c, for 'a Corinthian girl' = a prostitute.

veracity of his comments on this point have been rightly questioned.[36] The size of the Roman temple of Aphrodite on the Acrocorinth ruled out such temple prostitution; and by that time she had become Venus — the venerated mother of the imperial family and the highly respected patroness of Corinth — and was no longer a sex symbol.[37]

'All things are permitted', the self-justifying aphorism for the notorious conduct of the Corinthian Christians at dinners, concerned the 'intimate and unholy trinity' of eating and drinking and sexual immorality.[38] Gluttony and drunkenness were an accepted part of social life in Corinth, as were the promiscuous 'after-dinners'. For grand dinners such as the series of banquets given by the President of the Isthmian Games for the citizens of Corinth, travelling brothels could be brought in by the host to cater for guests after the dinner in the place where it was held.[39]

The élite who gave private banquets to which they invited clients as well as other guests provided not only for their physical hunger but also for their sexual appetites. It needs to be noted that 1 Corinthians 6:12-20 does not state that Christians actually went to brothels. They were having sexual intercourse with prostitutes in the context of the dinner.[40]

The Corinthian Christians who argued that everything was permitted for them rationalised the exercising of their privileges on the grounds of first-century Platonic anthropology, philosophical hedonism, and social conventions. An outline of the former argument is preserved where the body is said to have been ordained for pleasure and that the immortal soul was unaffected by any such conduct. In fact, the enjoyment of life was what 'Nature' intended, bearing in mind that 'Nature' and 'God' could be used synonymously.[41] Gluttony could be justified because 'food is for the belly,

---

36. Strabo, *Geography* 8.6.20c and Athenaeus, *Deipnosophists* 13.573c-574e. Strabo passed through Corinth in 44 B.C., the year of its foundation, and again in 29 B.C. For discussion see J. Murphy O'Connor, *St. Paul's Corinth* (Wilmington: M. Glazier, 1983), pp. 55-56.

37. See p. 10.

38. Citing A. Booth, 'The Age for Reclining and Its Attendant Perils', in W. J. Slater, ed., *Dining in a Classical Context* (Ann Arbor: University of Michigan Press, 1991), p. 105. Dio Chrysostom, *Or.* 77/78.28, 30.

39. Dio Chrysostom, *Or.* 77/78.4.

40. The term 'prostitute' (πόρνη) was used of the professional engaged in 'casual' sex. For discussion see D. Montserrat, *Sex and Society in Graeco-Roman Egypt* (London: Kegan Paul, 1996), pp. 107-8.

41. J. H. W. G. Liebeschuetz, *Continuity and Change in Roman Religion* (Oxford: Clarendon Press, 1979), p. 208.

and the belly is for food', and by implication 'sex (fornication) is for the body, and the body is for sex (fornication)' (ἡ πορνεία τῷ σώματι καὶ τὸ σῶμα τῇ πορνείᾳ). The self-centred aphorism they espoused is brought out by the emphatic place of the personal pronoun 'for me' in the sentence πάντα μοι ἔξεστιν.

Dio Chrysostom responded to this form of argument which the élite espoused with a rhetorical question, 'Who needs more steadfast control than he to whom all things are permitted?' (τίνι δὲ σωφροσύνης ἐγκρατεστέρας ἢ ᾧ πάντα ἔξεστιν) (*Or.* 62.3). The end of the statement is what some Corinthian Christians also used to justify their conduct (6:12). This evidence supports the contention of Part 1 of this book that Christians were simply following the secular mores of the élite of Corinth.

While Dio argued for the cardinal virtue of 'self-control' (*Or.* 62.3), Paul put forward different objections. His arguments are preceded by the bridging section (6:9-10) where he lists those who will be excluded from the kingdom of God by reason of their lifestyle. He cites 'fornicators' (πόρνοι), 'adulterers' (μοιχοί), 'passive homosexuals' (μαλακοί), 'active homosexuals' (ἀρσενοκοῖται),[42] and also includes 'drunkards' (μέθυσοι), as he does in the previous list (5:11). He indicates that 'such were some of you, but you were washed, sanctified and justified'. Paul's subsequent discussion explains why gluttony, often epitomised by drunkenness followed by immorality at banquets, was proscribed for Christians.

Who in Corinth could make the affirmation, 'All things are permitted to me'? It would certainly not be the prerogative of those without status. Was there a time in the lives of those who possessed status in Roman Corinth when they saw themselves free from constraints? We know that those who received the Roman *toga virilis*[43] around their eighteenth year were seen to have reached 'the age for reclining' at banquets and were also exposed to 'its attendant perils'.[44] Booth states that 'there were conventions attached at which license freely to participate in the *symposium* and *convivium*, license to accept invitations there to recline was to be granted'.[45] It was acknowledged that the donning of the *toga* was seen as

---

42. For discussion see appendix on pp. 116-19.

43. Cf. the use of *virilitas* as a common euphemism for the male sex organ; J. N. Adams, *The Latin Sexual Vocabulary* (London: Duckworth, 1982), p. 69.

44. See Booth, 'The Age for Reclining and Its Attendant Perils', pp. 105-20.

45. Booth, 'The Age for Reclining and Its Attendant Perils', p. 107.

the most important ritual — a symbol of adulthood and the assuming of responsibility for one's actions.

Writers saw this milestone of receiving the *toga virilis* as a persistent danger for young men.[46] Tacitus, for example, said, '[T]he elegant banquet ... along with the use of the *toga* ... are the enticements of Romanization, to vice and servitude' (*Ag.* 21). Nicolaus of Damascus in his life of Augustus records that at that age he was not 'to be in attendance with the young men as they get drunk, nor to remain at drinking parties past evening, nor to have dinner ... [and he] abstained from sex just at the time when young men are particularly sexually active'.[47]

In Athens when 'the new adult, aged eighteen, usually acquired the right to accept invitations to recline ... he was considered sufficiently mature to cope with sexual advances'.[48] Xenophon says, 'Hercules has reached the *ephebic* age' (equivalent to that of receiving the *toga virilis*), and he had the freedom of choice and must select 'between the joys of eating, drinking, and lovemaking ... and edifying toil' (*Mem.* 2.1.21).

Cicero wrote of those who argued against the view 'it is permitted' (*licitum est*). 'If there is anyone who thinks that youth should be forbidden affairs even with courtesans, he is doubtless eminently austere, but his view is contrary not only to the licence of this age, but also to the custom and concessions of our ancestors. For when was this not a common practice? When was it blamed? When was it forbidden? When, in fact, was it that what is allowed was not allowed? (*quod licet, non liceret*).'[49]

It is significant that Plutarch, in 'On Listening to Lectures', 37C-D, writes to the young Nicander who had reached adulthood, '. . . now that you are no longer subject to authority, having assumed the male toga (τὸ ἀνδρεῖον ἱμάτιον)', i.e., the *toga virilis*. He goes on to explain that young men 'as they lay aside the garb of childhood ... straightway become full of unruliness.'

The problem which confronted Paul concerns young men reaching the age of reclining when promiscuity was theirs both by choice and convention. The accusation he brings against them is that they are committing

---

46. Booth, 'The Age for Reclining and Its Attendant Perils', p. 107; and T. Wiedemann, *Adults and Children in the Roman Empire* (London: Routledge, 1989), p. 91.

47. F. Jacoby, *Die Fragmente der griechischen Historica* (Berlin: 1926), II, 90.

48. Booth, 'The Age for Reclining and Its Attendant Perils', p. 117.

49. *Pro Caelio* 20.48. For a discussion of such conduct in Rome, see E. Eyben, *Restless Youth in Ancient Rome* (E.T. London: Routledge, 1993), pp. 231-33.

'fornication' (6:13). He states that those who commit a sexual act with a prostitute thereby create a 'one flesh' relationship and cites Genesis 2:24 and not, as one would expect, the appropriate charge of adultery if they were already married (6:15-16). In the latter case they would have broken the one-flesh relationship they had in marriage. The injunction, then, is not to flee 'adultery' — he has already drawn a distinction between fornicators and adulterers (6:9) — but to flee fornication.[50] Furthermore, the action is not described as adultery, i.e., a sin against a wife, but clearly as 'a sin against his own body' (6:18).[51]

He also may be indicating, as did other writers, that while youths maintained that 'all things was permitted for them', they had to be warned of the persistent dangers into which they could fall. 'Assumption of the *toga virilis* was on the one hand recognised to bestow freedom to recline [at dinner], and on the other to render desirable some restraint and guidance'.[52] Juvenal observes how a youth can learn the sin of gluttony from his father (*Satire* 14.7-10). The Roman *convivium* fostered 'a degree of decadence associated not only with the pleasures of the palate but also of the pillow'.[53] Seneca the Younger expressed his concern that the luxurious banquet and immorality were 'symptoms and causes of decadence in the young' (*Ep.* 95.24). Persius recalled the choices in sexual experimentation on assuming the *toga virilis* — 'At the age when the path of life is doubtful, and wanderings, ignorant of life, parted my trembling soul into the branching of crossways' (5.34-44).

The strong adversative 'but' used on both occasions in 6:12 was Paul's way of giving clear warnings against choosing the path of gluttony and whoring that epitomised conduct at banquets attended by young men who had gained the freedom of adulthood. If Christian youths affirmed that they had come of age and all was now permitted, Paul countered with

50. For a discussion of OT allusions which are the basis of Paul's reply see B. S. Rosner, 'Joseph and Paul Fleeing Immorality', *Paul, Scripture and Ethics: A Study of 1 Corinthians 5–7* (Leiden: E. J. Brill, 1994), ch. 5. A clear distinction needs to be drawn between the possible sources of the 'theological' background of Paul and the 'foreground', i.e., the problem and its background in secular Corinth.

51. See B. N. Fisk, 'ΠΟΡΝΕΥΕΙΝ as Body Violation: The Unique Nature of Sexual Sin in 1 Corinthians 6.18,' *NTS* 42.4 (Oct. 1996): 540-58 for an excellent discussion of Paul's argument on this point.

52. Booth, 'The Age for Reclining and Its Attendant Perils', p. 108.

53. Booth, 'The Age for Reclining and Its Attendant Perils', p. 106.

a statement that not everything was beneficial (συμφέρει), i.e., actually secured their well-being as Christians. Fornication, like drunkenness, was one of the grounds for exclusion from the kingdom (6:9-10).

Philostratus records that Isaeus in his early youth was 'the slave of eating and drinking . . . [and] was often in love' (*Lives of the Sophists* 513). Again, Paul warns of the addictive power of living on the basis of their aphorisms, in the face of the Christian's affirmation that 'for me everything is permitted'. Therefore, Paul asserts, as a personal choice he will not be enslaved by anything (6:12b). The linguistic relationship alluded to by Liddell and Scott between ἔξεστιν ('it is permitted') and the passive form of ἐξουσιάζω ('I am brought under the power') may be overlooked when seeking to understand Paul's response.[54] He has obviously framed it in order to counter their aphorism and not in any way to qualify it.

Among the sense perceptions referred to in Philo's summary of the justification of 'riotous living' was 'the appetite'. The Christian youth affirmed their right to gorge themselves at banquets. Paul, in response to their aphorism that food was destined for the stomach and the stomach was created for food and therefore gluttony was acceptable, countered with the argument that God will destroy both the stomach and food (6:13). It will be remembered that the opponents of the so-called lovers of virtue referred to the ascetic existence of such when compared to their own well-fed state, having noted that at death sense perceptions ceased (*Det.* 33).

Youth justified the enjoyment of sex on the grounds that nature had created the body with this sense perception. It was certainly the testimony of those who attended the Roman *convivium*. If the aphorism appears to have been that 'the body is for sex', Paul responded by introducing a central Christian theme — that the body was meant 'for the Lord', and 'the Lord was meant for the body'. He concluded with the command that the Christian men of Corinth were not justified in asserting their self-centred aphorism, for 'they were not their own [possession]'; they must 'glorify the Lord in their bodies' (6:19-20). Under no circumstances were they to engage in fornication with prostitutes, which, we have noted, was part of 'the after-dinners'. The interesting feature about the Christian men involved was that they defended their conduct by repeating secular aphorisms of the élite. It is also highly significant that they were socially in the

---

54. See p. 95 for the observation that the relationship between the noun ἐξουσία and the verb ἔξεστιν in 1 Cor. 8:9 and 10:23 is overlooked.

position to indulge in the lifestyle of young Corinthians by attending these banquets.

1 Corinthians 10:23

What is to be said about the background of 1 Corinthians 8:1–11:1 and the same aphoristic saying that is repeated in 10:23 except for the personal pronoun, 'for me'? I have already argued that the issue concerned was the determination of some Christians to exercise what they viewed as their right — Paul describes this forcefully as 'this right of yours' (ἡ ἐξουσία ὑμῶν αὕτη) (8:9). He never challenges that it is their right, but he does argue in the first instance that a right is not the sole criterion, or even the criterion to be used by Christians, in determining their conduct, even though it would have been the case with their non-Christian compatriots. It is important to note that it is a 'right' (ἐξουσία) some possess and not 'a freedom' (ἐλευθερία) to which Paul is referring. Some translators incorrectly render the former term thus. He does not use the term 'freedom' (ἐλευθερία) to describe what they possess, although the cognate, ἐλεύθερος, is found in 9:1.[55] There a distinction is observed between a right and a freedom which he clearly shows as he proceeds to argue that while he possesses certain rights as an apostle and is 'free' to exercise them, yet he chooses not to do so in the interests of the gospel (9:12).

The right which some Corinthian Christians exercised was to recline at a dinner in a pagan temple (8:10). It was not related to dining in the temple of Asclepius where one could eat a special diet as part of the prescription for recovery[56] or in the temple of Demeter which did not provide dining facilities in this period as it had done before the destruction of Corinth in 146 b.c.[57] This right related to the special privilege open to a limited number of the inhabitants to dine during the Games at nearby Isthmia on a number of occasions and came under the jurisdiction of Corinth. These were the Roman citizens of Corinth,[58] as the epigraphic evidence records. The custom which allowed all the Romans of Corinth to

55. See my *Seek the Welfare of the City,* pp. 166-68.
56. For a good example of curative eating in the Asclepion see *SIG³* 1170.
57. J. B. Salmon, *Wealthy Corinth: A History of the City to 338 BC* (Oxford: Clarendon Press, 1984), p. 403. For its use in Roman times see p. 164.
58. See my *Seek the Welfare of the City,* pp. 171-74.

banquet on a number of occasions would be perceived as 'a right'. We know that Lucius Castricus Regulus, as the President of the Games, celebrated their transfer from Corinth to Isthmia, possibly in A.D. 51. He gave a banquet for 'all the citizens'.[59] It is easy to see how the benefaction originally bestowed by Regulus to celebrate a particular event was subsequently seen as a right for citizens. It had been extended to several banquets by subsequent Presidents of the Games.[60] The Presidency of the Games was an honorary liturgy or civic office, to which one was elected by the citizens of Corinth. Candidates had to make election promises which they were required to fulfil by law if they secured the office.[61] They certainly could not hope to be elected to office if they offered less than their predecessor, so Plutarch records that Regulus established a benchmark to be bettered by subsequent Presidents of the Games.[62] The great temple of Poseidon at Isthmia was an integral part of the Games complex and would have been the place for the traditional banquets given by the President.

Just as there were perils in reclining at a private banquet (6:12-20), so too there were not dissimilar dangers open to those Christians who accepted the invitation to recline at the civic banquets associated with the Games. Some 'ate, drank and rose up to play' (10:7), which was the way that the LXX describes the banquet associated with idolatry and the 'after-dinner' behaviour in Exodus 32:6. The combination of the same verbs is on the grave of the founder of Tarsus according to Athenaeus and Strabo.[63] The nexus between reclining in the temple and idolatry becomes clearer as Paul commanded the Christians to flee from it, i.e., the dinners because, as he explains later, it was not possible for them to sit at 'the table of daemons' and drink of 'the cup of daemons' and to sit also at the table of the Lord and drink his cup (10:14, 21).[64]

---

59. See pp. 276-77. Kent, *Corinth*, 8.3, no. 153, cf. 151. The liturgy of the President of the Games was originally combined with that of the *aedile*, but because of the enormous wealth required to run the prestigious Isthmian Games privately, it had been separated from the latter office and was now regarded as the most senior of all the liturgies, even ranking ahead of that of magistrate.

60. *Moralia* 723A.

61. The fulfilling of election promises, *policitatio*, once appointed to office, was required by law.

62. *Moralia* 723A.

63. See p. 97. Athanaeus, *Deipnosophists* 530B; and Strabo, *Geography* xiv, 5, 9.

64. For later Jewish evidence of contamination for even putting one's head into an

Just as it is possible to overlook the semantic connection between ἔξεστιν and ἐξουσιάζω (6:12), so too the nexus between the term ἐξουσία, which Paul used extensively in 1 Corinthians 8–9, and ἔξεστιν (10:23) is not always recognised. What is a 'right' (ἐξουσία) can be expressed in the verbal form 'it is permitted' (ἔξεστιν). This being the case, Paul's extended 'defence' (ἀπολογία) (9:3) of his rights and his way of operating becomes explicable as he contrasts his conduct with theirs (10:23). They defend their 'right' (ἐξουσία) with the aphorism πάντα ἔξεστιν, but Paul spells out the way he operates in terms of what he aimed to achieve — 'but not all things are beneficial' (ἀλλ' οὐ πάντα συμφέρει) and 'but not all things build up' (ἀλλ' οὐ πάντα οἰκοδομεῖ). In this setting benefiting and enhancing the Christian's life must extend to that of the weaker brother. The reasons for this are the implications of exercising 'this right of yours', viz., the conscience of a weaker brother can be wounded; he stumbles and commits apostasy, having been enticed by the 'stronger' Christians to exercise his right also to recline in the idol temple (8:10-12).

Paul had such concern for the welfare and building up of others that he made the astonishing statement 'wherefore if meat makes my brother stumble, I will no more eat flesh (διόπερ οὐ μὴ . . . εἰς τὸν αἰῶνα), that I may not stumble my brother' (8:13). The command that follows Paul's strong adversative statements in 10:23 is put first of all in the negative — 'no one must seek his own [advantage]' (μηδεὶς τὸ ἑαυτοῦ ζητείτω) — and then in the positive — 'but the [good] of others' (ἀλλὰ τὸ τοῦ ἑτέρου).

The *imitatio* the Christians were meant to engage in had been supplanted by a secular aphorism, rationalised on the grounds that an idol was nothing and resulting in peer pressure on the 'weaker' Christians (8:10). S. Mitchell has noted 'that it was not a change of heart that might win a Christian convert back to paganism, but the overwhelming pressure to conform imposed by the institutions of his city and the activities of his neighbour'.[65] While Paul's argument began with an appeal not to entice the weaker brother to follow their example, he demonstrated to those who 'think they stand' that they will themselves fall into the trap of idolatry connected with such reclining if they continue to exercise their right

---

idol temple see *AZ* 54b and my discussion of other Jewish evidence as well in 'Theological and Ethical Responses to Religious Pluralism,' *TynB* 41.2 (1990): 207-26, esp. 215-19.

65. S. Mitchell, 'Christian Origins,' *The Rise of the Church, Anatolia: Land, Men, and Gods in Asia Minor* (Oxford: Clarendon Press, 1993), II, 10.

(which will invoke the Lord's jealousy) and live by the secular aphorism, 'everything is permitted' (10:12, 22).[66]

This is not the end of the matter. Paul again explained his own approach having commanded them not to give offence to non-Christians or Christians, 'even as I also please all men in all things (cf. 9:20-23), not seeking my own welfare (τὸ ἐμαυτοῦ σύμφερον; cf. συμφέρει, 10:23), but the welfare of many (ἀλλὰ τῶν πολλῶν), that they may be saved' (10:32-33). This is the *imitatio* of Paul modelled on Christ (11:1) and sharply contrasts to their defence based on the culturally axiomatic aphorism that 'everything is permitted'.

1 Corinthians 15:29-34

1 Corinthians 15 may have more to do with combating the widely held belief in the immortality of the soul and its implications for ethical conduct than the view that the Corinthians had an overrealised eschatology which had no place for the resurrection of their bodies.[67] Evidence abounds for the concept of the immortality of the soul. '[Friend, this] tomb Attica did win. But Italy [kept my body], and my soul went up on high.'[68]

One of the pivotal sections in 1 Corinthians 15 is in verses 29-34.[69] They contain the first set of imperatives to this point in Paul's argument and provide important clues concerning the conduct of Corinthian Christians. It has a significant connection with the only other, and indeed final, set of injunctions where Paul summarised the ethical implications of this discussion with his customary 'so then' (ὥστε) (15:58; cf. 11:34; 14:39-40).[70]

66. For a detailed discussion of 10:22 see B. Rosner, '"No Other Gods": The Jealousy of God and Religious Pluralism,' in A. D. Clarke and B. W. Winter, eds., *One God, One Lord: Christianity in a World of Religious Pluralism*, 2nd ed. (Grand Rapids: Baker; Carlisle: Paternoster, 1993), ch. 7.

67. For a helpful survey of the history of research see J. Holleman, *Resurrection and Parousia: A Traditio-Historical Study of Paul's Eschatology in 1 Corinthians 15* (Leiden: E. J. Brill, 1996), pp. 4-31.

68. *SEG* 37 (1987), no. 198. For commentary see E. A. Judge, *New Docs.* 9 (forthcoming). See also a discussion in *New Docs.* 4:6.

69. See the uncertainty as to its role in Paul's argument reflected in C. K. Barrett's comments in J.-N. Aletti, C. K. Barrett, M. Carrez, F. Montagnini, K. Müller, and W. Schrage, *Résurrection du Christ et des Chrétiens (1 Co 15)* (Rome: Abbaye de S. Paul, 1985), pp. 82-83.

70. Holleman, *Resurrection and Parousia,* does not discuss these ethical commands

1 Corinthians 15:29-34 is contrasted with the climax of 15:1-11, where Paul affirms how costly it was to bring the gospel to the Corinthians that they might believe (15:10-11).[71] He compares it with the self-indulgent lifestyle adopted by some Corinthian Christians, which he charged had actually deprived others of the knowledge of God (15:29-34).[72] We will defer discussion of the enigmatic statements concerning 'baptism' and 'wild beasts' in 15:29, 32 until we have explored the remainder of this critical *argumentum ad hominem* of 1 Corinthians 15 for understanding the issues involved.

(i) 'Eat and Drink for Tomorrow We Die' (15:32b)

In the first century B.C. Strabo saw a famous gravestone of antiquity during his travels in the East. The second citation, which is a textual addition, explicates further what was meant by the final statement in the first — 'but those numerous blessings have been left behind'. This inscription of the founder of Tarsus recorded the hedonistic lifestyle of a hero and its cessation at death.

> Sardanapallus . . . built Anchiale and Tarsus in one day. Eat, drink, play (ἔσθιε, πῖνε καὶ παῖζε),[73] because all things else are not worth this. Choerilus also mentions this inscription; and indeed the following verses are everywhere known: 'Mine are all that I have eaten, and my loose indulgences and the delights of love that I have enjoyed; but those numerous blessings have been left behind'.[74]

> Well aware that you are by nature mortal, magnifying the desire of your heart, delighting yourselves in merriments, there is no enjoyment for

---

and their relationship to 15:58, which he does not cite. He believes that the arguments *ad hominem* in 15:29-34 'are not focused on the debated issue but on the participants in the debate' (p. 41). 'They are not directed against any specific point of the Corinthian position on life after death. The strength of these arguments is their rhetorical power' (p. 47). He cites all these verses only in the opening chapter, 'Introductory Problems'. As his title indicates, he is interested in the resurrection and the *parousia*. It is being suggested in this discussion of élitist ethics that vv. 29-33 are central to the problem of the Corinthian Christians.

71. Cf. 2 Cor. 10:14, where he indicates that he was their founding apostle.

72. Paul begins another section of this discussion in 15:35ff. as he answers the important objections to the doctrine of the resurrection of the body — 'But some will say, "How are the dead raised?" and "With what manner of body do they come?"'

73. παίζω = 'play' amorously; cf. Xenophon, *Symposium* 9.2 and Gen. 26:8 (LXX).

74. Strabo, *Geography* 4.5.9.

you after death. For I too am dust, though I have reigned over Ninus. Mine are all the food that I have eaten, and my loose indulgences, and the delights of love that I have enjoyed; but those numerous blessings have been left behind. This to mortal man is wise advice on how to live.[75]

Philo expresses a similar sentiment in the citation found in *Det.* 33, where the senses are to be indulged to the full while life lasts because there are no bodily pleasures beyond the grave — 'Did nature create pleasures and enjoyments and the delights that meet us all the way through life, for the dead, or for those who have never come into existence, and not for the living?' In 1 Corinthians 15:32 Paul cites Isaiah 22:13 — 'we must eat and drink, for tomorrow we die' — as he draws out the implication of a similar argument reflecting that of the sophists in *Det.* 33-34. He frames his argument against the Corinthian Christians' belief that there was no resurrection of the body — 'If the dead are not raised', then the present is all important. They could 'eat and drink' not because they would die if they did not, but rather that the present moment was for banqueting, since their partying days would one day be over. The 'now' was the moment for pleasure.

(ii) 'Evil Company Corrupts . . .' (15:33)

Paul would have agreed that 'They who think that the sins of youth deserve indulgence are deceived' (*Rhetorica ad Herennium* 4.17.25). He commanded the Corinthians not to be deceived. This suggests that they believed that their future was not spiritually affected by their present actions. Furthermore, they felt that they would not be corrupted in any way by joining with the banqueting set of Corinth because the soul was unaffected by what they were doing in this present life. Their self-deception reflects a wrong view of the future of their bodies.

In 15:33 Paul cites Menander's *Thais.* 'Loose-bridled?[76] Pest! methinks, though I have suffered this, that none the less I'd now be glad to have her.[77] Sing to me, goddess, sing of such a one as she: audacious, beautiful,

---

75. Cited in LCL, VI, 341, n. 2.

76. ἄγγαρος = a term of abuse and a synonym for ἀκρατής, which is used of those without control of their passions.

77. ἔχειν τινά = have intercourse with a client; Adams, *The Latin Sexual Vocabulary*, p. 187.

and plausible withal:[78] she does you wrongs; she locks her door; keeps asking you for gifts; she loves none, but ever makes pretence. Evil companionship corrupts good character' (φθείρουσιν ἤθη χρήσθ᾽ ὁμιλίαι κακαί).[79]

Apart from the context of a prostitute in Menander's *Thais*, the terms themselves belong to the semantic field of sexuality, for ὁμιλία refers to 'sexual intercourse' or 'able in body for sexual intercourse',[80] κακός = 'bad' in a moral sense, ἦθος = 'moral character',[81] χρηστός = 'good', and φθείρω means either 'I destroy' or 'I corrupt'.

It is often said that this was a popular saying and Paul did not know its context when he cited it. A search of the *TLG* shows that it appears only in a fragment from Euripides[82] and in Menander on three occasions two of which are in a collected list of his sayings which were aphorisms without a context.[83] It also occurs once in *Thais*, a fragment of a play which took its name from prostitutes, *hetairai*, who served high-class clients.[84] The citation stated that sex is only being provided for money by the one who 'keeps asking you for gifts'. She loves none of her clients but makes pretence as she provides her services to them for money.

Given Paul's acquaintance with rhetoric (without attempting to argue where he may have acquired it),[85] it cannot be categorically asserted that he had not read the works of Menander. Malherbe has drawn attention to the evidence that 'Menander's writings were highly regarded in Paul's day and were frequently suggested as excellent reading for the aspiring rhetorician'.[86] Paul could have been well aware of the *Sitz im Leben* of

78. θρασεῖαν, ὡραίαν δὲ καὶ πιθανὴν ἅμα. θρασύς = 'audacious' in a bad sense and in Aristophanes, *Equites* 181, connected with πονηρός.

79. LCL, Fragments, 215-18. If the additional line, ὁ κρατής, ἄγγαρος ὄλεθρος ἡδέως ἄν μοι δοκῶ given in A. Körte and A. Thierfelder, *Menandri quae supersunt*, 2nd ed. (Leipzig: Teubner, 1959), II, 187, is accepted, then this adds yet further evidence that the company to which Menander referred definitely were prostitutes.

80. Herodotus, 1.182; Xenophon, *Symposium* 8.22; *Memorabilia* 3.11.14.

81. Aristotle, *Nicomachean Ethics* 1139a 1.

82. Euripides in A. Nauck, *Tragicorum Graecorum fragmenta* (Hildesheim: Olms, 1964), no. 895.

83. A. Meinecke, *Fragmenta comicorum Graecorum*, 2nd ed. (Berlin: de Gruyter, 1970), I, 73; and S. Jaekel, *Menandri sententiae* (Leipzig: Teubner, 1964), p. 80.

84. T. B. L. Webster, *An Introduction to Menander* (Manchester: Manchester University Press, 1974), pp. 14, 185.

85. See my *Philo and Paul among the Sophists*, pp. 237-41.

86. Malherbe, 'The Beasts at Ephesus,' *JBL* 87 (1968): 73. If Paul possessed such train-

this citation, and it would, therefore, have been highly apposite. Even if he were not, is there any justification for thinking that the situation that gave rise to the sexual permissiveness with prostitutes (6:12-20; 8:1–11:1) was not in Paul's mind as he struggled against the philosophical justification of the indulgence of the senses with their 'eating and drinking' and 'after-dinners'? He appeared to have had a particular sort of dinner in mind when he stated that, if there was no resurrection of the body, it followed that Christians might as well have become part of this clique in Corinth (15:32). These banquets were different from those private occasions to which they might have been minded to go and attendance at which he did not proscribe. He only prescribed that they respond in a courteous way if the issue of idol meat was raised at a private dinner (10:27-28).

Because of the promiscuous behaviour which we have already noted at banquets (6:12-20; 8:1–11:1), 15:33 should not be taken to refer to day-to-day contact with the unbelieving world — Paul had corrected any mis-understanding in a previous letter, 'Not at all meaning the fornicators of this world . . . for then you must needs go out of the world' (5:10). He was concerned with the evil company into which they have been drawn (15:33). It has resulted in a highly inappropriate lifestyle epitomised by gluttony, drunkenness, and promiscuous behaviour which replicated the behaviour of their non-Christian compatriots.

(iii) 'Awake Out of Drunkenness' (15:34)

Paul uses the aorist imperative of ἐκνήφω meaning 'come out of your stupor', 'become sober'. It can also mean 'to sleep off a drunken bout' or 'become sober again'. They were to come out of the haze of their self-indulgent lifestyle of banqueting epitomised by drunkenness (cf. 5:11; 6:10) and to act responsibly, i.e., 'righteously' (δικαίως). The command is supplemented with an injunction 'not to go on sinning' (μὴ ἁμαρτάνετε), a present imperative. The overall context refers to the dissipated lifestyle of some Christians; these commands calls them to disengage from it.

---

ing, then it is possible that he had read Menander's works. Plutarch, *Moralia* 712, says in a discussion of 'What kinds of entertainment are most appropriate at dinner?' that 'we could not chart our course more easily without wine than without Menander. Even the erotic ele-ment in Menander is appropriate for men who after their wine will soon be leaving to repose with their wives'. He refers to 'Menander's polished charm' and 'the praise' of this writer of New Comedy (*Moralia* 712D).

Such had been their preoccupation with themselves, the assertion of their own rights, and what they were permitted to do that self-centredness and preoccupation with personal pleasure meant that their energies had been dispersed. They took no thought for others and their need of 'the knowledge of God' which comes through the gospel (1:21). Since not all in Corinth believed (1:23-24), the Christians were to be instruments in making the gospel known to their compatriots. Because some asserted their right to be part of the banqueting élite of Corinth, their hedonistic lifestyle meant that they had taken no thought for their responsibilities to seek the spiritual welfare of their neighbours (10:24).

Paul's reorientation of his lifestyle was for the purpose of bringing the gospel to others (9:12, 20-23). The fact that 'he had laboured more abundantly' in Corinth meant that the Corinthians had become believers (15:10). They must do the same for others.

In the culture of this Roman colony, to shame others — either publicly or by letter — caused an acute 'loss of face'.[87] Paul had drawn attention to the fact that while some may not have thought that they had shamed others, their inappropriate behaviour was a shameful matter (7:36).[88] He had also indicated that on another important issue he did not arbitrarily set out to shame them; cf. 'I am not writing these things to shame you, but to admonish you as my beloved children' (4:14). However, in this case, his intention was to awaken in them a deep sense of shame (πρὸς ἐντροπὴν ὑμῖν λαλῶ) (15:34b). It was a stinging rebuke meant to cover them in shame so that they would abandon their sinful way of living and wake up to their gospel responsibilities to non-Christians.

(iv) 'I Fought the Beasts at Ephesus' (15:32a)

This statement has been interpreted either literally (he engaged in a struggle with wild animals in the arena in Ephesus) or figuratively (that he battled with either opponents in the city or with his passions).[89] The first suggestion can be ruled out because Paul was neither a fighter of wild beasts nor a citizen condemned *ad bestias*.[90] Those who argue that the reference is

---

87. D. F. Epstein, *Personal Enmity in Roman Politics 218-43 BC* (London: Routledge, 1989), p. 113 on wounded honour.

88. R. A. Kaster, 'The Shame of the Romans,' *TAPA* 127 (1997): 4-5. See pp. 243-46.

89. See Malherbe, 'The Beasts at Ephesus,' p. 71 for the options.

90. C. Roueché, 'Gladiators and Wild-Beast Fighters', *Performers and Partisans at*

to human opponents point to 1 Corinthians 16:8-9, where Paul reported on the great opportunities he had for ministry and also the 'many adversaries' in Ephesus.

However, Malherbe has assembled important evidence to demonstrate that there was a long-standing tradition from Plato onwards where 'human passions and the pleasures of the flesh are described as beasts that fight against man'.[91] Dio Chrysostom discussed the myth of Heracles, the purpose of which was 'to show the character of [human] passions, that they are irrational and brutish and that, by holding out the enticement of some pleasure, they win over the foolish . . . and bring them to a most sad and pitiable end' (*Or.* 5.16). He described these 'lusts' (ἐπιθυμίαι) in terms of 'savage beasts' to be destroyed but notes that if they were not thoroughly rooted out they 'soon afterwards overwhelmed and destroyed [men] by the remaining lusts'. Only Heracles, having epitomised gluttony in the fourth century B.C., was rehabilitated in the first century, and he alone managed to make his own heart 'pure, gentle or tame'. The discourse ends with Dio's own addition to the mythical account of young men who were enticed by a naked 'Libyan' woman posing as a prostitute who slew the young men who came to her. He did this, he says, for the sake of the 'young people' present (5.22, 24-27). Lucian also portrayed Heracles as a soldier fighting against pleasures in order to purify his own life (*Vit. Auct.* 8).[92]

Why does Paul introduce the clause with the phrase κατὰ ἄνθρωπον?[93] Elsewhere he indicates that it was to be understood metaphorically, this being a polite, popular way of speaking.[94] This would be consonant with the context, where Paul discusses his own ministry in Ephesus (15:30-32). He asked, 'Why do we ourselves also run risks every hour?' (15:30). Then he questions whether, 'as one would say' (κατὰ ἄνθρωπον), having

---

Aphrodisias in the Roman and Late Roman Periods, Journal of Roman Studies Monograph 6 (1996), ch. 5.

91. Malherbe, 'The Beasts at Ephesus,' p. 74.

92. Citation in Malherbe, 'The Beasts at Ephesus,' p. 74. His essay is a veritable gold mine of ancient material which discusses human passions and their defeat.

93. J. B. Lightfoot, *Notes on the Epistles of Paul from Unpublished Commentaries* (London: Macmillan, 1895), p. 186, 'as one would say'.

94. κατά, *BAGD* #5. It refers to an established rule in society (1 Cor. 9:8). It can illustrate a social convention (Gal. 3:15); indicate a human way of thinking (Gal. 1:11); and refer to a secular way of operating (1 Cor. 3:4). Rom. 3:5, where the phrase refers to a human way of thinking, comes closest.

'fought the beasts' was, in retrospect, a worthwhile thing to do — 'What is its profit to me?' (15:32a), given the Corinthian Christians' nonresurrection premise (15:32b).

There was no advantage to Paul having 'fought the beasts'. He had fought off human passions in Ephesus and died daily to these 'beasts'. All this was to no avail 'if dead [bodies] are not raised up' — the word is νεκροί without the article. The logical consequence was for Paul to imitate the Corinthians and go banqueting, for death came as the end point for such activities if the deeds done in the body were of no consequence. This would explain why he asks the question, 'What does it profit me if dead bodies are not raised?' and explains his ethical injunctions calling them to Christian service — 'Therefore, my beloved brethren, be steadfast, immovable, always abounding in the work of the Lord'. Significantly he concludes with the essence of his argument, 'knowing that your labour in the Lord is not void' (κενός) (15:58), and that subsequently 'each one may receive the deeds done in the body, according to what he has done, whether good or bad' (2 Cor. 5:10).

Was Paul's risky service and daily self-denial futile? He was, in the scornful words of Philo's adversaries who ridiculed those who did not indulge their senses, 'in training for dying'; he should be looked down upon because, according to the Corinthians, this enjoyment which Nature has given will cease at the grave. In the eyes of pagan thought he needed to take account of the reality of this life — 'knowing full well that you are but mortal, indulge your desire, find joy in your feasts. Dead, you shall have no delight'.[95]

(v) 'Baptism on Behalf of the Dead Bodies' (15:29)

This discussion occurs at the beginning of the *argumentum ad hominem*, and it is assumed almost *a priori* that the reference in 15:29 is to baptism on behalf of deceased ancestors or friends.[96] While it is not possible to

95. *Det.* 34; cf. *De Gig.* 14 and Plato, *Phaedo* 64A; cited in Athenaeus, *Deipnosophists* 336A-B.

96. R. E. DeMaris, 'Corinthian Religion and Baptism for the Dead (1 Corinthians 15:29): Insights from Archaeology and Anthropology,' *JBL* 114.4 (1995): 661-82, who sees the pagan Corinthians' preoccupation with the dead demanding that the Christians address the same issue and use baptism as their expression of their care for the dead. J. R. White, '"Baptism on account of the Dead": The Meaning of 1 Cor. 15:29 in Its Context,' *JBL* 116.3

weigh the many interpretations against each other, how might this verse be understood in the light of the discussion so far? It is possible to render the passage, 'Otherwise (ἐπεὶ τί) what shall those who are baptised on behalf of the dead bodies (οἱ βαπτιζόμενοι) do, if corpses (νεκροί) are not raised at all? Why then are they being baptised on behalf of them?'

This translation suggests that the recipients of baptism may not be other than the actual Corinthian Christians to whom Paul is writing. His two questions may be meant to question the futility of their own baptism and the theological significance attached to it. The sentence begins with the causal ἐπεί, which, with the future tense, means 'otherwise' (Liddell and Scott). The first question is not set in the present tense, i.e., 'what are you doing', but the future, 'what shall they do?' which suggests that their action was a futile one for them personally, given their view on the future of their own bodies. It is hard to see how it could affect the future of loved ones. 1 Corinthians 1:13-17a suggests that some significance had been attached to the baptisms of those involved in strife and jealousy.

Paul attached a theological and an ethical significance to baptism — a point which appeared to have eluded the Corinthian Christians — asking in the letter he wrote from Corinth, 'Are you ignorant that all who were baptised into Christ Jesus were baptised into his death? We were therefore buried with him in baptism into death: that like as Christ was raised from the dead through the glory of the Father, we might walk in newness of life' (Rom. 6:3-4). This argument is set in the context of those who felt justified in living in sin that grace might abound (6:1).

Two seemingly cynical questions were asked by some of the Christians (15:29-34): 'How could there be the resurrection of the body?' and 'What would a resurrected body be like?' (15:35). The fact that Paul proceeded to deal at length with these issues suggests that the resurrection of the body had greatly puzzled the Corinthian Christians. This is understandable since resurrection would have been a complete enigma to the first-century Gentile who believed in the immortality of the soul and the cessation of the body's senses at death.

The cause of the problem does not seem to be that of an over-

---

(1997): 487-99, has surveyed the views on this text and proposed that the reference is to the 'apostles' who in their ministry are dying (p. 498). The strength of his argument is that he seeks to link this passage with the earlier part of 1 Cor., esp. chs. 1–4, but the immediate context is ignored, as are indeed the ethical issues it represents.

realised eschatology but that these Christians, like many in their own day and generation, believed that the senses which surrounded the body ought to be indulged in this life. Their conduct showed that they felt no harm would be done because of the immortality of the soul, whose future for the Christians was made all the more secure because of Christ's resurrection. 1 Corinthians 15 does not necessarily imply that the Christians did not believe in the resurrection of Christ, but that they, like their compatriots, did not believe in the resurrection of their own bodies.

For those who reject the above line of interpretation and opt for some idea of vicarious baptism, it does not substantially alter the thrust of the argument that has been developed here. If the Corinthian Christians did not believe in the resurrection of the body, then if some were undertaking baptism on behalf of the deceased it was still an exercise in futility, just as it was for their own baptism, given their basic premise.

V. Conclusions

The idea must be rejected that the maxim of the secular élite that '[for me] all things are permitted' (which some Corinthian Christians espoused) was part of an ill-thought-out Pauline *paradosis*.[97] Paul himself emphatically rejected the aphorism which he twice cited with the use of the strong adversative ἀλλά (6:12; 10:23).

It has been argued that some of the Christians believed what most of their fellow Corinthians believed, i.e., that the soul was immortal and that this mortal life alone afforded pleasure. They differed from their compatriots only in that the Christians believed that their immortality was now guaranteed by the resurrection of Christ. Rather they would have differed with Paul, whose anthropology and the ethical imperatives of the Christian life were based on the resurrection both of Jesus and the Christian. This important connection is found not only in 15:1-34 but also in 6:12-20, where it plays an important role, for Paul affirms, 'But the body is not for fornication, but for the Lord; and the Lord for the body: and God both

---

97. See B. J. Dodd, 'Paul's Paradigmatic "I" and 1 Corinthians 6:12,' *JSNT* 59 (1995): 39-58; cf. Fee, *The First Epistle to the Corinthians*, pp. 251-52, who states that the aphorism 'is almost certainly a Corinthian theological slogan' and speculates, 'possibly the Corinthians had turned a Pauline position into a slogan for their own purposes'.

raised up the Lord, and will raise up us through his power' (6:13b-14). If the background evidence assembled in this chapter is apposite, then Paul's conflict with the Corinthian Christians' view is a combination of first-century Platonism and a form of hedonism or Epicureanism which was defended by first-century sophists as an ethic of the élite.[98]

The title of this chapter contains the phrase 'élitist ethics'. The question, raised in passing in the opening section of this particular chapter, should now be explored. Were any Christians among 'the élite' of Corinth? Some think that 1 Corinthians yields a negative answer to this question, but by sifting through the evidence a positive conclusion has emerged. We know that there were some, perhaps 'not many'. Certainly not many were among 'the wise, the well-born and the powerful' (1:26), but this was also true of the composition of a city in the first century. Elsewhere they are designated as 'the wise among you in this world' (3:18), with an ironical question concerning 'a wise man among you' who could arbitrate (6:5).[99] There were 'some' who as Roman citizens had a 'right', not just 'the freedom', to recline in a pagan temple (8:9-10);[100] there were 'certain among you' (ἐν ὑμῖν τινες) who argued that there was no resurrection of the dead (15:12). Paul accused them of being involved with the party-going Corinthian set whose status and wealth alone admitted them to take part in banqueting with its unholy trinity of eating, drinking, and sexual intercourse (15:32-4).[101] Some young Corinthians, i.e., Roman citizens who had assumed the *toga virilis*, had 'the right' to eat, drink, and fornicate at a banquet. There was a segment in the Corinthian church from among the sons of the 'not many' élite who were part of this banqueting set (6:12-20). They rationalised their conduct on the basis of what was permitted for them as members of a class who secured their freedom on the occasion of

98. See E. L. Bowie, 'The Importance of the Sophists,' *Yale Classical Review* 27 (1982): 29-59 for an extended discussion of their social status.

99. See pp. 59-60 for the argument that vexatious litigation was an activity of the élite.

100. See my 'Civic Rights, 1 Corinthians 8:1–11:1,' *Seek the Welfare of the City,* ch. 9.

101. B. Witherington III, *Conflict and Community in Corinth: A Socio-Rhetorical Commentary on 1 and 2 Corinthians* (Grand Rapids: Eerdmans; Carlisle: Paternoster, 1995), p. 306 says 'the "some" here are the same "some"' who are criticised there [1 Cor. 8-10] namely certain reasonably well-to-do Gentiles (likely males) who were arguing for the right to dine in temples', and argues thus on the grounds that they espoused an eschatology based on an imperial viewpoint.

assuming the *toga virilis,* and may have been simply following in their fathers' footsteps (10:7, 21). The proportion of the Christian community who argued this way cannot be ascertained, but that is not crucial, for as a class in Corinth they were 'the powerful' (1:26), i.e., that vocal and ruling minority whose views determined its civic life.[102] Some of them appeared to have operated in the same way in the Christian community, for in the civil courts the vexatious litigation which Paul discusses (6:1-8) was also an activity of the élite.[103] The description of their ethics as 'élitist' for some in the Corinthian church is therefore considered apposite.[104]

The opening section of this chapter examined how two combined philosophical outlooks were the foundation of a plausible argument which would have commended itself to the wealthy and self-indulgent in this colony so recently affected by the affluence of the Claudian era.[105] Some of the Christians had justified their conduct on the basis of what has been shown to be a philosophical argument recorded by the Alexandrian Jew Philo, and could be epitomised by secular aphorisms. It enabled some Corinthian Christians to continue to enjoy 'pleasures which carry the sweets of life to the all-welcoming soul by every channel of the senses', as it also had for their compatriots.[106]

These sections of 1 Corinthians are an example of what Judge sought, i.e., the aphorisms '[for me] everything is permitted' and 'eat, drink and be merry, for tomorrow we die' (6:12; 10:23; 15:32), which were sustained by an intellectual argument. The search for evidence of a sustained argument has taken us outside 1 Corinthians, but at the same time 1 Corinthians has provided something unexpected — Paul's arguments aimed at demolishing the theoretical basis for élitist aphorisms.

The quest has led us not to a *Vulgärethik* but surprisingly to the eth-

---

102. It is not certain that the same persons were necessarily involved in 6:12-20 and 8:1–11:1 since it has been argued that the former were young unmarried men, but they were from the same élite segment of society which could live by that aphorism. It was not impossible that some fathers were guilty of duplicity, as ancient sources noted, 'Parents are criticised for preaching chastity to their children but setting an example by adultery'. R. P. Saller, 'Corporal Punishment, Authority, Obedience in the Roman Household,' in B. Rawson, ed., *Marriage, Divorce and Children in Ancient Rome* (Oxford: Clarendon Press, 1991), p. 162.

103. See pp. 59-60.

104. This does not necessitate an examination of the philosophical school or schools of their day to which they might have belonged.

105. Williams, 'Roman Corinth as a Commercial Center,' p. 46.

106. Philo, *Det.* 33.

ics of the élite. Strabo wrote his *Memoirs* 'more particularly for those who are in high stations in life' at the time of the founding of Corinth as a colony (which he had also visited) and commented,

> the great masses of women and men cannot be induced by mere force of reason to devote themselves to piety, virtue and honesty . . . [our ancestors] maintained that poetry was sufficient to form the understanding of every age. In the course of time, history and our present philosophy were introduced; these however suffice but of the chosen few and to the present day poetry is the main agent that instructs our people.[107]

For our purposes it is important to note that a body of literature was written in the early empire; it was based on the view that history and philosophy could be, and was, harnessed to instruct the élite on how they should live. Dionysius of Halicarnassus wrote as he did in the time of Augustus in order to 'afford a great abundance of noble and profitable examples, not only to lawgivers and leaders of the people, but also to others who aspire to take part in public life and to govern the state'.[108] The eleven books of *Memorable Deeds and Sayings* were written in the time of Tiberius by Valerius Maximus exclusively to instruct the élite Roman gentleman on how to behave in his religious, private, and public life.[109] Plutarch's aim in writing *The Lives* 'was clearly to provide a repertoire of *exempla* for public men' in the Flavian period.[110] That the Corinthians would have aphorisms does not surprise us given their role in the instruction of the general population. What has been unexpected is that, in the Corinthian church, it is élitist aphorisms that Paul has to contend with.[111]

---

107. Strabo, *Geography* 1.1.23; 2.8. It should remain a matter of ongoing interest to New Testament scholars that early Christianity chose to produce both gospels and letters as the means of instruction.

108. *Roman Antiquities* 5.75.1. This is a history of the Roman people.

109. See the recent English translation *Memorable Deeds and Sayings*, LCL (Cambridge, Mass.: Harvard University Press, 2000), 2 vols. and a discussion of their intended audience by C. Skidmore, *Practical Ethics for Roman Gentlemen: The Works of Valerius Maximus* (Exeter: University of Exeter Press, 1996), pp. 103-7.

110. D. A. Russell, 'On Reading Plutarch's Lives,' *Greece and Rome* 13 (1966): 141.

111. *Pace* J. J. Meggitt, *Paul, Poverty and Survival* (Edinburgh: T & T Clark, 1998). Not only is the issue of the status of some Christians supported by a careful discussion of status terminology in 1 Cor. 1:26ff., cf. 7:17-24, but their ethical values also provide important information.

This chapter has shown that there were philosophical arguments for ethical conduct which justified the behaviour patterns of some Corinthian Christians whom it has emerged were drawn from the ranks of the élite. It would be a totally incorrect assumption that such conduct involved every adult male Christian. Rather it reflected the convictions of a socially influential minority whose ethics were exempt from any effective censure by others, including fellow Christians in the city up to this point, but certainly not by the apostle Paul. Here was an ἐκκλησία which, unlike the civic one, or that of an association, did not provide, let alone permit, an accepted two-tier system of ethical behaviour, including sexual ethics, to operate among its members — the élite and the non-élite. The appendix further supports this contention.

Roman Homosexual Activity and the Elite
(1 Corinthians 6:9)

The 'mores' of the élite of Roman Corinth have not been taken sufficiently into account when discussing matters affecting attitudes towards homosexual conduct. Greek words were borrowed by the Romans to describe one aspect of homosexual intercourse — the Romans transliterated Greek sexual terminology into Latin for conduct of which they did not approve. By exploring the significance of one of the Latin terms, *malacus,* important light is thrown on the meaning of μαλακός which helps in turn in deciphering the significance of the other term, ἀρσενοκοίτης, which Paul used (6:9). It emerges that under Roman law in this area of activity a double standard operated in favour of the élite of Roman society. It permitted the sexual penetration of non-Roman males by Roman citizens but under Roman criminal law punished those who penetrated Roman citizens. In contrast, Paul proscribed both aspects of homosexual activity.

Roman Law in Corinth and Homosexuality

The Argive petition concerning Corinth states what was true in Roman colonies. Roman law operated — 'in reliance on the laws they now have, they claim that their city has gained the advantages since they received the colony from Rome' (409D) — laws which as indicated elsewhere are not those of ancient Greece but rather 'those which it seems they took over from the sovereign city,' i.e., Rome (409A). As homosexuality came under

Roman criminal law it is important that we examine this before we proceed to discuss attitudes to it on the premise that Roman society was greatly influenced by Roman law.[112]

In a recent work on criminal law in Rome, Robinson, in his chapter 'Sexual Offences', devotes a section to homosexuality as an offence.[113] The *Lex Scantinia* (c. 149 B.C.), named after a plebeian tribune, Scantinius, is said to have dealt with homosexuality.[114] It is known to have been invoked 100 years later. In a letter to Cicero in September, 50 B.C., Caelius indicates that a charge has been made under that law as part of a vexatious campaign against him. At the same time he charged a fellow Roman citizen, Appius, in public under the same law, and notes with some satisfaction, 'the scandal of it has given Appius more pain than the fact of his being charged'.[115]

It was clearly in operation a century and a half later in the reign of Domitian where Suetonius reports that the emperor 'administered justice scrupulously and conscientiously' and cites as an example that he 'condemned several men of both orders [senatorial and equestrian], offenders against the Scantinian Law'.[116] When Augustus had earlier legislated in the general area of sexuality,[117] the law 'defined all sexual intercourse with peo-

---

112. See J. Crook, 'Introduction,' *Law and Life in Rome* (Ithaca, N.Y.: Cornell University Press, 1967), ch. 1, where he argues that compared with English society the Romans were much better acquainted with their law, and this certainly was true where Roman law dealt with marriage and sexuality.

113. O. F. Robinson, *The Criminal Law of Ancient Rome* (London: Duckworth, 1995), ch. V, pp. 70-71.

114. See S. Lilja, *Homosexuality in Republican and Augustan Rome* (Helsinki: Societas Scientiarum Fennica, 1982), pp. 112-21, who sought to argue the law was not concerned with homosexual crimes. C. A. Williams, *Roman Homosexuality: Ideologies of Masculinity in Classical Antiquity* (Oxford: Oxford University Press, 1999), pp. 119-24, argues that the law covered *stuprum* with males or females and cites in support three references to this alongside the section dealing with adultery in *lex Julia*. Williams' argument does not overthrow the fact that the law covered homosexual activity. See also F. X. Ryan, 'The *Lex Scantinia* and the Prosecution of Censors and Aediles,' *CP* (1994): 159-62.

115. Cicero, *Letters to Friends* 8.12 and 14. On vexatious litigation see D. F. Epstein, *Personal Enmity in Roman Politics 218-43 B.C.* (London: Routledge, 1989), pp. 90-100.

116. Suetonius, *Domitian* 8.

117. For a full discussion of the legislation see L. F. Raditsa, 'Augustus' Legislation concerning Marriage, Procreation, Love Affairs and Adultery,' *ANRW* 2.13 (1980): 278-339, and more recently J. E. Grubbs, '"Pagan" and "Christian" Marriage: The State of the Question,' *Journal of Early Christian Studies* (1994): 361-412.

ple of either sex who fell under the law as *stuprum,* a word which was in general use for any irregular or promiscuous sexual acts'[118] or what was known as 'debauchery', e.g., *stuprum cum masculo,* as in the following case. According to Quintilian, writing at the end of the first century, a legal case could be argued where someone 'debauched a free-born citizen *(ingenuum stupravit)* and the latter hanged himself, but that was no reason for the author to be awarded capital punishment as having caused the death; he will instead pay 10,000 sesterces, the fine imposed by law' (4.2.69). Lilja is forced to concede in her conclusion that all would be well for her interpretation of the *lex Scantinia,* i.e., that it did not cover homosexual crimes, 'if Quintilian had not referred to [this] law' cited here. It in effect undermines her whole thesis.[119] The penalty under that law may appear initially to be at variance with the Augustan *Lex Iulia,* which prescribed death for 'not only those who dishonour the marriage-bed with another but also those who indulge their ineffable lust with males', according to the *Institutes* (4.18.2-3). It is important to note that a concern was expressed in marriage documents that the husband did not engage in a sexual relationship with another male.[120] The *Lex Iulia* is dealing specifically with the homosexual conduct of a married man. We have already noted the double standards enshrined in Roman law in relation to incest and social status, and this penalty might well apply to the penetration of a Roman citizen by a married man where the activity dishonours the marriage relationship. It is also necessary to bear in mind that Augustan laws on marriage 'are known mainly in fragmentary and sometimes distorted form in the writings of later jurists and historians who cite them'.[121] While this is not true of all, it may well apply in this instance, given that there is evidence spread over nearly three centuries, including the first, for invoking penalties under the *Lex Scantinia* and against sexual intercourse between Roman citizens, even of the highest social orders, according to Quintilian. It is very clear that Roman law penalised certain homosexual acts in order to protect the rights of its free-born citizens. 'The qualification "free-born" highlights the fundamental difference between the attitude of Athenians and Romans . . . on this matter [homosexuality]. Whereas Solon had forbidden slaves to partake in homosexual practices, at Rome it was

118. S. Treggiari, *Roman Marriage: Iusti coniuges from the Time of Cicero to the Time of Ulpian* (Oxford: Clarendon Press, 1991), p. 264.

119. Lilja, *Homosexuality in Republican and Augustan Rome,* p. 133.

120. See n. 123.

only slaves and other non-citizens who could legitimately be used for them; and could be used without restraint. There was something sacred about the person of a Roman citizen.'[122]

Roman Corinthian Attitudes to Homosexuality

The Argive petition reminds us that the Corinthians followed the Roman 'custom' (νόμιμος) (409C). The sexual penetration of male slaves, some of whom were specifically purchased for the purpose, was approved by the Romans. However, Cato rebuked them because in Rome 'pretty boys fetched more than fields'.[123] In Roman Corinth Charicles was said to be 'only fond of the wrestling schools because of his love of "passive partners" (παιδικός)'.[124] What would the attitude of the élite members of Roman Corinth have been to homosexuality? Lucian reflects the concerns of the Romans about homosexuality when he wrote in a dialogue that it would be better that a woman invade the provinces of male wantonness (homosexuality) 'than that the nobility of the male sex should become effeminate and play the part of a woman' (ἢ τὸ γενναῖον ἀνδρῶν εἰς γυναῖκα θηλύνεσθαι) (*Amores* 28).[125]

How do we account for the élite's literary tastes on homosexuality? Wiedemann observes, 'In Latin poetry on homosexual themes, the characters frequently have Greek names, and the object of the poet's love is not a respectable boy of citizenship status but a *déclassé* or a slave.'[126] In Roman political oratory, including forensic rhetoric, homosexual passivity which was equated with effeminacy was the butt of humour and hubris. 'In the particular process of defining and enforcing the importance of masculin-

121. E. Fantham et al., 'The Age of Augustus,' *Women in the Classical World* (Oxford: Oxford University Press, 1994), p. 303.

122. L. P. Wilkinson, *Classical Attitudes to Modern Issues: Population and Family Planning; Women's Liberation; Nudism in Deed and Word; Homosexuality* (London: William Kimber, 1979), pp. 136-37. See Petronius, *Satyricon* 9-11, Juvenal, 6.33-37.

123. E. Eyben, *Restless Youth in Ancient Rome* (E.T. London: Routledge, 1995), p. 245.

124. Lucian, *Amores* 9. παιδικός = *pedico*, a passive homosexual. Cf. *P.Tebt.* 104, l. 20 (92 B.C.) where the marriage contract forbids the husband 'to have a male passive lover', παιδικὸν ἔχειν.

125. θηλύνω = become soft, i.e., to actually become a passive homosexual. γυνναῖκα is a derivative of ὁ γύννις = an effeminate male.

126. T. Wiedemann, *Adults and Children in the Roman Empire* (London: Routledge, 1989), pp. 30-31; Polybius, 31.25.4-5.

ity in Roman culture, public speakers found an easy target for their insecurities in the person of the effeminate male.'[127]

There was the open liaison between C. Vibius Maximus, a Prefect of Egypt (A.D. 107-12), and a 'still beardless . . . and handsome youth' who dined and travelled with him rather than attend school and the gymnasium.[128] He was a seventeen-year-old *ephebus*. The 'shameless conduct of the young man coming out of the bedchamber alone showing signs of intercourse with him', and then appearing before the assembled gathering who were waiting to give the *salutatio* to the Prefect, told against him in the advocate's speech. The young lover accompanied the Prefect to the praetorium and travelled with him on his assize around Egypt, and 'once accustomed to his shame this handsome and rich youth gave himself airs and became so impudent . . . in the presence of every one and laughed long and freely in the middle of the clients'. The recording in such detail is evidence that a homosexual liaison would only be apposite if the criminal act of the penetration of a young Roman citizen was among the charges being brought against Maximus. Because of his conduct, including his homosexual liaison with this youth, he subsequently suffered *damnatio memoriae*, with his name being removed from public monuments in Egypt.[129]

The Sexual Loanword

Discussions of sexual terminology need to be more nuanced than is sometimes the case in New Testament studies. Nowhere is this more needed

---

127. A. Corbeill, 'Moral Appearance in Action: Effeminacy,' *Controlling Laughter: Political Humor in the Late Roman Republic* (Princeton: Princeton University Press, 1996), ch. 4, citation 130. In this excellent chapter Corbeill shows that 'Extant evidence strongly supports the notion that our constructed effeminate male constitutes a real category of person to whom distinguishing and distinctive codes of behaviour can be ascribed' (p. 131).

128. These activities epitomised education (Lucian, *Amores* 45).

129. Maladministration was also alleged in *P.Oxy.* 471 (second century A.D.), which is incomplete with two columns. If the charges were vexatious, then allegations of effeminacy would be apposite (Corbeill, 'Moral Appearance in Action: Effeminacy,' p. 148) and not a charge of *muliero*, an act of *pedicatio* perpetrated against a boy which was presumably being brought under the *lex Scantinia*. R. Syme, 'C. Vibius Maximus, Prefect of Egypt,' *Historia* 6 (1957): 484, refers to the various charges, 'notably and lavishly the scandal of a *puer delicatus*', citing this papyrus and epigraphic evidence. For the prosecution of governors and prefects see p. 45.

than in the debate that has surrounded the two words used by Paul in 1 Corinthians 6:9 for homosexuality. The problems are highlighted by the vast number of words and allusions to sexual conduct, as the work by J. N. Adams on *The Latin Sexual Vocabulary* shows.[130] The *Sitz im Leben* is important. Terms used in *De Medicina* by the medical writer Aulus Cornelius Celsus in the reign of Tiberius, or the famous Galen in the following century, on sexual anatomy and activity, will be very different from those scratched on the walls of Pompeii which advertised the most ancient of trades. The discussions in Petronius' *Satyricon* or Apuleius' *Metamorphosis or the Gold Ass*, which are in the *genre* of the salacious historical novel, again used more ribald terms.[131] Geographical and cultural differences can account for variations in terms of different meaning assigned to the same term between Greece and Egypt, as Monserrat's work shows.[132]

Religious contexts also influenced choices where a more restrained *vox propria* would be used. Such language was not found in graffiti in Pompeii or Herculaneum. The Jewish works of Philo of Alexandria, a contemporary of Paul's, and *The Sentences of Phocylides* provide examples. 'Transgress not for unlawful sex the natural limits of sexuality. For even animals are not pleased by intercourse of male with male.'[133]

The Latin Borrowing of Greek Sexual Terminology

Cultural susceptibilities and moral attitudes played a highly significant role in the choice of terms as Adams' important observation shows.

> Forms of perversion [to the Roman mind] . . . tend to be ascribed particularly to foreign people, and those perversions may be described by a word from the foreign language in question. Various words to do with homosexuality in Latin are of Greek origin *(pedico, pathicus, cinaedus,*

130. London: Duckworth, 1982.

131. See J. Tatum, ed., *The Search for the Ancient Novel* (Baltimore: Johns Hopkins University Press, 1994); and G. Schnaling, ed., *The Novel in the Ancient World* (Leiden: E. J. Brill, 1996).

132. D. Monserrat, *Sex and Society in Graeco-Roman Egypt* (London: Kegan Paul, 1996), esp. pp. 107-8 on the different uses of πόρνη, παιδικός, and ἑταιρίς in the different geographical locations.

133. *The Sentences of Phocylides,* ll. 190-91. Κύπρις is used to describe an unlawful sexual act. Cf. Lucian, *Amores* 22, for the same animal analogy.

catamitus; cf. *malacus).* . . . But the sexual organs and ordinary sexual behaviour did not attract loanwords.[134]

Loanwords, then, can indicate that the Romans did not endorse activities represented by these terms.[135]

The Meaning of μαλακοί

The borrowing of the Greek term μαλακός indicates what the Romans thought of the activity to which it refers. The word refers to 'a soft person'.[136] The fact that it is in the masculine gender in the semantic field of sexuality is significant because the 'transfer to a male of terms strictly applicable to a female suggests effeminacy of the referent with extreme forcefulness.'[137] A private letter requests, 'Also send us Zenobius, the effeminate, τὸ μαλακόν, with drums and symbols and castanets, for he is wanted by the women for sacrifice: let him wear as fine clothes as possible' (*P.Hib.* 1.54) (third century B.C.). It was said that 'a man's character could be known from his looks' and when 'a rake' (κίναιδος) is brought in, even though his hands bore the signs of hard agricultural work, it was declared, 'He is effeminate' (μαλακός ἐστι).[138] Plutarch referred to two types of men 'who through weakness or effeminacy (μαλακία) are unable to vault upon their horses', i.e., consummate a marriage. Men who penetrated other men could be bisexual by definition, but here the reference is to effeminate men, i.e., passive homosexuals incapable of sexual intercourse with a woman.[139]

Plautus, *The Braggart Warrior,* provided a good example of the meaning of μαλακός in its transliterated form. Periplectomenus, who boasted of

134. Adams, *The Latin Sexual Vocabulary,* p. 228.

135. Although Celsus, *De Medicina* 6.18.1, comments on the superiority of the Greek sexual vocabulary to that current in Latin, he himself did not introduce loanwords. The reality was that the Greeks had not established any uniform terminology (Adams, *The Latin Sexual Vocabulary,* p. 227).

136. Williams, *Roman Homosexuality,* pp. 5-32 discusses the issue of 'softness' but makes no reference to the term *malacus.*

137. Adams, *The Latin Sexual Vocabulary,* p. 116.

138. Diogenes Laertius, 7.173. See also Vettius Valens (Teubner, 1986), 115, l. 31, μαλακὸς ἔσται.

139. Plutarch, *Moralia* 139B.

his youth, offered his services 'in every situation'. He could be a legal counsellor, the gayest dinner guest, a peerless parasite (client), or an incomparable cook. Finally he paraded himself as a receptive homosexual, using the terms *cinaedus* and *malacus*. 'There is no dancer who can dance as seductively as I' *(tum ad saltandum non cinaedus malacus aequest atque ego)*, line 668. The reference to this is unmistakable, as he combines it with the term *cinaedus* (κίναιδος).[140] A powerful myth existed that 'Any person who touched the stone of a *kinaidion*-fish[141] will become impotent or carries the stone unwillingly will become soft' (μαλακίζομαι), i.e., 'made effeminate'. Gleason points out that we learn what was deviant, i.e., what made the person effeminate. It was not the gender of the sexual object — 'A man who actively penetrates and dominates others, whether male or female, is still a man'. He engaged in active homosexual penetration but he was not 'soft'.[142]

Plutarch wrote that the one who uttered the abuse was charged with effeminate practices (μαλακία) and the subsequent discussion contrasted him with a lady — 'she refrained from [sexual] "commerce" with men, though you are a man' (πλείω χρόνον ἐκείνην ἀπ᾽ ἀνδρὸς οὖσαν ἢ σε τὸν ἄνδρα) (*C. Gracchus* 4.4).[143] Vettius Valens wrote, 'a hermaphrodite is a catamite, an effeminate' (ἀνδρόγαμος ἔσται κίναιδος, μαλακός) who belonged to those who were regarded as lusting unnaturally (πασχητιῶν).[144]

In a dialogue with a young student of rhetoric from Corinth early in the second century A.D., Epictetus challenged him not to look like 'half-man and half-woman' because he removed the hair on his body with pitch plaster in order to look like a 'smooth' man.[145] Epictetus identified him

140. μαλακία and κιναιδεία are almost synonymous (Plutarch, *C. Gracchus* 4 and Dio Cassius, 58.4). The latter term originally meant 'dancer' but because of his sexual orientation came to mean a passive homosexual. J. Colin, 'Juvénal, les baladins et les rétiaires d'après le MS d'Oxford', *Atti delle Accademia delle Scienze di Torino* 87 (1952-53): 329-35; Corbeill, 'Moral Appearance in Action: Effeminacy', pp. 135-39; Williams, *Roman Sexuality*, pp. 175-83, who makes the important point that a *cinaedus* is a grown man and not a boy.

141. The term is also used of fish (Pliny, *Natural History* 32.146).

142. M. W. Gleason, *Making Men: Sophists and Self-Presentation in Ancient Rome* (Princeton: Princeton University Press, 1995), p. 65, citing Kyranides 1.10.49-67.

143. Corbeill, 'Appearance in Action: Effeminacy', p. 148.

144. Vettius Valens, *Anthologies* 113.22. Cf. Lucian, *Amores* 26, where 'the man who makes attempts on a young man of twenty seems to me to be unnaturally lustful (πασχητιάω) and pursuing an equivocal love' because, as he explained, he is fully grown and covered with bodily hair.

145. Williams, *Roman Homosexuality*, pp. 127-32, as a sign of 'softness'.

with a κίναιδος and asked him whether Corinth would acknowledge his citizenship of their colony when he looked like that sort of person, let alone to appoint him to public office. If he married, would he 'introduce them [his own sons] into the body of citizens as plucked creatures too?'[146]

In addition to using a standard term, κίναιδος, as a synonym for μαλακός, there was another word, παθικός. It refers to those who are sexually passive in a homosexual relationship. It was transliterated by some authors into Latin as *pathicus*, where it also described the passive, and also despised, homosexual.[147]

What is an antonym for μαλακός? Literary sources provide indications of how an individual author may choose to express the dichotomy of homosexual roles. Philo in his discussion of pederasty suggests that 'in former days the very mention of it was a great disgrace, but now it is a matter of boasting 'not only to the active but the passive partners' (οὐ τοῖς δρῶσι μόνον, ἀλλὰ καὶ τοῖς πάσχουσιν) (*Spec.* 3.37). He used first a metaphor that was not inherently sexual to convey the meaning.[148] The verb δράω is descriptive, meaning 'to be active', while πάσχω means 'to be affected' by passions or feelings. In Lucian, *Amores* 27 the 'active lover' is ὁ διαθείς and the passive person, the 'one who has been outraged' (τῷ ὑβρισμένῳ), which reflected his view that homosexual intercourse gave no pleasure at all to the young passive person whereas in a heterosexual liaison equal pleasure is enjoyed.

Is Paul's antonym for μαλακός in 6:9 the term ἀρσενοκοίτης? In an excellent article concentrating on the latter term, David Wright refuted the interpretation that it referred to 'male sexual agents', i.e., male prostitutes for either male or female clients, but rather to a male who lies with another male. He also drew attention to the neglected linguistic connection with the LXX translation of Leviticus 18:22, μετὰ ἄρσενος οὐ κοιμηθήσῃ κοίτην γυναικός, and especially in 20:13, where the word order of the latter's prohibition is ὃς ἂν κοιμηθῇ μετὰ ἄρσενος κοίτην γυναικός.[149] It is against a male who 'beds' or lies in bed with a male as he would with a woman.[150]

146. Epictetus, 3.1.31-34.

147. Corbeill, 'Appearance in Action: Effeminacy', p. 137; and Adams, *The Latin Sexual Vocabulary*, 189-90. See Juvenal, 2.99.

148. Adams, *The Latin Sexual Vocabulary*, p. 193.

149. 'Homosexuals or Prostitutes? The Meaning of ΑΡΣΕΝΟΚΟΙΤΑΙ (1 Cor. 6:9, 1 Tim. 1:10),' *VigC* 38 (1984): 125-53.

150. Cf. Lucian, *Dialogue with the Courtesans* 6.1, 'make someone into a woman' (τὸ

The verb κοιμάω with μετά was also used in Classical Greek to refer to having sexual intercourse with another person.[151] Paul is seen to have invented the word ἀρσενοκοίτης by combining two words from Leviticus 20:13,[152] ἄρσενικος meaning 'male' (ἀρρένικος in its Attic form).[153] Paul joined this with κοίτη, which means 'bed' and of itself had sexual connotations (i.e., Num. 5:20) — he used the term in Romans 13:13 to denote sexual debauchery. Did he read the LXX and as an interpreter of Scripture combine the two words from Leviticus 20:13 because they expressed a specific role in homosexual intercourse?

Given the Romans preoccupation with 'the nature of the masculine self' over the effeminate behaviour of males,[154] the meaning of ἀρσενοκοίτης for a male engaging in sexual penetration of another male would have been explicable for a Corinthian audience. Furthermore, the citing of the term μαλακός first, with its very strong connotations of passive homosexuality, would have automatically expected a word describing an active homosexual. It was not a reference to a male prostitute. If Paul had been seeking a specific term proscribing that profession, the LXX's choice of ὁ πορνεύων in Deuteronomy 23:17 would have provided him with an appropriate one (cf. 1 Cor. 6:15).[155] If ἀρσενοκοίτης had meant something other than an active homosexual person, Paul would have been proscribing only passive homosexuality and thereby would have reflected the values and attitude of Roman society on this issue.

This interpretation helps answer the question why Paul used two words to describe homosexual persons (6:9), rather than one general term. He referred to the passive and active partner in homosexual intercourse

---

γυναῖκα γενέσθαι ἐκ παρθένου). The concept of turning someone into a woman by penetration, i.e., making him effeminate, reflects the major Roman concern about the homosexuality of its citizens.

151. A person spends a night in bed with a female prostitute μετὰ χαμαιτύπης τὴν νύκτα κοιμᾶσθαι (Timocles, *Comicus* 22.2).

152. It is not possible to state categorically that a first-century Christian author invented a word because, as the CD-ROM of the *TLG* has shown, some New Testament words were not *hapax legomena* since almost the entire body of literary texts from Homer to the sixth century A.D. can now be searched. The ongoing recovery of papyriological evidence may yet unearth a pre-Pauline example.

153. *P.Oxy.* 38 (first century A.D.).

154. Corbeill, 'Appearance in Action: Effeminacy,' p. 128.

155. The word for the female prostitute ἡ πόρνης appears six verses later. ὁ πόρνος was used of a male prostitute (cf. Athenaeus, *Deipnosophists* 13.572).

because Roman society and literature observed such a distinction. Those who engaged in homosexual activity assumed either one role or the other. Latin transliteration of the Greek term was an indicator that passive homosexual activity did not have Roman endorsement for its citizens.[156]

In summarising the issue of homosexuality in Roman society, Williams concluded his extensive work on the subject by stating that what was important for the Roman male was that he played 'the insertive role and not the receptive role in penetrative acts . . . there was a further consideration: Were his sexual partners slaves or free? Free born Romans . . . were officially considered off-limits . . . and any sexual relations with such persons would constitute acts of *stuprem* . . . liable to the censure of moralists [and] to legal penalties.'[157] Everything was permitted for him with the exception of penetrative acts with a male Roman citizen.

Unlike Roman society, Paul proscribed both roles for Christians. While active homosexual intercourse was tolerated in certain circumstances in Roman Corinth, Christians were not to add them to the list of sexual mores which some might have wanted to defend with the aphorism 'for me everything is permitted' (6:12; 10:23). Intercourse in 6:12-20 is with female prostitutes and not males, as the gender of the noun makes clear (v. 15-16). However, some Christians may have shared the same attitude as their secular Roman counterparts on active homosexual intercourse, but despised passive activity while accepting the legitimacy of its practice on the person of non-citizenship status. The Christian élite could neither justify nor claim any special privileges or exemptions under the banner 'all things are permitted', regardless of Roman law and the moral mores of Corinth.

156. The linguistic evidence produced in this chapter contradicts the unfounded conclusion of J. Boswell, *Christianity, Social Tolerance and Homosexuality* (Chicago: The University of Chicago Press, 1980), p. 341: 'The argument that in 1 Corinthians 6:9 the two words "μαλακοί" and "ἀρσενοκοῖται" represent the active and passive partners in homosexual intercourse is fanciful and unsubstantiated by lexicographical evidence.'

157. Williams, *Roman Homosexuality*, pp. 225-26.

CHAPTER 6

Veiled Men and Wives and Christian Contentiousness (1 Corinthians 11:2-16)

'Obliged to Unveil . . . and Obliged to Veil' (11:7, 10)

Husbands and wives veiled or unveiled their heads in certain situations in Corinthian society. Examples of this are also found in 1 Corinthians 11:2-16 where Christian men wore veils while praying and prophesying, but Christian wives did not even though they were engaged in the same activity. In this chapter we shall (I) explore who among men in pagan society covered their heads with their *togas* while they prayed; (II) examine the evidence which indicates that Paul's reference is to 'wives' and not 'women'; and the reasons why he requires them to wear the sign of their marital status, i.e., a veil, because of the promiscuous conduct of the 'new' Roman wife who dressed 'unveiled' in the early empire; (III) deal with the implications of a formal gathering of Christians for their 'public' meetings in a private household and the way outsiders might secure information about them; and (IV) seek to understand why some Christians wanted to be contentious over this matter.

I. Men of Status Covering Their Heads

It is surprising that this passage was, and continues to be, regarded as a discussion about 'the veiling of women'. Paul clearly begins with the veiling of men (11:4), and returns to the problem some three verses later. It was in a ground-breaking essay by D. W. J. Gill, an ancient historian whose academic expertise includes Roman statue types, that the significance of the

Roman convention of men covering their heads while praying and offering up libations was made clear for New Testaments scholars.[1]

Gill's argument is based on statue types where men were depicted with the toga drawn over their head, the *capite velato*, while praying or offering up a libation to a god or gods. Evidence of this is found in Corinth. He discusses the well-preserved statue of Augustus from the first-century Julian Basilica, as well as one of Nero. There a former emperor is dressed as a Roman magistrate offering up a sacrifice and wearing a veil.[2] Gill points out that the statue type is not unique to Corinth but belongs to one of approximately twenty which have been found in various places with this emperor portrayed as a sacrificant. Evidence for this practice is widespread in the Empire. He concludes that it was part of Augustus' propaganda and was meant to project a particular image of the emperor. Portrayed 'in the manner of a Roman magistrate',[3] this skilful propaganda presented him in combined religious, legal, and civic roles as head of the Empire. This image was promoted in Rome also — it was not merely for provincial consumption — and likewise appeared on coins. The latter is a sure sign that this portrayal was meant for popular consumption.[4]

Not all participants drew the *toga* over their heads, only those taking a leading part in a local pagan rite, i.e., sacrificing or praying. Gill produces important epigraphic evidence from Corinth which confirms what is known from elsewhere — that the social élite undertook this function.[5] He suggests that this specific role hardly fits the context of 11:3 because the text implies that it is open to every man in the congregation.[6] However, in a subsequent discussion of prophesying during worship Paul states that 'two or three prophets must speak' and the remainder of the congregation, including those who prophesy, were to discern or weigh up what was said

1. 'The Importance of Roman Portraiture for Head-coverings in 1 Corinthians 11:2-16,' *TynB* 41.2 (1990): 245-60.

2. See Plate No. 3, p. xvii.

3. Gill, 'The Importance of Roman Portraiture,' 247, citing R. Gordon, 'The Veil of Power: Emperors, Sacrifices and Benefactors,' in M. Beard and J. North, eds., *Pagan Priests: Religion and Power in the Ancient World* (London: Duckworth, 1990), p. 211, and A. Wallace-Hadrill, '*Civilis princeps*: Between Citizen and King,' *JRS* 72 (1982): 32-48.

4. Gill, 'The Importance of Roman Portraiture,' 247, citing P. Zanker, *The Power of Images in the Age of Augustus* (Ann Arbor: University of Michigan Press, 1988), p. 127, fig. 103c.

5. Gill, 'The Importance of Roman Portraiture,' 248-50.

6. Gill, 'The Importance of Roman Portraiture,' 248. This is based on the statement that Christ is the head of every man (1 Cor. 11:3).

(14:29). There is no need to conclude that only the élite prophesied; rather, when they did so in the Christian gathering they covered their heads after the manner of the pagan priests. The possibility cannot be ignored that those Christians who were not among the élite also chose to follow this custom when they undertook to pray or prophesy. The Augustan statue type combines the dress of a magistrate with the action of a priest who drew the toga over the top of his head.

II. 'New' Wives and the Sign of Marital Status

'New' Wives

A radical change took place in Republican and early Imperial values concerning Roman wives; this first became apparent at the time of the founding of Roman Corinth.[7] An essay on Roman wives, 'The "New Woman": Representation and Reality', demonstrates 'new patterns of female behaviour and its influence on the celebration of love and submission of women'.[8] 'Both in ostensibly factual texts and in imaginative writing a new kind of woman appears precisely at the time of Cicero and Caesar: a woman in high position, who nevertheless claims for herself the indulgence in sexuality of a woman of pleasure.'[9]

That freeborn Roman wives should seek to compete with those from whom they were traditionally differentiated, viz., foreign women and freedwomen, can be explained for a number of reasons. The sexual propriety demanded of the wife contrasted starkly with the culturally acceptable unfaithfulness of husbands with casual sexual companions provided for guests at the dinners of the élite.[10] Foreign women and freedwomen plied their charms as *hetairai* during the banquets and provided sexual pleasures in the 'after-dinners' for their individual dinner companions, who were husbands of Roman matrons.

7. See R. A. Bauman, *Women and Politics in Ancient Rome* (London: Routledge, 1992) on their 'liberation' and the role of élitist women in public life. See also E. D'Ambra, 'Virgins and Adulterers,' *Private Lives, Imperial Virtues: The Freeze of the Forum Transitorium in Rome* (Princeton: Princeton University Press, 1993), ch. 3.

8. E. Fantham et al., 'The "New Woman": Representation and Reality,' *Women in the Classical World* (Oxford: Oxford University Press, 1994), p. 280.

9. Fantham, 'The "New Woman,"' p. 280.

10. See pp. 228-29.

This double sexual standard could be most insensitively rationalised in the conventional speech delivered by the orator at the marriage bed of the newly wedded couple before guests left the room so that the marriage could be consummated. A later book on conventional speeches, *Menador Rhetor*, which enshrined earlier discussions on the subject, classified this oration as 'the bedroom speech' (κατευναστικός).[11] Plutarch, writing in the first century A.D., provides an example of such a speech delivered to two young friends. It demanded of the woman religious faithfulness to her husband's gods and the acceptance of his casual sexual encounters with a maid-servant or with high-class prostitutes at dinners. The last activity was rationalised on the grounds that these sexual liaisons were a means of gratifying lust, for he loved his wife and it would be inappropriate for him to find this sexual release with her, so he informed this new bride.[12] Many girls married in their early or mid-teens men who were some ten years older than themselves.[13] The inevitable revolt by Roman wives of social status against accepted, but totally inequitable, values can be readily understood. The ethics of these 'new' women' are reflected in the poems of Catullus and Propertius, the erotic poems of Ovid, as well as a discussion by Sallust, who wrote of Sempronia, a married women with children, that she was

> able to play the lyre and dance more skillfully than an honest woman should, and having many other accomplishments which minister to voluptuousness. But there was nothing which she held so cheap as modesty and chastity. Her desires were so ardent that she sought men more often than she was sought by them ... she was a woman of no mean endowment; she could write verse, bandy jests and use language which was modest or tender or wanton.[14]

He himself took as his mistress a noble woman, ten years his senior, of whom Cicero also wrote. She was 'the daughter of one of Rome's noblest

11. D. A. Russell and N. G. Wilson, *Menander Rhetor* (Oxford: Clarendon Press, 1981), VII, 147-59.

12. Plutarch, 'Advice to the Bride and Groom,' 140B, D.

13. P. Veyne, 'The Roman Empire,' in P. Veyne, ed., *Histoire de la vie privée; E.T. A History of Private Life* (Cambridge, Mass.: Harvard University Press, 1987), p. 20 where he indicates that a girl was regarded an adult at age fourteen. 'Men then call them "madame" (*domina, kyria*) and seeing that there is nothing left for them but to share a man's bed, they dress themselves up and think of nothing else.'

14. Sallust, *Catiline* 25.

families, claiming the sexual freedom of a woman of no social standing to lose, and making no effort to conceal her behaviour — "a woman not just noble but notorious"'. A subsequent lover, Caelius, was accused of 'passions, love making, adulteries, visits to Baiae, beach picnics, parties and revelling, songs, choruses and boat-trips'.[15] It is clear that 'new women' pursued wealthy men.[16] Ovid, in his *Art of Love*, undertook to instruct not only men but also women.[17]

Plutarch also made comments on the 'new' women. He referred to those who were 'bored by uncompromising and virtuous men, and take more pleasure in consorting with those who, like dogs and he-goats, are a combination of licentiousness and sensuality'.[18] He also warned husbands that 'those who are not cheerful in the company of their wives, nor join with them in sportiveness and laughter, are thus teaching them to seek their own pleasures apart from their husbands'.[19]

While it has been said, 'We shall never know to what extent women of an established family endorsed the life of pleasure described by the elegists, or the degree to which the poet's own actions matched their profession of enslavement to love', the nexus is established between the activities of 'new' women and the unprecedented move to regulate private morality in society. Augustus legislated on marriage, remarriage and divorce.[20] The reason for this was his concern about promiscuous marital unfaithfulness among Roman women of social status. Augustus thought that the licentious and adulterous conduct of married women with younger single men who were avoiding marriage was responsible for the falling birth rate among Roman citizens and the breakdown of family values.[21] The legislation not only made adultery by a woman a criminal offence which, as we have already noted, could be initiated only after her husband divorced her, but it also

---

15. Fantham, 'The "New Woman,"' p. 284, citing Cicero, 'For Caelius,' 32, 35.

16. Propertius, 1.5.59-60, 67-68; 2.16.

17. *Art of Love*. For a discussion of Ovid see E. Greene, 'Sexual Politics in Ovid's Amores,' *The Erotics of Domination: Male Desire and the Mistress in Latin Love Poetry* (Baltimore: Johns Hopkins University Press, 1998), ch. 4.

18. Plutarch, 'Advice to Bride and Groom,' 7, *Moralia* 139B.

19. Plutarch, 'Advice to Bride and Groom,' 15, *Moralia* 140A.

20. Fantham, 'The "New Woman,"' p. 290. For a fulsome discussion see L. F. Raditsa, 'Augustus' Legislation concerning Marriage, Procreation, Love Affairs and Adultery,' *ANRW* 2.13 (1980): 278-339.

21. Fantham, 'The "New Woman,"' p. 290.

made 'the condoning of adultery by an "injured" husband an offence open to criminal prosecution and punishable by expulsion from society.'[22] This severe penalty of exile and loss of property for the unwillingness of a husband to curb or punish his wife pressurised him into taking action against the profligate behaviour of his 'new' Roman wife.

The conduct of subsequent Julio-Claudian emperors (and at times their wives) did not always provide a high moral paradigm for these 'new women' to abandon the behaviour of those who competed against them for their husband's amorous attention. Even in the time of Augustus, the conduct of his daughter Julia proved that legislation did not prevent the élite from committing adultery.[23]

'Ordinary anonymous citizens might continue to be chaste or promiscuous unnoticed, but respectability was now enforced in the public eye'.[24] The legislation of Augustus was resisted at the time of its introduction — Suetonius records that the knights 'persistently called for its repeal at a public gathering'.[25] It would prove impossible to control powerful 'new' Roman wives by legislation, even with such severe penalties. 1 Corinthians 5 itself provides evidence of the illicit sexual behaviour of a wife with a younger man, i.e., her stepson.[26]

Women or Wives

Can the ambiguous term γυνή be translated with confidence as 'wife' in 11:2ff.? The range of semantic terms available to describe the status of the female gender were 'a girl' (παῖς), 'a betrothed' (παρθένος), 'a wife' or 'a woman' (γυνή), and 'a widow' (χήρα). The status of those described as 'a woman' began between the age of fourteen and sixteen years. First-century Roman women married in their early or mid-teens; the legal minimum age for girls was twelve.[27] Soranus, in his medical textbook *Gynaecology*, stated that the time to begin sexual intercourse was after the onset of puberty,

22. Fantham, 'The "New Woman,"' p. 290.
23. Fantham, 'The "New Woman,"' p. 292.
24. Fantham, 'The "New Woman,"' p. 290.
25. Suetonius, *Augustus* 34.2.
26. See pp. 47-49.
27. B. Rawson, 'The Roman Family,' in B. Rawson, ed., *The Family in Ancient Rome: New Perspectives* (London and Sydney: Croom Helm, 1986), pp. 21-22.

which, he observed, was aged fourteen. He outlined the risks for those who had intercourse before the onset of menstruation and therefore discouraged marriage before that age (1.33). A single girl aged sixteen years or younger would not speak in a public meeting and is therefore unlikely to have prayed and/or prophesied in a meeting, so the term Paul used would not include the pre-teen or the unmarried woman in her early teens.

The very mention of the word 'veil' by Paul would automatically indicate to the Corinthians that the females under discussion in this passage were married. As S. Treggiari has pointed out in Latin 'the verb used of the woman marrying, *nebo*, is related to *nubes*, a cloud, and means literally "I veil myself"'.[28] The marriage ceremony involved what was called in Greek 'veiling the bride' (τὴν νύμφην κατακαλύψαντες).[29] Both Tacitus and Juvenal describe the taking of 'the veil of a bride' as one of the essential components of marriage.[30] It was the social indicator by which the marital status of a woman was made clear to everyone. So Paul did not use a generic term to refer to women of indeterminate marital status, but the combining of the two terms 'veil' and 'woman' indicates that she was married. The widow would no longer wear the marriage veil.

Paul's initial discussion of this issue also seems to rule against translating the term 'woman', without reference to her marital status. The head of every man is Christ, he states (11:3); he does not argue that the head of every woman in the Christian gathering is the minister, but rather that the head of every wife is the husband. Because any reference connecting a woman and a veil would immediately alert a first-century reader to the fact that she was a married woman, there are secure grounds for concluding that the issue here was married women praying and prophesying without their veil in the Christian meeting.

'New Wives' and Adulteresses

The presence of an unveiled woman accompanied by a man in public signalled that she might not be his wife. At a typical banquet a woman (not

28. S. Treggiari, *Roman Marriage: Iusti Coniuges from the Time of Cicero to the Time of Ulpian* (Oxford: Clarendon Press, 1991), p. 163.

29. Plutarch, 'Advice to the Bride and Groom,' 138D.

30. Tacitus, *The Annals* 11.27.1; 15.37.9; Juvenal 2.119ff.; 10.333ff.

necessarily his wife) seated next to a married man would be his social and sexual companion, *hetaira*, for that evening.[31]

A married woman did not normally wear her veil in her own household, so that the wife of the patron of the church, or the patroness in the case of Cenchreae (Rom. 16:1), might not have felt that it was necessary for her to wear a veil for a Christian gathering being held in her own home. A wife visiting the house of a friend would not be expected to continue to wear her veil once she had entered it. However, the crux of the issue in 1 Corinthians 11:2-16 was not the problem of protocol for married women attending a public meeting in a private household. The text does not suggest that every wife present at the meeting removed her veil, any more than every man covered his head. Rather there were those who were deliberately removing their veils while praying and prophesying — 'Every woman praying and prophesying with her head uncovered' (πᾶσα δὲ γυνὴ προσευχομένη ἢ προφητεύουσα ἀκατακαλύπτῳ τῇ κεφαλῇ) makes this clear with the participial construction and the dative of manner (11:5).[32]

Paul made a startling statement about the unveiled wife. He said that her behaviour was 'one and the same thing as a woman who has been shorn' (ἕν ἐστιν καὶ τὸ αὐτό τῇ ἐξυρημένῃ) (11:5). It is known, e.g., that in Cyprus the law prescribed that 'a woman guilty of adultery shall have her hair cut off (ἐπορνεύετο) and be a prostitute', i.e., like a foreigner or freedwoman who provided sexual favours at a dinner. Therefore Paul equated not wearing a veil with the social stigma of a publicly exposed and punished adulteress reduced to the status of a prostitute.[33]

Even more surprising is Paul's imperative, 'If a woman is not veiled, she must also be shorn' (11:6a). An adulterous wife would be shorn or have her head shaved as a punishment intended to humiliate her publicly (11:6b). He was, in effect, accusing the Christian wife who removed her

31. For a discussion of this point see pp. 84-85.
32. The construction explaining the activity of the men with the use of participles to describe their activity is followed by a further participle, 'having his head covered (κατὰ κεφαλῆς ἔχων). In v. 5 Paul has used an alternative construction, i.e., the dative of manner, to describe the same situation.
33. Dio Chrysostom, *Or.* 64.3; and T. A. J. McGinn, *Prostitution, Sexuality and the Law in Ancient Rome* (Oxford: Oxford University Press, 1998), p. 147. 'The *Lex Julia* lowered the status of the wife found guilty of adultery to that of a prostitute.' He defines it as 'the concept of an obligation, in the minds of laymen as well as lawyers, which seems to have retained the connotation of some sort of invisible rope around the neck . . .' (p. 5).

veil when praying and prophesying of parading like one of the profligate 'new' Roman women. If she did this while participating in a leading way in an open meeting, then she publicly dishonoured her husband (11:5) and ought to bear the public stigma. Paul then argued the converse, that if it was shameful for a wife to be shorn or shaven, then the only alternative was to wear the marriage veil (11:6c).

The Corinthian congregation was also called upon to judge how the action of the unveiled wife appeared (11:13). Paul used an adverb 'seemly' (πρέπον), indicating that it was a matter of decorum — an issue of supreme importance in Roman society. For a Christian wife to indicate that she placed herself among the high-class 'new' Roman women grossly misrepresented the teaching of Christianity on marriage. A Christian man had already done this by committing incest with an older woman and was to be excommunicated from the community because of his conduct.[34]

It is of interest that all statues, except one, of Roman women found in Corinth portrayed them with heads unveiled.[35] It could be that they were carved showing full features with no marriage veil because these were displayed in private houses. Gill notes a famous portrait of a husband and wife found in a house in Pompeii where both are bareheaded.[36] Only high-class Roman women had their statues carved; the presence of only one veiled statue suggests that it was a statue type and therefore may have had nothing to do with the portrayal of the 'new' Roman wife. If it had, it would have resulted in a complete loss of *dignitas* for a husband who had allowed his wife to be portrayed thus in his own household where he was, by convention, the head.

Was Paul at this point being discriminatory in his treatment of wives while ignoring the inequitable situation of philandering husbands? He had already proscribed the conduct of husbands and wives, demanding fidelity on the part of both. Neither could engage in sexual encounters outside marriage because they no longer had 'authority' over their own sexuality, having surrendered themselves exclusively to their spouse (7:2-5).[37] In addition, he not only proscribed fornication by men, but also sexual liaisons

---

34. See pp. 56-57.

35. F. P. Johnson, *Sculpture 1896-1923, Corinth* 9, American School of Archaeology at Athens (Cambridge, Mass.: Harvard University Press, 1931).

36. Gill, 'The Importance of Roman Portraiture,' 253.

37. For discussion see pp. 227-28.

between engaged couples.[38] He also warned the community not to be deceived in this matter; Christians who were involved in adultery and other sexual misdemeanours would be excluded from the kingdom of God (6:12-20; 7:35-36; 6:9-10).

Obligations

In the discussion of men, wives, and the veil, Paul used the verb expressing obligation (ὀφείλω) (11:7, 10). While translators render this verb with the mild 'ought', it does not do justice to the powerful significance represented by that term in Graeco-Roman society. Roman law devoted a whole section to *The Laws of Obligations*.[39] It was this concept that indicated the first call on any person's actions in his or her relationships with others, for they always involved obligations. The 'politics' of friendship were about reciprocal obligations, as were client/patron relationships.[40] Former slaves had obligations to their masters (including financial support should the latter fall on hard times), and punitive measures were in place if they failed to fulfil them at all times.[41] It could result in the re-enslavement of freedmen for *libertus ingratus*, i.e., ingratitude towards their patron for failing to meet his annual obligations to his former master. This was very much an issue in the principate of Claudius.[42] Masters also had obligations to their slaves.[43]

Obligations were binding and, according to Seneca, failure to meet

38. For discussion see pp. 243-46.

39. For the wide-ranging issues covered by it see A. Watson, *The Law of Obligations in the Later Roman Republic* (Oxford: Clarendon, 1965); R. Zimmerman, *The Law of Obligations: Roman Foundations of the Civilian Tradition* (Cape Town: Juta, 1990).

40. See J. W. Hewitt, 'The Development of Political Gratitude,' *TAPA* 55 (1924): 35-51; B. Rawson, *The Politics of Friendship: Pompey and Cicero* (Sydney: Sydney University Press, 1978); and R. P. Saller, *Personal Patronage under the Early Empire* (Cambridge: Cambridge University Press, 1982).

41. See A. Watson, *Roman Slave Law* (Baltimore: Johns Hopkins University Press, 1987), p. 9.

42. W. W. Buckland, *The Roman Law of Slavery: The Condition of the Slave in Private Law from Augustus to Justinian* (Cambridge: Cambridge University Press, 1908), pp. 422ff.; and more recently Watson, *Roman Slave Law*, p. 17.

43. K. R. Bradley, 'Loyalty and Obedience,' *Slaves and Masters in the Roman Empire: A Study of Social Control* (Oxford: Oxford University Press, 1987), ch. 1.

them was 'a sin';[44] any lapse could create enmity relationships. Relationships constituted the essence of *societas*. The first-century concept of obligation, especially Paul's use of it in ethical discussion, has not been taken into account sufficiently by New Testament scholars. The invoking of the term in 11:2-16 provides the most powerful argument that could be used in correcting conduct in the first century.

Paul told men that they were obliged not to have their heads veiled because they were detracting from the image and glory of God that each one 'bears' — the verb ὑπάρχω was used to describe their origin (cf. Gen. 1:26-27). To draw attention to their secular status at the very time they were praying to God (who restored that image in them) and prophesying on His behalf meant that not only had they dishonoured Christ as their head (11:4), but also they had failed to meet the obligation they owed him (11:7). Paul had already indicated that the Christian derived his significance through the sufficiency of Christ (1:14-9) and Christ had been made their 'wisdom, both [their] justification and sanctification, and redemption' (1:30). Their conduct constituted a serious breach of their obligation to God.

For the first-century woman, the most obvious outward sign of marriage was the wearing of the veil (11:10a).[45] Therefore 'she was obliged to have the authority [or sign of marriage] on the head'. Paul is not saying here that the husband as head 'exercises authority' over his wife, otherwise he would have used the verb ἐξουσιάζω; simply that the woman is obliged to wear on her head that which signified to all and sundry that she was married.[46]

Nature Teaches Us

The Stoics and others, including the Jew, Philo of Alexandria, Paul's contemporary, discussed at length the question — 'nature (φύσις) is the origin and guarantor of culture'.[47] Paul declared what Roman custom also de-

---

44. Seneca, *De beneficiis* 1.13, 4-8, 13.

45. The phrase διὰ τοῦτο refers to vv. 8-9; cf. 11:30.

46. It is sometimes overlooked that immediately after this Paul inserts an extremely important caveat in 11:11-12 with the adverb 'except' (πλήν). He argues that there was the interdependence of man and wife, for neither was without the other 'in the Lord', and that God was the originator of both, for 'all things come from Him'.

47. D. Jobling, "'And have dominion. . . .'": The Interpretation of Genesis 1:28 in Philo Judaeus,' *JSJ* 8.1 (1977): 79.

creed — that it was dishonouring for a man to wear his hair long, for even 'nature' taught this (11:14). Dio Chrysostom indicated that young men sheered off their locks at puberty, comparing that to the action of horse-breeders who cut the manes of mares when they were ready to mate. When a young slave boy reached puberty the master 'caused his long girlish locks to be cut'.[48] This happened in the case of the freeborn Roman youth as soon as he began to grow facial hair and prepared to receive the *toga virilis*. In the early second century A.D. the philosopher Epictetus asked a young student of rhetoric from Corinth, who was a Roman citizen, about his sexual identity, given that he removed his bodily hair with pitch plasters and looked like 'a smooth man', i.e., a homosexual (κίναιδος). Bodily hair was an indicator of the male gender, Epictetus argues, and 'nature' (φύσις) had bestowed it, differentiating between the sexes. Its removal denied nature and gave a customary signal of homosexuality.[49]

While there are statues from Corinth with males wearing long hair,[50] Gill points out that these are usually male deities.[51] It should also be noted that the only others depicted wearing long curly hair were from the Facade of the Captives in the forum in Roman Corinth. To portray these men wearing their hair thus was the way the Roman conquerors indicated that all the men in the facade were 'weak', i.e., captives of the mighty Roman army. It implies that they were 'soft' or 'effeminate'.[52] This differed from the standard Roman portrayal of the Barbarian.[53]

The adult male inhabitants of Roman Corinth did not wear their hair long, for to do so indicated their denial of their masculinity — they were parading as homosexuals.[54] Veyne draws attention to a statue found in Nero's villa at Anzio which he believes was either an original from the fourth or third centuries B.C. or a Roman copy. Even though he was garbed as a woman and wearing long hair, Veyne concluded that because the person was flat-chested he was a young man who had reached puberty (ὁ

48. Veyne, 'The Roman Empire,' 79.

49. Epictetus, 3.1.25-31.

50. A point misunderstood by C. L. Thompson, 'Hairstyles, Head-covering, and St. Paul: Portraits from Roman Corinth,' *Biblical Archaeologist* 51.2 (1989): 99-115, but corrected by Gill, 'The Importance of Roman Portraiture,' 257.

51. Gill, 'The Importance of Roman Portraiture,' 257.

52. See Plate No. 5, p. xix.

53. Plate No. 4, p. xix, for the standard statue type of the Barbarian.

54. For Roman attitudes to passive homosexuality see pp. 116-18.

ἀμφιθαλὴς παῖς). It reflected something of Nero's sexual interests, but it would not have been accepted by Roman men as a portrayal of manhood.[55] According to Dio Chrysostom, philosophers traditionally wore long hair and a cloak but no tunic;[56] for other men to wear hair long was a denial of their masculinity — something that none wished to do because of the social stigma attached to parading as passive homosexual Romans.[57]

Unlike the man whose hair was shorn, a woman whose hair was cropped or shorn had been publicly humiliated as an adulteress (11:5-6). Paul contrasts this with a woman whose long hair was seen as her glory, and given to her for a covering. Corinthian Roman statues of women support this, for all portray them with long hair lavishly styled according to the convention of the day.[58] It was, however, inappropriate for grown men to have long hair (11:15).

All first-century cultures possessed means by which the polarity of the sexes was defined with various conventions;[59] hair length was one such feature in Roman Corinth, as 11:14-15 accurately noted.

III. The 'Public' Meeting and 'the Messengers'

Pagan worship was largely an individual activity, and citizens did not normally worship together in a formal service.[60] The exception was the worship of civic gods, including the deified reigning emperor and those deceased who were honoured at an annual feast day. Because, in pagan

55. On his 'marriage' to the freedman, Pythagoras at a public banquet and his castration and penetration of Sporos, a young Roman freedman, after the death of Poppaea see M. T. Griffin, *Nero: The End of a Dynasty* (London: Batsford, 1984), pp. 164, 169; and for the discussion of the former see the account in Tacitus, *Annals* 15.37. On his sexual relationship with Lucius Silanus, a young Roman citizen of noble birth, see also Tacitus, *Annals* 16.8-9.

56. Others who wore a cloak but no tunic under it and had long hair could be identified as philosophers, for, as Dio Chrysostom, *Or.* 72.2 explains, it was 'customary with the philosophers'.

57. Veyne, 'The Roman Empire,' 78. On Nero's bisexuality see n. 54; for the discussion of Roman attitudes to homosexuality see my appendix to Ch. 5, pp. 110-20.

58. Gill, 'The Importance of Roman Portraiture,' pp. 251-56.

59. Cf. Philo, *Virtues* 20, 'men ought to have nothing to suggest unmanliness' in their dress.

60. On the widespread practice of asking the gods to curse opponents as a private religious activity but one not always performed in a temple see Ch. 8.

religion, a corporate meeting of adherents was not something that was normally associated with cultic practices, Roman citizens in Corinth may have been puzzled with a 'religion' that had such a regular 'meeting' (ἐκκλησία) as its essential characteristic.[61] They would certainly have been surprised by the use of the political term ἐκκλησία for a 'gathering' which was not that of an association but rather a religious one, yet possessed no statue of their divinity.[62]

Christians apparently met once a week to worship, as did the Jewish community. O. F. Robinson has drawn attention to the legal prohibition against associations meeting no more than once a month because of concern about sedition in the minds of the Roman authorities. He indicates that Jews had been granted specific exemption to meet every Sabbath. As a Roman legal historian, Robinson makes an important observation — 'the Christians could hardly have formed legal *collegia,* since they needed to meet weekly'.[63]

So what technically was the Christian gathering in the eyes of the Romans? To them a Christian meeting must have been something of an enigma, if not a real concern. We have some idea of how early Christians were first perceived by Romans in Antioch. According to E. A. Judge, the term 'Christians' (Χριστιανοί) was coined by the Romans — 'they were first named Christians' (Acts 11:26). '[The term] can hardly be invented by orthodox Jews since it concedes the messiahship of Jesus. Its suffix implies the word was coined by speakers of Latin. . . . The suffix -*ianus* constitutes a political comment. It is not used of the followers of a god. It classifies people as partners of a political or military leader, and is mildly contemptuous.'[64]

The label was not a self-designation. It was a perception of the movement, not by Jews who would not have conceded the title, but by Romans. The weekly gatherings might well have been seen as the activity of an 'asso-

61. They also had no statues of which they could say, as they did of their deities, 'Here is Apollo', believing that there dwelt the divinity. They were subsequently to be accused of atheism because of this.

62. For a discussion of this widely used secular term see my 'The Problem with "Church" for the Early Church', in D. Peterson and J. Pryor, eds., *In the Fullness of Time: Biblical Studies in Honour of Archbishop Robinson* (Sydney: Lancer, 1992), ch. 13.

63. Robinson, *The Criminal Law of Ancient Rome*, p. 80.

64. E. A. Judge, 'Judaism and the Rise of Christianity: A Roman Perspective,' *TynB* 45.2 (1993): 355-68, cited on p. 363.

ciation' *(collegia)* whose purposes could allegedly be seditious because they broke the monthly rule. '*Collegia* represented a threat to public order rather than a standing offence, but they could be repressed severely'.[65] If 'Christians' was a somewhat derisory designation, then their meetings could only be viewed with a measure of curiosity at best, and suspicion at worst. They had no god but rather followed a leader, either a political or military one.

How could others monitor such a movement? That Christians met in private houses meant that their weekly meetings were all the more suspicious in the eyes of the Roman authorities. A legal decision by the noted Roman jurist, the governor of Achaea, Gallio, 'the friend of Claudius', declared that disputes with the Christian movement were an internal 'Jewish' matter. This was an unexpected ruling for the Christian community in Corinth and meant that weekly meetings during his governorship could not be condemned as a contravention of the Roman law governing associations (Acts 18:12-17). However, this ruling did not mean that, like those of Caesar's wife, their activities would automatically continue to be seen as above reproach. After Gallio left Corinth following his brief rule of the province, each subsequent governor exercised that all-powerful *imperium* as he himself judged fit.[66]

The vestibules of Roman houses were open to the street, and it was here that clients of wealthy patrons gathered for the morning *salutatio*. The house was specifically designed to be open to *politeia*.[67] As such, an outsider could come in. We know that this was precisely what they did, and were meant to do, in the Christian gathering (14:23). Whether it was out of interest in the message or in order to report on what these unknown gatherings were all about, 'the meeting' (ἐκκλησία) was open to all who wished to witness its proceedings.

We do not know what the 'public' role of wives in a secular association would have been, but there is important evidence of the prejudiced attitude to them in a public setting. Valerius Maximus, writing in the Principate of Tiberius, asked, 'What business has a woman with a public meeting? If the ancient custom be observed, none.' However in his *Memorable Deeds and Sayings* he could cite a number of instances where they

65. Robinson, *The Criminal Law of Ancient Rome*, p. 80.
66. See p. 45.
67. See pp. 186-87.

spoke in public venues. Sempronia, the wife of Scipio Aemilianus, who did so in the first century B.C., was an exception and only did so because of exceptional circumstances. We know nothing of the details of the case except that it was clearly a grave matter which resulted in her being brought before a Tribune of the Plebs.[68] He does provide three examples of 'Women who pleaded before magistrates for themselves and others'.[69] He cited examples of *Matrona Docta*, and all attracted derisory or patronizing comments. Maesia of Sentinum pleaded her case in a professional way by 'going through all the forms and stages of a defense not only thoroughly but boldly'. She did so well that she was acquitted at the first hearing. 'Because she bore a man's spirit under the form of a woman, they called her Androgyne.'[70] Carfania became a byword for 'women of shameless habit'. A wife of a senator, Licinius Buccio, was 'ever ready for a lawsuit and always spoke on her own behalf . . . because she had the impudence to spare . . . constantly plaguing the tribunals with "barkings" to which the Forum was unaccustomed, she became a notorious example of female litigiousness'. Hortensia pleaded the cause of women 'resolutely and successfully'. Before the Triumvirs in 42 B.C. she won 'the remission of a greater part of the impost' of a heavy tax imposed on the 'order of matrons'. No man would argue their case, and she was said to have revived her 'father's eloquence'. Valerius Maximus noted that none of the male descendants of that house even equalled her or her father for eloquence. In the Christian meetings wives certainly did participate in a public way with prophecy and prayer.

One of Paul's arguments for the veiling of married women while praying and prophesying was 'because of the messengers' (διὰ τοὺς ἀγγέλους). While it has been traditional for this to be translated 'because of the angels',[71] the term was also used of a 'messenger'. The word 'messenger' in the first century did not necessarily imply that he was only the bearer of messages. It was also used of the conveyor of information about those he visited to the person on whose behalf he had been sent. The role of the messenger in the ancient world was not confined to the delivery of verbal or written information from a sender. For example, Epictetus, writ-

---

68. *Memorable Deeds and Sayings*, 3.8.6; Sallust, *Catiline* 25.

69. *Memorable Deeds and Sayings*, 3.8.1-3.

70. For a discussion of this prejudice among men of 'a male mind in a female body' see E. A. Hemelrijk, Matrona Docta: *Educated Women in the Roman Elite from Correlia to Julia Domna* (London: Routledge, 1999), pp. 89-96.

ing in the early second century A.D., records, 'What messenger is so swift and so attentive as the eye?' (2.23.4). Moreover, a messenger could be sent 'as a scout' to report back, as Epictetus also noted (3.22.23-24). In discussing the role of the Cynic philosopher he observed that the present time can be compared to a war situation where the Cynic cannot operate as he would normally do; if he did he would destroy his role as 'the messenger, the scout, and the herald of the gods that he is' (3.22, 69-70). After Domitian banished the philosophers from Rome, a young man from Nicopolis was sent to Rome to spy out the land on their behalf, as Epictetus reports (1.24.3-10). Philosophers had been banished from Rome from time to time by a number of emperors, hence the need for a messenger to report back to those exiled from the capital of the Empire. The role of information-gatherer who reports back to the sender appears to be what Paul is concerned about.

It would not have been the first time that a person or persons in a Christian meeting gathered information concerning the way it operated. Paul spoke of 'false brethren who sneaked in to spy out (παρεισῆλθον κατασκοπῆσαι) our liberty, that they might bring us into bondage' (Gal. 2:4). In Corinth the messengers had no Christian pretensions, unlike those in Galatia. Those with civic status or wealth whose curiosity was aroused about the Christian faith would not go to any meeting without having a client or others first carry back reports of its activities. The treason trials under Tiberius had left an indelible fear on every Roman because guilt by association had had catastrophic consequences.[72]

Furthermore, it was the duty of citizens to take cognisance of any unusual activities in the city. Associations were singled out for special attention, given that any allegations of sedition had critical implications for the whole of the city, whose privileges could be withdrawn at any time by the imperial authorities.[73] Rome had long ago banned pagan religions such as Bacchanalism and destroyed the temple to Isis in Rome. More recently Tiberius had restricted the activities of the Druid priests, and Claudius

71. See most recently J. D. BeDuhn, '"Because of the angels": Unveiling Paul's Anthropology in 1 Corinthians 11,' *JBL* 118 (1999): 295-320 where he makes the unlikely suggestion that 'Paul is attributing the separate formation of woman from man to a creative act of angels, not of God' (p. 308).

72. B. Levick, 'Tiberius and the Law: The Development of *maiestas*' *Tiberius the Politician* (London: Thames and Hudson, 1976), ch. 12.

73. Robinson, 'Offences against the State,' *The Criminal Law of Ancient Rome*, ch. 6.

subsequently abolished that religion altogether.[74] In the case of a colony with special loyalty to Rome, watching strange or foreign religions was all the more important. Concern about the 'messengers' as information gatherers on Christian meetings is explicable.

'For this reason', Paul states, the wife is under obligation to wear the sign of her marriage as she prays and prophesies because of what its absence signaled to the inquisitive outsiders — she portrayed herself as the promiscuous Roman wife, i.e., an unashamed adulteress (11:10).[75]

IV. Contentiousness in the Congregation

Paul concluded with a statement about 'any person, either male or female,' for he used the gender-inclusive term 'anyone' (τις) — 'if anyone has a mind to be contentious' (εἰ δέ τις δοκεῖ φιλονείκος εἶναι). The term 'contentious' (φιλονείκος) throws important light on the attitude of the men and women discussed in this passage.

Plutarch provides good illustrations from his eighty-one uses of the term. On the problems of frank speech in 'How to tell a flatterer from a friend', he contrasts the sophist's admonition of friends in private and before a crowd of witnesses and spectators; they were the virtuoso public orators of the day, who 'seek for glory in other men's faults, and to make a fair show before spectators'. He states that in seeking to correct a friend 'some regard must be paid to the contentiousness and self-will that belong to vice' (71A). In the search for ameliorating terms to secure improvement, Plutarch suggests that in place of the censure 'Don't be jealous of your brother', it would be better to state 'Don't be contentious with your brother' (73F). The implication is that the brothers are argumentative because of sibling rivalry.

In an essay devoted to 'Progress in Virtue' Plutarch requests that men use discourse for the improvement of others rather than for financial gain or to acquire a reputation as the sophists did.[76] He wants the 'spirit of con-

74. Robinson, *The Criminal Law of Ancient Rome*, p. 95.

75. *Pace* D. E. Blattenberger III, *Rethinking 1 Corinthians 11:1-16 through Archaeological and Moral-Rhetorical Analysis*, Studies in the Bible and Early Christianity 36 (Lewiston: Edwin Mellen Press, 1997), p. 68 where he concludes, 'In each case the focus is on the hair rather than the veil'.

76. For a discussion of these characteristics of the sophists see my *Philo and Paul among the Sophists*, pp. 49-50, 95-97.

tention and quarrelling over debatable questions' (τὸ φιλόνεικον καὶ δύσερι περὶ τὰς ζητήσεις) to be laid aside in order that learning and the imparting of something beneficial can be secured' (80B). In the same essay he speaks of a man 'imbued with a spirit of contentiousness and envy (φθόνος) towards his social betters' — the latter word refers to seeking to do positive harm and was not simply an attitude of hostility (84E).[77]

In 'How to Profit from One's Enemies' he reminds Cornelius Pulcher, a leading citizen of Corinth at the time, that it is the nature of public life (πολιτεία) to bear with 'envy or jealous rivalry or contention' (φθόνος, ζῆλος, φιλονείκος) (86C); that there is no way of getting rid of 'strifes, envies and contentions' (φθόνος, ἔρις, φιλονείκος) (92B). His 'Advice about Keeping Well' informs those who participated in public life (πολιτεία) that they should devote themselves to 'good and necessary ends' rather than the stress of 'politics' which was motivated by 'a spirit of insolence, envy or rivalry (ἐπηρεάζοντες ἑτέροις ἢ φθονοῦντες ἢ φιλονεικοῦντες) against others' (135E).

Plutarch commends the great advantages of a learning situation where contentiousness is absent, with 'listeners with nothing to distract them and eager to seek and gain information . . . all strife and contention is banished and a sympathetic hearing and freedom . . . is granted' (431D). Again in 'On the Control of Anger' Plutarch cautions, 'allow no place to anger . . . in learned discussions, for it turns love of learning into contentiousness' (462B).

In these six essays from his enormous corpus, Plutarch uses the term 'contentious' to indicate how disruptive it was in educative situations, a client/patron relationship, and the politics of the city. All these situations find a close parallel in the attitudes and activities of the Christian community in Corinth.

Paul's use of the term indicated that in the Christian gathering some had a mind to be contentious — not over the issue of praying and prophesying (the latter gift Paul described as the means of building up, comforting and consoling the congregation, 14:4) — but over the wearing and not wearing of 'the veil' (11:2-16). If men drew the veil over their head as the

---

77. For an informative discussion of this term which indicated that a person was seeking actively to harm another, see K. M. D. Dunbabin and M. W. Dickie, '*Invidia rumpantur pactora*: Iconography of *Phthonos/Invidia* in Graeco-Roman Art,' *JbAC* 26 (1983): 10.

élite had traditionally done when leading pagan cultic activities as part of their liturgical responsibilities, then they were deliberately drawing attention to their social status. It was a strong signal to other members of the congregation of their social prestige, as it was to any outsiders present.

Certain wives were also making a statement about themselves by deliberately removing the marriage veil when praying and prophesying. Paul accuses them of conduct like that of the 'new' élite Roman women, for they were abandoning the readily definable sign of their married state. The implication was that as 'leaders' in the service they were misrepresenting to the outsider the Christian attitude to marriage. While we have no evidence from the passage as to why they removed the veil, they may have argued that if men made a statement by covering their heads as élite liturgical performers, why should not wives likewise make a similar statement with theirs.

In the case of men, Paul has argued that they dishonoured Christ, their head, by drawing significance to social status; in the case of wives, they dishonoured their Christian husbands. They created a wrong impression for those who took information to others outside the community. There was the replication of secular status in the meetings and the toleration of 'new' Roman wives also leading in an essential role. This sort of conduct on the part of wives could be identified with the long-remembered Bacchanalian worship in Rome that had been proscribed. The wrong signals given to the messengers concerning the nature of the Christian gathering were not lost on Paul, even if they were on them.[78]

Paul ended his discussion by contrasting their unswerving loyalty to his traditions (11:2) with those who wanted to be contentious about these issues. He reminds them that there was no apostolic tradition that could be cited endorsing this; furthermore, there was no parallel custom in any of the churches (11:16).

Paul had already drawn attention to the presence of 'strife' and 'jealousy' in the community, with the 'Paul party' playing off against the 'Apollos party', as well as vexatious litigation (1:11-12, 3:3-4, 4:6, 6:1-8). The next issue Paul dealt with was the intrusion of a party spirit into the Lord's Supper and the problem of divisiveness emerging again in other worship situations (11:18-19; 12:14-25). Just as Plutarch's use of the term for 'contentious', along with other terms of divisiveness, described the de-

---

78. Robinson, *The Criminal Law of Ancient Rome*, p. 95.

structive effect of power politics in secular meetings or teaching contexts, so, too, Paul used it alongside other words to describe contention in a similar situation of strife in the Christian community.

Gill tentatively suggested that the reason for this conduct was 'members of the social élite were wanting to establish a Roman element into their worship.'[79] It would seem rather that there were some who wished to draw attention to their own status and themselves as they addressed God or spoke in his Name. The above evidence also points to the power struggle among the élite within the congregation. The issues were merely symptomatic of the wider problem of strife, zealousness, party spirit, schism, and contentiousness in the Christian community. Paul feared these might still be present when he wrote 2 Corinthians 12:20 — 'strife, zealousness, angry tempers, disputes, slanders, gossip, arrogance, and disturbances'. In this he was no less sanguine than Plutarch, who visited Corinth and, in his essay on 'How to Profit by One's Enemies' dedicated to Cn. Cornelius Pulcher, the distinguished Corinthian, observed that city government 'which has not had to bear with envy or jealous rivalry or contention — emotions most productive of enmity — has not hitherto existed' (86C).[80] The Christian ἐκκλησία in Corinth has shown itself after Paul left to be no different. The problem underlying the two issues of 1 Corinthians 11:2-16 was yet another example of the replication in the Christian community of the contentious conduct of those involved in the power politics in the body politic in Roman Corinth in the first century.[81]

79. Gill, 'The Importance of Roman Portraiture,' p. 260.

80. On his distinguished career in public office in Corinth, see Merritt, *Corinth*, 8.1, nos. 80-83, and Kent, *Corinth*, 8.3, nos. 138-43.

81. New Testament scholarship on this passage would have benefited greatly from the help of social historians in placing it in its first-century Roman cultural setting. Its use last century in an attempt to resolve a controversy over headship in the church seems to have been misplaced. That the significance of men covering their heads was almost always glossed over in the discussions shows how crucial it is to deal with the two problems together for the interpretation of the whole section.

CHAPTER 7

'Private' Dinners and Christian Divisiveness (1 Corinthians 11:17-34)

'When You Gather It Is Not to Eat the Lord's Dinner' (11:20)[1]

Why did the Corinthian Christians behave as they did towards one another at the Lord's Dinner (δεῖπνον) and what actions on their part caused Paul to dissociate their celebration from that instituted by Jesus? It is suggested that the answer lies in the fact that they behaved at this dinner in the same way as other Corinthians behaved at theirs. In order to demonstrate this it is proposed (I) to offer an alternative reconstruction of the debacle that occurred at the Lord's Dinner to the received reconstruction of the events; (II) to consider the significance of Paul's alteration of the word order of the Dominical sayings in the tradition; and (III) to argue that the behaviour of some of the Corinthians can be accounted for, because at the Lord's Dinner they followed the socially accepted convention of 'private' dinners in secular Corinth. An appendix challenges the usual translation of καὶ μέρος τι πιστεύω as 'I partly believe it' (11:19) and argues that Paul's comments about divisions did not reflect scepticism about the report he received on their conduct at that dinner.

---

1. This is a revised and expanded version of parts of my 'The Lord's Supper at Corinth: An Alternative Reconstruction,' *RTR* 37 (1978): 73-82. The chapter incorporates new primary sources and, in addition, explores the different conventions at dinners in the ancient world.

I. Reconstructing the Debacle at the Lord's Dinner

The usual reconstruction of the events lying behind the celebration of the Lord's Dinner is based upon the meaning given to two key words and a clause, viz., 'I take before' (προλαμβάνω), 'in eating' (ἐν τὸ φαγεῖν) (11:21), and 'I wait for' (ἐκδέχομαι) (11:33). This construction indicates that some, presumed to be the rich, commenced their own meal before the others arrived, eating and drinking to the point of satiation. The latecomers, presumed to be the poor or the slaves, arrived to an empty, or near empty, table and were embarrassed. Paul's solution was that they should wait for the latecomers and if some were really hungry and could not wait, they should eat at home.[2] Some have also seen the injunction in 11:34 as the apostolic imprimatur for the beginning of the removal of the Lord's Dinner from the context of a meal.

There are a number of difficulties with this reconstruction. Does it make sense to argue that, by waiting for one another, you overcame the difficulty of the have-nots being hungry if, as Paul correctly reported, each took his own dinner (11:21)? Was it really the case that the have-nots were put to shame because others had simply begun eating their own meal ahead of others? Paul treats it as more than a breach of social etiquette. Was it not that the have-nots had no food to eat at the Dinner?

What of the injunction that if 'anyone is hungry, let him eat at home (11:34)? Did this include 'the have-nots' or only those who had been imbibing too much? If it is to the drunken members of the Christian community, how much was Paul's injunction (11:33) a real solution for the embarrassment felt by the others? If it is to 'the have-nots', then why didn't they bring their own food to the meal as the others did? Does the injunction in 11:34a absolve the rich from responsibility towards the poor by removing any concern for them through changing the occasion from a meal to a simple memorial service?

Another reconstruction is based on these three key words or phrases and appears more in harmony with what we know of the social background. It was in the presence of 'the have-nots' that the others 'devoured' (προλαμβάνω) their own dinner, and they did so during the Lord's Dinner

---

2. See, e.g., S. M. Pogoloff, *Logos and Sophia: The Rhetorical Situation of 1 Corinthians*, SBL Dissertation Series 134 (Atlanta: Scholars Press, 1992), pp. 267-71.

(ἐν τὸ φαγεῖν). The Christians who were 'the haves' should have welcomed those have-nots by sharing their food with them (ἐκδέχομαι).

a. 'To Take Before', 'to Take', or 'to Receive'? (11:21)

It is usual to translate the verb προλαμβάνω as 'take before' — προ meaning 'before' and λαμβάνω, 'to take'. Of the three occurrences of this verb in the New Testament neither of the other two have this meaning. Mark 14:8 conveys the sense of 'to anticipate', and Galatians 6:1 the idea of 'being overtaken by a fault'.[3] We find all three meanings in literary, papyriological, and epigraphic sources, but is there external evidence of an identical social situation such as that in verse 21? If there is, it may well provide us with its meaning, for a word used in an identical situation should be weighed as carefully as its occurrences elsewhere in the New Testament.

In the contexts of eating there are occurrences where the verb may or may not carry a temporal sense. They concern how to overcome the effects of over-imbibing wine, and the use of citron to avoid poisoning. In *Deipnosophists* advice is given about overindulgence, especially concerning the drinking of potent wine with meals. In order to avoid the consequences of this, it suggests that pure water should be drunk before eating. 'If this is too troublesome, let him take before dinner some sweet wine' (γλυκύν ὑδαρῆ θερμόν προλαμβανέτω). Advice is later given 'that citron is to be eaten' before any food (ὅτι δὲ καὶ προλαμβανόμενον τὸ κιτρίον).[4] However, the sense of these passages requires that the verb be translated 'to take before', as it would in any context where one item was to be taken in advance of another.

Of the papyri collections published to date, only one refers to food eaten at a festival, *P.Cairo.Zen.* 59562, l. 12. The words following the verb in line 12 are missing, as indeed is the entire next line except for the definite article. The papyrus, if sections (b) and (c) belong together, deals with food for the king at the festival. The use of the aorist imperative suggests the taking of food, not necessarily for eating, but for providing a substantial amount of food for the king. However, as this papyrus is only a copy of

---

3. The word occurs only once in the LXX, where it also means to overtake (Wis. 17:16).
4. Athenaeus, *Deipnosophists* 2.445c; 3.84.

the instruction, we cannot be sure, and only the discovery of the original letter would make it clear whether the recipient of the order is permitted to eat some of the food himself or simply to supply stores for the king.

In a mid-second-century-A.D. inscription from the famous temple of Asclepius at Epidauris in Achaea, προλαμβάνω is used in connection with the taking of food. This testimony of healing by Marcus Julius Apellas, c. A.D. 160, stated, 'When I arrived at the temple he told me for two days to keep my head covered, and for these two days it rained; to 'take', i.e., to eat cheese and bread (τυπὸν καὶ ἄρατον προλαβεῖν), celery with lettuce, to wash myself without help, to practice running, to take lemon peels and to soak them in water (κιτρίου προλαμβάνειν τὰ ἄκρα) . . . to take milk with honey (γάλα μετὰ μέλιτος προλαβεῖν). When one day I had drunk milk alone he said, 'Put the honey in the milk so that it can get through'.[5] The use of this verb for eating food has drawn comment by the initial editor, who noted three possible meanings of this term — (i) 'to take before'; (ii) 'to take' on the grounds the inscription should have read on all three occasions προσλαμβάνω and not προλαμβάνω; and (iii) 'to take'. It certainly makes no sense to translate any of the uses of the verb in this inscription as 'to take before'.[6]

That there could be three errors by the inscriber is a possibility, although the most recent editors of the inscription do not take up Dittenberger's suggestion of προσλαμβάνω.[7] Luke uses that verb for the taking of food (Acts 27:33, 36). There Paul urged his fellow passengers 'to take' some food (μεταλαβεῖν) because they had been without food 'having taken nothing' (προσλαβόμενοι) and 'they ate' (προσελάβοντο) some food. Besides, there is a variant reading in 1 Corinthians 11:21 with προσλαμβάνω namely A, together with approximately twenty cursives, e.g., 3, 31, 46, 106, 108, 114, 120 (Tischendorf's numbering). There are, however, difficulties in accepting A and the cursives against all other texts. An examination of A shows that the verb is divided with προς at the end of a line. -ος is written

5. *SIG*[3] 1170, ll. 7, 9, 16.
6. W. Dittenberger, the editor suggests this possibility (*SIG*[3] 328). The translation cited in the next note does not comment on the term but translates it without any temporal sense.
7. E. J. and J. Eidelstein, *Asclepius: Collection and Interpretation of the Testimonies* (Baltimore: Johns Hopkins University Press, 1998), no. 432. The translation of the passage is primarily mine based on that in my M.Theol. thesis, 'The *oikos* Controversy in the Lord's Supper, 1 Corinthians 11:17-34' (1976).

in smaller letters, and one cannot be sure if *omicron* and *sigma* are the work of the original copyist or a corrector. The hands appear to be identical and, from the previous section commencing in chapter 10, the copy is the work of the 'third' copyist who tended to squeeze letters at the end of a line. He might well be both the copyist and the corrector, and the error may have been made at the point of correction by adding a sigma. Although A belongs to the Alexandrian type texts, the sigma is missing from significant texts such as B and a. Certainly in our earliest manuscript P[46], which is also Alexandrian, the copyist has πρό at the end of the line of 1 Corinthians 11:21. He consistently breaks words at the end of lines syllabically. For example, προσευχομένη in 1 Corinthians 11:5 is broken off after the sigma, even though he extended three letters beyond the end of the previous line's margin to do so. Therefore it cannot be argued that he completed a line with omicron and meant to begin the next line with the sigma. The problems regarding A as the correct reading are far too difficult to overcome, as is the supposition that the inscription in all three places where this verb occurs should have read πρός and not πρό-. The textual variant is rejected in spite of the precedent for the use of πρός in Acts 27:33, 36 for the eating of food.

It has been suggested by MM and BAGD that the prefix πρό- had lost its temporal force by the first century. They both refer to the same Asclepian inscription in connection with this verse. The former states, 'One naturally thinks of 1 Corinthians 11:21, where no part lies in the "forestalling" of others: the gravamen of Paul's charge is that there was "no Lord's Dinner to eat", "everyone devours *his own* supper at the Meal"' (italics theirs). The latter refers to the use of the verb 'where the temporal sense of πρό is felt very little, if at all' and translates verse 21 as, 'everyone takes his own dinner'.[8] Some recent commentators on 1 Corinthians have not taken up either of these lexical comments on the nontemporal interpretation. For instance, C. K. Barrett indicates that the interpretation is governed by the meaning he attaches to verse 33, 'to wait for'.[9] (See section c.) It is readily seen how the usual view is sustained, i.e., that the Corinthians took their food beforehand and hence they must wait for the latecomers. However, the epigraphic evidence for the use of προλαμβάνω with its non-

8. MM, p. 542, BAGD, p. 708.
9. C. K. Barrett, *The First Epistle to the Corinthians* (New York: Harper and Row, 1968), p. 262.

146

temporal sense in an eating context may alter this. Fee takes account of my argument in an earlier discussion and concludes, 'In this case the lack of further description by Paul makes a clear-cut decision impossible', although he favours the view that the verb should be interpreted as 'devours'.[10]

We also note the use of λαμβάνω (11:23) for the taking of bread on the part of Jesus. If 'take' had simply been the meaning in 11:21, then why did not Paul use λαμβάνω there also? Jeremias has shown with regard to the use of λαμβάνω ἄρτον that 'it belongs to those verbs which in a Semitic language describe, in a way which is cumbersome and superfluous for our idiom, a movement (or attitude) which is preparatory to the action on which the stress lies'.[11] The elevation of the bread was simply preparatory to the saying of grace. The same idiom is found in classical Greek.[12] In 11:24, then, λαμβάνω describes Jesus' action before saying grace, while the verb in 11:21 describes the eating of food by the Corinthians. The former verb belongs to the group of verbs relating to the beginning of a meal with grace; the latter refers to the actual eating of food. The former, then, is something of a pleonasm, while the latter is the main verb. Would not Paul have found the use of the same verb inappropriate to describe both the activity of Jesus and the behaviour of some Corinthians? He took and gave it to others, while they all took food in their own hands and ate it themselves.

G. Theissen wishes to translate this verb as 'receive' in support of his thesis that the rich at the Lord's Dinner received a different quality and quantity of food from that of the poor. He assembles evidence of different quantities being served to the rich at pagan festivals, but it is difficult to integrate this evidence into the Corinthian situation in 11:17-34.[13] How are we to understand the meaning of the word for hungry in verse 21b? On Theissen's argument the amount served to the poor left them hungry. He suggests that they also ate separately from the rich. Although Theissen's

10. G. D. Fee, *The First Epistle to the Corinthians* (Grand Rapids: Eerdmans, 1987), p. 542 on my early discussion 'The Lord's Supper at Corinth: An Alternative Reconstruction,' 74. For his view that the verb should be interpreted as 'devours', see pp. 542, 568. See also the acknowledgement of the nontemporal use of the verb while ignoring the implications in the discussion in S. J. Kistemaker, *1 Corinthians* (Grand Rapids: Baker, 1993), pp. 390-92, n. 68.

11. J. Jeremias, *The Eucharistic Words of Jesus* (E.T. London: S.C.M., 1966), p. 175.

12. B. A. Mastin, 'Jesus Said Grace,' *SJT* 24.4 (Nov. 1971): 449-55.

13. G. Theissen, 'Social Integration and Sacramental Activity,' 153-55.

data are significant for a general appreciation of pagan festivals, one has to agree with Malherbe in his critique of Theissen's thesis when he writes, 'Theissen's efforts to interpret the situation are not always convincing'.[14]

Why then did Paul use πρό rather than simply λαμβάνω? We note a tendency in Greek to join this preposition to others for the purpose of strengthening the meaning.[15] A case can be made out for this in *koine* Greek, where δίδωμι can mean 'give up' while προδίδωμι means 'betray'. Did Paul choose the verb in 11:21 to stress the selfish and unfeeling character of their action? MM translates the verb as 'devours'. Johnson had previously suggested that it should be translated 'pounces'.[16] He may have been influenced by a comment of Plutarch in *Symposium* 2.10, who himself said of the table manners of the participants at a pagan festival where there was elbowing, snatching of food, and finger battles — 'It is monstrous and dog-like'. Marcus Julius Apellas uses the term in the inscription to describe compulsion, although in his case it was not greed as in the case of the Corinthian Christians but divine promptings in his search for healing. Paul did not describe what had happened in a neutral sense, for his opening statement says that he could not, under any circumstances, praise them (11:17) — even though he had already done so for following certain of his apostolic traditions (11:2). In this situation he condemned their greed in 'taking' their own food at the dinner without any thought of sharing with those who had none. The pejorative sense of 'devours' seems to best fit the whole context.

b. ἐν τῷ φαγεῖν — 'In Eating' or 'During the Eating' (11:21)

The significance of the articular infinitive and its relationship to the main verb προλαμβάνω confirms the nontemporal interpretation of the latter. The aorist articular infinitive occurs only once in all of Paul's epistles (1 Cor. 11:21), once in Hebrews, and nine times in Luke. It is argued that 'the present infinitive is normally used to mean "while", but Luke also has the aorist, whereby the translation shifts from "while" to "after that"

---

14. A. J. Malherbe, *Social Aspects of Early Christianity* (Baton Rouge: Louisiana State University Press, 1977), p. 84.

15. Liddell and Scott, p. 1465, for example.

16. E. Johnson, 'The Table of Demons,' *ET,* 2nd ser. 8 (1884): 247.

(therefore = aorist participle or ὅτι with the aorist)'.[17] Examples are cited. They classify Luke 3:21, 8:4, 9:34, and 11:37 as examples of actions occurring simultaneously with the main verb. Only Luke 19:5 is translated as meaning 'after his return', and BDF does not comment on 1 Corinthians 11:21. BAGD classifies ἐν with the articular infinitive as introducing 'an activity whose time is given — "when", "while", "during" . . . with the aorist infinitive the meaning is likewise "when". That lexicon does not, however, comment on 11:21.

The fundamental significance of the aorist in such a construction is not generally thought of as durative but as punctiliar. When an aorist is declared as 'punctiliar' it 'does not represent the initial or final point of the action. . . . A segment of time is involved, and it is the nature of this segment as a whole and its particular character that evokes the use of the aorist'.[18] Moulton states that ἐσθίειν by itself is durative in its force while φαγεῖν is constative.[19] Moule suggests that what Moulton means with respect to the latter can be described as 'a line reduced to a point by perspective'.[20]

Burton argued that the aorist articular infinitive marks 'the time at which the action expressed by the principal verb takes place and simply marks in general the time of the event denoted by the principal verb, leaving the context to indicate the precise nature of the chronological relation'. He suggests that in 11:21 'the action of the Infinitive cannot be antecedent to that of the principal verb'.[21] Having regard to the arguments of BAGD, Martin, Moulton, and Burton, it is suggested that the use of the aorist articular infinitive is meant to convey the idea in 11:21, that it was during the meal that each took or devoured his own dinner.

Can this conclusion be further reinforced by information from the Jewish liturgical background? If the church was following the Jewish cus-

17. BDF #404(2).

18. W. J. Martin, 'I Corinthians 11:2-16: An Interpretation,' in W. Ward Gasque and R. P. Martin, eds., *Apostolic History and the Gospel* (Exeter: Paternoster, 1970), p. 235.

19. J. H. Moulton, *A Grammar of New Testament Greek*, I, 3rd ed. (Edinburgh: T & T Clark, 1908), 111. For examples of ἐν τῷ ἐσθίειν in this sense see Plato, *Gorg.* 499d, 'pleasure in eating', and LXX Lev. 22:16 and 2 Kings 4:40, 'while they were eating out of the pot'.

20. C. F. D. Moule, *An Idiom Book of New Testament Greek* (Cambridge: Cambridge University Press, 1959), p. 11.

21. E. Burton, *Syntax of the Moods and Tenses in New Testament Greek*, 3rd ed. (Edinburgh: T & T Clark, 1889), pp. 50-51.

tom of breaking bread before the meal was eaten, we would conclude that the breaking of bread in remembrance of Jesus' death was the signal that the meal had begun.[22] After they had concluded the main meal, they would have drunk from the common cup. They may well have followed the order of the events Paul quotes in the Institution Narrative (11:23-25).

Did they follow the order of the Passover? Paul definitely uses technical terms in 1 Corinthians without offering any explanation as to their meaning. In 10:16 he refers to 'the cup of blessing which we bless', the cup over which Jesus pronounced the meaning of his death. He speaks also of 'the bread which we break'. While the latter could refer to an ordinary meal, it certainly referred to the Passover. Reference is also made to 'Christ our Passover' and the call 'to keep the feast not with the old leaven of malice and wickedness' (5:8). The use of this as an exhortation in the context of the immoral person means that the Corinthians had to be well acquainted with Passover language if they were to understand precisely to what Paul was alluding.

We know that the Corinthians had a number of Jewish converts in their congregation, including Crispus, the former leader of the Jewish synagogue. It is probable that he and other Jews would have followed the outline of the Passover either fully or in a modified form for the Lord's Dinner. The breaking of bread would have constituted the beginning of the meal proper, having been preceded by a common cup, the entrée, the Passover Liturgy, and a second cup. After the meal the cup of blessing, over which Jesus spoke his words of reinterpretation, would be drunk.[23] This would also fit into the reconstruction we have proposed, with the action of the main verb fitting into the context of the meal.

There would be good reason for using the Institution Narrative as an outline for the form of service to be followed in Corinth. If we reject the idea of the Lord's Dinner being modelled on the Passover as Jesus reinterpreted it, what model would Paul have followed in contextualising the Christian Passover in a Gentile and Jewish congregation? A pagan model would have been unacceptable to Jewish converts and somewhat out of keeping with what we know of Paul's observance of Jewish cultic activities.

The cumulative evidence from the religious background of both Paul and some of his Corinthian converts, the Passover allusions in 1 Corinthi-

---

22. C. F. D. Moule, *Worship in the New Testament* (London: S.C.M., 1961), p. 19.
23. J. Jeremias, *The Eucharistic Words of Jesus* (E.T. London: S.C.M., 1966), pp. 85-86.

ans, and the grammatical considerations would suggest that we translate the aorist articular infinitive as indicating the time during which the activity of the main verb took place. Thus it was during the meal that each one 'took' or 'devoured' his or her own dinner.

c. ἐκδέχομαι — 'To Wait for' or 'To Receive' (11:33)

The only other occurrence of ἐκδέχομαι in the Pauline corpus is in 1 Corinthians 16:11 where Paul is 'expecting' Timothy to come to him 'with others'. At the beginning of the letter Paul adds the preposition ἀπο to ἐκδέχομαι where he states that Christians are those who 'wait for (ἀπεκδεχομένους) the revealing of our Lord Jesus Christ' (1:7). The latter term, when found elsewhere in Paul, is used of the eschatological hope.[24] If Paul had meant 'wait for', then the appropriate word would have been the one he used in 1:7, viz., ἀπεκδέχομαι. There is no instance in the New Testament where the word is used in the context of a meal. Liddell and Scott indicate that in that context this word means 'to receive, 'to entertain' at a feast.

It is important to note that this word in the LXX was used to express the concept of hospitality, not only in its simple form δέχομαι but in most of its composite forms including ἐκδέχομαι (3 Macc. 5:26). W. Grundmann draws attention to its use for the time-honoured and sacred character of receiving others.[25] In the papyri it is used also for the entertaining of an important official, which included the provision of food (P.Tebt. 33, l. 7). Given the meaning of the term in literary sources, including the LXX and in nonliterary ones of receiving and sharing, there are good grounds for translating the imperative as 'receive one another' in the sense of sharing food and drink.

How well does this meaning resolve the issues Paul outlined in verses 18-21? By receiving one another they share their resources with those who 'have not' and thus alleviate the acute embarrassment felt by those who came without food to the Lord's Dinner. They also respond to one another in precisely the same way Jesus responded to the needs of everyone present in his body given 'for you' (11:24). When Paul declared that it was not the

24. Rom. 8:19, 23, 25; Gal. 5:5; Phil. 3:20.
25. TDNT, II, 51.

Lord's Dinner (11:20), he did not mean in liturgical terminology that it was sacramentally defective, but rather their own action invalidated it because they acted towards the needs of others in exactly the opposite way Jesus did.

By receiving one another, they acted in a way consistent with the keeping of the Passover if, as it has been argued here, this is the model that lies behind the Corinthian Lord's Dinner. It would be inconceivable for Paul, or any Jewish Christian, to exclude any who actually sat at table from full participation in the Passover. The Messianic Passover provided an adequate precedent for Jewish Christians in Corinth.

By receiving one another, they acted towards one another in the way Paul outlines in 1 Corinthians 12:25, where he calls upon them to show the same care for everyone. The context suggests that they showed care towards some, but not others — the 'less comely parts' of the fellowship. This problem is also reflected in the dinner if we take the statement of 'not discerning the body' (v. 29) to mean that they failed to recognise whom they were shaming.

If it is true that 'the haves' ate their own dinner within the context of the Lord's Dinner in the presence of 'the have-nots' (while the latter partook only of the 'sacramental' bread broken before the meal began and waited while the others ate until the meal concluded, drinking with them from the cup of blessing), then it makes sense to argue that Paul's solution had to involve the sharing of 'the haves' dinner with those who were hungry in order to alleviate the shame the latter felt as the 'have-nots' (11:33).

The receiving of one another went some way in helping to resolve the problem of the divisions to which Paul referred (11:18). If they were simply to 'wait for one another', it is difficult to see how the first indictment against the Corinthians concerning the parties would be resolved. He was aware that parties existed, and as he had sought to abolish the Apollos and Paul parties (4:6ff.), he did the same with his apostolic injunction (11:33).

The reasons outlined above furnish grounds for accepting this meaning of ἐκδέχομαι (11:33). Because ὥστε signals the apostolic injunctions to remedy the situation (14:39; 15:58), we are certain that these verses were meant to resolve the situation Paul described in 11:18-21, even if only temporarily. Paul's suggestion that he needed to deal with other matters relating to the Lord's Dinner when present (11:34b) indicates that the resolution of the problem was difficult and perhaps touched the current economic problem aggravated by social structures of Corinthian society as it related to 'the haves' and 'the have-nots'.

II. The Pauline Interpretation of the Words of Jesus

In reconstructing the situation insufficient attention has been paid to the fact that Paul has changed the word order of the Institution narrative and the reason for that.[26] The text reads τοῦτό μού ἐστιν τὸ σῶμα τὸ ὑπὲρ ὑμῶν, which is not the word order in the synoptic gospels.[27] The personal pronoun μου has been shifted to an earlier part of the sentence and appears next to the neuter demonstrative pronoun τοῦτο. If translated literally it would read, 'This of mine is the body [given up] on your behalf'.

It is assumed that 'this' refers to 'bread' (ἄρτος) *per se*, which in Greek is masculine, while the demonstrative pronoun is neuter. To what does that demonstrative refer? A survey of the use of the neuter demonstrative pronoun in the Pauline corpus shows that of seventy-four occurrences of τοῦτο, in sixteen instances it refers to an action.[28] Is Paul, by repeating the words of the Institution Narrative (11:23ff.) that referred to the action of the Jesus on their behalf, doing so in order to contrast it with their conduct?[29] Paul also provides examples of the use the neuter demonstrative pronoun for the sake of emphasis where an infinitive or a noun follows as a predicate.[30] If that was the case here, then how do we account for the place of μου in the sentence which normally fills this emphatic role.[31] 1 Corinthians 9:18 is the only exact parallel in Paul for 11:24, 'What then is my re-

26. It is surprising that commentators do not deal with this issue; e.g., Fee, *The First Epistle to the Corinthians,* makes no comment at all.

27. Matt. 26:26; Mark 14:22; Luke 22:19, all of which read τοῦτό ἐστιν τὸ σῶμά μου.

28. In 1 Cor. itself we see evidence of the continuative use of the neuter demonstrative to refer to action; 6:6 refers to κρίνετε, 8 to ἀδικεῖτε (wrong) and ἀποστερεῖτε (defrauding); 7:37 to τηρεῖν (to keep her); 9:17 to εὐαγγελίζωμαι (preaching). See also Rom. 12:20; 2 Cor. 1:17; Eph. 2:8; 6:1; Phil. 3:15; Col. 3:20; 1 Thess. 4:3; 5:18; 1 Tim. 2:3; 4:16; 5:4; Philem 18. This use of the neuter demonstrative is well attested in Classical Greek but has not been highlighted by New Testament scholars, *pace* J. C. Callow, 'To What Do *touto* and *tauta* Refer in Paul's Letters?' *Notes on Translation* 70 (1978): 2-8, where he confesses 'to complete bafflement' on the whole subject.

29. In the actual text the reference could be to the action of breaking, ἔκλασεν.

30. G. B. Winer, *Grammar of New Testament Greek* (E.T. Edinburgh: T & T Clark, 1870), p. 200. See 2 Cor. 2:1; 7:11; 13:9.

31. There are one hundred and twenty-nine occurrences of this personal pronoun in the postnominal position in Paul, two in genitive absolute clauses and four in an immediate pronominal position for emphasis. In 1 Cor. 4:17 Paul uses the personal pronoun twice: μου τέκνον, also postnominally ὁδούς μου; 9:27, μου τὸ σῶμα; 2 Cor. 4:16, μου λαός, citing the LXX; Col. 4:18, μου τῶν δεσμῶν.

ward?' (τίς οὖν μού ἐστιν ὁ μισθός). Paul is giving great emphasis in that discussion to his decision to waive his rights to receive a wage for his gospel activity (9:1-18). Whether in 11:24 the neuter demonstrative is used to refer to action or is used for emphasis and/or μου is used to further stress the point cannot be finally determined, but the interpretation is the certain — 'this is *my* body [given] on your behalf'.[32] What is clear is that if this is what Jesus did 'on behalf of you [Corinthians]', then you must 'do this in remembrance' of him (11:24). This is further emphasised with a contrast with other accounts which read, 'this cup is the new covenant in my blood'. Paul writes literally, 'this cup, the new covenant [one], is in my blood' (τοῦτο τὸ ποτήριον ἡ καινὴ διαθήκη ἐστὶν ἐν τῷ ἐμῷ αἵματι) with an emphatic personal pronoun (11:24) — 'this new covenant cup is in *my* blood'. Paul's point was that at the Lord's Dinner they acted on their own behalf by consuming their own food, but the example of Jesus taught that Christians were obligated to act likewise for others, especially in the very dinner which recorded his self-giving sacrifice for its participants.

It becomes clear that Paul's purpose in quoting the eucharistic words was not simply to repeat a tradition that he had already delivered to them but to explain why that tradition did not endorse their conduct but condemned it — '*For* I received from the Lord . . .' (11:23). By rearranging the word order of parts of that tradition he explicated the significance of Jesus' action as a servant giving himself up on their behalf to incorporate them into the New Covenant. His action thoroughly condemned their own self-centred conduct exhibited at the very dinner which Jesus instituted for them to remember his death. Little wonder that Paul declares that this cannot be the Lord's Dinner (11:20), for that imposed the obligation to imitate Christ in their relationships (cf. 11:1).

III. The Lord's Dinner as a 'Private' Banquet

The ancient world described a whole range of dinners that one could attend. There was a 'free dinner' (ἀσύμβολον δεῖπνον). A traditional saying

---

32. For some of the complexities of word order see A. Wifstrand, 'A Problem concerning the Word Order of the New Testament,' *Studia Theologica* 3 (1951): 172-84. His discussion of Paul is too brief, but he does note, 'The word to which it is added is accentuated by the enclitic' (182-84, cited on 183).

by the fourth-century-B.C. comic poet Amphis on the sheer folly of coming after a free dinner had commenced was cited by the second-century-
A.D. writer Athenaeus — 'whoever is late for a free dinner you may guess
would desert very soon the ranks in battle', i.e., the person is a fool.[33] In the
same place the latter also cited Antiphanes, a poet of the same period as
Athenaeus — 'That it is the life the gods lead, when you can dine at others'
expense with no thought of the reckoning', i.e., reciprocity.[34] There were
dinners with the distribution of the 'meat privilege' (γέρας) where choice
cuts were given to those of highest status in the community together with a
'meal of equal parts' where the animal was 'divided entirely into pieces of
equal weight, which are distributed by lottery.'[35] In contrast the subscrip-
tion dinner (ἔρανος) was one where the guests paid towards the cost of the
food. There were also dinners where guests actually brought the food with
them and ate it themselves. This was designated a 'private dinner'
(ἀσύμβολον δεῖπνον).[36]

When it comes to the early empire there is a debate concerning two
types of dinners. In Question Ten of 'Table Talk' in Plutarch's *Moralia*
there is a discussion between Hagias and Lamprias on the specific issue of
whether the ancients 'did better with portions served to each, or people of
today, who dine from a common supply'.[37] Hagias indicates that there was
a division of opinion in his own day, for when he held public office 'most
of the dinners were "portion-banquets" (τὰ πλεῖστα τῶν δείπνων δαῖτες
ἦσαν) and each man at the sacrifices was allotted his share of the meal.
This was wonderfully pleasing to some, but others blamed the practice as
unsociable and vulgar and thought the dinners ought to be restored again
to the customary style when my term as *archon* was over . . . this division of
meat into shares kills sociability and makes many dinners and diners with
nobody any body's dinner-companion when each takes his share by weight
as from a butcher's counter and puts it before himself.'[38] According to

33. Kock, ii. 248, frag. 39, cited by Athenaeus, *Deipnosophists* 1.8C.
34. Kock, ii. 248, frag. 243, cited by Athenaeus, *Deipnosophists* 1.8D.
35. M. Detienne, 'Culinary Practices and the Spirit of Sacrifice,' in M. Detienne and
J.-P. Vernant, eds., *The Cuisine of Sacrifice among the Greeks* (Chicago: University of Chicago
Press, 1989), p. 13 for a discussion of this convention.
36. Homer, *Od.* 7.102. The word δαιτυμών when used in the plural could also indicate
this, according to Liddell and Scott.
37. *Moralia* 642E.
38. *Moralia* 642E-643A.

Lamprias who responded to Hagias, Homer's observation of the behaviour of civilised men at the dinner was invoked — the first century often cited Homer as a precedent for disputes concerning conduct.[39] 'Now of meat, also, portions were equally divided, whence he calls banquets "equal" because of the equality observed. Dinners were called *daites* (δαῖτας) from *dateisthai*, "to divide" (δατέομαι) and the wine as well as the meat was equally apportioned'.[40] He also cited with approval Hesiod, who shared pride of place with Homer as an authority for first-century writers, 'But where each guest has his own private portion, companionship perishes'.[41] Subsequent discussion refers to the ostentatious behaviour of the rich with showy dining rooms of thirty couches or more, making for 'unsociable and unfriendly banquets'.[42] In the first century the pros and cons for 'equal' or 'portion' banquets and those who dined from a common 'table' were being weighed.

At this point of time archaeological explorations provide limited hard evidence from Corinth. One convention allowed only Roman citizens and ordinary inhabitants to be invited to an 'official' dinner at the Isthmian Games.[43] Nothing is known of the practices at that 'State' dinner, although one could speculate that it was either an 'equal dinner' or that some social distinctions in terms of rank within Roman society may have been observed. Plutarch records his own attendance at a private over against an official banquet at the Isthmian Games but provides no clues as to etiquette.[44]

Plutarch's sentiments can be contrasted with those of some of the Corinthian Christians, for he observed that 'nothing unseemly or unbecoming a gentleman could be seen so long as the goddesses Portion and Lot presided with equity over dinners and drinking parties'. That the proof

39. See S. J. Myres, *Homer and His Critics* (London: Routledge and Kegan Paul, 1958); and R. J. Morley, 'The Past in Clement of Alexandria: A Study of an Attempt to Define Christianity in Socio-Cultural Terms,' in E. P. Sanders, ed., *The Shaping of Christianity in the Second and Third Centuries: Jewish and Christian Self-Definition* (Philadelphia: Fortress Press, 1980), I, 193: 'the idea of antiquity implies superiority: once a culture has been demonstrated to be the most ancient, it has also been demonstrated to be the source of all others', hence the use of Homer as the most ancient authority.

40. Athenaeus, *Deipnosophists* 1.12C.

41. Hesiod, *Works and Days* 722, cited in *Moralia* 644C.

42. *Moralia*, 679B.

43. For a discussion of this occasion see Ch. 12.

44. See pp. 277-78.

of his assertion is true is 'the fact that even now at sacrifices and public banquets, because of the simplicity and frugality of the fare, each guest is still served his equal portion of the meal'.[45]

In light of the above evidence on dining, Paul's comments suggest that some Corinthian Christians saw the Lord's Dinner as a 'private dinner' (ἀσύμβολος δεῖπνον) and not an 'equal' or 'free' one, for they brought their own food with them and ate it themselves.[46] Paul may well have established the observation of the Lord's Dinner with participants bringing their own food or may himself acted as the 'father' of the family. How had their observance deviated after he left, and brought such a strong condemnation (11:27)? It would seem that there were things that happened after Paul left Corinth. The first was the divisions among them which naturally spilt over into any church gathering including the celebration of the Lord's death (11:17-18; cf. 1:10-12; 3:1-4; 12:25); the second and connected reason may have been the immediate social difficulty of a food shortage.[47] The latter might have been cited as an excuse not to share, for it is known how anxious 'the haves' were in times of famine as they feared the attack by the *plebes* on their grain hoards and their property generally — it will be argued that Corinth was in the midst of such a grain shortage when Paul writes (7:26).[48] The city officials took action to ensure that there was a temporary 'corn dole' administered through 'the superintendent of the grain supply' who was specially appointed for the task to alleviate some of the tensions and the rioting that was associated with famines.[49] Some Christians seem to have made no move at the dinner to share with the 'have-nots' during this grain shortage.

If the precedent for the Corinthians' Lord's Dinner was the Jewish Passover, as it was when it was first instituted,[50] then it would be totally in-

---

45. *Moralia* 644C-D.

46. G. Theissen's argument that at the Lord's Supper there were different portions of food handed out does not fit with the text which indicates that some were hungry, *The Social Setting of Pauline Christianity: Essays on Corinth* (Philadelphia, Fortress Press, 1982), pp. 145-74.

47. See pp. 220-21 for a discussion of 1 Cor. 7:26.

48. See pp. 223-24.

49. See pp. 222-23.

50. Paul's use of Passover imagery without needing explication and his reference to the third cup of wine in the Passover meal as 'the cup of blessing which we bless' and 'the bread which we break' again without explanation suggests that all the congregation was well aware of the Passover precedent for the Lord's supper (5:7 and 10:16).

congruous for some family members not to share their resources, especially in this type of situation. Given that Jesus organised the Passover for his disciples whom he called upon to see themselves as 'brothers', i.e., 'family', the Corinthian celebration could hardly be called the Lord's Dinner if it was observed as a 'private' banquet.[51] In spite of the teaching of Jesus some 'brothers' in Corinth were left without food. The actual behaviour of 'the haves' at that meal was totally indefensible, for while immorality was absent, the other two hallmarks of Corinthian secular dinners were present. There was drunkenness, which Paul singled out to epitomise the overindulgence with food and wine (11:21; cf. 15:34).[52] Some of the Corinthians ended the meal inebriated, and the third 'cup of blessing' was equated with 'after-dinners' wine.[53] Paul's assertion that their celebration was not the Lord's Dinner is explicable (11:20), for it had degenerated into a 'private dinner' where the social 'haves' devoured their own meal and drank themselves into stupor with their own wine, while the hungry low-class 'have-nots' were left looking on as slaves did at private dinners. Paul records that the actions of the 'haves' reflect their despising the very nature of the gathering, i.e., 'the church of God' and shaming the 'have-nots' (11:22).[54] In behaving thus some Christians replicated the dinner 'etiquette' of their secular counterparts.

51. Matt. 23:8. For a continuity of the perception of 'brothers', i.e., 'family' see Lucian (c. 120-190), 'The Passing of Peregrinus', 13, who reported of Christians, '... their first lawgiver [Jesus] persuaded them that they are all brothers of one another ... '.

52. Cf. 15:34 and pp. 100-101.

53. See this technical term in Plutarch, *Moralia* 710E. For this sort of conduct at Corinthian dinners, see pp. 83-84.

54. See J. J. Meggitt, *Paul, Poverty and Survival* (Edinburgh: T & T Clark, 1998), p. 120 for the somewhat unusual suggestion that Paul's reference to 'the have-nots' was to certain persons 'not having the bread and the wine of the eucharist' and not a reference to their social status over against that of 'the haves' (cf. 1 Cor. 1:26-28). On his premise he then argues that they are 'behaving *as though* they are eating τὸ ἴδιον δεῖπνον and not the Lord's supper. That Paul complains of some being drunk does not *necessarily* indicate that there must have been more wine present than the single cup of the Lord would allow: his description *may be* a caricature, part of the "biting rhetoric" that is characteristic of this particular section of the epistle' (p. 191 [italics mine]). With such interpretations Meggitt attempts to revive in part what was the 'new' reading of a century ago of the low status of all early Christians by Professor A. Deissmann, who, on taking up the New Testament chair at the University of Berlin, joined the German Workers' Party. He then proceeded to recast the social status of early Christians using the concept of 'the Proletariat', which was then gaining fashion. Deissmann's tremendous contribution to New Testament philology was not matched by his eisegesis on this subject.

'I Partly Believe It' or
'I Believe a Certain Report'? (11:18)

The discussion of the Lord's Dinner commences with what happened when the Corinthian Christians came together — it was not for their spiritual enhancement; the gathering was, in fact, detrimental to that purpose. Paul gave two reasons for his concerns (11:18-19, 20-21). 'For first of all, when you come together in the meeting, I hear that divisions (σχίσματα) exist among you'. He adds the following enigmatic sentence — καὶ μέρος τι πιστεύω. It is usually translated either as 'and I partly believe it' or 'and in part I believe it'.

If this is what Paul was really saying, then it is astonishing that he should have written as he did in 1:10–4:21 and 11:17-34. There he not only names the source of his information as 'those of Chloe's household' and reports what they have said — 'that there are contentions among you' (ὅτι ἔριδες ἐν ὑμῖν εἰσιν) (1:11b) — but also indicates why they have said it. He explains clearly what he means by this report of divisions, 'I am saying this' (λέγω δὲ τοῦτο) that each member of the congregation has divided on 'party lines' because 'each one of you is saying (ἕκαστος ὑμῶν λέγει), "I belong to Paul", and "I belong to Apollos", and "I belong to Cephas", and "I belong to Christ"'. He repeats this (3:3-4) and charges them with immaturity, i.e., being 'carnal' and 'operating in a secular way' because of their 'strife and jealousy'.[55] Again he gives his reason for these charges: 'for when

---

55. See my *Philo and Paul among the Sophists* (Cambridge: Cambridge University Press, 1997), pp. 170-74.

one says "I belong to Apollos", and "I belong to Paul", are you not men', i.e., behaving as pagan Corinthians do on these matters. He describes what is happening as 'strife' (ἔρις) (1:11); and as 'jealousy and strife' (ζῆλος καὶ ἔρις) (3:3). He uses the term 'divisions' (σχίσματα) (11:18) to describe the results of their internal strife, having already made mention in his appeal (1:10) that there should be no 'divisions' (σχίσματα) in their midst. Even a superficial reading of 1:10–4:21 indicates that Paul not only believed the report from those of Chloe's household but also condemned their behaviour as culturally driven and immature (3:1-4). Using Scripture, he argued against it (1:19, 31; 2:9; 3:19-20), instructing them 'not to go beyond the things that are written', i.e., Scripture (4:6), and citing his own example (2:1ff.) as a remedy based in part on a proper perception of the complementary ministries of Apollos and himself (3:5ff.; 4:1ff.). He wrote to admonish them as his children (4:14) and rebuke the arrogant (4:18). He concluded with a threat not dissimilar to that issued by the emperor as 'the father of the colony' of exercising his [apostolic] rod as father of the congregation if they did not repent of their behaviour (4:21).[56] How could he say all this about them in this extended rebuke if, as 11:18 appears to suggest, he was acting on hearsay which he only partly believed?

Furthermore, the consequence of their behaviour was that they were declared 'guilty of the body and blood of the Lord' and, as a result, God's judgement had already fallen on certain members of the congregation (11:27, 30). Some might argue that it was only for the second reason that they were attracting such judgement, i.e., if 'therefore' (οὖν) is the second reason (1:20-21).

How have New Testament scholars dealt with this enigma? Schmithals concludes, 'If one compares this passage [11:18] with Paul's statements in 1–4, it is simply inconceivable that both attitudes toward the disputes could come from the same epistle'. For him this is clear proof of the fragmentary nature of 1 Corinthians.[57] He argues for the composite character of 1 and 2 Corinthians on the grounds of 11:18 and states categorically that Paul is quite indefinite on the nature of the divisions, hence 11:2-34 is prior to 1–4.

56. On the weight of this 'imperial threat' see E. M. Lassen, 'The Use of the Father Image in Imperial Propaganda and 1 Corinthians 4:14-21,' *TynB* 42.1 (1991): 127-36.

57. W. Schmithals, *Gnosticism in Corinth* (E.T. Nashville: Abingdon, 1971), pp. 90-91. For his full treatment see 'Die Korintherbriefe als Briefsammlung,' *ZNW* 64 (1972): 263-88.

What other conclusions have been drawn from the usual interpretation? One commentator suggests that 'Paul expresses himself cautiously. Relying only on hearsay, he guards himself so that no one can accuse him of speaking rashly'.[58] Theissen believes that Paul is carefully distancing himself from his informants because others who wrote to him were from the upper class. He responds bearing this in mind 'as if only partly willing to credit what he has heard, but perhaps that is mere diplomacy'.[59] Allo resorts to 'an understatement in which an affirmation is expressed by the negative to the contrary'.[60]

Mitchell provides a solution based on rhetoric. For her, 11:18 is 'mock disbelief' on Paul's part and 'a further, more honest and weary concession by Paul to the realities of political life — the inevitably of factions'.[61] She cites Quintilian in support of the idea that Paul is using the rhetorical device of *dissimulatio*. 'There is also the device of *dissimulatio* (εἰρωνεία) when we say one thing and mean another, the most effective of all means of stealing into men's minds and a most attractive device, so long as we adopt a conversational rather than a controversial tone' (9.1.29). Although this is actually Cicero being cited by Quintilian and not his own comment, the latter subsequently states, 'he will desire his words to be taken in a different sense from their literal meaning' (*Inst.* 9.43).

Paul, we are arguing, is not at all uncertain about the difficulties, and 11:18 should read, 'And I believe a certain report'. This is based on the meaning of the phrase μέρος τι in literary and nonliterary sources as well as its occurrence elsewhere in the New Testament; the use of μέρος as a noun in relation to τι and πιστεύω; its connection with Paul's explanation in the following sentence concerning the 'necessity' of divisions; and his previous discussion of the Corinthian Christians' behaviour earlier in his letter.

μέρος carries a wide range of meanings in the New Testament as it does elsewhere in literary and nonliterary sources.[62] For example, it can re-

58. S. J. Kistemaker, *1 Corinthians* (Grand Rapids: Baker, 1993), p. 387.

59. Theissen, 'Social Integration and Sacramental Activity: An Analysis of 1 Cor. 11:17-34,' *The Social Setting of Pauline Christianity*, p. 163.

60. E.-B. Allo, *Saint Paul: Première Epître aux Corinthiens*, 2nd ed. (Paris: LeCoffre, 1956), p. 270.

61. M. M. Mitchell, *Paul and the Rhetoric of Reconciliation: An Exegetical Investigation of the Language and Composition of 1 Corinthians* (Louisville: Westminster/John Knox, 1992), pp. 152-53 for evidence of this device.

62. See Liddell and Scott and Moulton and Milligan.

fer to 'the line of business' or 'trade' (τὸ μέρος) (Acts 19:27) or a faction or party — 'Paul perceived that the one party, τὸ ἓν μέρος, were Sadducees', Acts 23:6 (cf. *P.Flor.* 1.47, l. 17). Paul uses μέρος in the Corinthian correspondence as a noun to refer to 'a matter' — ἐν τούτῳ τῷ μέρει (2 Cor. 3:10); and again of the collection — ἐν τῷ μέρει τούτῳ (2 Cor. 9:3).[63] In *P.Ryl.* 127 (A.D. 29) the term also refers to a legal matter, 'Wherefore I request you to order the Archephodus of Euhemeria to inquire into the matter' (ἀναζητῆσαι ὑπὲρ τοῦ μέρος); cf. *BGU* 168, line 24 (second century A.D.). Menander also uses 'this matter' (τούτου τοῦ μέρους) to refer to a legal case which he had been discussing.[64]

In Luke 11:36 the exact phrase refers to 'having no part' dark (μὴ ἔχον μέρος τι) with reference to the body. In Acts 5:2 the identical phrase is again used, where it is translated as 'and they brought a certain part' (καὶ ἐνέγκας μέρος τι) and refers to money and the deception of Ananias and Sapphira in bringing only a portion of their gift. These are the only three occasions in the New Testament where μέρος is linked to τι, and it makes no sense to translate either Luke 11:36 or Acts 5:2 adverbially.

What, then, are the options for 1 Corinthians 11:18? Paul originally referred to a report concerning divisions which had been brought by 'those of Chloe's household'. As he had been 'informed' (ἐδηλώθη) of them (1:11), it would be reasonable to infer that in 11:18 he was making reference to the verbal report given to him. However, the sentence in 11:18 cannot be translated as 'I believe a certain party' (those of the household of Chloe) because πιστεύω would require the genitive, i.e., 'I believe [the report of] a certain party'. μέρος is in the accusative. πιστεύω followed by the accusative should be translated as 'I am convinced of'[65] 'a matter' or 'a report', which is one of the meanings of μέρος. If so translated, then it would refer to the report from members of Chloe's household to whom Paul has already made reference (1:10). The issue of divisions in which 'each one' (1:12) is declaring their loyalty exclusively to Paul or Peter or Apollos affected the way in which Christians related to each other in the meeting. When he discussed the use of spiritual gifts in church (12:25), Paul expressed his continuing concern that there should be no divisions.

The indefinite pronoun τι 'has an indefinite quantity that is never-

---

63. BAGD b.θ.
64. Menander, *Epitrepontis* 234; cf. 228, 230, where the reference is to a legal case.
65. BAGD 1.a.

theless not without importance',[66] and therefore the phrase μέρος τι should be translated as 'a certain matter' or 'a certain report'. New Testament Greek knows of the postpositional τι, as in Acts 5:2, 'and they brought a certain part' (καὶ ἐνέγκας μέρος τι). In addition to the above discussion, Paul goes on to explain that he is not surprised, 'For (γάρ) it is necessary that there should be divisions in your midst in order that (ἵνα) the genuine may be manifested' (11:19).

Far from being uncertain, as some translations and commentators have suggested, Paul is convinced of the truth of the report, which must have included information on both the nature of the divisions mentioned in 1:12 and the conduct of Christians at the Lord's Dinner.

66. BAGD 2.c cites 1 Cor. 16:7 and compares it with 11:18. The indefinite can be placed either before in Acts 3:2 or after the noun; cf. *SIG* 976, l. 15 and 1240, l. 8.

CHAPTER 8

Religious Curses and Christian Vindictiveness (1 Corinthians 12–14)

'You Were Led Away to Dumb Idols . . .' (12:2)

Some twenty-seven ancient curse tablets, made of lead and known as ἀραί inscriptions, have been unearthed in recent years in Corinth and its environs. Fourteen were found on the slopes of the Acrocorinth in the precincts of the temple of Demeter and Persephone where such curse tablets were traditionally buried by worshippers;[1] three were located in the Apsidal building;[2] another at the east end of the Gymnasium South Stoa;[3] four in the underground bath complex known as 'the Fountain of the Lamps';[4] three in tombs excavated near the National Highway north of Corinth;[5] two

---

1. For a discussion see R. S. Stroud, 'The Sanctuary of Demeter on Acrocorinth in the Roman Period,' in T. E. Gregory, ed., *The* Corinthia *in the Roman Period,* Journal of Roman Archaeology, Supp. No. 8 (Ann Arbor: University of Michigan, 1995), p. 72; also N. Bookidis and R. S. Stroud, *Demeter and Persophone in Ancient Corinth* (Meriden: Meriden-Stinehouse Press, 1987). I am extremely grateful to Professor Ronald S. Stroud, Department of Classics, University of California, Berkeley, who has so kindly given me access to his edition of the curse tablets prior to their publication and also the permission to reproduce his reconstructions of these texts in this essay. Except for the curse against athletes and a larger text (see n. 7), all other curse inscriptions on Corinth apart from the Demeter collection are awaiting publication by Dr. D. R. Jordan.

2. J. Wiseman, 'The Gymnasium Area 1967-68,' *Hesperia* 38 (1969): 70.

3. J. Wiseman, 'The Gymnasium Area 1967-68,' *Hesperia* 38 (1969): 70, n. 10.

4. J. Wiseman, 'The Gymnasium Area of Corinth, 1969-70,' *Hesperia* 41 (1972): 33.

5. D. R. Jordan, 'A Survey of Greek *Defixiones* Not Included in the Special *Corpora,*' *GRBS* 26 (1985): 167.

in the Sacred Glen in Isthmia;[6] one from a well west of the Sanctuary of Poseidon;[7] and a substantial tablet of about twenty-two lines east of the theatre.[8] All await publication.[9] They are but a small part of a large body of extant evidence of the widespread custom of invoking a deity in pagan
religion to grant a curse against an adversary in the Graeco-Roman world.

There were at least four areas of life where religious curses were used
— (i) rivalry in sport; (ii) love; (iii) *politeia* including litigation; and
(iv) the world of commerce.[10] An examination of the evidence shows the
cultic and literary conventions observed in this prominent and characteristic activity of pagan religion which was used to bring divine curses upon
rivals and hopefully to overthrow them.[11]

Could this evidence, and the practice it represents, cast some light on
the enigmatic statement '*anathema* Jesus' (12:3)? This statement has given
rise to a variety of possible explanations by New Testament scholars, most
of which fail to satisfy.[12] That a person in the Christian gathering would

6. O. Broneer, *Isthmia*, II (Princeton: American School of Classical Studies in Athens,
1973), 115.

7. See D. R. Jordan, 'Inscribed Lead Tablets from the Games in the Sanctuary of Poseidon,' *Hesperia* 63 (1994): 111-26. Of the five tablets, four are ballots and one is a curse
against other athletes in a race.

8. *SEG* 37 (1987), no. 268 (3rd-4th century A.D.), which indicates that it 'invokes
Hekate, Persephone, and the chthonic gods in general to punish some wrong-doer, whose
bodily parts are listed from head to toe' (p. 88).

9. In the extant Corinthian curse inscriptions we have one Latin text, Stroud, No. 12.
Latin curse formulae are known to have been derived from the Greek. J. H. W. G.
Liebeschuetz, *Continuity and Change in Roman Religion* (Oxford: Clarendon Press, 1979),
p. 138.

10. See D. R. Jordan, '*Defixiones* from a Well near the Southwest Corner of the Athenian Agora,' *Hesperia* 54 (1985): 205-55 for texts dealing with wrestling (nos. 1-5), athletics
(no. 6), lovers (nos. 7-9). On curses which influence the outcome of litigation and business,
see *SEG* 37 (1987), nos. 219, 224, 681.

11. For the most recent discussion see C. A. Faraone, 'The Agonistic Context of Early
Greek Binding Spells'; H. S. Versnel, 'Beyond Cursing: The Appeal to Justice in Judicial
Prayers'; and J. J. Winkler, 'The Constraints of Eros,' in C. A. Faraone and D. Obbink, eds.,
Magika Hiera: Ancient Greek Magic and Religion (Oxford: Oxford University Press, 1991),
chs. 1, 3, and 8 respectively.

12. See D. A. Carson, *Showing the Spirit: A Theological Exposition of 1 Corinthians 12–
14* (Grand Rapids: Baker, 1987), pp. 27-30 for a summary of positions. For some, the solution has been to abandon the search for a plausible explanation. Carson himself suggests, 'if
Paul's interest lies rather in establishing who truly has the Holy Spirit, then the pressure to
identify a precise and believable background is reduced' (p. 31).

actually say 'Jesus [is] a curse' or 'Curse Jesus' has had to be explained as an ecstatic utterance, because no Christian person in his or her right mind would actually make such a statement in the presence of the Christian congregation. While Witherington makes reference to the curse inscriptions found in the temple of Demeter and Persephone as he explores the options, he dismisses any parallel because 'all [worshippers] direct curses against particular people who lived in Corinth'. He, like other commentators, assumes that it is Jesus who is being cursed.[13] Is that assumption correct, or was Jesus seen as a God who could be invoked to deliver a curse against particular persons in Corinth, and, if so, why?

The purpose of this chapter, then, is to suggest that the Corinthian curse tablets, along with those found elsewhere, throw important light on the text (12:3a). Paul's comments also describe a major aspect of first-century religion which he summarises in 12:2 and which shows the influence of pagan thinking on the religious perceptions of the Corinthian Christians, thus demonstrating the thesis of this book.

In order to do this it is proposed (I) to examine the widespread use of curses in pagan religion in order to harm one's adversaries and in which the name of a god was invoked on leaden curse tablets placed in temples; (II) to record the use by subsequent generations of Christians of the 'name' of God, Jesus, or the Trinity when they invoked curses for the purpose of retaliating against others; (III) to suggest that, in the light of the genre of the curse tablets, 'Jesus' is the subject, for it is he who grants the 'anathema', thus making sense of the immediate and overall context of chapters 12–14 where the purpose of the gatherings should have been not to diminish others, but rather 'to edify, comfort and console' (14:3); and (IV) to argue that the Corinthian Christians operated in much the same way as their fellow citizens did.

---

13. B. Witherington III, *Conflict and Community: A Socio-Rhetorical Commentary on 1 and 2 Corinthians* (Grand Rapids and Carlisle: Eerdmans and Paternoster, 1995), p. 256, n. 9.

I. Pagan Religion and Cursing

(a) Paganism and Cursing

While most popular perceptions of classical religion have been coloured by aesthetically pleasing statues of gods and goddesses, and the neoclassical revival epitomised in Keats' 'Ode to a Grecian Urn', an underbelly of first-century cultic activity reveals a very different picture.[14] One feature which stands out is the powerful hold over the pagan mind of cursing others and being cursed. The procedure involved writing the text on lead and either defacing the tablet or driving a nail through it while cursing the opponent. It was then buried in the ground, placed in a well, bath, fountain, or in the temple of Demeter and Persephone.[15] These actions were accompanied by the verbal imprecations where the god or goddess was called upon to curse an adversary. It was a widespread phenomenon, with over a thousand examples having already come to light.[16]

The gods invoked belonged to the dominion of death or the underworld. Demeter was the goddess of the earth who came to be associated with the depths of the earth, while Persophone/Kore, her daughter, was the wife of the god of death. In the order of frequency of invocation, Persophone/Kore is ranked only behind Hermes, and Demeter comes behind Hecate, Hades/Pluto, and Ge.[17]

---

14. See D. W. J. Gill, 'Behind the Classical Facade: Local Religions of the Roman Empire,' in A. D. Clarke and B. W. Winter, eds., *One God, One Lord: Christianity in a World of Religious Pluralism*, 2nd ed. (Carlisle: Paternoster; Grand Rapids: Baker, 1993), ch. 4 for the shattering of this myth.

15. For a list of locations of the temples of Demeter and Kore in which they have been found see D. R. Jordan, 'Two Inscribed Lead Tablets from a Well in the Athenian Kerameikos,' *Ath. Mitt.* 95 (1980): 231, n. 23.

16. Jordan, '*Defixiones* from a Well near the Southwest Corner of the Athenian Agora,' p. 207. For a list see Jordan, 'A Survey of Greek *Defixiones* Not Included in the Special Corpora,' pp. 151-97.

17. Versnel, 'Beyond Cursing: The Appeal to Justice in Judicial Prayers,' p. 64.

(b) Curse Tablets in Corinth and Isthmia

Recent finds of curse tablets in Corinth provide evidence that what was true of other cities also applied in Roman Corinth.[18] The use of curses in the name of the gods was an accepted religious convention. It was used when a person could not 'control' a situation and resorted to divine help to gain personal advantages over adversaries. The following examples from Roman Corinth support this.

Side A of an Isthmian curse against other competitors has sketches of four men with the imperative 'control' (κάτεχε) written across their chests, a verb frequently used elsewhere. The writing on side A has been largely obliterated, but the following words are discernible — 'May they not prevail in running Friday but (?) indeed . . .' (μὴ ἰσχύσοισαν δραμεῖν προσάββατον ἀ<λ>ὰ (?) καί). Side B has a wedge with magical letters on it.[19]

One of the interesting features of the tablets found in the temple of Demeter and Persephone in Corinth is the absence of the verb in three of the fourteen curses. Two identical texts do not contain any verb. They read, 'Maxima Pontia, for destruction' (Μαξίμαν Ποντίαν ἐπὶ [κατ]εργασίᾳ).[20] In addition, there is a particularly interesting lead tablet where a verb is to be assumed. Side A of the text reads, 'I entrust and consign Karpime Ballia, weaver of garlands, to the Fates who exact justice, so that they expose her acts of insolence, to Hermes of the Underworld, to Earth, to the children of Earth . . . Hermes of the Underworld [grant] heavy curses' ('Ερμῆ χθόνιε τὰ μεγάλα).[21]

On Side B, the same devotee also seeks fertility for herself and invokes the 'names' both to accomplish this and, at the same time, to destroy her enemy, Karpime Babbia, who may be a rival lover. It reads, 'The names of Ανανκε, Βεβεζαπαδαιεισεν[.] γειβεβεοαερα, make me fertile. The mighty name (τὸ μέγα ὄν[ο]μα) the one carrying compulsion,

18. For the report and description see N. Bookidis, 'The Sanctuary of Demeter and Kore on Acrocorinth: Preliminary Report IV,' *Hesperia* 41 (1972): 304; and R. S. Stroud, 'Curses from Corinth,' *AJA* 77 (1973): 228.

19. Jordan, 'Inscribed Lead Tablets from the Games in the Sanctuary of Poseidon,' pp. 116-25.

20. Stroud, nos. 1 and 4, where a verb such as παραδίδωμι might be used.

21. Vacat. 0.05 m. (no. 1, l. 8), Bookidis and Stroud, *Demeter and Persephone in Ancient Corinth*, p. 30, for the translation of one side of a curse tablet.

which is not named recklessly unless in dire necessity. Come then, mighty name (μέγα ὄν[ο]μα), make me fertile and destroy Kerpime Babbia, weaver of garlands, from her head to her footsteps with lasting destruction' (ll. 10-17).

Because the two curses involve the same person, Stroud, after the publication of Side A,[22] now tentatively suggests that the texts of the two curses be joined together to read, 'I pray to you, Hermes of the Underworld, [that] the mighty names Ανανκε, Βεβεζαπαδαιεισεν[.] γειβεβεο-αερα make me fertile' (ll. 9-11). His reason for joining together τὰ μεγάλα and ignoring the space of 0.05 metres which ends the first tablet is that Side B begins with ὀνόματα τῆς Ἀνανάκης . . . , and later in the text τὸ μέγα ὄν[υ]μα is followed by κ<αρ>πίσαι με (l. 14). His linking of the two texts has some grammatical justification in that prayers of entreaty are followed by the aorist imperative, and this one reads 'fertilise me'. However, this makes the text disjointed. If Hermes of the Underworld was alone being invoked to make the petitioner pregnant, then Stroud's subsequent suggestion would make sense. The subjects of the verb 'fertilise me' are the names Ανανκε, Βεβεζαπ-αδαιεισεν[.] γειβεβεοερας. Two lead inscriptions numbered by Stroud as 8A and B follow the same pattern, so that the use of both sides of the tablet for the cursing of Karpime Ballia is not unusual, nor is the use of separate sentences on each side.[23] In the first it is the destruction of the Babbia that is sought, while in the second fertility for the petitioner and destruction of her adversary are both implored. There are also two categories of curse inscriptions — one specifies the punishments that await the guilty person and the other does not. They are both represented in the two curses on the same tablet, one on each side of it. Strubbe classifies the first as 'non-specific' and the other as 'specific'.[24] The latter is presented on Side B and the former on Side A in this, and there the verb is assumed.

The extant Corinthian inscriptions which have been examined in this section show that the gods were invoked to curse a person. The form of the curse does not necessarily require a verb to be written and therefore provides a possible precedent for 1 Corinthians 12:3a.

22. See n. 21.
23. A. Audollent, *Defixionum Tabellae* (Paris, 1904), no. 7 (Caria).
24. J. H. M. Strubbe, "'Cursed be he that moves my bones,'" *Magika Hiera*, p. 33.

II. Christian Curses in the Post-apostolic Church

R. K. Ritner noted that 'unfortunately for scholarly preference and popular sentiment, however, ritual cursing has been shown to occupy a prominent position within all official ancient Near Eastern religious traditions.'[25] But while there is evidence that curses were widespread, is there any evidence that subsequent generations of Christians engaged in the use of curses against those who had offended them or constituted some threat to them or their loved ones? As we shall see, there is ample evidence that the early Christians in Egypt engaged in such practices, as did some in Corinth in subsequent generations.

a. Coptic Christian Texts

A recently published set of Christian Coptic texts demonstrates that they did not shake off the cultural convention of pagans. Not only are enemies cursed, but even the person who opened a grave was liable for a divine curse. While the circumstances that gave rise to such anger are not revealed, the petitioner believed that God, the Lord Sabbaoth, the God of heaven and earth, will 'perform my judgement against all those who oppose me'. He calls upon God 'to bring down' not only the man but also his son, David, and 'render him friendless, in prison, like a bronze chain, as I produce the trusty words.' This document is, in fact, a counter-curse, for he is responding to those who had sought to curse him.

> Any person, every one, who adjures bad things upon me and every one who calls my name evil, and those who curse me . . . God will perform my judgement against them all. . . . you shall bring all of them down. . . . The cherubim, the seraphim, the ten thousand angels and archangels shall appeal to the God of heaven and earth and he shall perform my judgement against everyone who opposes me. Any one who curses me, you must bring down and abandon him to demons. Yes true, beloved saviour.[26]

25. R. K. Ritner, 'Curses,' in M. Meyer and R. Smith, eds., *Ancient Christian Magic: Coptic Texts of Ritual Power* (San Francisco: Harper, 1994), p. 183. For later Jewish evidence see J. Naveh and S. Shaked, *Magic Spells and Formulae: Aramaic Incantations in Late Antiquity* (Jerusalem: Magnes Press, 1993).
26. Ritner, 'Curses,' no. 88.

He does not end there, but calls upon God to do his bidding in bringing down all the sufferings of Job and to abandon his enemies to the demons, whom he likens to those who said, 'His blood is upon us for three generations'.

Another document contains a widow's curse, in which the Trinity is invoked. 'Bring judgement on our behalf, quickly'.[27] In yet another curse against a number of violent people the petitioner says, 'Lord, my God . . . 'You must strike. . . . You must hinder. . . . You must bring upon them the anger of your wrath. . . . You must curse the one who has committed this act of violence. . . . You must quickly overthrow. . . . Yes, Lord Sabbaoth, you must bring judgement on his behalf, quickly'.[28]

Elsewhere the Father, Son, and Holy Spirit, the God of Abraham, Isaac, and Jacob, together with the four creatures around the throne and the twenty-four elders, are all party to the demand to 'strike' a number of people and their children in a petition that ends with the sign of the cross against 'Jesus Christ'.[29]

There are forensic curses against perjurers and litigants where Christians are involved in civil actions. In the case of the latter, the Lord God and Jesus (who is described as 'the voice that was raised upon the cross, until the seven unbroken seals were undone through him'; cf. Rev. 5:1-4) are invoked to make the opponent tongue-tied in court.[30]

A mother delivered a very strong curse against a young lady who had captured the affections of her son and who clearly had failed to please her prospective mother-in-law. The unfortunate young lady would not be heard by God, be without hope in this world, childless, demon-possessed, ill, feverish, a 'chill and numbness of heart and an itching' together with continual menstrual problems and die. The aggrieved mother's petition sought that this 'judgement [be] performed quickly' by the God who sits on the chariot, with the cherubim, the chief archangel, the twenty-four elders, and four creatures who support His throne. All this is done 'through the power of these names'.[31]

Other texts touch on requests to bring sickness; one seeks prosperity

27. Ritner, 'Curses,' no. 89.
28. Ritner, 'Curses,' no. 90.
29. Ritner, 'Curses,' no. 91.
30. Ritner, 'Curses,' nos. 92, 94.
31. Ritner, 'Curses,' nos. 92, 93.

in business, and another in litigation.[32] Vindictiveness is sought; especially evident is one instance where Mary's curse against Martha ends, 'My Lord Jesus Christ, you must bring her down to an end. Yes, Jesus Christ, you must dissipate her hope so that no one desires to assist her'.[33]

Could it be argued that these petitioners were marginal Christians with little or no understanding of the Christian faith? It is obvious that these petitioners are not ignorant of biblical history as they cite characters from the Old and New Testaments as well as incidents of God's judgement or deliverance. Some show a substantial understanding of Christian theology with references to the 'consubstantial Trinity'.[34]

b. Anatolian Christian Grave Curses[35]

An interesting set of inscriptions from Anatolia (the majority of which come from Phrygia and Bithynia) covering A.D. 250-350 provides additional information on the use of curses by Christians. In form and content they are derived from pagan and Jewish grave curses in the region, and they are concerned with the disturbing of burial sites. A sarcophagus from Termessos reads, 'no other is it allowable to bury someone [here]. For that, the perpetrator will pay to Zeus Solymos 2,000 denarii also he will reckon with the dead' (1.16; *Tam* 3.1, 813). A Jewish inscription reads, 'I want no other to dismantle it. Otherwise, he will answer to the judgement [of God] and pay 1,000 denarii to the synagogue, and 500 to the [city?] treasury' (1.20; *Tam* 4.1, 376). Another Jewish inscription invokes 'the curses which have been written in Deuteronomy' (Akmonia 1.23, *MAMA* 6, 335a). In a Christian inscription, 'If anyone should try to inter another he will pay to the imperial fiscus 2,500 denarii, and more important than that he will reckon with God' (3.3). Another states that in the event of the grave being disturbed 'he will give account to God and be cursed. Come Lord' (ἀνάθεμα ἤτω μαράνα θάν, 4.1). The editor has noted that the wording comes in part from 1 Corinthians 16:22.

32. Ritner, 'Curses,' nos. 96, 106, 109.
33. Ritner, 'Curses,' no. 100.
34. Ritner, 'Curses,' no. 88.
35. On their use in Asia Minor see G. J. Johnson, *Early Christian Epitaphs from Anatolia* (Atlanta: Scholars Press, 1995).

c. Corinthian Christian Grave Curses

Lest it be thought that a later generation of Christians in Corinth escaped this pagan practice, their grave inscriptions in the late Roman and early Byzantine periods (A.D. 267-668) show that they operated no differently[36] but followed a widespread pagan practice.[37] Threats were issued against any disturbance of grave sites and, in some instances, attempts were made to protect them by invoking either God's judgement or a divine curse.

No. 539 warns against opening the grave and thereby 'involve themselves in penalties', and no. 620 decrees, 'If [anyone] infringes the property of the owners, or (opens the sepulchre), let him be (ἐχέτω) punished as a traitor'. Another specifies, 'If anyone should dare to open without my consent this burial place which I bought from [————] I swear before God [by the eternal judgement] of God [————]' (no. 643). A divine curse is specifically invoked in no. 644 — 'A sepulchre belonging to Makedonia, who has become (a woman) of blessed memory. If anyone tries to open it without the consent of its owners, may the curse of Annas and Kaiaphas be upon him' (ἔστω αὐτῷ τὸ ἀθνάθεμα Ἄννα καὶ Καιάφα). Annas and Caiaphas, who were two chief instigators of the execution of Jesus, were represented in iconography as permanent dwellers in Hell.[38] A gravestone of a mother and her three offspring also pronounces a curse (ἀνάθεμα) on any who disturbs the grave.[39] Judas's punishment is apparently invoked in another — 'If anyone except for my (kinsmen) dares in future [to open this (sepulchre), let him have the] punishment [of Judas]' (no. 660).[40] One of the most vigorous states that 'if they have children, may they bury them, if they have nurslings may they be bereft, and they experience the mercy of God from nobody. May Satan enter their house and utterly destroy them'.[41]

---

36. See Kent, *Corinth*, 8.3, nos. 522-685 for inscriptions on Christian tombs.

37. For discussion see Strubbe, '"Cursed be he that moves my bones,"' ch. 2.

38. Kent, *Corinth*, 8.3, no. 644.

39. *SEG* 37 (1987) no. 195, ll. 6-7. On the variant in spelling see n. 54.

40. For a discussion of the use of the Judas curse see B. McLean, 'A Christian Epitaph: The Curse of Judas Iscariot,' *Orientalia Christiana Periodica* 58 (1992): 241-44; and P. W. van der Horst, 'A Note on the Judas Curse in Early Christian Inscriptions,' *Hellenism-Judaism-Christianity: Essays on Their Interaction* (Kampen: Kok, 1994), ch. 10.

41. Merritt, *Corinth*, 8.1, no. 137.

III. Paganism and the Curse in 12:3a

(a) Paul's Description of Paganism

While later Corinthian Christian curses do not prove that this is what happened in Corinth when Paul was there, they leave open that possibility. Paul begins with a very succinct statement about pagan religion — 'You know that, when you were heathen, you were led away to dumb idols as you would be led' (ὅτι ἔθνη ἦτε πρὸς τὰ εἴδωλα τὸ ἄφωνα ὡς ἂν ἤγεσθε ἀπαγόμενοι) (12:2). As Kistemaker observes, the verb is in the imperfect and indicates that there were repeated occurrences, hence the translation 'as you would be led'.[42]

Paige suggests that 'the leading' had to do with a cultic procession in which the devotees were preceded by priests, and that Paul is saying that they were really being carried away captive in a way which they did not understand, i.e., by the power of the gods.[43] There were, of course, religious processions in Roman cities.[44] Paige's proposal does not resolve the relationship of verse 2 with the following verse. It is connected by 'therefore' (διό), and verse 3 should be seen as having some relationship with their conduct.[45] In some way 12.2 epitomises popular pagan activity, while the beginning of the next verse establishes the aspect of paganism to which he refers.

(b) 'Jesus [Is] a Curse' or 'Jesus [Grants] a Curse'?

In the light of the presence of religious curses in the ancient world, the Corinthian evidence of curse tablets, the behaviour of Corinthian Christians in later centuries, and the evidence from Christian Copts, there is every justification in asking if it makes sense to translate this sentence without a

42. S. J. Kistemaker, *Exposition of the First Epistle to the Corinthians* (Grand Rapids: Baker, 1993), pp. 413, 416. ἦτε . . . ἀπαγόμενοι is a periphrastic construction, while ὡς ἂν ἤγεσθε is a imperfect indicative with the particle implying 'as you would be led'.

43. T. Paige, '1 Corinthians 12.2: A Pagan *Pompe*,' *JSNT* 44 (1991): 57-65.

44. E.g., Ephesus; G. M. Rogers, 'The Procession of Statues,' *The Sacred Identity of Ephesos: Foundation Myths of a Roman City* (London: Routledge, 1991), ch. 3.

45. *Contra* Carson, *Showing the Spirit*, p. 27, who suggests that verse 2 on pagan religion should be taken with verse 1 and 'therefore' is a resumptive.

verb with 'Jesus' as the subject and 'a curse' as the object. There has been no hesitation on the part of translators to render ΚΥΡΙΟΣ ΙΗΣΟΥΣ as 'Jesus [is] Lord' (12:3b), yet when it comes to 12:3a, ΑΝΑΘΕΜΑ ΙΗΣΟΥΣ, the usual translation is 'curse Jesus', implying that it is Jesus who is being cursed by some Christians.

Regarding the absence of the verb, it has been observed that in early evidence curse formulae may 'consist solely of lists of names, [which] strongly suggests that a verb of binding was uttered aloud sometime during the ritual', especially with the perforation of distortion of the lead tablet. In later developments verbs might be used,[46] but there are still examples of their absence.[47] In tomb curses the verb was also deleted — '[I adjure] you by the god' (τὸν θεόν σοι) — which was adopted in its abbreviated form later but not exclusively by pagans.[48] So the absence of a verb in 12:3 is not without precedent even among Corinthian pagan curse tablets.

When the LXX introduced each one of the covenant curses of Deuteronomy 27:15-20, it did so without a verb, using rather the noun ἐπικατάρατος to render the Hebrew 'cursed be he . . . '. As is the case in many aspects of this Greek version, its choice of literary conventions etc. can be explained on the basis of contemporary usage in Egypt.[49] It is of interest to note that none of the extant Jewish inscriptions against those who violated graves in Asia Minor uses the term *anathema*.[50]

An important first- or second-century-A.D. Greek curse inscription was found in the nineteenth century at Megara, which is located between Athens and Corinth.[51] The curse is clearly a pagan one which invokes

46. Faraone, 'The Agonistic Context of Early Greek Binding Spells,' p. 5. See also his list of binding verbs, prayer formulae, etc. (p. 5).

47. Faraone, 'The Agonistic Context of Early Greek Binding Spells' (p. 5).

48. Strubbe, '"Cursed be he that moves my bones"' (p. 35).

49. See J. A. L. Lee, *A Lexical Study of the Septuagint Version of the Pentateuch*, Septuagint and Cognate Studies 14 (Chico: Scholars Press, 1983); and R. K. Ritner, *The Mechanics of Ancient Magical Practice*, Studies in Ancient Oriental Civilization 54 (Chicago: Oriental Institute of the University of Chicago, 1993).

50. See J. H. M. Strubbe, 'Curses against Violation of the Grave in Jewish Epitaphs of Asia Minor,' in J. W. van Henten and P. W. van der Horst, eds., *Studies in Early Jewish Epigraphy* (Leiden: E. J. Brill, 1994), pp. 106-27, where terms such as 'the curses, αἱ ἀραί, that are written in Deuteronomy', 'the law of the Jews', 'the judgement of God', 'eternal scourge from the immortal God', and 'the sickle of curse' are found.

51. A. Audollent, *Defixionum Tabellae* (Paris, 1904), no. 41.

Persephone, Hecate, and Selene.[52] Side A, line 4, has 'we curse' (κατα-γράφομεν), and a synonym is used in lines 5-6, 'we curse them' (ἀναθε-ματίζομεν αὐτούς), and again in lines 8-9, 'we curse the people' (τουτοὺς ἀναθεματίζομεν).[53] He curses every part of the body on side A and on side B indicates that the reason for the curse relates to a false accusation of his not having paid a debt and the infringement of his rights. Before the curse concludes on side B it prefaces the final imprecation with 'we curse for punishment and retaliation and revenge [κατα]γρα[φ]όμεν [εἰς] κο-λάσε[ις . . .] καὶ [τι]μ[ωρ]ί[αν]' (ll. 10-12). Then, on a single line, spaced off and in large lettering compared with the rest of the curse inscription, it has the single word, ΑΝΑΘΗΜΑ.[54] It stands alone without any verb, and is translated 'a curse'.

If, then, the copula is assumed, as translators do in the statement, κύριος Ἰησοῦς in 12:3b, it means that the preceding words could be translated 'Jesus is a curse'. If the LXX convention is a guide, then the text could be rendered 'Jesus curse' (cf. 1 Cor. 16:22). If, in the case of the curse tablet against Karpime Babbia, Ἑρμῆ χθόνιε τὰ μεγάλα is translated following the literary convention of not providing a verb as in the Corinthian tablet, 'Hermes of the Underworld [grant] a curse', then it would not be unreasonable to render ΑΝΑΘΕΜΑ ΙΗΣΟΥΣ as 'Jesus [grants or gives] a curse'. Paul would not have needed to insert the verb given the strong precedent for its absence.

---

52. Any attempt to attribute Jewish influences to it were refuted by A. Deissmann, *Light from the Ancient East* (E.T. London; Hodder & Stoughton, 1927), in 1909. *Light from the Ancient East*, pp. 95-96, *contra* Versnel, 'Beyond Cursing: The Appeal to Justice in Judicial Prayers', p. 65.

53. Deissmann, *Light from the Ancient East*, p. 95 suggests ἀναθεματίζομεν τουτοὺς on side B, ll. 8-9, along with the orginal editor while ἐνωνπα[ρατίτ]ομεν τουτο[ύς] is the rendering of Audollent, *Defixionum Tabellae*, p. 76.

54. For reasons for the variation in the vowels see Audollent, *Defixionum Tabellae*, p. 77, and for a summary of the discussion Moulton and Milligan, p. 33. A Christian grave-stone in Corinth has ἀνάθεμα; *SEG* 37 (1987), no. 195, ll. 6-7. As Liddell and Scott indicate, the term ἀνάθημα was derived from the cognate ἀνατίθημι. In its philological development it acquired the verbal form of ἀναθεματίζω. For examples of the former verb in curse inscriptions from Caria see Audollent, *Defixionum Tabellae*, nos. 4 A, l. 1; B, l. 10; 7, A, l. 1; 13, l. 1.

(c) Textual Variants

The suggested translation would be possible if Ἰησοῦς was a secure reading. It needs to be remembered that an error can easily be made in the writing of the *Nomina Sacra* because only three letters were used.[55] Two textual variants should be explored. If it read Ἰησοῦ, then it could be either a vocative, dative, or genitive. The vocative would mean that the sentence should be translated 'O Jesus, [grant] a curse', while the dative would read 'let a curse be on Jesus'. In the case of the genitive it would read 'let a curse of Jesus be [on X]', but support for this reading is not strong.[56]

The textual support for Ἰησοῦν is good and has been read as 'call Jesus a curse' because verbs which 'designate as' or 'call' are followed by a double accusative.[57] The best textual evidence supports the nominative and can be translated as 'Jesus is anathema' (RV), or, as is being suggested here, 'Jesus [grants or gives] an anathema'.[58] Both the evidence and the reason for the absence of a verb in some curse inscriptions have already been noted and the latter rendering is preferred.[59]

For those whose translation of ΚΥΡΙΟΣ ΙΗΣΟΥΣ and ΑΝΑΘΕΜΑ ΙΗΣΟΥΣ is determined by a parallelism between the two statements, it is interesting to note that P[46] and other witnesses do not have an exact parallel in 12:3, for there in v. 3a 'Jesus' is in the accusative and in v. 3b in the nominative. This suggests that no exact parallel was deemed essential in those texts — an argument against translating v. 3a and v. 3b in exactly the same way. It is suggested that a good case can be made for a translation determined by what is known of the literary genre of curse tablets and not by an argument based on what we judge to be parallelism.

(d) Jesus Grants Curses — The Theological Connection

Why would some Christians have thought it appropriate to invoke the name of Jesus, when subsequent generations of Christians in Egypt used

55. See C. H. Roberts, 'Nomina Sacra: Origins and Significance', *Manuscript, Society and Belief in Early Christian Egypt* (London: The British Academy, 1979), ch. 2.
56. See F 629 *pc* lat.
57. P[46] D G. BAGD #157 (2); cf. Mark 10:18, τί με λέγεις ἀγαθόν.
58. A B C 6. 33. 81.
59. See p. 168.

'divine' names? The Corinthian curse tablets contain references to the 'Lord gods of the underworld' (κύριοι θεοὶ κ[α]ταχθόνιοι) (no. 8A), and also 'Lord, expose them. Gods of the underworld, Gods' (κύριε φανέρωσαν αὐτούς. θεοὺς καταχθονίους. θεοῖ) (no. 8B). It would not have been diffi-cult for a former pagan to draw the conclusion that Jesus, who had con-quered the underworld in his death and resurrection, could substitute for the gods, especially Hermes of the underworld whose particular domain they had once believed was his.[60] The editor of the Christian Coptic texts has drawn attention to the fact that 'the voice calling from the cross refers to the powerful words of the crucified Jesus that are cited frequently in texts of ritual power, and the seven seals may be considered undone through the death and descent of Jesus into the underworld'.[61]

This supports the view that the Christianisation of Hermes of the Underworld was in the minds of some converts who saw that now his tasks were performed by Jesus. Christians could confidently invoke him in order to see the fulfillment of their curses. In addition, Paul had already made reference to what was seen as a credal statement applied to the eat-ing of idol food in the pagan temple. It was that 'for us . . . there is only one Lord, Jesus Christ, through whom are all things, and we exist through him' (8:6).[62] The invocation of Jesus 'through whom are all things' is ex-plicable.

If this interpretation is accepted, what does it tell us about the Co-rinthian Christians who did this? It suggests that, like their successors in late Roman Corinth and Coptic Egypt, they invoked the second person of the Godhead, Jesus, to curse others for the purpose of punishing or disadvantaging rivals. They appeared to have behaved no better than their pagan counterparts, or subsequent generations in Corinth or Cop-tic Egypt.

If the translation 'Jesus [gives] a curse' or 'Jesus [grants] a curse' is correct, then how does it throw light on the immediate context? No 'spiri-tual person' speaking by the Spirit of God can say that 'Jesus grants a curse', as one would have believed formerly that a pagan god could do, anymore

60. In no. 13 A Herakleides is invoked — 'I bind Secunda Postumia to Herakleides, to all men, her mind, her wits, her hands, her knees, the entire body I bind Postumia Secunda to all men'.

61. Ritner, 'Curses,' p. 198.

62. See my 'Ethical and Theological Responses to Religious Pluralism in Corinth: 1 Corinthians 8–10,' 219-22.

than it is possible to make the basic Christian confession that Jesus is Lord, except by the Spirit. It is interesting that Paul uses the verb δύναται, i.e., 'has the power', with respect to the latter statement. The issue of curses implied the possession of power on the part of the deity and the capacity or power of the speaker to invoke the deity to curse another.

A possible parallel to this verse exists in the incident where the traditional adversaries of the Jews, the Samaritans, refused the ministry of Jesus and the disciples inquired whether it was appropriate to invoke a curse upon them by calling down fire from heaven — 'Lord, do you wish we ask (κύριε θέλεις εἴπωμεν) to call down fire from heaven in the tradition of Elijah'? It was greeted with a rebuke to which was added in the variant reading, 'and he said, "You do not know of what manner of spirit you are (οἵου πνεύματος ἐστέ)"' (Luke 9:54-55).

There are two more examples of cursing, both of which Paul uses. In the midst of the concluding greetings to the Corinthians he states, 'If anyone does not love the Lord, let him be anathema (ἤτω ἀνάθεμα)' (16:22), invoking a 'Deuteronomic' curse. In Galatians 1:8-9 he also invokes curses on those who preach another gospel, even if the proclamation was being made by an angel from heaven. What then is the difference between Paul's imprecations and those of the Corinthians? Traditional interpretations of 1 Corinthians 12:3 say that in the case of the latter some Christians were actually cursing Jesus. The thrust of this chapter is that some Christians were invoking Jesus to punish, restrain, or disadvantage others. Paul, by contrast, reminded them that those who did not love the Lord their God, and introduced an alternative gospel, could not expect the grace of the Lord Jesus (16:23). Does this understanding of 12:3 provide a backdrop for the subsequent discussion?

(e) Jesus Grants a Curse and the Wider Context

Paul proceeded to argue that while there are diversities of gifts, service, and work, they derive from the same Spirit, the same Lord, and the same God (12:4-6). He added that 'the same God is at work in every way in all [men]' (τὰ πάντα ἐν πᾶσιν) (12:6b). There is, therefore, a consistency in the way the Godhead works.

In the following section he indicates precisely what the Spirit does, implying that those who are invoking the name of Jesus to disadvantage others cannot be speaking 'in the Spirit'. He indicates the purpose of the work of the Spirit — 'to each one has been given the revelation of the Spirit for the welfare [of others]' (πρὸς τὸ συμφέρον) (12:7). Gifts are given to secure the welfare or the blessing of others and not for their disadvantage. The following verses explain this further: 'For to one is given through the Spirit the word of wisdom, and to another the word of knowledge according to the same Spirit, to another faith in the same Spirit, to another workings . . . and the one and the same Spirit works all these, dividing to each one severally as He wills' (12:8-11).

Not only does one Spirit give diversity of gifts, it is also true that there is only one body in Christ into which all were baptised and made to drink of one Spirit (12:12ff.). That unity of purpose with the diversity of gifts is essential for the unified functioning of the Christian community. In the overall context of chapters 12–14 the Godhead is the originator of the gifts by which they function together in the Christian meeting, for all are one; therefore some cannot withdraw their gifts because they are now limbs or essential bodily parts. God's intention is that there should be no schism in the body, but that the members should have the same care one for another (12:25). Such should be the relationship of Christians to one another that in both suffering and rejoicing all empathise because of the body of Christ and their part as limbs in it (12:26-7). Gifts must therefore be exercised in the context of love, and not malice (1 Cor. 13).

That which builds up, encourages, comforts, and consoles (14:3), and not that which diminishes others, must be emphasised in the gathering of God's people. The call to childlikeness in regard to wickedness perhaps becomes explicable in the light of the above (14:20). Certainly the demands that all must be done for building up (14:26), that all are to learn, and that all are to be encouraged by activities in the meeting draw attention to the differences between pagan and Christian practice. In the former individuality and self-centredness pursue personal advantage at the expense of others (and at times to their detriment). In contrast, all adherents to the Christian faith must seek the advantage of other members of the Christian community (14:31).

How does this interpretation fit into 1 Corinthians as a whole? We have already noted the circumstances in which pagans used curses — rivalry in sports, love, litigation, politics, and commerce. In 1 Corinthians there is definite evidence of rivalry and dissension among Christians over

Paul and other teachers (1:10–4:21, especially 4:6). An exploration of the precedent for this can readily be found in secular Corinth.[63] Vexatious litigation had been undertaken between Christians which had established their relative social status in either the congregation or in the wider social context of Corinth (6:1-8). The use of vexatious litigation for this purpose was a well-established secular convention.[64] Clearly, rivalry or divisiveness was evident in the Lord's Supper (11:18). Why should it stop there and not express itself in other gatherings, if it is assumed that 11:2-16, 11:17-34, and 12–14 relate to different services? What better way to deal with rivalry in the services (chs. 12–14), to which Paul alludes in 12:25, than to resort to invoking Jesus, who controls all things, to disadvantage one's rivals? They would have resorted to this device in their pre-Christian days, especially in the world of *politeia* which included the ἐκκλησία of the secular association and the citizens. Why not do so in the Christian ἐκκλησία? It was necessarily restricted to cursing Christians, but they could, as they would have done previously, curse non-Christians with whom they were in conflict or in situations of rivalry.

IV. Conclusions

This discussion suggests that the basic premise that there is no precedent for oracular imprecations in first-century Graeco-Roman religious activities is incorrect.[65] It also challenges the usual reconstruction that it was within the Christian meeting that there was an uncontrolled ecstatic utterance in which Jesus was actually cursed. Forbes' monograph shows that prophecy and glossolalia in the Christian community find no precedent in inspired utterances in Graeco-Roman religion.[66]

63. For discussion see Ch. 2 and more fully my *Philo and Paul among the Sophists.* Curses were invoked against public orators, as noted by Faraone, 'The Agonistic Context of Early Greek Binding Spells,' p. 16.

64. See Ch. 4.

65. E.g., G. D. Fee, *The First Epistle to the Corinthians* (Grand Rapids: Eerdmans, 1987), p. 580, n. 48 suggests that there is no evidence for such oracular imprecations from pagan antiquity (at least none is noted in Aune, *Prophecy*): '. . . there is no good reason to doubt that they could have occurred in the "inspired utterances" of pagan religion.'

66. C. Forbes, *Prophecy and Inspired Speech in Early Christianity and Its Hellenistic Environment,* WUNT 2.75 (Tübingen: J. C. B. Mohr, 1995). He states that he did not attempt 'a full explanation or exegesis of the "cursing of Jesus"' (p. 320).

Those who wish to argue that Paul in writing 12:3a was simply creating a hypothetical situation in order to contrast the Christian affirmation in 12:3b, need to explain the nexus between 12:2, which discusses an 'addictive' phenomenon of paganism ('as you would be led'), and the verse which is connected by διό. This chapter seeks to establish the nexus between pagan religion and the ancient phenomenon of cursing by investigating the literary form which was influenced by uttering the curse when the nail was plunged into the lead inscription.

The Christian faith with its unique use of vocabulary (such as 'build up' to describe the purpose of its religious gathering) was to be distinct from first-century paganism. Nothing could identify this distinction more clearly than, on the one hand, the religious phenomenon of 'pulling down' others by means of curses and, on the other hand, seeking the welfare of others through love. The latter is Paul's deep concern, and his introduction excludes the possibility of a person speaking 'in the Spirit of God' resorting to this typical pagan imprecation as a means of gaining the advantage over others in adversarial relationships.

Does this discussion throw any light on the issue about which the Corinthians wrote in 12:1? It concerns the marks of a spiritual or Christian person. Paul makes it clear (12:2) that people speaking 'in the Spirit of God' no longer act as they formerly did when they were led away to dumb idols. He wished them to know that no person, i.e., presumably no Christian, 'speaking in the Spirit of God' said 'Jesus [gives or grants] a curse', as they might previously have done. The power to invoke the gods to curse others belongs to paganism and is therefore not an utterance located 'in the Spirit of God' even if uttered by a Christian. However, the declaration that 'Jesus is Lord' is an utterance that can only be made in the power of the Holy Spirit. The 'manifestation' of the Spirit in the Christian was for the blessing of others and was one of the hallmarks of a spiritual person.

And what was the nexus between the connective διό in 12:3, a description of an aspect of paganism and a 'Christian' curse? The former use of curses against one's adversaries was an acceptable precedent for some Corinthian Christians and was seen as a legitimate use of Jesus' power for the purpose of impeding adversaries either within or outside of the Christian community. It would seem that this was at least part of the issue raised by the Corinthians concerning the spiritual person (12:1). In addressing it Paul takes the opportunity not only to condemn this practice, but also to teach about the use of 'speaking' gifts given by the Spirit.[67]

This chapter has not engaged in a full exposition of 1 Corinthians 12–14, but rather demonstrated the thesis of this book. It has been argued that the inroads of paganism were seen in the way Christians reacted to others in an adversarial situation whether in their Christian ἐκκλησία or outside of it. We noted in the introduction that there were four areas where curse inscriptions were used. A reading of 12:3a in its immediate context and that of 1 Corinthians as a whole can help us see how some Christians acted in a thoroughly 'Corinthian way' when it came to handling conflicts, divisions, and retaliation against adversaries within their religious mind-set.

---

67. It is not being suggested that Christians used lead inscriptions on which to write curses or that they went to customary sites such as temples, but that they 'Christianized' the curse convention.

CHAPTER 9

Secular Patronage and Christian Dominance
(1 Corinthians 16:15-16)

'The House of Stephanas . . . Set Themselves to Minister' (16:15)

Any investigation into the ethical conduct of citizens in the first century would be deficient if it did not include an examination of the fundamental social structures in which the dynamics of social interactions were played out. In Corinth the most powerful one germane to the Christian church was private patronage. While that 'institution' operated from the household, its activities were not directly related to the domestic well-being of its inhabitants. It existed to promote the political ambitions of the patron and aimed at expanding his influence in *politeia* through his clients.

This chapter will argue that many Christian patrons operated in the same way in the Christian community as they did in *politeia*. As a result they were responsible in part for sustaining the underlying conflicts in 1 Corinthians. Paul specifically commended a Christian patron because of the demonstrable benefits his household had bestowed on the Christian community. In the case of Stephanas, the traditional role of patronage had undergone a radical Christian transformation; this was also true for the patroness Phoebe from nearby Cenchreae. Both Stephanas and Phoebe were there to serve others — others were not there for them, which was the traditional role of clients. E. A. Judge has made an astute observation concerning Paul's strategy in 1 and 2 Corinthians in relation to patronage. 'The Corinthian letters show him in head-on confrontation with the mechanisms [of patronage] by which it imposed social power. . . . His positive response to this collision was to build a remarkable new construction of social realities that both lay within the fabric of

184

the old ranking system and yet transformed it by a revolution of social values.'[1]

Elsewhere I have explored how Paul revolutionised the benefaction tradition by demanding that Christian clients no longer remain in 'the old ranking system' as the full-time paid retainers of patrons but rather become benefactors. He sought not the transformation of the client relationship in Thessalonica but its abolition. As a paradigm for those who did not '*wish* to work' (θέλει ἐργάζεσθαι), Paul laboured with his own hands to support himself, even though he had the apostolic right not to do so (2 Thess. 3:6-9). Freeborn clients came from that strata of society whose members' 'hands have never known work'.[2] After Paul left Thessalonica, it proved difficult to sustain this requirement in that community (2 Thess. 3:10) as some strongly resisted his command. As a result there was the need subsequently to 'command . . . in the name of our Lord Jesus Christ' the withdrawal of fellowship from those who, as clients, traditionally 'walked disorderly and not after the tradition which they received from us' (2 Thess. 3:6; cf. 1 Thess. 4:11-12).[3] For Christians it was not the transformation of the role of clients but its demise. In its place Paul enjoined all Christians, including former clients, to work and thereby have the wherewithal to undertake 'good works', i.e., benefactions, for those in need — a role that was the traditional domain of the élite.[4] All able-bodied Christians were to be benefactors to others rather than clients.[5]

1 Corinthians 16:15-18 provides evidence of the fruit of a Pauline revolution for the obverse side of the client/patron relationship, i.e., the role of the Christian 'patron'. Paul cites the house of Stephanas as an example because it set itself 'for ministry' (εἰς διακονίαν)' (16:15). In a later letter sent from Corinth he also commended Phoebe, the patroness 'of many' (including himself), who came from Corinth's eastern port and satellite town, Cenchreae. She was a 'deaconess' (διάκονον) of the church there and

---

1. 'Cultural Conformity and Innovations,' *TynB* 35 (1984): 20-21, cited on p. 23.

2. 'From Secular Client to Christian Benefactor,' in my *Seek the Welfare of the City* (Grand Rapids: Eerdmans; Carlisle: Paternoster, 1994), ch. 3.

3. Winter, *Seek the Welfare of the City,* pp. 51-53.

4. For evidence of these words as synonyms see my *Seek the Welfare of the City,* pp. 34-35.

5. See 'From Secular Clients to Christian Benefactors, 1 Thess. 4:11-12 and 2 Thess. 3:6-13,' and 'Widows and Legal and Christian Benefactions, 1 Timothy 5:3-16,' *Seek the Welfare of the City,* chs. 3 and 4, esp. pp. 34-35.

carried this letter to the Christians in Rome (Rom. 16:1-2). Paul spoke of her as a 'patroness' because of the change of focus, similar to that in the house of Stephanas in Corinth, in the activities of her house in Cenchreae.

Social status had become irrelevant because 'the saints' were now the focus of ministry in the house of Stephanas and not the hired retainers who had been used for the personal aggrandisement of their patrons in *politeia*. Paul sought appropriate acknowledgement from other Christians for the paradigmatic role that this house had played in their community (16:15-18). This was in contrast with the conventional acknowledgement of patrons whose clients greeted them with the daily *salutatio* in the vestibules of their houses before processing to the forum, the council chamber, or the courts.

This concluding chapter of Part I of this book examines the traditional role of patronage, its detrimental effect on the Christian community, and the new focus for Christian patrons which Paul commended. It is proposed to explore (I) the traditional role of private patrons in *politeia*, (II) the activities of the Christian patron in the politics of the church, (III) the new role of the patron Stephanas in the service of the Corinthian Christians and the patroness Phoebe in the service of the Cenchreaean congregation (Rom. 16:2); and (IV) the conversion of patronage in the Christian community.

I. The Private Patron in the Service of *Politeia*

a. The Role of the Household in Politeia

In a number of books on architecture, Vitruvius, the later first-century-B.C. writer, drew attention to an important feature of the houses of those with status. They were concerned not only with visual impact but also with space for conventions surrounding the patron/client relationship.[6] The architectural requirements of a patron were different from those of a client. He stated that clients did not need 'wonderful entrance-halls, vestibules and courtyards, since their social obligations consist in going to pay respects to others rather than receiving their own clients'.

---

6. E. J. Owens, *The City in the Greek and Roman World* (London: Routledge, 1991), p. 145.

> Those of the highest status, who are involved in politics and the struggle for office and have to appear in public, must have high and impressive entrance-halls, wide courtyards and wide porticoes lined with trees to show off visibly how important they are. Furthermore, their libraries and halls should be built as magnificent as public ones, since these men often need to preside over public meetings and cases requiring arbitration or legal judgements in their homes. (*On Architecture* 6.5.1-2)

By implication such things were essential for patrons and their role in civic life. These comments draw attention to the fact that the heads of households were citizens of status and played strategic roles in *politeia*. This might involve them in civic activities in their own homes, e.g., the role of an private arbiter as an alternative to appearing before a judge and jury in civil litigation such as Paul recommends to the Corinthian Christians (1 Cor. 6:1-8).[7] Vitruvius also suggested that the facilities of a large private house could be made available for public meetings.

The ideals of the ancient city were that its citizens should own enough of the means of production to secure their economic independence so that 'they could afford the leisure for full participation in active politics'.[8] In large cities such as Corinth, a rich patron whose steward managed his local commercial interests could secure independence. A few might be 'appointed' patrons of their city.[9] Aelius Aristides noted that some 'men enjoy the official status of being public friends with [patrons of] foreign cities'.[10] Most were the patrons of private households. Wealth and status provided a political power base in Corinth.

---

7. On the legal provision for an officially appointed arbiter see *Lex Irnitana*, ch. 86, and the discussion in J. A. Crook, *Law and Life in Rome* (Ithaca, N.Y.: Cornell University Press, 1967), pp. 78-81. See also D. F. Epstein, *Personal Enmity in Roman Politics 218-43 BC* (London: Croom Helm, 1989), for his absence in the Republic. For its relevance to Christians in Corinth, see pp. 67-68.

8. J. Gardner and T. Wiedemann, *The Roman Household: A Sourcebook* (London: Routledge, 1991), p. 68.

9. J. Nicols, '*Tabulae patronatus*: A Study of the Agreement between Patron and Client-community,' *ANRW* 2.13 (1980): 535-59.

10. *Or.* 46.23.

b. The Role of Private Patrons

The ideal of independence had to be modified with an interdependence secured from a network of 'friends' who could lend their resources or manpower to other households in exchange for exclusive loyalty. The importance of the client to the patron has been described thus.

> The aristocratic social milieu of the Republic continued into the
> Principate, and with it the basic notion that a man's social status was re-
> flected in the size of his following — a large clientèle symbolizing his
> power to give inferiors what they needed. If a man's *clientela* was indica-
> tive of his current status, his potential for mobility depended on the ef-
> fectiveness of his patron whose wealth and political connections could
> be indispensable. Partly because of the unchanging social structures and
> values, financial institutions appear to have continued to rely largely on
> patrons, clients and friends for loans and gifts in time of need, and assis-
> tance in financial activities.[11]

Clients were not drawn from the lower levels of society, but, as in Corinth,
were citizens. Roman free men, like their patrons, were those 'knowing
nothing of labour' (πόνον οὐκ εἰδόντος).[12] Patrons devoted themselves to
the running of the city in a number of ways, through annual honorary
public offices to which they were elected by citizens, through active participation in the political decision-making processes of the Council of the
city, or by voting in the secular meeting of the People (δῆμος).

The daily routine of patrons and clients gives some indication of
how much they functioned as a social unit and as a class apart from manual labourers and artisans who worked in their shops and workshops. Clients arrived at the house of their patron at dawn in order to be ready to
greet him when he appeared for the morning *salutatio*. This activity could
last until the second hour when they departed for the forum with the patron in the lead and his clients walking in procession. The courts operated
from the third hour and in certain circumstances could continue to the
tenth hour. If the patron was involved, his clients accompanied him. The
fourth and fifth hours were devoted to financial and other business by the

11. R. P. Saller, *Personal Patronage under the Early Empire* (Cambridge: Cambridge
University Press, 1982), p. 205.
12. Philo, *Det.* 34.

patron, again attended by his entourage of clients. By the sixth hour all would process to the baths, which were at their hottest for the sake of the élite members of society.[13] After that they moved in procession back to the patron's house if dinner was being provided. This was a long-drawn-out affair, in some cases lasting very late into the night.[14] Certainly, 'clients could be expected to accompany their patron to the ninth hour'.[15] This was the routine that consumed a client's day.

As Laurence has pointed out, 'A key part of élite display was the movement through the city with the entourage of clients'.[16] By means of these processions the strength of the power base of a particular patron was advertised and felt by other patrons, their clients, and citizens as well.

It is not necessary to go beyond the New Testament corpus to catch a glimpse of the activities of clients.[17] Paul instructed clients on two occasions to cease their activities; not to operate in a disruptive or disorderly way (ἀτάκτως) (2 Thess. 3:6, 11); to 'be ambitious to be quiet', in contrast to being political activists who were ambitious for the advancement of their patron (1 Thess. 4:11); to attend 'to his own affairs' (τὰ ἴδια), unlike the client who devoted his daylight hours to attending to the affairs of his patron as an alternative to working with his own hands — being a paid retainer enabled a client to avoid this (1 Thess. 4:11). He was 'to operate in an honest way towards outsiders, and have need of 'nobody',[18] i.e., no patron (1 Thess. 4:12).

Like disciples of sophists, clients of patrons stirred up strife in the rough-and-tumble of educative and political life respectively. The latter were not at all inactive on their patron's behalf during the annual elections to the honorary civic offices for the running of the city. In the cut and thrust of public debates and civic legislation they lobbied vigorously for

13. See G. G. Fagan, *Bathing in Public in the Roman World* (Ann Arbor: Michigan University Press, 1999), for a discussion of the social role of Roman baths and for the presence and sometimes payment of clients publicly in them by their patron; see esp. p. 217 for evidence.

14. R. Laurence, *Roman Pompeii: Space and Society* (London: Routledge, 1994), pp. 124-29.

15. Laurence, *Roman Pompeii*, p. 140.

16. Laurence, *Roman Pompeii*, p. 131.

17. For a detailed discussion of the meaning of these terms see my 'From Secular Client to Christian Benefactor,' *Seek the Welfare of the City*, pp. 46-53, 57-59.

18. μηδενός can be either masculine or neuter. Given the discussion in the previous verse, the context suggests that with respect to working and the impression given to the outsider of Christians, the term is best rendered as 'nobody'.

their patron. The division of Corinth into 'tribes' for the purposes of voting in the ἐκκλησία and for the honouring of benefactors, apart from that role by 'the Council and the People',[19] meant that a patron and his clients played an active role in political processes. As his paid retainers, clients operated at their patron's behest, and through these mechanisms the patron 'imposed social power' for his own political ends.[20]

II. Private Patrons in the Politics of the Church

At the beginning of his reign one of Augustus' first acts was to curb the power of associations because of their perceived political subversiveness.[21] He limited their meetings to once a month. It is significant that the weekly meetings of the Jewish synagogue were specifically exempted in that legislation. The Romans saw the Jewish synagogue meetings (ἐκκλησίαι) as gatherings somewhat comparable to those of an 'association'.[22] Christian meetings could also be identified with those of an association because they were not dissimilar to those of the synagogue.[23] That was the perception of the noted jurist Gallio in his judgement on the Jews versus Paul in Corinth during his brief governorship of the province (Acts 18:12-17). The term ἐκκλησία, used by associations, had political connotations given its origins in *politeia*, where it was used primarily to describe an official gathering — an ἐκκλησία was a formal meeting of 'The People' (ὁ δῆμος). It was an apposite one for Christians to use, but it carried culturally endorsed conventions associated with it.[24] This made it easy for Christians who were pa-

19. Of the ten Corinthian tribes known from inscriptions, two were named after the mother and wife of Julius Caesar, another after a legate and friend of his, and five after close friends and associates of Augustus; Kent, *Corinth*, 8.3, p. 23, n. 18.

20. Judge, 'Cultural Conformity and Innovations', 23.

21. See W. Cotter, 'The *Collegia* and Roman Law,' in J. S. Kloppenborg and S. G. Wilson, eds., *Voluntary Associations in the Graeco-Roman World* (London: Routledge, 1996), p. 78.

22. Cotter, 'The *Collegia* and Roman Law', p. 77.

23. Robinson, *The Criminal Law of Ancient Rome*, p. 80. For discussion see pp. 134-35.

24. Cf. Acts 19:32, 39. See my 'The Problem with "Church" for the Early Church,' in D. Peterson and J. Pryor, eds., *In the Fullness of Time: Biblical Studies in Honour of Archbishop Robinson* (Sydney: Lancer, 1992), ch. 13. On ancient associations see Kloppenborg and Wilson, eds., *Voluntary Associations in the Graeco-Roman World*.

trons to make use of the conventional mechanisms of social power which they had long exercised elsewhere.

It can be appreciated with what ease the 'politics' of the secular associations and civic life could be replicated by the heads of leading Christian households in the Christian 'meeting' (ἐκκλησία). Power games could be played by leading figures in this Christian 'association' as they were in similar contexts in Corinth. Christian patrons in search of their 'social' place in a Christian 'association' could be forgiven for making such a connection, as they thought about 'the rules of engagement' with one another for control of the organisation. Roman society was concerned with the preservation of *dignitas*, especially by men of social status, in their interactions in such gatherings, and its loss could result in feelings of shame, enmity relationships, and open conflicts carried forward into the civil courts, associations, and the secular ἐκκλησία.[25]

It must be remembered that Paul never had to repeat to the Corinthians the same tradition about clients that he delivered to the Thessalonians. Can it be assumed that because Paul remained in Corinth for at least eighteen months compared with his short stay in Thessalonica, he succeeded in abolishing the 'profession' of clients among the Corinthian converts? It is known that he provided an example by working with his own hands in Corinth, as in Thessalonica, for he also chose not to exercise his apostolic right for support in the latest field of his endeavours (1 Thess. 2:9; 2 Thess. 3:8; 1 Cor. 9:4ff.). In 1 Thessalonians, which was written from Corinth, Paul reminded his recipients of his tradition concerning clients delivered while he was there — 'even as we charged you' (1 Thess. 4:11), although without the sharpness found in 2 Thessalonians 3. The issue was, therefore, foremost in Paul's thinking in Corinth. After he left the Roman colony, the issue of clients *per se* did not raise its head directly in his correspondence.

It would seem that while he succeeded in abolishing the role of clients for Corinthian Christians, the patronage system proved a far more complex entity for Paul to reform, as events after his departure demonstrated. It appeared not to have undergone any long-term effective transformation, except for Stephanas and Phoebe. D. W. J. Gill located the

---

25. Epstein, *Personal Enmity in Roman Politics 218-43 B.C.*; and for the continuity of the problem in the Roman empire see R. A. Kaster, 'The Shame of the Romans,' *TAPA* 127 (1997): 1-19.

existence of the élite in Corinth from 1 Corinthians.[26] His conclusions concerning their presence in the church enable us to explore those situations where patrons may have been manipulating the Christian community in the only way they knew, having learned well the intricacies of domination from secular society. It would have been possible for patrons to exercise influence, not through 'clients', but directly in meetings because of their social status. This would explain a number of features in church life reflected in Paul's letter.

While the rise of 'dissension' (ἔρις) and divisions (σχίσματα) over former teachers can be accounted for in terms of the disciple/teacher paradigm in secular education, the person or persons qualified to lead these 'parties' from within the congregation has not been highlighted. In the secular assembly, all citizens identified themselves by a particular tribe usually named after imperial personages.[27] Citizens voted according to tribes in that assembly, and the power-broking role of patrons, with the assured votes of their clients, was a critical factor. It is significant that church members identified themselves by an important teacher. The text states that 'each one of you on the one hand is saying "I belong to Paul", and on the other hand "I belong to Apollos", and "I belong to Peter"' (ἕκαστος ὑμῶν λέγει ἐγὼ μέν . . . δέ . . . δέ . . . δέ), although it was Apollos who was requested to return to Corinth, and not Paul (1:12, 16:12).[28] So while the disciple/teacher perception is explicable because of the educational parallel, the organised reaction in the church after Paul left can only be accounted for by the traditional leaders of parties, i.e., the patrons, who in this case led factions in the name of the significant figures in early Christianity, Paul, Apollos, and Peter. The patrons were 'household' based (1:14-16).

These divisions (σχίσματα) naturally surfaced whenever Christians gathered together, in the same way they did in the secular counterpart. Therefore it comes as no surprise that they emerged at the Lord's Supper and resulted in 'factions' (αἱρέσεις) (11:18-19). It was not unknown for pa-

---

26. 'In Search of the Social Elite in the Early Church,' *TynB* 44.2 (1993): 336.

27. While the names of all the tribes in Corinth are not known, epigraphic evidence has yielded the names of ten tribes to date, Atia (mother of Augustus), Agrippa (daughter of Augustus), Aurelia (the mother of Julius Caesar), Calpurnia (wife of Julius Caesar), Domitia, Hostilia, Livia (mother of Tiberius), Maneia, Vatinia, and Vinicia.

28. For the precedent of 'zealots' of even deceased teachers see my *Philo and Paul among the Sophists*, p. 129, citing Dio Chrysostom, *Or.* 55.1, 3, 5, where Socrates can be called a 'zealot' of Homer if the reader objects to the term 'disciple'.

trons and clients to eat in front of others, and for patrons to provide poorer-quality food for their clients at banquets. This was a means of enforcing social control over individual clients. In the Lord's Supper Paul mentioned first of all 'the divisions', and then proceeded to rebuke those Corinthians who were devouring their own meal and imbibing their own wine in the presence of others (11:18-21). They were shaming the 'have nots', i.e., those who did not 'have' houses as a safety net in times of dearth in Corinth (11:22).[29]

Even if such activities (11:17-34) were not part of the same gathering (chapters 12–14), the manipulation of power was again reflected in the discriminating care bestowed on some at the expense of others. Paul specifically commanded the giving of more abundant honour to 'uncomely parts' that were 'feeble' and 'that part which lacked' (12:21-22). He did this in order 'that there should be no divisions in the body, but (ἀλλά) that they show the same care towards others' (12:25). The text does not suggest that there were some who did not care for anybody, but that they were selective to whom they showed it. The discussion preceding this indicates that some felt they had no need of others (12:20-21). The attitudes expressed reflected the mind-set of the patrons, who were used to giving special attention to those whom they courted, or those clients whom they specially favoured with their carefully controlled largesse. By contrast, Paul's view of the relationship of Christians to other Christians was such that when 'one suffered, all [and not just a few] suffered [with him or her]. When one was honoured, all the members rejoiced' (12:26). Christians were to see other members of the community in a new light. They were not association members but were an ontological reality where each was an 'organ' in the body of Christ. In pulling down the strongholds of prestige and power, Paul was eliminating the controls it provided for 'the comely parts' and reconstructing the way in which 'all' were to respond to very diverse situations in the seasons of life, showing 'the *same* care for one another' (12:25). Paul was seeking to wrest the community from the grasp of the patrons, who sought to exercise their control over other Christians.

Again, élite men prayed and prophesied in the service with their heads covered (11:4). They were among the 'not many' wise, well-born, and powerful Christian men who were drawing attention to their status by this display of social power (1:26). In 'an association' clients may not be as

29. For discussion see pp. 233-36.

essential for exercising influence — they were in *politeia*, with voting by citizens in Tribes in the assembly and the casting of 'lots' by jurors in the courts — because patrons were used to pulling rank in the secular sphere with social inferiors. Having operated thus for years in the secular ἐκκλησίαι, they would have had no problem in replicating such behaviour in the Christian ἐκκλησία.[30]

The litigious spirit among the Christian élite has also been discussed (6:1-8). This was the normal way of conducting power struggles between the patrons in the secular sphere. They had resorted to this activity with other Christians, 'brother taking brother to court' (6:6). In a vexatious action, once the jury decided who possessed the superior status, then it would be plain to all in the Christian community who were the socially superior in the intricate pecking order among the élite and therefore the more politically powerful.[31] Such a declaration would not have gone unnoticed in the secular or Christian ἐκκλησία. The decision to engage in a vexatious civil action was not only for retaliatory purposes because of the loss of *dignitas* but also for declaration by their secular peers who were regarded as the socially and politically superior contestants.

This would appear to be the extent of patronal influence in the Corinthian church, which reflected the mechanisms of patronage. However, J. K. Chow also sees the influence of patronage in 1 Corinthians 5–6, 8–10, and 15:29 and classifies the patrons in each case as rich, powerful, political, and priestly respectively.[32] Such a classification is artificial and misleading, as all patrons were rich, powerful, politically active, and could undertake priestly liturgies.[33]

---

30. For discussion see Ch. 6.

31. For discussion see Ch. 4, esp. p. 62.

32. J. K. Chow, *Patronage and Power: A Study of Social Networks in Corinth*, SNT Supp. 75 (Sheffield: Sheffield Academic Press, 1992), pp. 130-66.

33. It is unlikely that the man involved in incest was a patron, as it has been argued that his father was still alive (see pp. 47-49). It is also true that the young men of 1 Cor. 6:12-20 were not patrons, as it was around the age of eighteen that they assumed the *toga virilis* and were too young to function in that capacity, given that they were below the minimum age for participating in liturgies, which was normally twenty-five years.

III. The Patron and Patroness in the Service of the Church

Stephanas and His Household and House

In seeking to understand the role of the house of Stephanas which Paul commended, it is important to ascertain who made the decision to serve 'all the saints' (16:15). To help understand this it is necessary to examine the household terminology used by Paul, viz., οἰκία and οἶκος.

In 1 Corinthians 1:16 Paul refers to the baptism of the 'household of Stephanas' (τὸν Στεφανᾶ οἶκον) and in the same letter writes about the 'house of Stephanas' (τὴν οἰκίαν Στεφανᾶ) (16:15). Was there a distinction between οἰκία and οἶκος? G. Theissen concludes, 'Wie man sieht, sind und hier synonym'.[34] C. K. Barrett also argues that the terms were synonymous,[35] as does BAGD. A. Schreiber also appears to assume this.[36] If this generally accepted conclusion is correct, then it might be felt that the use of οἶκος four verses later when Aquilla and Prisca send their greetings 'with the church in their house [better 'room' within the house]' (σὺν τῇ κατ᾽ οἶκον αὐτῶν ἐκκλησίᾳ) (16:19) confirms the conclusion. However, Paul never used οἰκία interchangeably but always οἶκος to describe 'the house church'.[37] In the discussion of the Lord's Supper Paul used both terms: 'have you no houses for the purpose of eating' (μὴ γὰρ οἰκίας οὐκ ἔχετε εἰς τὸ ἐσθίειν) (11:22), and 'If anyone is hungry, let him eat at home' (εἴ τις πεινᾷ ἐν οἴκῳ ἐσθιέτω) (11:34). This might also fortify the conclusion that Paul made no distinction.

34. G. Theissen, 'Soziale Schichtung in der korinthischen Germeinde, Ein Beitrag zur Soziologie des hellenistichen Urchristentums,' *ZNW* 65 (1974): 249; E.T. 'Social Stratification in the Corinthian Community: A Contribution to the Sociology of Early Hellenistic Christianity,' *The Social Setting of Pauline Christianity* (Philadelphia: Fortress, 1982), p. 87. See also A. Chapple, 'Local Leadership in the Pauline Churches: Theological and Social Factors in Its Development: A Study of 1 Thessalonians, 1 Corinthians and Philippians' (Ph.D. diss., University of Durham, 1984), p. 398, who assumes the same.

35. C. K. Barrett, *A Commentary on the First Epistle to the Corinthians* (London: A & C Black, 1971), p. 48.

36. A. Schreiber, *Die Germeinde in Korinth: Versuch einer gruppendynamischen Betrachtung der Entwicklung der Gemeinde von Korinth auf der Basis des ersten Korinthbriefes* (Münster: Aschendorff, 1977), p. 131. 'In 1 Kor. 16,15 wird das Haus (οἶκος) des Stephanas als Erstling Archajas bezeichnet'. He has wrongly noted that 16:15 has οἶκος and not οἰκία.

37. E.g., Rom. 16:5, again of the meeting in the home of Aquila and Prisca (Col. 4:15 and Philem. 2).

However, in the Appendix (pp. 206-8) papyriological evidence indicates that where the terms 'house' (οἰκία) and 'household' (οἶκος) occurred in the same document, contract, or private letter, they were never used synonymously. Likewise, in the survey of the large corpus of one late first-century literary author, Dio Chrysostom, these words were not used interchangeably.

On the basis of this survey it can be concluded that in 16:15 the term οἰκία did not refer to the 'household', but that it was the 'house of Stephanas' which made this important decision. While the service would have involved all who resided in that household, it was, in effect, the decision of Stephanas as the *paterfamilias*, perhaps in consultation with his immediate family. They resolved to put the resources and members of their household at the service of the needs of the saints. As that would have been the prerogative of the head of the house and perhaps the senior members of the 'inner' family, the term οἰκία was an apposite one to have chosen. It distinguished between those who had the authority to decide and all those belonging in this social unit who, as 'the household of Stephanas', would carry out the particular service described by Paul.

Gill suggests that there is 'a hint' that Stephanas was a member of the élite 'because his household is mentioned', endorsing Theissen's view.[38] For a house to make a commitment to serve the needs of the Corinthian church, especially if the city was in the midst of a famine, would mean that it was a well-resourced one.[39] In the three Corinthian famines of this period, we know that Tiberius Claudius Dinippus was appointed by the Council of Corinth to be in charge of grain relief for the whole city. His liturgies taken as a whole indicate that he was a man of great wealth who subsidised grain in times of shortage and, in addition, personally financed the Isthmian Games.[40] It would require manpower and money for Stephanas to support the needs of the saints, for all the members of this household were assuming the role of 'stewards',

38. D. W. J. Gill, 'In Search of the Social Elite in the Early Church,' *TynB* 44.2 (1993): 336. Theissen, *The Social Setting of Pauline Christianity,* p. 87 argues with respect to the house of Stephanas, 'Reference to someone's house is hardly a sure criterion for that person's high social status, but it is a probable one, particularly if other criteria point in the same direction'.

39. See p. 223.

40. See my 'Secular and Christian Responses to Corinthian Famines,' *TynB* 40 (1989): 95-99, and pp. 217-20 in the following chapter of this book.

distributing from the largesse of the patron's store to the needs of the 'household of God'.

Paul drew attention to the house of Stephanas as 'the firstfruits of Achaea' (ἀπαρχὴ τῆς Ἀχαΐας) (16:15) and, in doing so, was pointing out the most senior house in this province in terms of Christian conversion.[41] While he retained the old ranking system in drawing attention to this fact, at the same time he does not suggest that any deference must be afforded it because of that. Submission to it was called for, not because of any rank or status it might have secured in the secular world as 'first',[42] but because of its commitment to the service of the saints and to any others who were emulating that house. In his pre-Christian times, it was the clients who were committed to the service of Stephanas on a daily basis, but an incredible inversion had occurred. The patron and the adults from his immediate family now committed 'themselves to serve' God's people, many of whose social status would not have qualified them as clients in ordinary circumstances in Corinth. The family of Stephanas would no longer operate as a political unit in competition with other households, as they would have done in secular Corinth and as some among the Christian households were still doing.

Paul then noted, 'And I rejoice at the coming of Stephanas and Fortunatus and Achaicus: for that which was lacking on your part they supplied' (16:18a). This would suggest that more than Stephanas had personally experienced this 'house' conversion, if Fortunatus and Achaicus possessed social status. We cannot be certain if they were heads of households similar to Stephanas'. However, the same ministry they had to Paul in Ephesus, they rendered to the Corinthian church. Paul indicated with reference to Stephanas and others that they had 'refreshed my spirit and yours'.[43]

Having the House set themselves 'for the purpose of service' (εἰς διακονίαν) resulted in substantial exertion in meeting the needs of 'the saints' — Paul used the verbs 'to exert' (συνεργέω) and 'to slave' (κοπιάω).

41. 'You know the house of Stephanas, that it is the firstfruits of Achaea.' The verb 'to know' here means 'you are acquainted with the fact that . . .' (Liddell and Scott, B.1).

42. On intercity quarrels over the issue of primacy that occupied much of the ancient world, see C. P. Jones, *The Roman World of Dio Chrysostom* (Cambridge, Mass., and London: Harvard University Press, 1978), pp. 78, 86ff.

43. For a discussion of this important terminology see A. D. Clarke, '"Refresh the hearts of the saints": A Unique Pauline Context,' *TynB* 47.2 (1996): 275-300.

These endeavours have been said to relate to the needs of the poor and hospitality of the travellers.[44] Paul had already referred to some in the church as 'the have-nots' (11:22). What options would have been open to a Christian resident in Corinth in difficulty? For non-slave labourers and artisans there was the possibility of support through the links of kinship and free loans which provided a safety net against starvation. An alternative was sheltering under the personal patronage of the wealthy.[45] This would have further fuelled the divisions in the church along household lines with loyalties to leading patrons, for the 'giving and receiving' of money could thereby establish patron/client relationships with its loyalty obligations.[46]

If Corinth was experiencing a grain shortage at the time of his writing, then the 'have-nots' could have been given grain or have been able to purchase an amount, however meagre, at a low price. The city had to guarantee its own safety and civil order, with rich benefactors satisfying the needs of the 'have-nots'. Wealthy citizens as part of the community might have contributed financially to the subsidy, as this was done in order to protect their own goods from being plundered.[47] This would have tided over the non-slave labourers and artisans and enabled them to subsist in a time of grain shortage.

It is not known what steps Paul had in mind to remedy the situation when he promised, 'and the rest I will command when I come' (11:34b). If this related to the needs of some and not simply the further regulation of the Lord's Supper — the latter appears to have been resolved in the letter (11:28-34). He may have felt reluctant to disclose his hand about the remaining matters (11:34b) until he returned to Corinth, anticipating some resistance to his plans for meeting the needs of the Christians, given the divisions in the church (11:18). In the meantime the house of Stephanas and others ministered to the needs of the saints in Corinth by providing for

44. Chapple, "Local Leadership in the Pauline Churches," pp. 403ff.

45. Garnsey, *Food and Famine*, p. 80.

46. S. C. Mott, 'The Power of Giving and Receiving: Reciprocity in Hellenistic Benevolence,' in G. F. Hawthorne, ed., *Current Issues in Biblical and Patristic Interpretation: Studies in Honor of Merrill C. Tenney* (Grand Rapids: Eerdmans, 1975), pp. 60-72, esp. p. 63: 'the expression of gratitude placed a valid claim for further benefits upon the benefactor'. C. B. Welles, *Royal Correspondence in the Hellenistic Period: A Study in Greek Epigraphy* (New Haven: Yale University Press, 1934), p. 108 comments, in discussion of *SIG* 533 (218 b.c.), 'gratitude for one favour is the best method of securing another'.

47. See pp. 222-23.

them during this difficult time. This 'ministering' may have been the solution Paul had in mind (11:34), but his reluctance to set up such a mechanism for the whole church by letter may have been governed by the internal divisions, which would only have been aggravated by such a move, creating client relationships to further those divisions.

This 'conversion' of the role of the House of Stephanas from power-broking to serving the needs of the saints is an example of what Judge implied when he argued that Paul's aim had been 'to build a remarkable new construction of social realities that both lay within the fabric of the old ranking system [personal patronage of a head of a House] and yet transformed it by a revolution of social values [for the needs of all the saints]'.[48]

b. Phoebe, Servant and Patroness of the Cenchreaean Church

Herodes Atticus, the leading benefactor and the most famous sophist of the Second Sophistic around whom Philostratus wrote his work on *The Lives of the Sophists*, resided in Corinth for a period in the early second century.[49] That city honoured him because he built the beautifully covered Odeon next to the theatre, and he overtly honoured himself by erecting a statue to his wife in which she was praised for possessing 'moderation', that great virtue which epitomised the Roman woman. In that same inscription he portrays himself as possessing all the civic virtues.[50] There was, however, another modest yet powerful Roman woman of Corinth. Almost a century before Herodes, and almost a decade prior to the founding of the Corinthian church, she proved to be a most remarkable patroness and benefactress. Even though she contributed nothing to Corinth according to the extant Corinthian inscriptions, yet she warranted acknowledgement by the Council and the People of Corinth.[51]

In A.D. 43 an inscription was erected to Iunia Theodora, 'a Roman cit-

48. Judge, 'Cultural Conformity and Innovations,' p. 23.

49. G. Anderson, *Philostratus: Biography and Belles Lettres in the Third Century* A.D. (London: Croom Helm, 1986), p. 4.

50. See Kent, *Corinth*, 8.3, no. 128; see also no. 129.

51. For the inscription see *BCH* 83 (1959): 496-508. For an English translation and commentary on the text see R. Kearsley, 'Women in Public Life in the Roman East: Iunia Theodora, Claudia Metrodora and Phoebe, Benefactress of Paul,' *TynB* 50.2 (1999): 189-211.

izen resident in Corinth, a woman of the greatest honour, living modestly (ζῶσα σωφρόνως)', the same term used of Herodes' wife, which Judge calls a 'discreetly feminine quality'.[52] She was specifically commended by the People of Patara for not ceasing to offer 'hospitality to all the Lycians and receiving them into her house' in Corinth and described with the accolade 'a woman of the greatest honour'. The People of Myra also had good cause to commend her for her hospitality at the time of their arrival in Corinth. The Federal Assembly of the Lycians honoured her with the benefactor's title and a gold crown — 'a Roman, a fine and noble woman devoted to the nation' ('Ρωμαίᾳ γυναικὶ καλῇ καὶ ἀγαθῇ καὶ εὐνόῳ τῷ ἔθενει)[53] because she was a benefactress of the federation. It again takes up the fact that she was 'full of good will to all travellers whether private individuals or ambassadors sent by the nation' who arrived in Corinth, for which she was rewarded with 'a crown and a portrait painted on a gilt background'.[54] A decree of the Lycian city of Telmessos records that she 'welcomes into her own house Lycian travellers and our citizens . . . supplying them with everything; displaying her patronage (προστασία)[55] of those who are present'.[56]

Iunia Theodora was honoured for her contribution not to Corinth, but to the cities of Lycia, Patara, Telmessos, and Myra and the federal assembly in Lycia in Asia Minor. She operated from Corinth as a federal and a civic patroness, in contrast to a private one, in commercial matters for other cities.[57] A first-century city constitution provides an interesting insight into the appointment of a city patron. The *Lex Irnitana* prescribes

52. The last description of her is interesting because it implies that she was not a 'new' Roman woman who had wealth but no morals. For discussion see pp. 123-26.

53. *BCH* 83, ll. 12-14, 19-20, 23-24, 47-50, and 75-77. Judge, 'Cultural Conformity and Innovations,' p. 21.

54. For a discussion of these benefaction terms see my *Seek the Welfare of the City*, pp. 26-33.

55. For a discussion of the use of such terms in Latin and Greek and their adoption in the first century see Judge, 'Cultural Conformity and Innovations,' pp. 17-22.

56. The inscription was composed in the genre of the Greek and not the Roman benefaction tradition and is the smallest-lettered inscription recovered to date at the site. The contrast was so obvious when compared with the normal-sized lettering of official Corinthian inscriptions to men who operated as the colony's benefactors.

57. On the role of civic patrons see Nicols, *Tabulae patronatus*, pp. 535-59; and R. P. Duncan-Jones, 'Patronage and City Privileges — The Case of Guifi,' *Epigraphische Studien* 9 (1972): 12-16. For a parallel case see *CIL*, no. 8837 (A.D. 55), where a legate operated as a civic patron for the Roman colony of Julia Augusta Tupusuctu.

Concerning the co-opting of a patron. No one is publicly to co-opt a patron for the *municipes* of the *Municipium Flavium Irnitanum* or to confer the power of patronage on anyone, except by a decree of the majority of the *decuriones* which has been passed when not less than two thirds of the *decuriones* are present and they have cast their votes by ballot on oath. Whoever publicly co-opts otherwise or contrary to these rules a patron . . . or confers the power of patronage on anyone, is to be condemned to pay 10,000 sesterces . . . and whoever has been co-opted a patron against this statute or had the power of patronage conferred on him, is not thereby to be a patron of the *municipes* of the *Municipium Flavium Irnitanum*.[58]

This legislation sought to curb enthusiastic citizens co-opting a patron on his own initiative, no doubt causing acute embarrassment to the city and a great loss of *dignitas* to the person concerned. We know of a number of people on whom the title of city patron was conferred.[59] The benefactions of Junia Theodora were quite remarkable in terms of hospitality, and the inscription reflects that.[60] She facilitated the needs of Lycians who arrived in Corinth in either an official or private capacity. She was fully honoured by the rulers of those cities possibly for furthering Lycian links with Corinth. She acted for the Lycians in Corinth for commercial purposes as the city and federation patroness as well as their hostess.

Another woman was living in the environs of Corinth at exactly the same time as Iunia Theodora, and that was Phoebe. A cognate of the term 'patronage' which was used of Iunia was invoked by Paul to describe this Christian lady (Rom. 16:2). She was a 'patroness' (προστάτις) not of a particular ethnic group, but rather of 'the saints' (Rom. 16:2). She may have been a hostess to many as Iunia was, but she functioned in the service of the church in Cenchreae as a διάκονος, which was very much a servant role.[61]

58. The *Lex Irnitana*, ch. 61. For the text and commentary see J. González, The *Lex Irnitana: A New Flavian Municipal Law,' JRS* 76 (1986): 147-243.

59. Nicols, *Tabulae patronatus*. In Corinth Gaius Iulius was patron of a Corinthian tribe; West, *Corinth*, 8.2, no. 68. On patrons of colonies see Pisidian Antioch, *ILS*, 9485; Luna, *ILS*, 233; Iulia Augusta Taurinorum, *ILS*, 2701.

60. Cf. Titus Pomponius Bassus, a Senator from Rome, who was appointed the city patron of Ferentinum c. A.D. 101, and the city fathers had a 'tablet of hospitality engraved with this decree placed in his house'; *CIL*, 6.1492, ll. 23-24.

61. See J. N. Collins, *Diakonia: Re-interpreting the Ancient Sources* (Oxford: Oxford

Paul writes, 'Receive her in the Lord worthily of the saints, and assist her in whatsoever she may have need of you', the reason being that 'she herself has been a patroness to many' (Rom. 16:2). His call was for a response to her needs in Rome in order to secure reciprocity for her ministry in Cenchraea, because from her home she had been a patroness to many.[62] He used προσδέχομαι to describe the reception he sought for her from the Roman church that was 'in the Lord, worthily of the saints'. That verb was used to describe the welcoming of foreign emissaries or offering hospitality. For example, Euripides asked, 'What Athenian house shall offer you hospitality? (τίς σε πύργος Ἀτθίδος προσδέξεται;).[63] If the latter meaning is what Paul had in mind as he sought appropriate Christian reciprocity for her as a guest, then Phoebe's service in the church may have related to hospitality which met the needs of many, as did Iulia Theodora's. Like Stephanas, Phoebe did not manipulate the traditional role of patronage as others sought to do in the Christian community. The saints were not there to serve her ends, but she was there to serve their needs, and that without the normal discrimination based on rank or status in the patronage system.

Paul emphatically states that 'he himself' (ἐμοῦ αὐτοῦ) has also been the beneficiary of her 'patronage' (Rom. 16:2b). When he wrote his letter to the Christians in Rome from Corinth, he mentioned that his host (ξένος) was Gaius, whom he had baptised in his early ministry there (Rom. 16:23; 1 Cor. 1:14); so he was not living in the home of Phoebe. She lived in the eastern port of Corinth which Paul visited, and there he had his hair shorn as a vow (Acts 18:18). A church was established there, and Paul's role in that is unknown. He had experienced the patronage of Phoebe, who acted not as his host but as a sponsor for his ministry in ways that he does not specify. Financial support certainly cannot be ruled out, or the important networking which was at the heart of relations in the Roman world. Phoebe was not the first woman whom Paul named as a fellow worker in

University Press, 1990); and A. D. Clarke, 'Pauline Ministry in the Church,' *Serve the Community of the Church,* First Century Christians in the Graeco-Roman World (Grand Rapids and Carlisle: Eerdmans and Paternoster, 2000), ch. 9, esp. pp. 233-43 for a repudiation of Collins' thesis that it refers to someone of status and is not a term denoting low standing and involving a servant role to others.

62. On a helpful survey of this port see R. M. Rothaus, 'Kenchreai, Eastern Port of Corinth,' *Corinth: The First City of Greece: An Urban History of Late Antique Cult and Religion* (Leiden: E. J. Brill, 2000), ch. 4.

63. Euripides, *Phoenissae* 1706; see also Sophocles, *Oedipus Tyrannus* 1428.

his apostolic ministry (cf. Phil. 4:3), but the only one to whom he gives the title of 'patroness'.

While there may have been striking similarities in the roles of these two contemporary Corinthian women, the contrast between the two is also important to note. Iunia Theodora was a 'city' patroness who used her Corinthian home as the base for her role in *politeia* on behalf of the Lycians. In that, her role in patronage was not unusual, and she was appropriately honoured as civic benefactress, albeit by distant authorities for entertaining and helping visitors from cities across the Aegean Sea — their honours were commended to 'the magistrates and the people' of Corinth. Her patronage was different in that she did not operate as a civic patroness to the Corinthians. Her contemporary, Phoebe, was a private patroness, and her role in relation to serving the church, if reciprocity is implied in Romans 16:2, earned her the title of patroness from Paul. The other description of her shows a transformation of her focus as she adopted a servant role (διάκονος) in the Cenchraean church (Rom. 16:1). In this she was no different from Stephanas, whose house's endeavours were 'for the purpose of service' (εἰς διακονία) for the needy in the Corinthian church (1 Cor. 16:15).

IV. The Conversion of Patronage

Under Paul patronage values had been inverted, with a patron and patroness now serving people without respect for their *persona* and their usefulness for any personal political aspirations typical of patronage.

The assistance and acknowledgement that Paul sought for both was again transformed by the very nature of the Christian community whose members Paul addresses as 'brothers' or 'beloved brothers' in *familia* language that was only reserved in Roman society for siblings, either born in the family or adopted. They were no longer the fawning and flattering parasites of private patrons, subservient to their ambitions and daily agendas, but they were family — the family of God.

Paul issued two injunctions to the Corinthian Christians in relation to the house of Stephanas and Stephanas himself. The first was 'to be subject to such', and the second required that they 'acknowledge such' men as he and Fortunatus and Achaicus (16:16, 18). Whatever he meant by these two statements, they cannot mean that the Christian community should become the clients of Stephanas or that they must participate in some form of *salutatio,* daily or otherwise, to him as their patron as an expression of exclusive loyalty. Having disavowed that in relation to teachers, he would hardly have encouraged it in relation to a particular member of the congregation. The term 'to such' is plural, so that more than Stephanas was involved, and the possibility is further ruled out when he required them to be in subjection also 'to every one who helps in the work and labours' (16:16b). Paul expanded the circle beyond the patrons to include 'everyone' (παντί) who met the needs of the saints. This would include not only the household of Stephanas but also all Christians who laboured for the community.

Was Paul contrasting those who presented a paradigm of service with those heads of households who sought to operate as 'political' patrons in the church and struggled to win primacy over others, thereby dominating the community? (See pp. 190-94.) If so, in this passage Paul was calling for a rejection of the overtures of the power-broking Christian patrons. Rather, church members were being encouraged to line themselves up with those who had set themselves for the benefit and blessing of the Christian community. No form of recognition or acknowledgement was to be given to the former because of their misuse of their power and wealth as Christians. Paul commanded Christians to acknowledge the ministry of those whose resources were being used to meet the needs of God's people and not to embrace those who were manipulating others for their own inappropriate purposes, even though they were operating according to the sophisticated norms of secular conventions in Corinth. Without affecting 'the fabric of the old ranking system' Paul was certainly transforming it with a revolution in the use of the resources of patrons.

This contrasts with the conventions in the Diaspora synagogues. For example, Asia Minor inscriptions record the gifts to the synagogue of benefactors and a benefactress, none of whom were Jews, according to Rajak.[64] In an important essay she has argued that the role of *archisynagogos* was not a cultic one but 'had far more to do with patronage and philanthropy',[65]

64. T. Rajak, 'The Synagogue within the Greco-Roman City,' in S. Fine, ed., *Jews, Christians and Polytheists in the Ancient Synagogue: Cultural Interaction in the Greco-Roman Period* (London: Routledge, 1999), ch. 9.

65. T. Rajak, 'The Jewish Community and Its Boundaries,' in J. Lieu, J. North, and T. Rajak, eds., *The Jews among the Pagans and Christians in the Roman Empire* (London: Routledge, 1992), pp. 9-28.

and that this role had been much influenced by secular categories in *politeia* in the early empire.[66]

Judge completed his important article with the observation that by the use of 'building' terminology (e.g., οἰκοδοκέω) for religious purposes — a unique use in contemporary religious language — Paul turned away from the power/destructive model of patronage relations to the service/ submission syndrome where 'the constructive spirit' of love contributed to the good of others in contrast to the 'puffed-up' spirit which 'demolishes' the life of the community.[67] The latter observation expresses the corrosive effects of private patronage on the church, as witnessed in various places in 1 Corinthians. The comment on the constructive effects of love that served the good of others was apposite for the new role for Christian patronage. Paul had immediately preceded his endorsement of the ministry of the house of Stephanas with the injunctions, 'Watch, stand fast in the faith, quit yourself like men, be strong, let all that you do be done in love' (16:13-14). The last command was by no means an aphorism of private patrons in *politeia* or of those leading persons who did not seek to minister as servants to the Christian community but rather engaged in a struggle to secure their own patronal domination of it by conventionally accepted 'political' manoeuvres.

That Paul should have effectively concluded his discussion of the whole of his letter thus, apart from his personal signature, would suggest that this was no incidental issue as it might first seem. It was not part of the *Varia* that sometimes appears in the concluding section of some of Paul's letters. Untransformed patronage exercised by some leading members of the congregation was the means by which relational difficulties were created and aggravated after Paul left Corinth. This was the culturally accepted way of perpetuating relational difficulties. Therefore, drawing Part I of this book, which has examined the effects of social ethics on the Christians in Corinth, to a close with the topic of power of patronage is apposite. It explains the means by which the current state of tensions at the time of writing to Paul were sustained.

---

66. T. Rajak and D. Noy, '*Archisynagogos:* Office and Social Status in the Graeco-Roman World,' *JRS* 83 (1993): 75-93.

67. Judge, 'Cultural Conformity and Innovations,' p. 24.

The Meanings of οἰκία and οἶκος

The following survey of evidence indicates that where both words occurred in the same document, contract, or private letter, as they do in 1 Corinthians, they were not used synonymously. Likewise, in the survey of a large corpus of a late first-century and early second-century literary author, Dio Chrysostom, these terms were not used as synonyms either, even though the various orations were written over a long period from A.D. 70 to c. 107.[68]

a. Papyriological Distinctions

The period survey dates from the late second and first centuries B.C. to the end of the second century of the Christian era. Some thirteen papyri are examined, which provide a good spectrum of usages.

Menches complains of a raid carried out on his house, οἰκία, and the lock on his mother's οἶκος having been broken open. In this context the latter term has been said to refer to an *insula,* although the reference could be to a room. The distinction between the two terms in this papyrus has been noted by the editors of *P. Tebt.* 46 (113 B.C.).[69]

---

68. See Jones, *The Roman World of Dio Chrysostom,* pp. 133-40, for the dates of various orations.

69. *TDNT,* V, 131; MM 441; B. P. Grenfell, A. S. Hunt, and J. G. Smyly, *The Tebtunis Papyri* (London, 1902), p. 153. The word *insula* is used in a broad sense. For a discussion of variations in meanings and the debate see A. G. McKay, *Houses, Villas and Palaces in the Roman World* (London: Thames and Hudson, 1975), p. 83 and footnotes.

In a private letter from a freedman to his patron a distinction is made between the garden and the house, οἰκία (l. 27), and in l. 37 both terms are used. οἰκία describes the place, where the meal takes place, the house, while one is received into the household, οἶκος. The former term is also used in l. 35, and while the line is not complete, the word refers to the house (*BGU* 1141) (10 B.C.).

There are four marriage contracts where a distinction is drawn between the house, οἰκία, from which the wife is not to absent herself without her husband's permission, and the οἶκος, the household whose reputation the wife is not to injure through any misconduct. This is a common clause in four contracts, viz., *BGU* 1050 (Augustus), *BGU* 1052 (13 B.C.), *P.Tebt.* 104 (92 B.C.), and *P.Oxy.* 497 (early second century A.D.), and indicates how the terms are normally used, with a contrast between the physical house and the members who live there.

In a loan with the right of occupancy of a house, οἶκος refers to the house as distinct from the roof, pylon, court, entrance and exit, and all other appurtenances of the house, οἰκία. This legal document draws a distinction between the house 'proper' and the whole of the property. In *P.Oxy.* 1641 (A.D. 68) οἰκία is used because it was originally the plural of οἰκίον and was used to describe all the buildings.

A testatrix bequeaths her house and all its appurtenances to her son. However, the document subsequently refers to a sister to whom an οἶκος is left in the event of her separating from her husband. The latter refers to an *insula* or room within the property. A distinction between the two words is observed in *P.Oxy.* 104 (A.D. 96).

In a document transferring property both terms are used in both ll. 11-13 and 16-17, and the editors of the collection note that 'οἰκία is a "house" in the ordinary sense of the term; οἶκος is a separate dwelling or tenement in a large building or *insula* corresponding to our "flat"' (*P.Fay.* 31) (A.D. 129).[70]

In a letter from Cornelius to his son Hierax, greetings are sent also from all the household, οἱ ἐν οἴκῳ. His father exhorts Hierax not to offend

70. B. P. Grenfell, A. S. Hunt, and D. G. Hogarth, *Fayum Towns and Their Papyri* (London, 1900), p. 142. οἶκος is used to describe 'dwelling units' in Corinth in an inscription dated c. A.D. 170; Kent, *Corinth*, 8.3, no. 306. These are to be built for the athletes at the Isthmian Games. The inscription uses ξενία, 'guest rooms', to describe the 'units' or even 'rooms', referred to as οἶκοι (ll. 12, 15). The latter term has a number of usages related to property, but is not used to describe the whole of the property.

any of the people who are living with him in the house, οἰκία, which is also shared by the members of his son's household (σου καὶ τῶν σῶν). He encourages his son to work hard at his studies and to provide money out of his own pocket for his household until the father sends some (*P.Oxy.* 531) (second century).

In a declaration of property οἰκία refers to a house with a courtyard. Reference is made to property located elsewhere which consists of ἐπιοικία καὶ οἶκοι which is translated as 'outhouses and buildings'. The nature of these buildings is not indicated, but they could be part of a complex. They are obviously different from the house referred to earlier in the papyrus (*P.Mich.* 540) (A.D. 53).

In a division of inherited property from both father and mother οἰκία is used thirteen times to refer to the houses. A single room within a brother's dovecote is referred to as οἶκος on two occasions (*P.Mich.* 554) (Domitian).

In a letter of Dorian to his son Serenus, the greeting comes from the whole household, οἱ ἐν οἴκῳ, and reference is made to the old farm building that belongs to the house, οἰκία (*P.Mich.* 212) (second or early third century A.D.).

In conclusion, where the terms occur in the same document they are never used synonymously by the writers. οἰκία refers to the whole property and not to the members of a household. οἶκος is used of an *insula,* a room, part of the property, viz., the house, to distinguish it from the roof, pylon, court, and entrances, all of which were described by the former term, and the household, by which the writers mean the members and not the whole property. The variety of uses to which the latter term is applied is governed by the nature of the document, i.e., legal, private, etc. and the immediate context.

b. Literary Distinctions

A near-contemporary author has been chosen in order to show that what was true in nonliterary sources also applied in a literary one as well. In Dio Chrysostom's eighty orations οἰκία refers to a building fifty-three times. On three occasions it is used of the mighty House of Pelops in 11:51 and 66:6, and of the House of Nero and Domitian in 66:6. This is in keeping with the classification in Liddell and Scott of the house or family from which lineage is traced. The philosopher is someone who rules over himself or a house or the greatest state (49:3), and here Dio is referring to an equivalent of the house of Pelops.

οἶκος refers to a household on seven occasions (8:25, 15:8, 36:36, 38:15[2], 62:2, and 69:2), and follows Homer when he spoke of a household; twice the reference is to the dining room (7:83), which is a better translation than house (30:44). Liddell and Scott cite the term for a room and instance a dining room; once it is used of the appurtenances with θυρία, ἑστία (4:12), once of public buildings (4:13; Liddell and Scott, §3); once of the home of the gods (36:36), and once of the world (30:28). These words are not used interchangeably by Dio in his corpus.[71]

In light of the above, it can be concluded that the diagrammatic summary provided by Cluck of intersecting circles, in which he suggests that terms such as household, family, and relations were described as either οἶκος or οἰκία, can be misleading.[72] Samples of literary and nonliterary evidence in the early empire show that both terms, when used in one letter or one corpus, were not synonyms, and the context determines what is meant by the respective terms.

c. Gospel Distinctions

Was this distinction also observed by Christian writers? A comparison of the synoptic gospels is helpful, for there are occasions where the words appear in common sources.[73]

The terms appear in Mark twenty-eight times. There are ten occa-

---

71. As M. O. Knox, '"House" and "Palace" in Homer,' *JHS* 90 (1970): 117-20 observes in Homer, we do get the range of meanings which signify the houses of various classes of people with δόμος, δῶ, δῶμα, οἶκος, and μέγαρον and the plurals δόμοι, δώματα, οἶκοι, οἰκία, and μέγαρα. The word μέγαρον can be used of the living room and not the whole house. It has been suggested that the word οἶκος would 'originally have meant an estate, and/or the family or group of people cultivating it, and only secondarily an actual house' (p. 119), '. . . when a household or family is spoken of, the word is οἶκος' (p. 119, n. 131). It is interesting that in Homeric times οἰκία could mean domicile, i.e., he made his home in X, and it could refer to a specific house or several houses (120).

72. H.-J. Klauck, 'Die Hausgemeinde als Lebensform im Urchristentum,' *Münchener Theologische Zeitschrift* 32 (1981): 1-15.

73. P.-Y. Brandt and A. Lukinovich, 'οἶκος and οἰκία chez Marc comparé Matthew at Luc,' *Biblica* 78.4 (1997): 525-33.

sions where Matthew agrees with Mark and eight times with Luke. Only once is there a disagreement with both Matthew and Luke in 5:38, where Luke and Matthew both agree — εἰς οἶκον for Mark and εἰς οἰκίαν for Matthew and Luke. It relates to the entering of the house of the ruler of the synagogue, and all three use εἰς. Mark favours εἰς οἶκον where there are no parallels with the other synoptic writers (3:20; 7:17, 30; 8:3; 9:28; 10:10). One exception is in 7:24, where he uses εἰς οἰκίαν to indicate that the woman comes to the house where Jesus is and εἰς οἶκον when the woman returns to her house. Where there are no parallels Mark uses ἐν οἴκῳ (2:1) and ἐν οἰκίᾳ (9:33; 14:3). In 3:27 εἰς οἰκίαν is used to describe the entry of the thief and agrees with Matthew; but Luke uses αὐλή (11:21). In both Matthew and Mark the thief spoils the house, οἰκία, while in Luke he simply divides the spoils. It would be correct to assume that οἰκία includes the αὐλή. The latter was the open court or quadrangle round which the house was built, having a corridor all round, from which were doors leading into the men's apartments.

d. Epistle Distinctions

Paul correctly uses the term οἰκία to describe 'those of the House of Caesar' (οἱ ἐκ τῆς Καίσαρος οἰκίας) (Phil. 4:22).[74] It was not a reference to the imperial family but to those connected with it, including a vast number of slaves and freedmen who worked for the emperor both in Rome and throughout the empire.[75] An earthly house is a metaphor for the human body, which has philosophical allusions to first-century Platonism (2 Cor. 5:1; Philo, *Det.* 32). In the wider Pauline corpus it is used of buildings, i.e., for a great or wealthy house in which there are vessels of honour (2 Tim. 2:20). 2 Timothy 3:6 speaks of false teachers who creep into houses and lead silly women astray and in the same discussion refers to 'merry widows' with little better to do than to go about to different houses (1 Tim. 5:13).

74. 'The House of Nero and Domitian' (Dio Chrysostom, 66:6). 'Even if Agrippa had not been a king, yet as a member of Caesar's household . . .' (Philo, *Flacc.* 35), and 'Helicon, an abominable execrable slave who had been foisted for ill into the imperial household' (αὐτοκρατορικὴν οἰκίαν) (*Legat.* 166).

75. For a discussion of Caesar's household see P. R. C. Weaver, *Familia Caesaris: A Social Study of the Emperor's Freedmen and Slaves* (Cambridge: Cambridge University Press, 1972).

In the Pauline corpus οἶκος is used of the 'house churches', which, it is presumed, gathered in 'a reception room' of Christians (Rom. 16:5; Col. 4:15; Philem. 2). It is used twice of the household of Onesiphorus (2 Tim. 1:16; 4:19). Elsewhere in the Pastorals it refers to one of the areas of responsibility, i.e., the members of one's own household (1 Timothy 3:4; 3:5), specifically mentions children and the wider household (3:12), equates the household of God to members of the church and not a building (3:15), and emphasizes the responsibility towards children or grandchildren as a primary expression of piety — their own household, which also includes parents (5:4). In 1 Timothy 5:3-6 both terms occur and their use is explicable, for οἶκος refers to members of a household and οἰκία to physical buildings.

Paul uses both terms in his discussion of the Lord's Supper (1 Cor. 11:17-34). He responds to those who devour their own food in the context of the Supper with a series of questions which are meant to indict them. 'What![76] Do you not have houses for the purpose of eating and drinking (μὴ γὰρ οἰκίας οὐκ ἔχετε εἰς τὸ ἐσθίειν καὶ πίνειν)?[77] The answer is, 'Of course you have' (11:22).[78] In his closing injunctions he commands that if anyone is hungry that person must eat at home (ἐν οἴκῳ), i.e., in his own dining room (11:34). He repeats the phrase ἐν οἴκῳ (14:35), and in that context it refers to asking 'at home' in contrast to the interrogation of prophecy 'in church'.

Paul refers to the place of a Christian gathering in Ephesus as the οἶκος of Aquila and Priscilla, which indicates the place where the actual meeting was held in their home (1 Cor. 16:19). It might be more precise to call this the meeting in their reception room, for in the house of those with status this was a large area.[79]

76. 'The assentient γάρ in answers, although originating in the causal use, is to all intents and purposes simply a particle of affirmation'; M. Thrall, *Greek Particles in the New Testament* (Leiden: E. J. Brill, 1962), p. 44.

77. See pp. 144-48.

78. The affirmative answer to this rhetorical question is conveyed by the use of μή and οὐκ, following classical usage (BDF #427 [2]).

79. See p. 186.

PART II

THE INFLUENCE OF SOCIAL CHANGE

CHAPTER 10

The Present Crisis and the Marriage Bed (1 Corinthians 7:1-5)

'It Is Good for a Man Not to Touch [His] Wife' (7:1)

'It is good for a man not to touch [his] wife' (7:1). Was that what the Corinthians wrote about, and, if so, why? This chapter begins by examining
the problem which, it is argued, gave rise to this question. It had to do with
difficulties which were experienced by all the inhabitants of Roman Corinth (7:26). A careful analysis of the evidence for this crisis will set the
scene for the next two chapters, because it affected two issues raised in
1 Corinthians 7.

In order to pursue this, we shall discuss (I) 'the present distress' to
which Paul refers (7:26) and its effect on Roman Corinth and the Christian
community; (II) the use of language when referring to one's wife and the
semantic field of sexual intercourse from literary and nonliterary sources
in order to understand the question raised in 7:1; and (III) the sexuality of
marriage, the distinctive teaching on the authority of husband and wife
over each other's bodies and Paul's warning against sexual abstinence in
marriage. An appendix will spell out the grammatical reasons why the
concession which Paul made in 7:6 does not refer to 7:2-5.

I. 'The Present Distress' for Corinth and the Church

(a) Present Distress and Grain Shortages in Corinth

After Paul left Corinth a set of inscriptions unique to the first century A.D. was erected to one of its leading citizens, Tiberius Claudius Dinippus.[1] They record the high public offices which he held during the formative period of the church.[2] No other first-century benefactor in Corinth had such honours bestowed upon him. 'The Council and the People' erected an inscription in honour of him, and the extant evidence shows that ten of the twelve Tribes which comprised the administrative divisions of that city did likewise with identical wording. This suggests that maybe all twelve did so, and the remaining two may yet come to light. The only difference between these eleven Latin inscriptions is in the abbreviations of the various leading civic offices that he filled. As all were listed in the same order, it is right to see this great show of gratitude as occurring at the same time.[3] What gave rise to this unprecedented and highest possible public display of honour for this Corinthian benefactor? Corinth had honoured its benefactors for comparable public offices before, but never like this. The answer may lie in the fact that Dinippus was three times 'curator of the grain supply' *(curator annonae)*, which made him responsible for the relieving of grain shortages in times of famines.[4]

1. A. B. West, *Corinth: Results of Excavations conducted by the American School of Classical Studies at Athens 1896-1926* (Cambridge, Mass., 1931), 8.2, no. 86-90; J. H. Kent, *Corinth*, 8.3, nos. 158-63; J. Murphy-O'Connor *St. Paul's Corinth: Texts and Archaeology* (Wilmington: M. Glazier, 1983) did not include the inscriptions to Dinippus in his collection.

2. '*duovir, duovir quinquennalis*, augur, priest of Britannic Victory [military tribune of Legion VI], Hispanenesis, chief engineer, curator of the grain supply three times, [*agonothetes*] of the Neronea [Caesarean and of the Isthmian and Caesarean games]'; Kent, *Corinth*, 8.3, no. 158.

3. Great benefactors of the second century to whom Corinthian inscriptions were erected were the great Athenian sophist Herodes Atticus and the Epidarian Cornelius Pulcher. The latter held similar offices to Dinippus, including *curator annonae*, ἐπιμελητὴς εὐθηνίας; *IG* 4.795; and B. D. Merritt, *Corinth: Greek Inscriptions 1896-1927* (Cambridge, Mass.: American School of Classical Studies at Athens, 1931), 8.1, no. 76. He was honoured in other inscriptions (ibid., nos. 80-83). In nos. 76 and 80-81 the character of the letters is the same. Nos. 82-83 supported statues erected at the same time. They were not, however, all erected on the same occasion (see West, *Corinth*, 8.2, nos. 71-72), nor with the same wording as in the case of Dinippus.

4. In West, *Corinth*, 8.2, no. 92; and Kent, *Corinth*, 8.3, no. 161, the fragments do not

How important was this in the eyes of the city? The traditional ascending order of precedence for honorary public offices placed the Corinthian magistrates immediately below the President of the Games.[5] This would have been even more so, since Dinippus again occupied the magistracy in the important year when permanent members of 'the Council' were appointed. In all the extant inscriptions to Dinippus, however, *curator annonae* was placed next to the most prestigious office, viz., the President of the Games, and not after his magistracies. The placing of the *curator annonae* in this order of 'seniority' by the Corinthians would have signalled that the alleviation of the city's grain shortage or famine on three occasions was seen as a benefaction of enormous significance for the welfare of the city.

What does a comparison with other holders of this office in Corinth and elsewhere reveal? Although in the first and second century A.D. others in Corinth accepted the office of *curator annonae,* no other person is known to have held this office more than once.[6] When Boulargos of Samos held office three times in the mid-third century B.C., there was a chronic dearth of food.[7] This crucial office was filled only in times of famine. Its importance is shown in that a series of intermittent and severe grain shortages in Corinth were such that the inhabitants had to look to a leading citizen, not once but on three different occasions, to come to their rescue. The whole political structure of the city expressed its heart-felt appreciation in the fullest way possible. Again, not only the Council and the People but also all of the tribes individually erected their own inscription in this unprecedented display of honours by Corinth. He had rescued the city from hunger and the accompanying social distress it inevitably caused.

What were the various offices Dinippus undertook, and can we date them? He began as chief engineer of the Council, *praefectus fabrorum.* He

---

preserve the record of his term as the superintendent of the grain supply but it can be assumed, given its mention in the other inscriptions cited in n. 1.

5. In Corinth the games were of such importance that its president took precedence in status over the magistrates; J. Wiseman, 'Rome and Corinth 1,' *ANRW* 2.7.1 (1979): 500.

6. For holders of the office in the first and second centuries A.D. apart from Dinippus and Cornelius Pulcher see Kent, *Corinth,* 8.3, nos. 164 (70-100), 170 (c. 125), 177 (164), 127 (late second century), and nos. 169, 188, 227, 234-36, 238; Merritt, *Corinth* 8.1, no. 94, and West, *Corinth,* 8.2, nos. 83 and 91, all of which are too fragmentary to date.

7. P. Garnsey, *Famine and Food Supply in the Graeco-Roman World: Responses to Risk and Crisis* (Cambridge: Cambridge University Press, 1988), p. 14, citing *SEG,* 2, no. 366.

'jumped' the important office of *aedile*, the chief administrative and financial position in Corinth, which would normally have followed that. He held the office of one of the two magistrates, *duumviri*, who were elected annually and were executive and judicial officers of the Council. He also secured the crucial office *duoviri quinquennales*, for the year when the census was taken (which was every five years) and the magistrates nominated new members of the Council. Technically this was the most senior position in rank in a colony. Dinippus was President of the Games celebrated in A.D. 55, which would have involved him in the enormous expense of staging them, as well as personally bearing the cost of the constant entertainment of dignitaries.[8] The President of the Games had become the most senior honorary office because of this.[9] He was also elected curator of the grain supply on three occasions. As the *curator annonae* was only appointed in times of need, A. B. West suggests that 'it is possible that Corinth had a *curator annonae* on more than one occasion during the reign of Claudius'.[10]

Records indicate that Greece was affected by famine from the middle to the end of the forties, and also in 51. J. Wiseman suggests that Dinippus may have been *curator annonae* during that year.[11] There is no extant evidence of any other holders of this office during the late 40s and 50s. The precise dates when he held the office are not certain, although it would have been before the Games of 55. It has been suggested that Dinippus held the office of magistrate in 51/52. The seniority of the presidency of the Games held in 55 over the former position makes the earlier date of 51/52 more likely.[12] Because of the enormous expense of hosting

8. Plutarch, *Quaes. conviv.* 723A. 'During the Isthmian games, the second time Sospis was president, I avoided the other banquets, at which he entertained a great many foreign visitors at once, and several times entertained all the citizens.'

9. Wiseman, 'Rome and Corinth 1,' pp. 497-500. See Epictetus, *Discourse* 111.1.34, where the President of the Games is the most senior honorary public office, having displaced in seniority the office of magistrate because of the enormous importance of the games. On this issue of rank and status see E. A. Judge, *Rank and Status in the World of the Caesars and St. Paul* (Christchurch: University of Canterbury Publications, 1982).

10. West, *Corinth,* 8.2, p. 91.

11. Wiseman, 'Rome and Corinth 1,' p. 500, invokes West, *Corinth,* 8.2, p. 70 in support of his argument that 'It is not at all improbable that Dinippus' service was rendered during this time' and elsewhere places the date as c. A.D. 51.

12. A variety of dates have been suggested, i.e., West, *Corinth,* 8.2, no. 52, A.D. 52-53 and Kent, *Corinth,* 8.3, p. 26, A.D. 57-58. The former's dating is based on A. Bagdikian, 'The Civic Officials of Roman Corinth' (M.A. thesis, University of Vermont, 1953). However, for

the Games, it was improbable that he would have undertaken any two of the three offices of magistrate, president, or *curator annonae* at the same time. This could narrow the famines down to early 51 and between late 52 and early 55.

What were the dates for the formation of the church in Corinth? Claudius expelled the Jews from Rome in A.D. 49. Paul's arrival is calculated as late 49 or early 50 and his ministry lasted 18 months, during the latter part of which the proconsul Gallio was appointed governor of Achaea. Gallio was to have held this office from 1 July 51, for twelve months. Did he fulfil the office for the whole period? A note from his brother Seneca records that 'when, in Achaea, he began to feel feverish, he immediately took ship, claiming that it was not a malady of the body but of the place'. Pliny, in noting Gallio's hypochondria, indicated that he needed a long sea voyage to recuperate after his consulship. Whether the Jews sought a decision against the Christians soon after he assumed office,[13] or whether Gallio remained in Achaea 'more than five months from June to the end of October',[14] Paul's encounter with him can be placed between July and October, 51. The period between Paul's departure from Corinth and the writing of 1 Corinthians is considered to be not more than three years.

Dinippus could well have exercised the office of *curator annonae* once during Paul's stay in Corinth. The latter's concern not to be a burden to the church could have been related in part to the famine in the city.[15] That all the Tribes of Corinth erected inscriptions in addition to that of 'the Council and the People' suggests that his benefactions were seen as both timely and generous. More than that is not known from the archaeological evidence presently available. The important point to note is that

---

the list of magistrates known to have held the office of magistrate and who issued local Corinthian coins bearing their name during the period, see M. Amandry, *Le monnayage des duovirs corinthiens*, BCH, Supp. XV (Paris and Athens: Ecole Francaise d'Athènes, 1988), p. 76. As no coins were struck during of magistracy of Dinippus, the most likely date is 51/52; Amandry, pp. 22 and 74, n. 563.

13. C. J. Hemer, *The Book of Acts in the Setting of Hellenistic History* (Tübingen: J. C. B. Mohr [Paul Siebeck], 1989), pp. 251-53.

14. Murphy-O'Connor, *St. Paul's Corinth*, p. 147, citing Seneca, *Letters* 104.1 and Pliny the Elder, *Natural History* 31.62 on his illness, and Suetonius, *Claudius* 15 on his impulsive behaviour.

15. 2 Cor. 11:9 in addition to the reason furnished in 1 Cor. 9:12.

food crises in Corinth were alleviated during the period of the early days of the church on three occasions in the traditional way by the appointment of a curator of the grain supply.

b. Present Distress in the East in the Forties and Fifties

It is important in discussing 'famine' in the Principates of Claudius and Nero to note that the term reflects the situation created by grain shortages. These shortages resulted in a steep rise in price on the market through a crop failure or a regional dearth from a succession of crop failures.[16] 'Even in richest corn-growing provinces . . . cases of local famine were frequent'. The reason for this is that many of the major cities in the East were located in agricultural areas which were not capable of fully supporting them with grain.[17] The planting of the Roman colony of New Corinth in 44 B.C. was not the result of a feasibility study undertaken to assess the adequacy of the agricultural infrastructure.[18] Corinth's commerce had greatly expanded in the intervening one hundred years, as had its population, which was estimated at some 100,000.[19]

Apart from the epigraphic evidence from Corinth, we possess literary and nonliterary evidence. Eusebius records, 'In his time [Claudius'] famine seized the world'.[20] In P. *Mich.* 594 (Sept.-Oct. 51) there is a list of arrears for Egyptian taxes of 1,222 people who defaulted in 45/46, increasing to 1,678 the following year and declining in 47/48. In 50/51 there were still default-

---

16. M. Jameson, 'Famine in the Greek World,' in P. Garnsey and C. R. Whittaker, eds., *Trade and Famine in Classical Antiquity* (CPS Supp. 8, 1983): 6, speaks of 'the temporary shortage of grain in the Greek cities' when comparison is made with the vast famines in China and Africa experienced this century. F. F. Bruce, *The Acts of the Apostles* (London: Tyndale Press, 1952), p. 239, comments that 'famine' is not perhaps the most appropriate term, but that 'dearth' should be used.

17. M. Rostyovtzeff, *The Social and Economic History of the Roman Empire*, II (Oxford: Clarendon Press, 1957), 600.

18. 'Another Caesarian colony founded for economic or social reasons was the most celebrated of them all, Corinth. . . . Its *coloni* were freedmen for the most part . . . and this, taken in conjunction with its siting, shows that the colony could not have been agrarian. It was manifestly intended to revive the mercantile glories of the city that Mummius had destroyed in 146.' Salmon, *Roman Colonization under the Republic*, p. 135.

19. Engels, *Roman Corinth*, pp. 79-84.

20. *Ecclesiastical History* 11.8.

220

ers. It has been calculated that more than half of the male population in Philadelphia in Egypt had defaulted.[21] Other papyriological evidence also presents the same picture. *SB* 7461(45) indicates that taxpayers were unable to meet their obligations and fled the city to another Nome to which a request was made for them to be brought back under armed guard.[22] In spite of Egypt's reputation as a grain bowl for Rome and the East, its inhabitants suffered financial hardship and shortage of food in this period.[23]

P. Garnsey notes that there were 'flooding and food shortages which affected numerous states in Greece ... in the 40's and 50's'.[24] Of this period Eusebius refers to (λιμὸς Ἑλλάδος) when the price of grain was extremely high.[25] Suetonius verifies that the food shortages of A.D. 51 were the result of 'crop failure' *(sterilitas)*, and does not limit it to one location.[26]

This evidence adds to the epigraphic witness of Dinippus and allows that in Corinth there were grain shortages three times during the reign of Claudius and the early Principate of Nero.[27] J. Wiseman places at least one such occasion when Dinippus was *curator annonae*, and this was during Gallio's proconsulship of Achaea in A.D. 51.[28]

In addition to crop failures there was constant pressure from Rome

21. G. M. Browne, *Documentary Papyri from the Michigan Collection, X, ASP* 6 (Toronto, 1970), pp. 64-67. For subsequent problems see *P.Cornell* 24 (A.D. 56) and *P.Ryl.* 595 (A.D. 54-55), and discussion by J. F. Oates, 'Fugitives from Philadelphia,' *Essays in Honour of C. Bradford Welles, ASP* 1 (New Haven, 1966), pp. 87-95, who assesses the Egyptian economic crisis and cautions against projecting Egypt's problems onto the whole empire without external evidence.

22. On the use of soldiers for collecting taxes see H. I. Bell, 'The Economic Crisis in Egypt under Nero,' *JRS* 28 (1938): 5-6.

23. North Africa was the predominant supplier of grain for Rome's insatiable need to support those entitled to the monthly grain dole in the imperial city; see Garnsey, *Famine and Food,* p. 255.

24. There were problems in Acraephia, Greece in the forties (*IG* 7.2712). Only the benefactions of one man helped the city to survive and thrive; J. H. Oliver, 'Epaminondas of Acraephia,' *GRBS* 12 (1971): 233-36. See discussion also by Garnsey, *Famine and Food,* p. 261.

25. *Eusebi Chronicorum,* II (Berlin, 1886), 151.

26. *Claudius* 18, 'a scarcity of grain because of long-continued droughts'.

27. For discussion, including the *terminus ad quem* of the honorary public offices of Dinippus, see pp. 217-19.

28. Wiseman, 'Rome and Corinth 1,' p. 505. See also West, *Corinth,* 8.2, no. 70; and V. P. Furnish, 'Corinth in Paul's Time: What Can Archaeology Tell Us?' *Biblical Archaeology Review* 15 (1988): 19, who notes, 'According to inscriptional evidence uncovered by archaeologists, a severe famine occurred in 51 A.D.'

to feed those vast numbers of its inhabitants who were traditionally entitled to the monthly corn dole regardless of need. It was granted on the
grounds of their citizenship and residence in the imperial capital.[29] Short-
falls in the harvest aggravated the problem for cities in the East, as the failure of the emperor to meet the needs of Rome was of such political consequence that it had, of necessity, first claim on existing supplies. Thus a
second-century emperor reminded the city of Ephesus, 'bearing in mind
the necessity that first the imperial city should have a bounteous supply of
wheat procured and assembled for its market.'[30]

c. The Social Distress Caused by Famine

A second-century-A.D. Ephesian inscription notes in its preamble the expected response to famine. 'Thus it happens at times that the populace is
plunged into disorder and riots.'[31] Other sources also observe that there
were always accusations by the mob of mismanagement, or profiteering by
the corn dealers, and, as a result, 'grave social disturbances occurred, riots
and demonstrations were common.'[32] Seneca, writing of the problems in
Rome in A.D. 41, says, 'we were threatened with the worst evil that can be-
fall men even during a siege — the lack of provisions . . . [and Gaius's poli-
cies were pursued] very nearly at the cost of the city's destruction and famine and the general revolution that follows famine.'[33]

Of problems in A.D. 32 Tacitus wrote, 'the excessive price of grain all
but ended in rioting [in Rome] and large demands were made for several
days in the theatre.'[34] Apollonius of Tyana observes such a rampage when
he arrives in Aspendus of Pamphylia where the population was forced to
eat vetch during the Principate of Tiberius:

> an excited crowd of all ages had set upon the chief magistrate and was
> lighting a fire to burn him alive even though he was clinging to the

29. G. Rickman, 'The Corn Distribution,' *The Corn Supply of Ancient Rome* (Oxford:
Clarendon Press, 1980), ch. 7; and Garnsey, *Famine and Food*, pp. 198ff.
30. *IEph* 215, ll. 1-3, cited in Garnsey, *Famine and Food*, p. 255; see also pp. 231-32.
31. *IEph* 215, ll. 1-4.
32. See Rostyovtzeff, *The Social and Economic History of the Roman Empire*, II, 146.
33. Seneca, *Brev. vit.* 18.5, cited in Garnsey, *Famine and Food*, p. 222.
34. *Annals* 6.13.

statue of the emperor. The chief magistrate plucked up courage and said 'So-and-so and So-and-so' naming several 'are to blame for the famine that has arisen, for they have taken away the grain and are keeping it in different parts of the country.' A hue and cry thereupon arose among the Aspedians to make for these men's estates.[35]

Apollonius rescued the magistrate by persuading the speculators to release grain to the citizens.

Garnsey observes that 'the fear of famine rather than famine itself was enough to send people on the rampage, as in 57 B.C. or A.D. 51'.[36] Dio Chrysostom in c. A.D. 70-80 encountered such a mob in his hometown who had attempted to storm his estate because of the rise in the price of grain and the allegations that hoarding was being practised. He rebuked them the following day in the assembly as he reminded them of their intention 'to stone them [him and rich fellow citizens] and burn their houses, with a view to consuming in one conflagration if possible them and their children and their wives'. He argues that they were reacting irrationally because the cost of grain had risen to a price comparable to that in other places and 'it is not so high as to make you desperate'.[37] 'Hungry people do not listen to reason', Seneca observed, and his nephew, Lucan the poet, said, 'The grain supply provides the mainsprings of hatred and popularity. Hunger alone sets cities free, and reverence is purchased when rulers feed the lazy mob: a hungry population knows no fear'.[38]

d. Present Distress and the Corinthian Christians

Tacitus declared that A.D. 51 was an 'ominous' year. 'There were earthquakes and subsequent panic in which the weak were trampled under foot'. In addition, he notes, there was once again a shortage of corn and, as a

35. Philostratus, *The Life of Apollonius of Tyana* 1.15, and comments by C. P. Jones, *The Roman World of Dio Chrysostom* (Cambridge Mass. and London: Harvard University Press, 1978), p. 21; and G. Anderson, *Philostratus: Biography and Belles Lettres in the Third Century A.D.* (London: Croom Helm, 1986), p. 191, on the reliability of Philostratus and his sources.

36. Garnsey, *Famine and Food*, p. 31.

37. *Or.* 46:10-12, citation #11, and discussion by C. P. Jones, 'Riot at Prusa,' *The Roman World of Dio Chrysostom*, ch. 3 and for the dating of the oration p. 134.

38. *On the Shortness of Life* 18.5 and *Pharsalia* 3.55-58.

39. Tacitus, *Annals* 12.43.

consequence, famine. He records that all this was construed by some as 'a supernatural warning'.[39] Just as some pagans made deductions from these portents, so too did Corinthian Christians. Do we have evidence? 1 Corinthians 7:26 records the 'present distress' (ἐνεστῶσαν ἀνάγκην) being experienced in Corinth. While some have sought to argue that 'present' means 'impending' and therefore 'immediately impending', as Conzelmann has suggested — the word 'present' means what it says.[40]

Is this a reference to distress in the city's life caused by three acute grain shortages and the attendant social unrest? Thucydides speaks of situations where cities were forced to face conditions of dire necessity (διὰ τὸ μὴ ἐς ἀκουσίους ἀναγκὰς πίπειν) which included 'severe famine' (λιμὸς ἰσχυρός), and thus makes a connection between the 'distress' and famine. Dionysius of Halicarnassus in the early empire recorded an extreme situation with 'great famine in the city, and "trouble" (στάσις) and perplexity (ἀμηχανία) as to what should be done'.[41] The language which Paul used seems to suggest that Corinth experienced some difficulties, and literary and nonliterary evidence points to yet another famine with the attendant social dislocation and anxiety that it caused.

Agabus' prophecy of a famine was seen to have been fulfilled (Acts 11:28),[42] and from the time of the worldwide food shortage under Claudius there was a heightened expectation of the *parousia* as witnessed in the Thessalonian letters of Paul.[43] Did the Christians see this as the beginning

---

40. H. Conzelmann, *1 Corinthians* (E.T. Philadelphia: Fortress, 1975), p. 132, n. 13, seeks to resolve the questions as to whether ἐνεστώς means 'present' or 'impending' by suggesting 'imminent'. He argues that in some passages it means present and in others 'immediately impending'. He notes that 1 Cor. 3:22, Rom. 8:38, and Gal 1:4 refer to the present. He observes that 'each particular instance must be interpreted according to its context' and therefore accepts 'impending' (if ἐνεστώσης is the correct reading) (*P.Lond.* 904, l. 20). However, as G. D. Fee, *The First Epistle to the Corinthians* (Grand Rapids: Eerdmans, 1987), p. 329 argues, 'the term "present" invariably means what is already present in contrast to what is yet to come', and supplies supporting evidence. It is a perfect participle. See also W. Deming, *Paul on Marriage and Celibacy: The Hellenistic Background of 1 Corinthians 7*, SNTSMS 83 (Cambridge: Cambridge University Press, 1995), p. 186, n. 300.

41. Thucydides, 3.82.2, 85.2; Dionysius of Halicarnassus, *Roman Antiquities* 9.3-4.

42. For a discussion see my 'Acts and Food Shortages,' in D. W. J. Gill and C. Gempf, eds., *The Book of Acts in Its Graeco-Roman Setting*, The Book of Acts in Its First Century Setting (Grand Rapids and Carlisle: Eerdmans and Paternoster, 1994), ch. 3, esp. the discussion of the inscription, which speaks of a 'worldwide' famine.

43. 1 Thess. 4:13–5:11; 2 Thess. 2:1-12.

of the eschatological birth pangs? There was a nexus between such catastrophes and these birth pangs in the early church. Mark records 'there will be earthquakes in various places, there will be famine; this is but the beginning of the birth pangs'.[44]

In the 'Little Apocalypse' of Mark 13 not being pregnant or suckling a child was a blessing for a woman because of the coming crisis.[45] Because of the nexus between the famine and the tribulation, did the Corinthians seek confirmation that sexual abstinence was the appropriate response in order to avoid pregnancy? The use of 'self-restraint', abortion, and infanticide were the usual methods of contraception in the ancient world.[46] Abstention from sexual intercourse in marriage would have been the only acceptable means of birth control available to early Christians.[47] Is this the thinking that rests behind the request of the Corinthians for confirmation of their action?

II. *Familia* and Sexual Language

Does 7:1b confirm that the question is about sexual abstinence between husband and wife? The report of the Corinthians' view on the subject was — καλὸν ἀνθρώπῳ γυναικὸς μὴ ἅπτεσθαι. Can this question be read as, 'It is good for a man not "to touch" i.e., have sexual intercourse with [his] wife'? This rendering of the sentence makes use of a personal pronoun which is not in the text, and the translation of γυνή as 'wife' and not 'woman' for either is possible. Both literary and nonliterary precedents exist for this rendering.

Plutarch writes to his own wife in a moving letter as he seeks to console her on the death of a much wanted and greatly loved daughter aged two years old. The letter is addressed, 'Plutarch to his wife' (Πλούταρχος τῇ γυναικί). Not only here but throughout this letter he does not make use of the personal pronoun as he addresses her as 'my dear wife' (ὦ γύναι) or (γύναι). The translator of Plutarch's letter rightly renders γύναι in the vocative as 'dear wife'. He refers to the wives of others in the letter as 'their

44. Mark 13:8; cf. Matt. 24:7-8.
45. Mark 13:17; cf. Luke 23:29.
46. See L. P. Wilkinson, 'Population and Family Planning,' *Classical Attitudes to Modern Issues* (London: William Kimber, 1979), ch. 1, esp. pp. 29ff.
47. *Coitus interruptus* was subsequently condemned; see, e.g., Epiphanius, 'Against the Origenists,' *Panarion* 1.4–4.1.

wives' again without the personal pronoun.[48] Elsewhere Plutarch refers to 'the adultery of your wife' (μοιχεία γυναικός) without using the pronoun,[49] and notes that 'he no longer touched her' (μηκέτι αὐτὸν ἄψασθαι) [i.e., sexually] even though he was still fond of her'. This is a reference to a woman with whom he had had a long-standing sexual liaison.[50]

The term γυνή for a 'wife' is to be found in nonliterary sources, e.g., marriage contracts.[51] It can be translated as 'wedded wife' (γυνὴ γαμετή) in contrast to a concubine, and a 'wife' (γυνή) for a woman who had lived in a recognised form of union but without a written contract as 'has been living with him as [his] wife'.[52] These are clear references to a man's wife without the use of the personal pronoun in both legal nonliterary sources and personal references in literary sources.[53] The ancient world had, of course, *familia* terminology, and the use of γυνή in I Corinthians 7:1 reflects this; in Greek marriage language a 'woman' referred to a 'wife'. Therefore the rendering of γυνή in 7:1 as '[his] wife' follows a well-established first-century semantic convention, as Dickey has clearly demonstrated.[54]

The verb 'I touch' (ἅπτομαι) is a euphemism for sexual intercourse, as indeed is the verb 'I have'.[55] These words were also used as synonyms in the semantic field of sexuality to refer to intercourse and have comparable synonyms in Latin.[56] It is appropriate, then, to translate 7:1, 'It is good for a man not to have sexual intercourse with [his] wife.'

III. Sexual Abstinence in Marriage

Having suggested the occasion that gave rise to the Corinthian Christians' comment and the meaning of the sentence in 7:1b, we ask next, Does this

---

48. *Consolatio ad uxorem* 608C, D, 609C, 610D, and 609B.

49. *De tranquillitate animi* 475B.

50. Plutarch, *Pompey* 2.3.

51. See, e.g., *BGU* 1052 (13 B.C.), ll. 14, 15.

52. *P.Ryl.* 154 (A.D. 66), l. 4.

53. Cf. also *Chariton* 5.10.7, 'may you be happy, wife (γύναι), for I call you [my] wife (γυναῖκα γὰρ σε κάλω), even though you love another'.

54. See E. Dickey, *Greek Forms of Address: From Herodotus to Lucian* (Oxford: Clarendon Press, 1996), pp. 86-88; on ἄνηρ for 'husband' see pp. 85-86.

55. G. D. Fee, '1 Corinthians 7:1 in the NIV,' *JETS* 23/24 (1980): 307-14.

56. J. N. Adams, *The Latin Sexual Vocabulary* (London: Duckworth, 1982), p. 184 for ἅπτω and *tango* and ἔχω and *habeo*, p. 187.

make sense of the following verses? Paul clearly disagrees with the Corinthians' suggestion (7:1) and takes an opposite point of view. He argues, firstly, that their conclusion does not take into account the problem of the possibility of 'immoralities' (pl. of πορνεία) within marriage (7:2). It is clear from the previous passage that some Corinthian Christians had not abandoned what has been called 'an intimate and unholy trinity' of eating, drinking, and sexual immorality (6:9-20); sexual indulgence by men after marriage was assumed in the first century.[57]

Paul's deep concern about adultery can be justified, not because of a mistaken view among some New Testament scholars that Roman Corinth was more immoral than other cities, but because of the consensus in the first century that adultery by a man was not wrong unless it infringed Augustus law, viz., where adultery involved a woman of high status.[58]

The call is to each married person to recognise that the essence of marriage rests in the mutual sexual obligation where 'each', i.e., 'every [husband] "must have" (ἐχέτω) to his own wife and each [wife] must have to her own husband' (7:2).[59] The word 'have' carried the same connotations in the ancient world as it does in the present-day marriage service, where the presumption of sexual consent and sexual intercourse is expressed in the sentence 'to "have" and to hold from this day forward'. However, here sexual access was not seen simply as the presumption of consent as in the marriage service but as a command.

The husband is told that he must fulfil his sexual obligations to his wife. The concept of obligation had first priority in decisions relating to the conduct of first-century men and women. A freedman had binding obligations to his patron, and there was discussion in the first century whether failure to meet them should not be countered as a criminal offence. So when Paul refers to an obligation,[60] it would be seen as a binding commitment on the part of both the husband and the wife. Paul is stating here that there is a binding commitment on the part of the husband to fulfil his sexual obligations to his wife. He then proceeds to tell the wife that she has exactly the same duty towards her husband (7:3).

Roman law implemented by Augustus saw the husband having au-

---

57. To cite Booth, 'The Age for Reclining and Its Attendant Perils,' p. 105. See n. 61.
58. See p. 52.
59. Adams, *The Latin Sexual Vocabulary,* p. 186, ἔχω and *habeo.*
60. See pp. 130-31.

thority over the wife so that any breach of sexuality fidelity on her part was an indictable criminal offence once he had divorced her for it.[61] Paul repeats that the wife does not have authority to do what she wants with her body sexually. Rather, she has surrendered herself to her husband, and he has that 'authority'.

However, what runs counter to much first-century practice is the fact that the Christian husband does not have authority over his own body, but his wife does. He therefore cannot indulge his sexual passions outside marriage, however much this may have been accepted in first-century society.

Plutarch, in what seems to us an extraordinary but traditional *encomium* delivered in the bridal chamber, suggested that adultery on the part of the husband was both acceptable and explicable. His comment comes in one of the traditional speeches delivered at a wedding and given the title 'the bedroom speech' (κατευναστικός). In delivering such a speech, 'Advice to the Bride and Groom', to two young friends, Plutarch not only 'lectured' the young bride on the need for prudence in spending money on clothing and other matters, but also provided justification for her new husband's possible adultery in days to come.[62] He shows how acceptable it was in his society, even among philosophers. He supported his argument by citing as a precedent the conduct of Persian kings who sat with their wives during the meal but dismissed them when the kings 'wish to be merry and get drunk'. They then sent for their music girls and concubines. Plutarch says, 'they are right in what they do, because they do not concede any share in their licentiousness and debauchery to their wedded wives'. He then explains to the young bride. 'If therefore a man in private life, who is incontinent and dissolute in regard to his pleasures, commits some peccadillo with a paramour or a maidservant, his wedded wife ought not to be indignant or angry, but she should reason that it is respect for her which leads him to share his debauchery, licentiousness, and wantonness with another woman' (140B).[63]

61. L. F. Raditsa, 'Augustus' Legislation concerning Marriage, Procreation, Love Affairs and Adultery,' *ANRW* 2.13 (1980): 278-339; and J. E. Grubbs, '"Pagan" and "Christian" Marriage: The State of the Question,' *Journal of Early Christian Studies* (1994): 361-412.

62. Plutarch, 'Advice to the Bride and Groom', *Moralia* 140B-D.

63. L. Goessler, 'Advice to the Bride and Groom,' in S. B. Pomeroy, ed., *Plutarch's 'Advice to the Bride and Groom' and 'A Consolation to His Wife': English Translations, Commentary, Interpretative Essays, and Bibliography* (Oxford: Oxford University Press, 1999), pp. 111-20.

This was hardly the appropriate occasion on which to justify adultery — it was not as if the young married couple were strangers but both were actual friends of Plutarch. However, adultery on the part of the husband was so condoned that it was considered entirely apposite to justify it to this young bride just before the guests, who escorted the young couple to their wedding bed, retired so that the marriage could be consummated and proof provided the following morning to the families.[64]

Another view was expressed by the Stoic philosopher Musonius Rufus (c. A.D. 30–c. 101-2):

> Men who are not wanton or immoral are bound to consider sexual intercourse justified only when it occurs in marriage and is indulged in for the purpose of begetting children (ἐπὶ γενέσει παίδων), since that is lawful, but unjust and unlawful when it is mere pleasure-seeking, even in marriage. But of all sexual relations those involving adultery are most unlawful, and no more tolerable are those of men with men, because it is a monstrous thing and contrary to nature. But, furthermore, leaving out of consideration adultery, all intercourse with women which is without lawful character is shameful and is practised from lack of self-restraint.[65]

Musonius argues how inappropriate it would be for a husband to have sexual relationships with his slave girl, condoning it no more than he could his wife involving herself with a male slave. His argument was based on the concept of the Stoic virtue of self-restraint.

The orator at the marriage bed is instructed to tell his hearers that one of the advantages of marriage is 'temperance'.[66] Elsewhere it is said of married men that 'such persons are thought (δοκοῦσιν) to have given up promiscuous sex and to look each to his own wife and to her alone'.[67] The distinction with Paul's comments is that he is not speaking about the advantages of marriage but, given the above interpretation, of the necessity

64. *Menander Rhetor* 406, 'when there will be so many witnesses on hand the morning after the initiation'.
65. Musonius Rufus, 'On Sexual Indulgence,' 86-87, translated by C. E. Lutz, 'Musonius Rufus: The Roman Socrates,' *YCS* 10 (1947): 3-147. Cited in S. Treggiari, *Roman Marriage: Iusti Coniuges from the Time of Cicero to the Time of Ulpian* (Oxford: Clarendon Press, 1991), p. 221. On earlier attitudes see pp. 199-200.
66. *Menander Rhetor* 406.
67. Dionysius of Halicarnassus, *Roman Antiquities* 2.263.

of sexual intercourse in marriage because of the problem of 'immoralities' (7:2). His comments must be seen in the light of the overarching theological referent of 6:9 (cf. 5:11)[68] where the sexual sins of fornication and adultery are not 'thought to have been given up' but must be abandoned, for Christians are deceived if they believe that such conduct will not exclude them from the kingdom of God.

Paul's teaching was based on ownership of the body. The husband's body was not his own to do with as he wished. The marriage relationship tied him into exclusive sexual relations with his wife. The single man's body is not his own but, as Paul has previously reminded the young Corinthians, it is a member of Christ (6:15), the shrine of the Spirit (6:19), and, having been bought with a price, the agent through which God is glorified (6:20). However, the reason for purity in marriage is that the husband's body actually belongs to his wife.

Any withholding of sexual consent on the part of either is seen by Paul as 'depriving' or 'defrauding' (ἀποστερέω) the other partner of their due right (7:5a).[69] The only concession for abstinence is when a decision to suspend conjugal activity was 'out of mutual consent' (ἐκ συμφώνου). The purpose for this is clearly defined, i.e., prayer and presumably fasting because of the urgent need for extended prayer; but the period is limited because it is only for a season (7:5). Abstinence must be only temporary and then the couple must 'again come together' (καὶ πάλιν ἐπὶ τὸ αὐτὸ ἦτε) in sexual union. The reason for resumption is that they will be tempted by Satan because of the lack of self-control on the part of either partner if abstinence is prolonged. Paul saw the danger of adultery as ever-present in the marriage and therefore forbade sexual abstinence except for an exceptional and temporary circumstance. Presumably the activity of extended prayer in the presence of God does not provide the temptation that abstinence for no acceptable reason would.

Finally, why would Paul mention the matter of praying and presum-

68. See my 'Homosexual Terminology in 1 Corinthians 6:9: The Roman Context and the Greek Loan-Word,' in A. N. S. Lane, ed., *Scripture and Interpretation: Historical and Theological Studies in Honour of David Wright* (Leicester: Inter-Varsity Press, 1997), p. 290, for a brief discussion of the overarching theological referent which forms the framework for the discussion of issues relating to avoiding fornication (6:12-20), adultery (7:2, 5), covetousness relating to social mobility (7:17-24), and idolatry (10:14).

69. The same verb used of 'defrauding' a brother by going to court and winning a vexatious case with damage being awarded to the winner (6:7). See pp. 70-71.

ably fasting (7:5b)? Was it that Christians were given to this as they interceded for the tranquillity of the city. There is an Old Testament precedent for that in Jeremiah 29:7, where prayer for the tranquillity of the city was enjoined on all so that 'in the peace of the city you may have peace'. It could well be that Corinthian Christians had read 'the signs of the times' such as earthquakes and famines as supernatural warnings, as did their fellow non-Christians. They had determined to abstain from sexual intercourse. They were forbidden by Paul to relinquish the marriage bed, and one possible reason suggested in this chapter for their thinking it was appropriate to do this was so that the wife would not become pregnant or be suckling a child (Mark 13:17). While Paul countenanced prayer and fasting, given the gravity of personal or wider circumstances, he teaches the temporary nature of sexual abstention. He also stresses the resumption of the essential obligation of the marital bed both as a fulfillment of the sexual obligation of both partners and as a deterrent against the temptation to marital infidelity.

Deming attributes the sentence, 'It is good for a man not to touch [his] wife', to a 'Cynic' view of marriage held by the Corinthian Christians.[70] He has been influenced in his conclusion by the meaning he attaches to the use of σχολή and σχολάζω in the Stoic/Cynic tradition which he has taken as his starting point. However, the history of the noun shows that, while initially it meant 'leisure', that meaning was replaced by the term εὐκαιρία by the first century B.C.[71] The former term was used from that time on for a 'school', which was anything but a leisurely experience for pupils.[72] Its change in meaning is explicable in that the prerogative of the rich enabled them not to have to work but to devote their lives to leisure time, and the verb did mean 'to have leisure' or 'spare time' or 'have nothing to do'. It also meant 'to devote' one's time to something such as agriculture, and among the rich 'to attend lectures'. Education was seen as a privilege available to those who did not have to work but whose parents gave them the opportunity to study, originally under private tutors, but by the first century in a school.[73]

70. W. Deming, *Paul on Marriage and Celibacy: The Hellenistic Background of 1 Corinthians 7*, SNTSMS 83 (Cambridge: Cambridge University Press, 1995), p. 122.

71. J. Glucker, *Antiochus and the Late Academy* (Göttingen: Vandenhoeck & Ruprecht, 1978), pp. 161-62.

72. E.g., see *P.Oxy.* 2190 (first century A.D.), l. 21.

73. See my *Philo and Paul among the Sophists*, p. 25.

However, what is being sought in Corinth is not abstinence from sexual intercourse for the 'leisure' of prayer, but, as has been argued here, abstinence in order to pray because of 'the present troubles' (7:26). The Corinthian Christians' question to Paul on the appropriateness of sexual abstinence in marriage may reflect the seriousness of their concern as they read the signs of the times such as earthquakes and serious famines and saw the attempts by secular authorities to stem the deterioration of social stability that epitomised the responses to grain shortages in the first century. Their own response reflected their Christian interpretation of what all these external uncertainties meant. 1 Corinthians itself may reflect the fact of insufficient food for some at the Lord's Supper brought about by the grain shortages and later records that there were those of the 'house of Stephanas' who 'set themselves the task of ministering to the saints', which again may relate to this problem (11:21; 16:15).[74] That they should entertain such a radical step is explicable in the light of dominical sayings concerning the signs of the times. They were in uncharted waters as a young Christian community facing this social distress, and they needed Paul's apostolic ruling on whether this was the right response to this external problem.

74. See Chs. 7 and 9.

The Forward Referent of the Neuter
Demonstrative Pronoun in 7:6

Does the discussion of this particular issue end at 7:5? There is diversity of opinion on the relationship of 1 Corinthians 7:6-7 to its wider context, and, as a result, widely differing interpretations of 7:1-24 have been offered, especially concerning 7:2-5. Some have suggested that the neuter demonstrative pronoun refers to marriage in 7:2, 'But because of the temptation to immoralities, each man must have his own wife and each woman must have her own husband.' Thus they have concluded that Paul sees marriage as a concession to the lack of self-control and a less desirable option for Christians.[75] Others see the phrase 'by way of concession' pointing to temporary sexual abstinence, and 'this' refers to Paul's whole response (7:2-5) to the question raised by letter by the Corinthian Christians (7:1). Paul is therefore seen to agree with what some understand as the Corinthians' position on celibacy in 7:1.[76] Others see this demonstrative pronoun referring back simply to 7:5, where Paul lays down the only grounds

---

75. F. Godet, *Commentary on the First Epistle to the Corinthians* (Edinburgh: T & T Clark, 1898), I, 325; W. H. Mare, *1 Corinthians* (Grand Rapids: Zondervan, 1976), p. 229; and G. G. Findlay, *St. Paul's First Epistle to the Corinthians* (Grand Rapids: Eerdmans, 1961), p. 824.

76. Including C. K. Barrett, *The First Epistle to the Corinthians*, 2nd ed. (London: A. & C. Black, 1971), p. 157; F. F. Bruce, *1 and 2 Corinthians* (London: Oliphants, 1971), p. 67; Fee, *1 Corinthians*, pp. 283-84; and most recently J. C. Poirier and J. Frankovic, 'Celibacy and Charisma in 1 Cor. 7:5-7,' *HTR* 89.1 (1996): 1-18.

for not fulfilling conjugal obligations for those married.[77] The resolution of some of the alternatives narrows down primarily to the role of the referent of the neuter demonstrative pronoun 'this' (τοῦτο) in 7:6. Commentators on 1 Corinthians have themselves seen how important 'this' is in determining the overall interpretation of the passage.

In this appendix it is argued on grammatical grounds that the neuter demonstrative pronoun 'this', when used with the verbs of saying as in 7:6, refers to the subordinate clause introduced by 'that' (ὅτι) or an implied 'that' as in 7:7a, and its place in the sentence gives a clue as to the importance of the forward referent. Paul's statements in 7:7b contain an overarching conceptual framework for the discussion of God's gifts of singleness and marriage in the subsequent sayings in 7:8-16, and he links these gifts with his standard teaching 'in all the churches' on other important issues of life's calling such as the individual Christian's ethnicity and social status in 7:17-24.

As a result the translation offered of 1 Corinthians 7:6-7 is, 'And this I am saying (τοῦτο δὲ λέγω) by way of concession and not of command, [that] I wish rather (θέλω δέ) all men were even as I myself, but (ἀλλά) each man has his own gift from God, one after this manner, and another after that'.

The Role of 'This' and ['That'] in 7:6-7

In Greek grammar the neuter demonstrative pronoun 'this' (τοῦτο) has a number of functions, illustrated not the least from the Pauline corpus itself.[78] It can refer to a neuter nominative or accusative noun, pronoun, or relative pronoun.[79] There are five instances where it agrees with the substantised infinitive or participle,[80] and on some sixteen occasions in the Pauline letters it refers to a verb, thereby denoting action.[81] It is also 'used

---

77. E.g., S. J. Kistemaker, 1 Corinthians (Grand Rapids: Baker, 1993), p. 214.

78. There is a lack of precision on the various uses of the neuter demonstrative pronoun in modern New Testament Greek Grammars, and this has led J. C. Callow, 'To What Do touto and tauta Refer in Paul's Letters?' Notes on Translations 70 (1978): 8 to confess to 'complete bafflement'. The uses are by no means as obscure as Callow suggests.

79. Rom. 7:15 (twice), 16, 19, 20; 1 Cor. 5:2; 15:53-54; 2 Cor. 12:14; 13:1; Gal. 6:7; Eph. 5:32; 6:8; Phil. 2:5; or the substantive 1 Cor. 10:28.

80. Rom. 14:13; 2 Cor. 2:1; 8:10; Phil. 1:22, 25. See BDF #290 (3), #413 (3).

81. Rom. 12:20; 1 Cor. 6:6, 8; 7:37; 9:17; 2 Cor. 1:17; Eph. 2:8; 6:1; Phil. 3:15; Col. 3:20; 1 Thess. 4:3; 5:18; 1 Tim. 2:3; 4:16; 5:4; Philem. 18.

as preparation for a subordinate clause', with ὅτι found or implied in twenty-five cases.[82] For example, in Romans 6:6 Paul says: 'and knowing this that (καὶ τοῦτο γινώσκοντες ὅτι)'; and in 1 Corinthians 7:26 he writes: 'Therefore I think this . . . that it is good for a person to remain as he is (νομίζω οὖν τοῦτο, ὅτι).' So common was this usage in classical and koine Greek that the conjunction ὅτι could be omitted before the subordinate clause, because τοῦτο was sufficient to indicate it. For instance, in Galatians 3:17 Paul states: 'And this I am saying (τοῦτο δὲ λέγω) [that] the law . . . does not annul a covenant', where 'that' is simply understood. Elsewhere, we read in Ephesians 4:17: 'Therefore I am saying this in the Lord [that] . . .'. 1 Corinthians 7 itself provides an instance of the same: 'and this I am saying (τοῦτο δὲ φημι) [that] the appointed time has grown short' (7:29). Accordingly, 'this' in 7:6 could well be preparation for the objective clause in 7:7.

It should also be noted that ὅτι is used with the neuter demonstrative pronoun in Paul, as it is by other writers, 'when the clause which follows is to receive special emphasis'.[83] There are examples of this in 1 Corinthians, as in 1:12: 'And I am saying this that . . . (λέγω δὲ τοῦτο ὅτι)'.[84] The placing of the neuter demonstrative pronoun at the beginning of the sentence gives even greater emphasis to what is being said, as in 15:50: 'This I tell you, brethren, that flesh and blood will not inherit (τοῦτο δέ φημι, ἀδελφοί, ὅτι . . .).'[85] Where ὅτι is implied, the neuter demonstrative pronoun occupies the emphatic first position in the sentence.[86]

The neuter demonstrative pronoun can also be followed by 'therefore' (ἵνα) in final purpose clauses, as in Colossians 2:4: 'I am saying this in order that no one may delude you.' An important example is again provided in 1 Corinthians 7:35, where Paul stresses, 'I am saying this for your benefit not in order to lay any restraint upon you but . . . (τοῦτο δὲ . . . λέγω οὐχ ἵνα . . . ἐπιβάλω ἀλλά . . .)'. Here the neuter demonstrative refers

---

82. BDF #290 (3). Rom. 2:3; 6:6; 13:11; 1 Cor. 1:12; 7:26, 29, 35; 15:50; 2 Cor. 5:14; 9:6; 10:7, 11; Gal. 3:17; Eph. 4:17; 5:5; Phil. 1:7, 9, 28; Col. 2:4; 1 Thess. 4:15; 2 Thess. 3:10; 1 Tim. 1:9; 2 Tim. 1:5; 3:1, apart from 1 Cor. 7:6.

83. G. B. Winer, *A Treatise on the Grammar of New Testament Greek* (E.T. Edinburgh: T & T Clark, 1870), p. 200. In fact it could be used without a verb for emphasis, i.e., 2 Cor. 13:9; Gal. 3:2.

84. 1 Cor. 7:26. See also Rom. 2:3; 2 Cor. 5:14; 1 Tim. 4:15; 2 Tim. 1:15.

85. Rom. 2:3; 6:6; 13:11; Eph. 5:5; 1 Thess. 4:15; 2 Thess. 3:10; 2 Tim. 3:1.

86. E.g., 1 Cor. 7:29; 2 Cor. 9:6; Gal. 3:17; Eph. 4:17.

THE INFLUENCE OF SOCIAL CHANGE

back to 7:32-34 and ἵνα introduces the purpose clause containing the aorist subjunctive. However, the possibility that 7:7 is a final purpose clause is ruled out because of Paul's use of the present indicative 'I wish' (θέλω).[87]

Also important to our discussion of 7:6-7 is the fact that ὅτι is a conjunction used to 'introduce the objective clause after verbs of seeing or knowing, thinking or saying'.[88] The following examples from the Pauline corpus demonstrate that this was not simply a classical Greek construction. 'Do you reckon this, O man, when you judge . . . that you condemn yourself?' (Rom. 2:3); 'And knowing this, that . . .' (Rom. 6:6); 'And this I am saying, brothers, that . . .' (1 Cor. 15:50); 'having judged this, that . . .' (2 Cor. 5:14); 'he must reckon this again concerning himself, that . . .' (2 Cor. 10:7); 'such people must understand this, that . . .' (2 Cor. 10:11); 'For this we are saying to you, . . . that . . .' (1 Thess. 4:15); and 'we commanded this to you, that . . .' (2 Thess. 3:10). Verbs of saying followed by an objective clause assume the conjunction (ὅτι). Again 1 Corinthians 7 provides examples: 'I am saying to the unmarried and widows [that] . . .' (7:8); and 'To the rest I am saying [that] . . .' (7:12). In 7:6, it is therefore grammatically possible that the verb 'I am saying' introduces an objective clause in the following verse, and the forward place of the neuter demonstrative pronoun in the sentence is meant to give special emphasis to what is to be said.

The particle Paul used to begin the subordinate clause in 7:7 is not ὅτι, but either γάρ or δέ (there is textual uncertainty).[89] If it were γάρ, then the sentence would read either 'I wish indeed (θέλω γάρ) . . .', or 'to be sure I wish . . .'.[90] However, the need to use 'indeed' to stress the fact seems unnecessary, given not only the use of τοῦτο for emphasis but its place at the beginning of the sentence, which highlights its importance even more.

If the correct reading is δέ, then there are two possible translations. 'And this I am saying . . . that I wish all men were as even I myself am', where there is a causal connection which is less direct than γάρ. Given the

87. In the discussion of final purpose clauses, BDF note that the use of 'the present indicative after ἵνα is, of course, only a corruption of the text' (BDF #369 [6]). They are referring to variants found in some NT texts, but they do not include 1 Cor. 7:7.
88. Liddell and Scott, p. 1265.
89. B. S. Rosner, *Paul, Scripture and Ethics: A Study of 1 Corinthians 5–7* (Leiden: E. J. Brill, 1994), pp. 151-52.
90. See BAGD #4 on the use of γάρ to mean 'indeed' or 'to be sure'.

236

preference of later Greek writers to replace γάρ by δέ,[91] the later textual evidence for δέ would be explicable, but the textual evidence is certainly early and seems to rule this out.[92]

If adverbial meaning was given to δέ, 'rather', as some have suggested for this verse,[93] then it would fit in well with the concluding statement in the sentence, as well as the use of τοῦτο with λέγω and an implied ὅτι. The verses would read: 'And this I am saying by way of concession and not command, [that] I wish rather all were as I myself.'[94] Paul goes on to observe in a statement introduced by the strong adversative, 'but (ἀλλά) each one has his gift from God, one of one kind and one of another'. He recognises that alternatives open to Christians are not a matter of preference, but are a personal gift from God for each individual.

There is an interesting near parallel construction in 7:25-26. After stating in 7:25 that he has no command from the Lord, he goes on to say in 7:26: 'I think therefore this to be good because of the present distress that it (ὅτι) is good . . .'.[95] In 7:6-7 and 7:26 verbs of saying or thinking introduce the subordinate clause; although ὅτι is absent in the former, it is present in the latter. Comparing what Paul writes in 7:6 (τοῦτο δὲ λέγω) and 7:26 (νομίζω οὖν τοῦτο), we see that the place of the neuter demonstrative in 7:6 puts stress on the Pauline concession which follows, while in 7:26 it introduces Paul's own conviction, as the subsequent discussion demonstrates. In 7:26 the connective οὖν makes it clear that the reference is forward, while in 7:6 the emphatic placing of the neuter demonstrative pronoun indicates the same.

91. See BAGD #4.

92. E.g., P46.

93. On the meaning 'rather' in relation to this verse, see Winer, *A Treatise on the Grammar of New Testament Greek*, p. 567. See also J. D. Denniston, *The Greek Particles*, 2nd ed. (Oxford: Clarendon Press, 1950), pp. 162 and 177 on the adverbial use of δέ. K. Callow, 'The Disappearing δέ in 1 Corinthians,' in D. A. Black, ed., *Linguistic and New Testament Interpretations: Essays on Discourse Analysis* (Nashville: Broadman Press, 1992), ch. 9, analyses the occurrences of δέ in 7:1-9 and notes the short-span contrast in 7:7b, but she ignores the particle in 7:7a altogether (p. 187).

94. B. M. Metzger, *A Textual Commentary on the Greek New Testament* (London and New York: United Bible Societies, 1971), p. 554 argues: 'The reading δέ, which is strongly supported, is preferable to γάρ, which appears to be a correction introduced by scribes who did not appreciate the nuance of opposition to the concession mentioned in ver. 6.' The discussion here would rule out the view of v. 6 containing a concession.

95. The verb followed by accusative and the infinitive (BAGD).

According to Hans Conzelmann, the imperatival aspect of 7:6-7 'must not be pressed'.[96] But the interpretation of 7:6-7 offered here has the advantage of giving proper weight to that verbal aspect when cognisance is taken of 7:2-5. If τοῦτο in 7:6 refers back to those verses as a kind of concession, then Paul's statement is a *non sequitur*. These verses clearly include commands: 'each man *must* have his own wife'; 'each woman *must* have her own husband'; 'the husband *must* render to his wife his [sexual] obligation, and likewise also the wife *must* render to her husband [her sexual obligation]' — 'You *must* not defraud one another', and 'you must be together again'. The referent of τοῦτο in 7:6 cannot be the plurality of commands in 7:2-5, since the neuter demonstrative pronoun is not plural (ταῦτα), a form Paul uses elsewhere to refer to pluralities. Again 1 Corinthians itself provides examples of this: 'I write these things (ταῦτα)' (4:14); 'I am not saying these things (ταῦτα)' (9:8); and 'I am not writing these things' (ταῦτα)' (9:15).[97] By contrast, the τοῦτο of 7:6 must refer to a single phenomenon.[98] As has been shown, there are good grammatical grounds for seeing τοῦτο as referring not to a previous imperatival verb; the concessive comment that follows stresses that, in contrast to 7:2-5, he is not commanding conduct in 7:6-7, although he will again do so in 7:8-24.

It is suggested here, then, that Paul in 7:6 is at pains to inform his readers in this way: 'And this I am saying by way of concession and not of command'. τοῦτο is used to give special emphasis to what he is about to say (which is not a command) and, as we have noted, it is positioned at the beginning of the sentence to underscore this further. As already noted, τοῦτο is normally proceeded by 'that' (ὅτι), although here, as in 1 Corinthians 7:29, the conjunction is understood. The referent of the neuter demonstrative pronoun, then, is forward looking, and its place in the sentence furthers the emphatic nature of Paul's concessive comment in the clause in 7:7: '[that] I wish rather all men were as even I myself.'

---

96. H. Conzelmann, *1 Corinthians* (Philadelphia: Fortress, 1975), p. 118. See D. E. Garland, 'The Christian's Posture towards Marriage and Celibacy: 1 Corinthians 7,' *RevExp* 80 (1983): 360, n. 23 on the imperatives, citing W. F. Orr, 'Paul's Treatment of Marriage in 1 Corinthians 7,' *Pittsburgh Perspective* 8 (1967): 12. Garland concludes that the reference of 7:6 is forward and not backward, but feels that if γάρ were the correct reading, then that verse would clearly refer forward to v. 7.

97. The exception is 12:20, where he is citing the LXX.

98. Cf. ταῦτα ἔλεγον ὑμῖν (2 Thess. 2:5); ταῦτα λάλει (Tit. 2:15).

The Role of 7:7 in 7:8-24

Paul recognises that, whatever the advantages of singleness, his 'wish' can never be his 'command' that is binding on all the Corinthians, because of the alternative gifts God gives to his people. What, then, is the place of 7:7 in the subsequent discussion? It appears to operate as the overarching reality in which the implications of those two callings represented by two different gifts of God for Christians are subsequently worked out. How Paul discusses the issues in 1 Corinthians 7 helps us to understand this. The matter that the Corinthians have themselves raised by letter in 7:1, and that Paul has dealt with in 7:2-5, is consciously distinguished from the rest. He makes it clear that he is now taking up issues on his own initiative, and not ones raised by them: 'this I am saying (τοῦτο δὲ λέγω)' (7:6). He himself is raising three related issues: 'I am saying (λέγω δέ)' (7:8); 'I am commanding (παραγγέλλω), not I but the Lord' (7:10); and 'to the rest I am saying' (τοῖς δὲ λοιποῖς λέγω ἐγώ) (7:12). What he is discussing is clear — viz., singleness and marriage in relation to widows and the unmarried (7:8-9), separation and reconciliation (7:9-10), and the marriage ordinance and divorce for those whose marriage partners are not Christians (7:11-16).

Before Paul deals with the next issue raised by the Corinthians' letter to him (7:25ff.), he concludes the whole discussion by repeating a summary of a major aspect of Paul's traditional teaching which he commanded, without exception in 'all the churches' (7:17-24). It begins with the statement: 'As the Lord has assigned to each, each as God has called, thus he must walk.' Ethnicity and social identity were the results of the providential oversight of God (7:18, 21, 23). Having stated this at the beginning of the passage, Paul repeats the command twice 'each in whatever calling, brethren, in this you must remain with God' (7:20, 24). Just as the gifts of singleness or marriedness is personally given by the Lord, so too, Paul seems to be implying, were these ethnic and social 'markers'. God's gifts and calling were personal, and Christians were to remain in the situations in which God had placed them. This meant that Christians were forbidden to undergo epispasm and circumcision or to sell themselves into slavery, for these would change their God-given cultural or social status (7:18, 23). These moves were undertaken in the first century for financial reasons or to overcome feelings of social stigma imposed by secular society.[99] Together with

---

99. For a discussion of 7:17-24, see my 'Social Mobility,' *Seek the Welfare of the City,*

an individual's marital status, they were personal 'gifts' or 'callings' from God. In this context the word for 'calling' (κλῆσις, which can also mean 'class') is a synonymous term for 'gifts', used in 7:7. So sandwiched between 7:6 and 7:17-24 are supplementary but very important issues, all of which Paul himself raises and which he relates to the gifts distributed to the individual by God himself.

In conclusion, resolving the function of the neuter demonstrative pronoun has been shown to be crucial for interpreting this passage. Its role is certainly critical in 1 Corinthians 7:6-7, for it occupies a pivotal place as Paul turns from the Corinthian request for an apostolic ruling in 7:2-5 to the apostolic and dominical sayings in 7:8ff., inserting his own 'concession' in 7:6-7a but not to anything he has said in 7:2-5. He then proceeds in 7:7b to provide the framework for the discussion of Christian conduct in relation to the different gifts and callings of God.

First Century Christians in the Graeco-Roman World (Carlisle: Paternoster; Grand Rapids: Eerdmans, 1994), ch. 8.

CHAPTER 11

The Present Crisis and the Consummation
of Marriage (1 Corinthians 7:25-38)

'He Who Marries . . . He Who Does Not Marry' (7:38)

The previous chapter explored (1) the question raised by social change about the appropriateness of sexual abstinence in the marriage bed because of the present dislocation in Corinth caused by the famine; (2) Paul's rejection of their proposal that it was good for a man not to engage in sexual intercourse with his wife. It was natural therefore, that a supplementary question (7:1) should be raised as to whether Christians who were betrothed should proceed to consummate their relationship by marrying, given the same present difficulty in Corinth (7:25).

In examining Paul's response in 1 Corinthians 7:25-38 it emerges that the relationship with the betrothed was not the same in each case, as each fiancée had set different parameters for a decision. In order to understand the dilemmas some faced over this issue we must explore (I) the predicament which some men had created for their own relationship; (II) the eschatological framework that Paul invokes in which the expectations of life (including married life) should be seen by Christians; and (III) the Christian obligations of single and married men and women.

I. Personal Dilemmas Aggravated by the Present Dislocation

It is possible to reconstruct the question the Corinthian Christians asked Paul even though he began by succinctly stating only 'concerning the virgins' (Περὶ δὲ τῶν παρθένων)¹ (7:25). Subsequent discussion reveals that he was not speculating about the situation, because the conditional clause (7:36a) has 'if' (εἰ) with the present indicative, which is an 'indicative of reality'. It should therefore be translated 'as you tell me', as BDF note.² It is different from the following conditional clause (7:36b), which is introduced by ἐάν with the present subjunctive.³ While BDF account for the use of the different particles and moods in 1 Corinthians 7:36 thus — the first conditional sentence notes what is happening 'as you tell me', and the second has a future reference⁴ — there are examples within 1 Corinthians itself where ἐάν followed by the present subjunctive refers to the present (e.g., 4:15; 5:11). Fee says of the two conditional sentences that 'Paul knew that an actual situation like this existed in the community' and in the case of the second suggests that it was 'reflecting something that might be so'.⁵ It is the case that where εἰ and ἐάν immediately follow each other 'one conjunction or the other manifestly proceeds from a different conception of the relation'.⁶ The problem raised by the Corinthians is actually summarised in the εἰ clause and is followed by Paul's understanding of what happens as a consequence of inappropriate behaviour in such instances in 7:36c (see section c).

1. J. Chadwick, *Lexicographica Graeca: Contributions to the Lexicography of Ancient Greek* (Oxford: Clarendon Press, 1996), pp. 226-29, suggests the term is not restricted to a 'biological' virgin but is used of a social one, i.e., a woman who is not married.
2. BDF #372.
3. In this case ἐάν is not a synonymous particle for εἰ which requires the present or perfect indicative. *Contra* A. T. Robinson, *A Grammar of the Greek New Testament in the Light of Historical Research* (New York: Hodder and Stoughton, 1914), pp. 1009-10. ἐάν can be used to express an indefinite relation to a present reality; cf. 'if you should have many guides' (1 Cor. 4:15; BDF #372), and the present subjunctive can refer to the future (#373) or to the present.
4. BDF #372 (i) a.
5. G. D. Fee, *The First Epistle to the Corinthians* (Grand Rapids: Eerdmans, 1987), p. 350, nn. 11, 12.
6. For a discussion of this usage see G. B. Winer, *A Treatise on the Grammar of the Greek New Testament* (Edinburgh: T & T Clark, 1870), pp. 370-71. See, e.g., in Acts 5:38: 'if (ἐάν) it should be of men it will be overthrown [a point which the result will decide] . . . but if (εἰ) it is from God [as Peter says it is] you will not be able to overthrow them'; also Xenophon, *Cyropaedia* 4.1.15; Isocrates, *Evagoras* 194; Luke 13:9; John 13:17; Acts 5:38; and Rev. 2:5.

The Present Crisis and the Consummation of Marriage

a. Unseemly Behaviour Towards His Betrothed (7:36a)

In laying out the first condition which should govern the decision to marry — 'If anyone considers he is behaving in an unseemly way towards his betrothed [as you write]' (εἰ δέ τις ἀσχημονεῖν ἐπὶ τὴν παρθένον αὐτοῦ νομίζει) (7:36a) — Paul records how the Corinthians involved wrote about their particular situation.

The verb translated 'to behave unseemly' (ἀσχημονεῖν) and its cognates can have strong sexual innuendoes.[7] Plutarch, writing in the late first century A.D., records that Philip of Macedonia was sitting down with his tunic pulled up in 'an unseemly way', exposing himself in front of slaves. The person who pointed this out to Philip was declared to be a true friend indeed.[8] Cato's wife was divorced because of her 'unseemly behaviour' (i.e., her adultery),[9] and a young unmarried girl faced her 'unseemly behaviour' (i.e., fornication) with decorum by undergoing an abortion.[10] Plutarch also makes reference to 'sundry amours, idle amusements with wine and women and other unseemly pastimes' (καὶ παιδιὰς ἑτέρας ἀσχήμονας).[11] Those who 'fall into passion (πάθη) and sins (ἁμαρτίας) . . . act discreditably (ἀσχημόνειν)'.[12] He also records that 'men should not strip off their clothes [in the baths] with women' (which was seen to be 'an impropriety'), nor 'would a *hetaira* allow her lover to behave "improperly" beneath the portrait of Xenocrates who was famous for his chastity'.[13]

Epictetus, a contemporary of Plutarch, uses the same verb to refer to a person who 'disgraced himself naked and out of doors'. Its cognate is used to describe sleeping beside a beautiful woman and having strong desires — behaviour classed among the 'unseemly deeds' which Epictetus condemns.[14]

---

7. The cognate noun was also used as a euphemism for αἰδοῖον, and the LXX uses the latter term in Lev. 18:7-17 on a number of occasions. It refers to uncovering 'the nakedness' of a number of persons with affinity relationships.

8. *Moralia* 178D.

9. Cato Minor, 24.3

10. 'Sayings of the Spartans,' 235C; in the same discourse reference is made to 'keeping brothels and 'other unseemly pursuits' (236B).

11. 'Dion', 7.4.

12. 'How to Study Poetry' (23E).

13. *Fragments*, 85, 97.

14. *Diss.* 22.15.3; 4.9.5.

Dio Chrysostom says of those who became dissolute and drunk at a private banquet, where 'after dinners' — as they came to be known — included sexual intercourse with courtesans, were behaving in an 'unseemly' way. A courtesan was declared 'indecent' because she uttered licentious phrases from her chamber.[15] ἀσχημονέω and its cognates could also describe 'unbecoming' or 'inappropriate' behaviour, judged to be so by the norms of that society.[16]

Josephus used the term to describe the unseemly behaviour of the lovers Salome and Syllaeus in the court of Herod. He explicates this by recording that 'passions clear by their gestures and looks' resulted in a sexual liaison. Elsewhere what was done to statues which were then carried into a brothel was described as 'things too indecent to be reported'. He also notes the behaviour of a Roman soldier in the temple guard at the Passover in Jerusalem who exposed himself and stooped down in an 'indecent' attitude.[17]

The survey of literary writers and nonliterary sources[18] contains some eighty-seven occurrences of this word and its cognates, and provides overwhelming evidence that, within the context of male and female relationships, the word 'to behave unseemly' has sexual connotations.[19]

Paul himself uses the cognate and its antonym in 1 Corinthians 12:23-24 to describe the private over against the presentable parts of the body. He discusses the organs of the body and then proceeds to note that the unpresentable parts (τὰ ἀσχήμονα)[20] of the human anatomy (i.e., the

---

15. Dio Chrysostom, *Or.* 30.41; 40.29. Cf. also unbecoming table manners at a banquet (*Or.* 30.35).

16. Used of the city fathers of Rhodes who were 'recycling' statues of deceased benefactors (*Or.* 31.68, 108, 119, 158); behaving in a disorderly fashion in the public place in Alexandria which no claims to high status could ameliorate (*Or.* 32.31, 39); Appian records Dolabella engaging in 'unseemly behaviour' as he talked about his public office immediately after the assassination of Julius Caesar (*BC* 2.18).

17. *AJ* 16.223; *AJ* 19.357-8; *BJ* 224.

18. For example, a man who kept a woman in his room and would not allow her out, even though she was free born, was seen to be a [sexual] impropriety (*P.Oxy.* 1837) (sixth century A.D.); dressing appropriately for a journey (*P.Zen.* 59477); a begging letter from a shamed person who was an educated but indigent scholar (*P.Zen.* 59599); shameful mistreatment of slave (*P.Ryl.* 144) (A.D. 38); a complaint of an insult and injury (*P.Ryl.* 150) (A.D. 40); and an assault in a temple (*P.Tebt.* 44) (114 B.C.).

19. See V. J. Rosivach, *When a Young Man Falls in Love: Sexual Exploitation of Women in New Comedy* (London: Routledge, 1998), pp. 53ff.

20. It describes homosexual intercourse as 'shameless' acts (Rom. 1:27).

reproductive organs) are treated with a greater modesty than the present-able ones (εὐσχήμονα) — the statues of Roman Corinth portrayed women and men clothed — in contrast to the Greek tradition of the naked human form.[21]

What could such conduct encompass? On the evidence of engaged couples S. Treggiari notes,

> There is unfortunately very little evidence which might cast light on how the relationship of an engaged couple was expected to develop before marriage. Were even young *sponsi* allowed time together, so that they might get to know each other? What were the standards of chaperon-age?[22]

'The virgin certainly needed to be protected from seducers, but the phobia of pre-marital sex with a *sponsus* does not seem to occur until the empire became Christian. Rather, the maiden was meant to warm to her future husband.'[23] Treggiari cites Ovid's *Amores*, 'Let me be read by the maiden who warms to see her betrothed', and notes that 'Ovid paints a picture of the degree of physical intimacy which a *sponsus* might expect'.[24] That reference is to a woman who complained of the nervousness of her suitor. 'He woos me less boldly and seeks few kisses and calls me his in frightened voice', which weighed against the evidence of the earlier Roman requirement of sexual respectability, *pudicitia*, hardly establishes Treggiari's point.[25] Musonius said that 'above all a woman must be chaste and self-controlled; she must, I mean, be pure in respect of unlawful love . . . and not a slave to desire'.[26]

For Paul's Corinth, where for one hundred and ten years Roman and not Greek culture had prevailed, the Latin term *pudicus* could be used of a

21. The museum on the excavation site in Corinth has examples of statues of Roman women with elaborate dresses and Augustus dressed as the magistrate offering up a libation. However, the statues of the two adopted sons of Augustus recovered from the Julian Basilica in Corinth are portrayed naked standing like Greek athletes, but because they were deceased they were represented as gods in the imperial cult.

22. S. Treggiari, *Roman Marriage* Iusti Coniuges *from the Time of Cicero to the Time of Ulpian* (Oxford: Clarendon Press, 1991), p. 159.

23. S. Treggiari, *Roman Marriage*, p. 159.

24. S. Treggiari, *Roman Marriage*, p. 160.

25. *Her.* 21.195-96.

26. Musonius, 'That women too should study philosophy' (3, ll. 17-19).

sexually respectable male, i.e., one 'who did not do certain things',[27] although the parameters set for sexually admissible conduct for each young man is naturally unknown.[28] However, in 7:36a Paul refers to a very important aspect of shame in Roman culture, i.e., shame felt when reflecting on one's personal conduct which had fallen short of one's own ideal.[29] It was not simply guilt because of a sexual misdemeanour with other women but it was with, or towards, his betrothed — 'he reckons (νομίζω) he is behaving in a sexually unseemly way with his betrothed'.

b. Full of Sexual Passion towards His Betrothed (7:36b)

A traditional rendering of the clause ὑπέρακμος, 'if she be past the flower of her age', is not a feasible rendering. According to a late-first-century-A.D. Ephesian doctor, Soranus, this was when menstruation, and thus childbearing, ceased (*Gynaecology* 1.20). It occurred after the age of forty and not later than fifty.[30] If ὑπέρακμος means 'past her prime', then Paul is saying that it was only after child-bearing capability had passed that Christian women were permitted to marry!

There are a number of examples of this word and its cognates which demonstrate that the term refers either to puberty on the part of a woman or 'full of passion' with reference to men. The idea of 'past their prime' is not to be found in the use of the term in or outside the semantic field of sexuality. In the third century B.C. a nonliterary text reads, 'and you know that . . . the vines surpass in vigour [or] bloom' (γίνοσκε δὲ ὅτι . . . τὰ οἰνάρια ὑπερήκμακεν).[31] Again from the same century, the cognate verb is used to refer to the excessive energy in human beings — those who 'pre-

27. For an excellent discussion of this issue see R. A. Kaster, 'The Shame of the Romans,' *TAPA* 127 (1997): 4-5.

28. See pp. 88-92.

29. Kaster, 'The Shame of the Romans,' 5.

30. D. W. Amunsen and C. J. Diers, 'The Age of Menopause in Cassical Greece and Rome,' *Human Biology* 42 (1970): 79-88; A. Wallace-Hadrill, 'Family and Inheritance in the Augustan Marriage Laws,' *Proceedings of the Cambridge Philological Society* n.s. 27 (1981), p. 59; and J. F. Gardner, *Women in Roman Law and Society* (London: Croom Helm, 1986), pp. 178-79.

31. *PSI* 6.666, l. 18 (iii BC), a meaning given by Liddell and Scott in the second edition of 1845.

sented an appearance of vigour exceeding that of a slave' (ὑπερακμάζοιεν τὴν οἰκετικὴν ἐπιφάνειαν). Apparently this was a well-known saying, for it is repeated in the late-second-century work of Athenaeus.[32]

In what is thought to be a first-century-B.C. work, *Praecepta Salubria*, ὑπέρακμος refers to someone who is on the lookout to be satiated (τῇσδε τὸ πλῆρες σκόπει πλήρης) and has sexual connotations.[33]

There are also late-first-century and early-second-century-A.D. works which bear witness to the meaning of the word and are used only half a century after Paul wrote 1 Corinthians. Suetonius' *Περὶ Βλασφημιῶν* uses the neuter plural of the noun as an adverb.[34] The ones who have out-run the age of youth (ἐκδρομάδες)[35] are referred to as 'those who are un-disciplined sexually (οἱ ἀκολασταίνοντες ὑπέρακμα), as those overtaken by time and yet now behaving like youths with their first-time beards', i.e., promiscuously.[36] This example is important, for it uses another term to describe those who have 'outrun the age of youth', while the adverbial form of our word refers to a person who is sexually active.

From the late first century A.D. comes evidence from an Ephesian doctor concerning women. Soranus, who was trained in Alexandria and also practised in Rome, discusses in his extended work *Gynaecology* the intensity of the menstrual flow. 'For in very rare cases limited "to those women past puberty" [after the onset of menstruation] a concentrated flow appears before defloration . . .' (καὶ ταύταις ὑπέρακμοις πρὸ τῆς διακορήσεως ἀθροῦν ἐπιφαίνεται, 1.22).[37] Later he makes it clear that the time to begin sexual intercourse is after the onset of puberty, which, he observed, was aged fourteen. He outlines the risks for those who have in-tercourse before menstruation begins (1.33). The word ὑπέρακμος was

32. Myro 2. C. Müller, ed., *Fragmenta Historicum Graecorum* (Paris: Didot, 1867), 4.460; and *Deipnosophistae* 14.657d.

33. Line 18. On the sexual connotations see, e.g., Epicurus, *Sententiae*, 40.

34. Suétone, *ΠΕΡΙ ΒΛΑΣΦΗΜΙΩΝ. ΠΕΡΙ ΠΑΙΔΙΩΝ*, J. Taillardat, ed. (Paris: Les Belles Lettres, 1967), 3.69. Cf. Eustathius, *Od.* 2.265-66 (12th century A.D.), where he cites Suetonius and states that this phrase refers to those who have passed the age of youth, but clearly they are not past menopause nor are they impotent. This late work is invaluable be-cause the author collected old *scholia* and lost works of earlier scholars and lexicographers.

35. Eubulus (IV BC) 11; cf. Eustathius, 1915.20.

36. For a discussion of the behaviour of élite young men who took the *toga virilis* see pp. 89-92.

37. For an English translation, see O. Temkin, *Soranus' Gynecology* (Baltimore: Johns Hopkins University Press, 1956).

used in this instance as a medical term to describe females who were past puberty (i.e., fourteen years old), but certainly not past child-bearing age.[38]

A Christian writer of the fourth century, Epiphanius, translates 1 Corinthians 7:36, 'If any man thinks that he behaves himself uncomely towards his virgin, and need so require, let her marry; she has not sinned'. This rendering is germane to his refutation of certain heretics *(Against Apostolics)* who reject marriage *per se*. Epiphanius uses the phrase 'concerning marriageable women' (περὶ παρθένων ὑπεράκμων) for those who had not sworn a vow of virginity to God. He specifically states that these 'marriageable women had remained virgins in their prime (ἐν τῇ ἀκμῇ) not because of a vow but because they cannot find men for marriage'. Only slightly later he uses the cognate of ὑπέρακμος to mean 'to be sexually passionate' — 'these [women] who are sexually passionate would fall into immorality through natural desires' (ἐκεῖναι ὑπερακμάζουσαι περιέπιπτον πορνείᾳ διὰ τὴν κατὰ φύσιν ἀνάγκην).[39] In translating the word again only fourteen lines later, F. Williams surprisingly renders the same verb ὑπερακμάζω as 'past their prime'.[40] This context relates to fathers who kept their daughters at home for a long time because of a dearth of marriageable Christian men. However, the text nowhere implies that the women commit fornication in old age (i.e., 'past their prime'). Rather, because they were not married, there was the danger that they could fall into this sin because of the inappropriate use of natural sexual drives.

Hesychius, the fifth-century-A.D. lexicographer, gave synonyms for ancient literary sources which had been substituted by later editors. He indicated that κατοργᾶν is synonymous with ὑπερακμάζειν.[41] The former verb refers to the heightened desire for sexual intercourse, with ὀργάω

38. Barrett, *The First Epistle to the Corinthians*, p. 184, believes that the term does not mean 'at the age of puberty'.

39. *Haereses* 2.385, l. 10, l. 24. G. W. H. Lampe, *A Patristic Greek Lexicon* (Oxford: Clarendon Press, 1968), p. 1437, wrongly cites both passages from Epiphanius as examples of the use of the verb 'to be past the prime' and the noun 'past the prime' of 'virgins', and also refers to 1 Cor. 7:36.

40. F. Williams, *The Panarion of Epiphanius of Salamis, Books II and III*, Nag Hammadi and Manichaean Studies (Leiden: E. J. Brill, 1994), XXXVI, 118. Williams renders the noun and the verb inconsistently. ὑπέρακμος he rightly translates as 'marriageable women' in the slightly earlier discussion, and the verb as 'being past their prime'.

41. *kappa*, 1845.1. See also *Suda, kappa*, 1089.1.

meaning 'to desire sexual intercourse', and κατά strengthening the force of the verb, according to Liddell and Scott.

It is also important to note that another term was used to describe those 'past their prime',[42] and that is παρακμή, with its cognate, παρακμάζω. For example, in the late-first-century and early-second-century writings of Plutarch, it refers to those whose political power is waning; of people's wrath subsiding; of courage that is past its prime; of men who are old and past their prime; of those who are passing their prime; and of those experiencing the abatement of [sexual] vigour caused by age.[43] In Xenophon it describes beauty passing its prime.[44] Alexander of Aphrodisias refers to being past one's prime when 'licentious activity of the body will cease [because of age]' (τῷ τὴν μὲν ἀκολασίαν παρακμάζοντος τοῦ σώματος παύεσθαι).[45]

Clearly the verbal form neither suggested that the person had reached menopause if a woman, nor impotence through age if a man. It was used to refer either to a woman who had reached puberty and therefore could engage in intercourse and safely conceive, or to the sexual drives or passions of either sex. Usually it referred to the man, and then to indicate the danger of being entrapped by immorality through his natural sex drives.[46]

Attempts by lexicographers to construct a meaning for ὑπέρακμος on the basis of ἀκμή or ἀκμαῖος and ὑπέρ are not linguistically secure, because ὑπέρ can have two meanings. Paul's term does not refer to those women who were past childbearing age. Had the latter been the case, then the cognate of παρακμή and not ὑπέρακμος was the apposite term. ὑπέρακμος has specific meanings in the semantic field of sexuality. It can only refer to the sexual passion of men and not to the fiancée's father, as section d will show.

42. Cf. T. C. Edwards, *Commentary on the First Epistle to the Corinthians* (London: Hodder & Stoughton, 1897), 200, who incorrectly states, 'The class. synon. of ὑπέρακμος is παρακμάζω'.

43. *Brut.* 8.3; 21.1; *Arat.* 36.3; *Oth.* 12.3; *Moralia* 364B, 453B.

44. *Symposium* 4.17; 8.14.

45. *In Aristotelis topicorum* 223.23 (c. A.D. 200).

46. Liddell and Scott, in their first edition of 1843, translated the term to mean 'beyond the bloom of youth', citing only 1 Corinthians 7:36. In the latest edition, they rendered the term as 'sexually well developed', citing in support 1 Corinthians 7:36, and Soranus, 1.22. However, the above survey of additional primary sources shows that Liddell and Scott have arrived at their conclusion on the basis of limited evidence — one occurrence in a gynaecological textbook. They see *exoletus* as the Latin equivalent of ὑπέρακμος, wrongly following J. J. Wetstein, *Η ΚΑΙΝΗ ΔΙΑΘΗΚΗ* (1752), II, 131. For an important discussion of some of the inadequacies of Liddell and Scott and examples for such a contention, see Chadwick, *Lexicographica Graeca*.

c. Consequences of Sexual Impropriety towards His Betrothed (7:36c)

What does Paul mean when he says καὶ οὕτως ὀφείλει γίνεσθαι immediately after ἐὰν ᾖ ὑπέρακμος? Neither 'and so it has to be' (NRSV) nor 'and he feels he ought to marry' (NIV) clearly explains what he is saying.

Paul uses καὶ οὕτως elsewhere in his corpus. 'Bear one another's burdens and as a consequence you will fulfil the law of Christ' (future tense); 'sin came into the world through one man, and death through sin, and as a consequence spread to all men'; after concluding that whoever eats the bread and drinks the cup of the Lord in an unworthy manner will be guilty of profaning the Lord's body, he then commands that 'a man must examine himself', which he follows with καὶ οὕτως — he must eat the bread and drink of the cup (imperatives). Its reference to what precedes (i.e., self-examination) determines how he must now participate in the Lord's Supper compared with the way he had done so before (Gal. 6:2; Rom. 5:12; 1 Cor. 11:27-28).[47] A highly apposite example is actually found in 1 Corinthians 7:17a where Paul notes that, as the Lord has apportioned to each person and each is called by God, thus (οὕτως) he must walk. Naturally, as a consequence ('and thus', καὶ οὕτως) he gives instruction in all the churches based on these truths (7:17b).

According to Liddell and Scott καὶ οὕτως is to be translated 'even so' or 'even on this supposition'. They also note that, when used with the infinitive, ὀφείλει means 'he/it is bound' and γίνεσθαι means 'to come to pass', 'to take place'. The present tense and the infinitive ὀφείλει γίνεσθαι occur together on a number of occasions, and a natural and a necessary nexus is implied.[48] BAGD draws attention to the use of οὕτως without καί when indicating the moral after giving examples, and in support cites Aristotle.[49] Paul indicates what will happen of necessity because of such unseemly behaviour, i.e., his sexual drives have been inflamed. The apposite translation is 'and thus it is bound to happen', i.e., because of passion deriving from unseemly conduct.[50] According to Menander Rhetor, engagements could be

47. See also the only other two occurrences in the NT, Acts 7:8; 28:14.
48. Sextus Empiricus, *Pyrr.* 3.63; *Math.* 10.133.6; Albinus, *Epitome of Plato* 9.1.8; Alexander of Aphrodisias, *De Fato* 194.4 and Ἀπορίαι καὶ λύσεις 71.27. Cf. E. de W. Burton, *Syntax of the Moods and Tenses in New Testament Greek*, 3rd ed. (Edinburgh: T & T Clark, 1898), p. 81 inserts [εἰ] unnecessarily between καί and οὕτως, translating 'and if need so require'.
49. 'So then do take care lest in your desire to avenge . . .' (*Art of Rhetoric* 1393A-B).
50. According to Kistemaker, *1 Corinthians*, p. 251, it 'probably means that his sexual

long. 'Remember your courtship, how long it took, how many years it was before you just managed to succeed, how the girl's parents gave consent only very late'.[51] It may have been the lengthy betrothal that resulted in the situation Paul described here, with its inevitable consequences.

d. Sexual Necessity and Sexual Desire of the Fiancé (7:37)

Information can also be gleaned from the conditions that Paul suggests would lead the fiancé not to need to proceed to marriage at this particular moment. He indicates that there are those 'having no necessity' (ἀνάγκη) to marry. This term can refer to 'natural need', i.e., 'needs of the stomach', according to Aeschylus.[52] It also has sexual references which are well attested, i.e., 'necessity to sexual union' and 'the wants of nature, you love, you seduce'.[53]

And what is to be made of the statement 'having control over his own desire' (ἐξουσίαν δὲ ἔχει περὶ τοῦ ἰδίου θελήματος)? When ἐξουσία is used with ἔχειν it means 'to have control over', and θέλημα is used in pagan sources for 'sexual desire'.[54] Paul is therefore referring to the will of the man and is discussing not only marriage but also the person's own sexuality.

It can be concluded that as a consequence of the young man's sexual impropriety, which he himself judged as unseemly conduct, he is full of sexual passion. Paul states that it is an inevitable consequence of his behaviour. He could only awaken his own strong sexual feelings because of the nature of his amorous contacts with his fiancée. It does not seem to be the case that the unseemly conduct of the young men amounted to actual fornication. At least Paul does not say so. He had already warned the Corinthians that they should not be deceived by this behaviour because those

---

drive controls the man and compels him to marry'; cf. H. Conzelmann, *1 Corinthians* (Philadelphia: Fortress Press, 1975), p. 135, who asks what is the meaning of the sentence, suggesting 'and it has to be so'.

51. D. A. Russell and N. G. Wilson, *Menander Rhetor* (Oxford: Clarendon Press, 1981), pp. 156-57.

52. Aeschylus, *Agamemnon*, l. 726.

53. Plato, *Republic* 458d; and Aristophanes, *The Clouds*, ll. 1075-76.

54. For examples and discussion, see W. G. Kümmel, 'Verlobung und Heirat bei Paulus, 1 Kor 7:36-38),' in W. Eltester, ed., *Neutestamentliche Studien für Rudolf Bultmann* (Berlin: Töpelmann, 1957), pp. 283-84 and n. 25; and *TDNT*, III, 52ff.

who persisted in this particular sin would have no inheritance in the kingdom (1 Cor. 6:9). He then proceeded to deal with young men's sexual escapades with prostitutes with whom they had established a 'one flesh' relationship. They had reached the age where they had taken the *toga virilis* and were following the dictum of youth that 'all things are lawful'. While he accused some of fornication and not adultery (1 Cor. 6:12-20),[55] he makes no direct charge against the former (7:25ff.).

The external problem mentioned in 7:26 had been complicated by the compromising behaviour of some, but not all, of the young men. Postponing marriage when some were burning with passion would be too much for them. For others there would be no difficulty.

Paul spells out the alternatives for fiancés:

verse 36	verse 37
Criteria	
(i) If anyone thinks he is not behaving appropriately towards his betrothed	(i) The one standing steadfast in his heart,
(ii) if he is full of passion (ἐὰν ᾖ ὑπέρακμος)	(ii) having no [sexual] necessity (μὴ ἔχων ἀνάγκην)[56]
Consequences	
and thus it is bound to happen, (καὶ οὕτως ὀφείλει γίνεσθαι)	and is having control over his own [sexual] desire
Commands	
he must do what he wishes, he is not sinning, they must marry	and he has determined this in his own heart to keep his own betrothed, he will do well.
Conclusions	
'so then' (ὥστε)	
he who marries even (καί) he shall do well	he who refrains from marriage he shall do better.

---

55. For my argument, see pp. 89-92.

56. *Contra* K. L. Schmidt, θέλημα, *TDNT*, III, 60, who parallels this and the next statement with ἐὰν ᾖ ὑπέρακμος.

II. Eschatology and Youth's Expectations of This Life

Paul responded by telling them to take cognisance not only of their own individual situations but also of a worldview that provided a new perspective for understanding the realities of life for married couples. This view was diametrically opposed to that held by their contemporaries in the sophisticated world of Corinth, as this section will show. Up to this point in 1 Corinthians 7 Paul provided an important context for the discussion of a number of issues, namely, God's individual gift of singleness or marriedness and the wider callings for individual Christians (7:7, 17-24).[57] In foreshadowing the criteria by which those involved would have to make up their own minds (7:27-28a; cf. 7:36-37), he briefly outlines a new perspective for Christian decision-making (7:30-31) by exploring the difference that an eschatological framework makes to the expectations of life for young people, before proceeding to an examination of Christian obligations for both married and single people.

In order to understand the significance of what Paul says, it helps if we examine first the predominant ideological or philosophical view of the nature of the world and destiny of humanity. This would have determined life's expectations of the young people in pre-Christian days. We will then consider the contrasting eschatological framework in which Christians were encouraged to think about this particular issue. Then follows the implications of this new worldview on first-century expectations of life for young people relating to marriage, the sorrows and joys of life, and the making of money — all of which are determined by a correct 'use' of the present world whose form was 'passing away'.

a. The Eternity of the World

While studies in social sciences, and anthropology in particular, attribute to 'culture' the emergence of different attitudes towards the world in which we live, underlying them are belief systems which go to the heart of perceptions upon which the important decisions of life are made. In the city of Corinth two systems competed for the minds of the nascent Christian community. One was so ingrained in the thinking of those who were

---

57. On the latter see my 'Social Mobility,' *Seek the Welfare of the City*, ch. 8.

brought up in this highly sophisticated Roman colony, which was the centre of 'Romanitas' in the province of Achaea, that it was regarded as *ipso facto* true. How it worked itself out in 'the way things were done' was not always consciously linked by the Corinthians with that belief system, although a clear nexus can be established.

The Philosophical Discussion

In the first century, sophisticated arguments surrounded the issue of the eternity of the world, and nowhere is this more so than in Philo's *De aeternitate mundi.*[58] He makes it clear that three traditional views had been entertained in philosophical discussion.

> Some assert that the world is eternal, uncreated and imperishable. Some on the contrary say that it is created and destructible. Others draw from both of these. For the latter they take the idea of the created, from the former that of the indestructible and so have laid down a composite doctrine to the effect that the world is created and indestructible. (*Aet.* 7)

According to Philo, the first perception was that of Aristotle (384-322 B.C.) (*Aet.* 10), while the second view was supported by Democritus (b. c. 460 B.C.), Epicurus (341-270 B.C.), and the majority of the Stoic philosophers (*Aet.* 8–9). Plato had argued that the world was 'created and indestructible' (*Aet.* 13). Philo personally believed that 'the cosmos has been created and should in theory come to an end, but is preserved from destruction by the will and providence of the creator'.[59] In the alternative range of possibilities discussed by the ancient philosophers, Philo's view has more in common with Plato's. Given the nature of the discussion in Philo's important philosophical work, it emerges that a predominant

---

58. Some of the misreading of this text has arisen from a failure to take cognisance of the fact that Philo structured his discussion along the lines of what was technically called a 'thesis' which fully examined the arguments for and against an idea. D. T. Runia, in an incisive essay, 'Philo's *De aeternitate mundi:* The Problem of Its Interpretation,' *VigC* 35 (1981): 105-51, laid to rest the view that Philo contradicted himself within this particular philosophical treatise compared with his view consistently expressed elsewhere in his corpus. For a summary of the discussion, see D. T. Runia, *Philo of Alexandria and the* Timaeus *of Plato* (Leiden: E. J. Brill, 1986), pp. 394-96.

59. Philo's *De aeternitate mundi* 132.

view of his own day filtered down into what A. Dihle had designated the *Vulgärethik.*[60]

After the collapse of the Roman Republic, the philosophical concept of a lasting world was reinforced by political propaganda indicating that the commencement of the Empire was, in effect, the beginning of a lasting *Reich.* The actual birthday of its first Principate, Augustus, was declared to be 'the equivalent to the beginning of all things'.[61] He had given it permanence as well as the *Pax Romana,* and this could only reinforce the concept of the continuity of this 'ordered world' (κόσμος).

The Architectural Replication

Recent studies in 'social' architecture have drawn attention to the fact that town planning and the buildings which comprise a city reflect historical and philosophical values as well as the ongoing human propensity to impose on life a sense of order which reflects value systems. This is most clearly demonstrated in the effect of postmodernism upon buildings, but it is no less true, although perhaps not quite as obvious, in the history of architecture. This is certainly the case for the Roman Empire.[62] They ardently believed in an ordered world, a *kosmos* (κόσμος), and the systematic planning of their cities and design of their buildings reflected their ideological view of the nature of things.

For example, in town planning the Romans adopted the orderly grid system in laying out their cities. The very city to which Paul wrote 1 Corinthians is a good example of the replication of the orderliness of the natural world in the plan for this new colony, surveyed and laid out in 44 B.C.[63]

---

60. For an appreciation of Dihle's vast work in this field, see E. A. Judge, '"Antike und Christentum" — Some Recent Work from Cologne,' *Prudentia* 5.1 (1973): 1-113. For a discussion in relation to 1 Cor. see pp. 76, 107-8.

61. Cited in S. R. F. Price, *Rituals and Power: The Imperial Cult and Asia Minor* (Cambridge: Cambridge University Press, 1984), pp. 54-56.

62. For a general discussion, see J. Metzler, M. Millett, N. Roymans, and J. Slofstra, eds., *Integration in the Early Roman West: The Role of Culture and Ideology* (Luxembourg: Musée Nationale d'Histoire et d'Art, 1995).

63. For a discussion of the recent recovery of the layout of Corinth based on the traditional grid system, see D. G. Romano, 'Post-146 B.C. Land Use in Corinth and Planning of the Roman Colony,' in T. E. Gregory, ed., *The Corinthia in the Roman Period,* Journal of Roman Archaeology Supp. Series 8 (Ann Arbor: University of Michigan, 1994), pp. 9-30.

The concept was borrowed from the Greeks, who likewise were committed to both the eternity and orderliness of the *kosmos*.[64]

Roman architecture signalled the same ideological commitment to the symmetry of buildings as well as the layout of city streets. The towering 'treelike' columns and the ceilings of major buildings, reproducing the natural world in stone, reinforced an ideological statement about the nature of this world.

The Roman writer, Vitruvius, who produced his work *De architectura* at the end of the Republic, recognised that this subject matter touched not only buildings, but also everything that related to the physical and intellectual life of humankind and its surroundings. It was for this reason that he begins his work with a discussion of first importance, namely, 'The Training of Architects' (1.1), and includes in the curriculum the study of philosophy. He does this not only because it makes an architect 'high-minded' and not money-minded, but also because it makes him focus on 'the nature of things' (1.7).[65]

Personal Continuity

There was an *a priori* assumption that eternity also rested in the human person with the ancient doctrine of the immortality of the soul. While the first century did not follow Plato's doctrine that the body was the prison house of the soul, continuity after death was firmly established as part of the *Vulgärethik*. The important question was, 'What difference did the doctrine of the immortality of the soul make to the way one perceived the present activities of life?' The verbatim presentation of the implications of the immortality of the soul for the present contrasts this disparagingly with another view, namely, a Jewish one. Philo repeats the view of his opponents, the sophists, in his discussion 'The Worse Overcomes the Better' (32-34).

The passage begins with a series of questions, the first one of which had modified Plato's view: 'Is not the body the soul's house?' (not a 'prison

64. J. B. Ward-Perkins, 'Hippodamos and the Classical Greek City', *Cities of Ancient Greece and Italy: Planning in Classical Antiquity* (London: Sidgwick and Jackson, 1974), ch. 3.

65. Bk. 9, Preface 17-18. He refers to Lucretius, *The Nature of Things*, elsewhere, as he acknowledges (9.17). For a wide-ranging discussion, see J. C. Anderson Jr., *Roman Architecture and Society* (Baltimore: Johns Hopkins University Press, 1997), esp. ch. 1, 'The Roman Architects'.

house'). It is followed by another: 'Why, then, should we not take care of a house, that it may not fall into ruins?' The argument then changes from the analogy of a 'house' to 'bodyguards and friends': 'Are not the eyes and ears and the band of the other senses bodyguards and friends, as it were, of the soul?' 'Therefore must we not value our allies and friends equally with ourselves?' he says, pushing the argument further. The next statement moves away from Plato to philosophical hedonism. 'Did nature create pleasures and enjoyments and the delights that meet us all the way through life, for the dead, or for those who have never come into existence, and not for the living?' 'And', the series of questions concludes, 'what is to induce us to forgo the acquisition of wealth and fame and honours and public office and everything of that sort of thing which secure for us a life not merely of safety but happiness?'

The questions thus conclude that the lifestyle of this view, and that which they oppose, provide conclusive proof of the validity of what has just been stated. Those who held a view of humankind contrary to the sophists lived radically different lives, and the lifestyles clearly distinguished the philosophical commitment — the despised were Jews. Those who presented the alternative views clearly articulated them on the basis of a particular philosophical basis — 'The lifestyle is the witness of these things' (μάρτυς δὲ ὁ βίος τούτων).[66]

b. The Duration and Form of this World

We have noted that in the Graeco-Roman world, a prevailing philosophical worldview profoundly affected the perception of the physical world, and with it a specific anthropology which answered questions concerning the immortality of the soul. Deductions that might legitimately be made from that ideological stance have also been seen to have had far-reaching implications for the conduct of life. Paul refers to an alternative view to the permanence of the world. He comments on its relevance in helping to determine an immediate concern as well as its significance for other impor-

---

66. 'The mode of life of these two classes is a witness [to the truth of what I say]' (2.225). The Loeb translators of the text are expansive in the rendering of this sentence although the translation captures the import of the argument that has preceded it, and the evidence which follows substantiates the nexus between ideology and ethics.

tant aspects of life as they unfolded (1 Cor. 7:29-31). There was 'a time to embrace, and a time to refrain from embracing' (καιρὸς τοῦ περιλαβεῖν καὶ καιρὸς τοῦ μακρυνθῆναι ἀπὸ περιλήμψεως) (Eccl. 3:5b LXX). How could they know whether for them this was the 'season' (χρόνος) or the 'time' (καιρός) (Eccl. 3:1)?

'The Time' (1 Cor. 7:29)

A number of important features need to be noted about Paul's statement that 'the time has been shortened'. First, Paul uses a grammatical construction in this opening section to alert his readers to the importance of what he is about to say. When the neuter demonstrative pronoun 'this' (τοῦτο) is used with verbs of saying, it draws attention to what is being said. In addition, Paul gives very special emphasis when he places the neuter demonstrative pronoun at the very beginning of the sentence in 7:29a:[67] 'And *this* I mean, brethren (τοῦτο δέ φημι, ἀδελφοί), [that] henceforth the time has been shortened so that . . . (ὁ καιρὸς συνεσταλμένος ἐστίν· τὸ λοιπόν ἵνα κτλ). Verbs of saying are followed by 'that' (ὅτι), or, where it is omitted, are understood, so that the first clause is epexegetical.[68] Paul is therefore underscoring the great significance of eschatology for the matter under discussion to the Corinthians.

Concerning the matter of 'the time', Witherington notes that συνεσταλμένος ἐστίν has to be translated as 'short' or 'shortened'.[69] The use of this perfect passive periphrastic fills the role of the perfect tense and means that the reference is to the eschatological era *per se,* and not to a short time now before the end of all things.[70] It is not 'short', but it 'has been shortened'.

Also, the phrase 'henceforth' (τὸ λοιπόν, 7:29) should not be linked with the ἵνα clause and rendered 'that henceforth those who have "women" . . .' No textual evidence supports the translation of the term

67. See a detailed discussion of this point on pp. 234-35.

68. Manuscripts D E F G include 'that', while the majority do not. Fee, *The First Epistle to the Corinthians,* p. 334, n. 1, suggests that it could be either epexegetical or causal. On the epexegetical use with the neuter demonstrative and verbs of saying, see p. 235.

69. See B. Witherington III, 'Transcending Imminence', in K. E. Brower and M. W. Elliott, eds., *Eschatology in Bible and Theology: Evangelical Essays at the Dawn of a New Millennium* (Downers Grove: InterVarsity Press, 1999), pp. 173-74.

70. BDF, #352.

within the parameters of the subsequent ἵνα clause concerning 'those who have "women"', as is done by translators and exegetes alike.[71] While there are textual variants concerning the actual place of 'henceforth', all locate it within the main sentence, either after[72] or before the verb (συνεσταλμένος ἐστίν).[73] There are interesting examples of the use of 'henceforth' (τὸ λοιπόν) in relation to 'time' (χρόνος). Aeschylus provides two apposite ones. An oath is sworn 'henceforth to the fullness of all time' (τὸ λοιπὸν εἰς ἅπαντα πλειστήρη χρόνον), and as a result of an oracle 'Corinth henceforth (τὸ λοιπόν) was to me unknown'.[74] In this verse Paul is drawing attention to Christian eschatology, which creates the overarching theological framework in which this and allied matters are to be judged by the Christian young people who have raised the issue.

'The Form' of This World (1 Cor. 7:31)

Paul's statement in verse 29 is further illuminated by verse 31 and helps to confirm our understanding of his eschatological comments. He explains the reason for his instructions (29b-31a): 'For the form of this world is passing away' (παράγει γὰρ τὸ σχῆμα τοῦ κόσμου τούτου). Witherington notes that 'he [Paul] is referring to a process already set in motion, not one about to begin or on the near horizon'.[75]

Verse 26 should also influence our reading of verse 29. In the case of the former verse, it has been argued in the previous chapter that the *Sitz im Leben* which gave rise to the question was the 'present dislocation' in the city itself (7:25-26) — the term 'dislocation' is used to describe social unrest connected with grain shortages. We have noted that there is firm evidence for grain shortages in Corinth on three occasions during this period.[76] The 'present' difficulties should not be taken to mean 'impending',

---

71. A. Robertson and A. Plummer, *1 Corinthians*, 2nd ed. (Edinburgh: T & T Clark, 1914), p. 155, do this, and wish to argue that Paul places words before the ἵνα construction for emphasis. The RV and NIV render it 'that from now on'.

72. E.g., P⁴⁶, ℵ A B D*.

73. E.g., D.

74. Aeschylus, *Eumenides* 763; cf. 1031; and Sophocles, *Oedipus Tyrannus* 795.

75. See B. Witherington III, 'Transcending Imminence,' in K. E. Brower and M. W. Elliott, eds., *Eschatology in Bible and Theology: Evangelical Essays at the Dawn of a New Millennium* (Downers Grove: InterVarsity Press, 1999), p. 173.

76. See Ch. 10. For a more detailed discussion of the importance of some ten extant

as some have unsuccessfully sought to argue.[77] Rather, what was happening in Corinth at that time was related to anxiety and the accepted social dislocation, along with threats of rioting that inevitably accompanied grain shortages.[78]

There are then, good grounds for suggesting that Paul provides a contrasting view to that of the eternity of the world and the soul (7:29-30). Furthermore, he was asserting that young Christians must now look from a new vantage point, i.e., Christian eschatology, at the immediate issue to hand and at other matters which could so readily entice or consume them, as they did their own compatriots.

c. Christian Expectations in This World

Young people were driven by the value systems and expectations of their secular society. Marriage in the first century was everything, for it secured the much-prized Roman ideal of domestic happiness.[79] Sorrow was a catastrophe for those who pursued joy. The accumulation of money in order to acquire more possessions was the assured way to 'secure for us a life not merely of safety but happiness' (Philo, *Det.* 32).

Paul deals with four issues, and, as Doughty notes in his helpful treatment of this passage, 'the eschatological language functions to raise up a particular understanding of Christian existence'.[80] Paul's primary concern here is not to deny the reality or the importance of marriage, sorrow, joy, or resources, but to indicate that they now assume a *relative* importance. They are not everything, for eschatology puts them in perspective. This contrasts

inscriptions to Tiberius Claudius Dinnipus erected by the Tribes of Corinth as well as 'the Council and the People', see my 'Secular and Christian Responses to Corinthian Famines', *TynB* 40.1 (May, 1989): 86-106. He was in charge of the famine grain relief on three occasions during this period, and this can be identified with the present difficulty in 7:26.

77. Conzelmann, *First Corinthians*, p. 132, *contra* Fee, *The First Epistle to the Corinthians*, p. 329, arguing on Pauline usage of the term.

78. As P. Garnsey observes, 'the fear of famine rather than famine itself was enough to send people on the rampage, as in 57 B.C. or A.D. 51'; *Famine and Food Supply in the Graeco-Roman World: Responses to Risk and Crisis* (Cambridge: Cambridge University Press, 1988), p. 31.

79. Treggiari, 'Coniugalis Amor', *Roman Marriage*, ch. 8.

80. D. J. Doughty, 'The Presence and Future of Salvation in Corinth,' *ZNW* 66 (1975): 69.

with the argument of those who hold to the eternity of the world and the soul and the importance of the pursuit of pleasure now, on the grounds that these things are inaccessible to the unborn and the dead.[81]

What Paul is saying about marriage (7:29b) is perhaps best assessed in the light of his treatment of the remaining issues in 7:30. Considering them first is a legitimate interpretative approach because he uses the same construction in 7:30 as he did in 7:29b for all four issues 'as if' (ὡς μή). He is not saying that sorrow is nothing and therefore Christians should not weep (cf. 1 Thess. 4:13). Those who weep are to recognise that the perspective of eschatological hope means that their sense of loss is somewhat ameliorated.[82] What has happened is not the end of everything. The same is true of 'joy', which is an aspect of life but again is not everything.[83] Because people's lives do 'not consist in the abundance of things they possess', securing them cannot be the goal of life. They give no lasting security, and therefore the Christian must take a very different attitude toward them because of the eschatological perspective. There is a proper 'use' of this world, but it is not to be 'abused', i.e., exploited, as if this were the only sphere of existence for the Christian (7:31a).

Given that Paul is not rejecting *per se* life's realities or expectations (7:30-31a), what then is to be made of the first issue he dealt with? He states as a consequence of 7:29a 'that *even* (καὶ) those who have "women" may be as those who have none' (ἵνα καὶ οἱ ἔχοντες γυναῖκας ὡς μὴ ἔχοντες ὦσιν). The reference here cannot be to a celibate marriage, for, however one reconstructs the background of 7:2-5, what the text says is inescapable — 'the husband must render to his wife her conjugal rights', the same applying to the wife with respect to her husband (7:3). Sexual abstinence is seen as defrauding the relationship and is therefore permitted for only one reason, and that temporarily. It must be followed by the resumption of sexual relationships (7:5), as shown in the previous chapter. Paul cannot be suggesting that marriage is nothing, even in contrast to the young people who, in secular society, regarded it as 'everything' because it gave im-

81. 'Did nature create pleasures and enjoyments and the delights that meet us all the way through life, for the dead, or for those who have never come into existence, and not for the living?' (Philo, *Det.* 33).

82. Cf. 2 Cor. 1:3ff., where God is said to be the God of all comfort, and Paul therefore comforts others with the same comfort he receives from God.

83. The pursuit of 'happiness' (ἡδονή), which is condemned in the NT (Luke 8:14; Titus 3:3; Jas. 4:1, 3; 2 Pet. 2:13), was a preoccupation of pagan life.

portant signals concerning social class.[84] Eschatology modifies all of the seasons of life.

To whom, then, is Paul referring (7:27-29)? The term γυνή can refer to either the female gender or a wife. The context helps to decide. The opening discussion (7:2ff.), where γυνή is used on five occasions, confirms this, and, as argued in the previous chapter, refers to a wife. After beginning the discussion with a reference to the fiancée (παρθένος) Paul introduces another term. It is suggested that in this case it refers to the fiancée — 'Are you bound to a γυνή?' If so, then that person must not seek to be released from the relationship. He then asks, 'Are you loosed from a γυνή? Do not seek a γυνή'. The term here refers to the fiancée, for the argument draws attention to an important reality concerning betrothal, i.e., engagement bound the persons together so that they could not break an engagement but rather had to divorce. Betrothal was then a far more committing relationship than it is now in most societies. The first issue, then, on which Paul gives instructions concerns maintaining the present status of those men who have written — a clearly stated principle he has just enunciated (7:17-24). They are not to break with their betrothed, and if they are not betrothed at this stage, then they must not proceed to enter into an engagement.

It is true that later Paul uses separate terms in order to make clear that he is referring to two classes of unmarried women, i.e., 'the spinster' (ἡ γυνὴ ἡ ἄγαμος) and the fiancée (παρθένος). They contrast with the one who is married (ἡ δὲ γαμήσασα). In the case of the first two, both are expected to care for the things of the Lord, which are described as being 'holy in body and in spirit'. The married woman is different, for she has obligations to her husband, as he does to her (7:33, 34). However an earlier point in the argument makes clear to whom he is referring. γυνή and παρθένος are synonymous in this section (7:27-29). This compares with the later comment where he wishes his readers to understand that all unmarried women are included, so he adds ἡ ἄγαμος to ἡ γυνή (7:34). This is further supported when he proceeds to discuss cases where fiancés have not behaved with probity towards their fiancées, who may now not be 'holy in body and spirit' (7:36). Therefore the conclusion in the penultimate paragraph is correct.

84. On the importance of rank and wealth, see Treggiari, *Roman Marriage*, pp. 90-100.

Note the way in which Paul lays out the normal expectations of life in Corinth, i.e., marriage, happiness, and acquiring possessions; he encourages the use, but not the abuse, of this present life. Sorrow and pain were seen as disasters which took the shine off domestic happiness, which was so idolised by the first-century Roman society. Paul enunciates life's expectations and seasons as seen through young people's eyes, but at the same time he puts them into a Christian eschatological perspective so that marriage will not be seen to be that which delivers everything now.

III. Christian Obligations for Singles and Marrieds

Up to this point we have explored the problem which some Christians had created for themselves and which was aggravated by external social difficulties in Corinth. The result was uncertainty concerning the appropriateness of proceeding with marriage at this stage. Paul seeks to help both the Christian fiancé and fiancée (7:32-35) understand that, regardless of the external factor (7:26) and an eschatological perspective that demanded realism in the expectations of what marriage would yield (7:29-32), a substantial change of obligations existed if they changed their marital status. He does this by contrasting the present responsibility of single Christian men and women with an added obligation for those who are married.

a. The Origins of Paul's Terminology

Much has been made of the meanings and significance of the terms Paul uses in this section.[85] The μέριμνα- stem occurs five times, and Deming accordingly concludes that these terms reflect Stoic influences. Certainly, μέριμνα is found in Hierocles, a second-century-A.D. Stoic when he discusses the 'cares' of the householder — experiences shared by all householders and not simply those who were Stoics.[86] However, it should be noted that his other examples are drawn from Posidippus and Menander, neither of whom was a Stoic. Posidippus wrote,

---

85. For a succinct survey see Deming, *Paul on Marriage and Celibacy,* pp. 203-4.
86. 53.30 v.A.

263

'What path of life should one pursue?' . . . at home anxieties (φροντίδες). You are married? You are not without cares (ἔχεις γάμον οὐκ ἀμέριμνος ἔσσεαι). You are unmarried? You live a still more lonely life. (οὐ γαμέεις ζῆς ἔτι ἐρημότερος)[87]

Metrodorus, whom Deming does not cite, takes a very different line based on the value of the path of singleness and marriage and commenting that childlessness means one is 'free from care':

> Pursue every path of life. . . . Are you married? Your house will be the best of houses. Do you remain unmarried? Your life is lighter (ζῆς ἔτ ἀλαφρότερος). Children are darlings; a childless life is free from care. (ἄφροντις ἄπαις βίος)[88]

The following maxims on marriage and singleness are to be found in the fragments of Menander, the fourth-century-B.C. writer of *New Comedy*. On attitudes towards singleness and marriage he wrote,

> 'If one is poor and wishes to live happily, while others do their marrying, hold aloof from marriage'; 'Marriage, if one will face the truth, is an evil, but a necessary evil'; and 'You who are resolved to marry must know this: You will have large benefits if you receive a small evil'.[89]

Of marriage Menander records,

> 'If you come to look at it, there is no such cosy combination, Laches, as is man and wife', and 'There is one genuine love-charm — considerate dealing (εὐγνώμων τρόπος) — by this a wife is apt to sway her husband.[90]

Of marriage obligations he said, 'To have a wife and to be father of children, Parmenon, carries many cares in life' (μερίμνας τῷ βίῳ πολλὰς φέρει).[91]

Two points need to be noted. The terms ἀμέριμνος and μέριμνα are Pauline choices for 'free from care' and 'concern for', and, as the above examples show, each is a synonym and antonym respectively for ἄφροντις

87. *Greek Anthology,* bk. 9, 359.
88. *Greek Anthology,* bk. 9, 360.
89. Menander, *Fragments,* 650K, 651K, 648K.
90. Menander, *Fragments,* 647K, 646K.
91. Menander, *Fragments,* 649K; cf. 1083.1, ὅταν τις ἡμῶν ἀμέριμνον ἔχῃ βίον.

and φροντίς. For a long time scholars have concluded that Stoicism was the quarry from which Paul hewed his ideas in 7:32-35. The occurrence of aphorisms on singleness and marriage comparable to those in 7:32-35 are also to be found in writers who are not Stoics or Cynics. Therefore the conclusion that Paul here is repeating sentiments from either school cannot be proved. Could it not just as legitimately be argued that Paul had drawn some of his discussion from Menander, a writer of New Comedy and known for his maxims?[92] After all, he not only cited Menander's *Thais* (1 Cor. 15:33), but it has also been suggested that Paul was aware of the context of that passage with its remarkable resonance with the *Sitz im Leben* of 1 Corinthians 15:33.[93] If it is argued that Paul borrowed Menander's ideas in 7:32-35, then these sayings are as strong a candidate, if not a stronger, than Stoic and Cynic sources.

The extant sayings of Sosiadis in the Delphic canon were clearly displayed for all to see. They provide evidence of popular aphorisms on matters relating to marriage — 'mind to marry' (γαμεῖν μέλλε), 'control yourself' (ἄρχε σεαυτοῦ), 'keep weddings in check' (γάμους κράτε), 'revere modesty' (αἰσχύνην σέβου), and 'get [sons] of the wellborn' (ἐξ εὐγενῶν γέννα).[94] Some of these pithy sayings are enigmatic, but others demonstrate that there was another reservoir of aphorisms on marriage which was part of the popular ethos of the ancient world rightly called a *Vulgärethik*.

b. Paul's Argument

Paul begins and ends his discussion with assurances that his comments arise from a genuine concern for them as Christians (7:32, 35). He had previously stated that what he said about the difficulties for those who decided to marry at this particular time arose because of his pastoral concern

92. His plays may well have been adapted by Roman writers for stage such as Plautus and Terence; F. H. Sandback, *The Comic Theatre of Greece and Rome* (London: Chatto and Windus, 1977).

93. See pp. 98-100.

94. Sosiades, 8, 14, 67, 74, 138. For a helpful collection of these and other important extant sayings see E. A. Judge, *Ancient Beginnings of the Modern World*, in T. W. Hillard et al., *Ancient History in a Modern University* (Grand Rapids and Cambridge: Eerdmans, 1998), pp. 473-75.

for them (φείδομαι) (7:28) in the context of the present social distress.[95] The *Sitz im Leben,* therefore, is different from that of the Stoics and Cynics.

> Clearly, the logic of 7:32-35 runs parallel to the 'Cynic' position on marriage, for . . . Cynics as well as Stoics who held a Cynic position both opposed marriage inasmuch as attending to the needs of a marriage relationship compromised their commitment to philosophy.[96]

'And I am wishing rather[97] that you are free from concern', i.e., their concern *per se* or their concern at this particular moment for you to be easy [free from care] ἀμερίμνους (7:32a). According to Moulton and Milligan, 'in 1 Corinthians 7:32 the verb that follows clearly does not suggest anxious care' (26). Cf. *P.Oxy.* 930 (2nd-3rd century A.D.), 'For my mind was easy with regard to him [the teacher, Diogenes] as I knew that he intended to look after you to the best of his power'. This was also said by Antipater of Sidon concerning a cupbearer called Helicon — 'The boy who bears your name pours out Italian wine from a fountain that causes you less care (οἰνοχοεῖ κρήνης ἐξ ἀμεριμνοτέρης). Rather would I drink one cup only from his hand than a thousand of Castalia.'[98] In an early edition Liddell and Scott suggested that the term referred to 'driving away care'.[99] It would seem that Paul was concerned to ameliorate the external problem of the famine which they have already experienced and had been aggravated by the inappropriate conduct some displayed in relation to their fiancées.

Paul lays out the binding obligations and commitments of Christian singles and marrieds. The horizon of the single man or woman is to be taken up with being pleasing to the Lord, while the married man or woman has responsibilities to their spouse, i.e., how the married person may please his partner (7:32-34).[100] This is, of course, not the only place

95. On this meaning of φείδομαι see Plutarch, *Moralia* 114C, *A.P.* 5.279.

96. Deming, *Paul on Marriage and Celibacy,* p. 199.

97. On the meaning δέ, 'rather,' see Winer, *A Treatise on the Grammar of the Greek New Testament,* p. 567; and J. D. Denniston, *The Greek Particles,* 2nd ed. (Oxford: Clarendon Press, 1950), pp. 162, 177 on this adverbial use of δέ. See also K. Callow, 'The Disappearing δέ in 1 Corinthians', in D. A. Black, ed., *Linguistic and New Testament Interpretations: Essays on Discourse Analysis* (Nashville: Broadman Press, 1992), ch. 9.

98. *Greek Anthology,* bk. 11.24.

99. Liddell and Scott, 1845². Cf. Pliny, *NH* 25.160: *amerimnon* transliterated as a name for the aizoüm plant meant 'carefree'.

100. How do these obligations differ from those in 1 Cor. 8:1–11:1, where what the

where Paul discusses the obligations of Christians, whether single or married, male or female. In the following three chapters he spells out obligations which are epitomised in the concluding imperative: 'be imitators of me, as I am of Christ' (11:1). It naturally involved the material and spiritual welfare of neighbours (10:24) — something of a radical new focus, for Roman society was not concerned for neighbours but advantageous networking. This discussion is a reminder that for a married person a single focus is no longer possible. Their Christian responsibility, expressed in the concept of pleasing the other person, is to their spouses.

Paul concludes this section by emphatically stating, 'and this I am saying is for your welfare (τοῦτο δὲ πρὸς τὸ ὑμῶν αὐτῶν σύμφορον λέγω οὐκ ἵνα . . .)',[101] and not to place a restraint upon you'. With a strong adversative he expresses what he believes is appropriate given the present distress — 'but (ἀλλά) for what is seemly and devoted in waiting upon the Lord without distraction' (7:35).[102] Immediately after this, Paul deals with a case where it is not possible to wait, and affirms that it would not be sinning to proceed with marriage even though deferring is the best option. 'So then, even he who marries does well (even if, as they write, he believes that he has behaved indiscreetly during the engagement), and he who marries does better' (7:38).

If the married had written about the suspension of conjugal activity

---

imitation of Paul and Christ means is discussed at great length? Paul contrasts the obligations in these chapters with those of certain Christians who are interested in the primacy of their own rights over any obligations to their weaker brother, the gospel, and their neighbour. There is no suggestion that these injunctions in 8:1–11:1 are not laid on all Christians regardless of their marital status or indeed gender — 'each person must seek the benefit of others' (10:24). It would seem that too great a distinction is being made between the obligations of single and married Christians, and this is influenced in part by the reading of a Cynic background into ch. 7. A very sharp dichotomy between the single and married Christian is not warranted when cognisance is taken of Paul's discussion which immediately follows this chapter.

101. On the emphatic use of τοῦτο at the beginning of a statement see p. 235.

102. In 7:35 much has also been made by scholars of the Stoic origins of another term, ἀπερισπάστως, 'without distraction'. Deming, *Paul on Marriage and Celibacy*, p. 199, suggests, 'In choosing the adverbial form of this word, Paul has selected an exceptionally rare word indeed.' He comments that it is used only four times before the third century A.D., outside Stoic authors, twice in Polybius, and twice in papyri. While the use of the adverb may be somewhat restricted, there is no reason why the statistics of its cognates cannot be cited for evidence of their currency outside the Stoic school.

which, in Paul's view, formed the essence of marriage (7:1b), then it was only natural that those contemplating the state of matrimony should raise the appropriateness of proceeding with the consummation of their relationship. 1 Corinthians 7:25ff. cannot be understood without taking cognisance of the cumulative argument which Paul develops and which is set within a critical 'present distress'. His response placed the decision not only in the Christian eschatological framework but also in the context of the issues of Christian and marital obligations as well as the assessment of the relationship of individual fiancés with their betrothed (bearing in mind that some thought they had behaved in an unseemly way towards them). It was an external problem that caused uncertainty and social unrest. It was further aggravated by inappropriate sexual intimacy on the part of some Christian fiancés who had good reasons to pause and ask Paul whether they should not now marry in spite of the difficult times Corinth was passing through.

CHAPTER 12

The Imperial Cult, the Games, and Dining in a Temple (1 Corinthians 8–10:21)[1]

'Sitting at Meat in an Idol's Temple' (8:10)

After Paul left Corinth two highly significant and related events appear to have occurred at about the same time. The first was the establishing of a federal imperial cult in Corinth as distinct from local imperial cults in the cities of Achaea. A federal, or provincial, cult was distinct from the imperial cult of an individual city. Its creation was initiated by the province and approved by the emperor and the Roman Senate.[2] As an annual event it was one important way for a province to demonstrate to the emperor and the Roman Empire its loyalty and support of *Romanitas*. It was an event of enormous significance for the province and its capital, and it brought with

---

1. Aspects of this chapter were published in '"The Imperial Cult" in "Acts and Roman Religion,"' in D. Gill and C. Gempf, eds., *The Book of Acts in Its Graeco-Roman Setting*, The Book of Acts in Its First Century Setting, Vol. II (Grand Rapids and Carlisle: Eerdmans and Paternoster, 1994), ch. 4, and in 'The Achaean Federal Imperial Cult II: The Corinthian Church,' *TynB* 46.1 (May 1995): 169-78, produced in conjunction with A. J. S. Spawforth's shorter version of his essay cited in n. 3. Further explorations have been published in 'Civic Rights, 1 Corinthians 8–11:1,' *Seek the Welfare of the City: Early Christians as Benefactors and Christians* (Grand Rapids: Eerdmans; Carlisle: Paternoster, 1994), ch. 9, and in 'The Imperial Cult and the Early Christians in Pisidian Antioch (Acts 13 and Galatians 6),' in T. Drew-Bear, M. Tashalan, and C. M. Thomas, eds., *First International Conference on Antioch in Pisidia* (Ismit: Kocaeli Press, 2000), pp. 60-68. A monograph which covers all of the NT, *The Imperial Gods and the First Christians: Conflict over the Beginning of All Things*, is in preparation.

2. S. R. F. Price, *Rituals and Power: The Imperial Cult and Asia Minor* (Cambridge: Cambridge University Press, 1984), pp. 66-67.

it great prestige. Enthusiastically embraced in the Roman colony of Corinth and promoted within the province by the Federal League of Achaea, it required financial contributions from all the cities in the province. Argos, in the southern part of Achaea, complained about the substantial financial levy imposed on them.[3]

There is, however, a misconception about the imperial cult among New Testament scholars — that it may have flourished during the reign of Augustus was downplayed by the rest of the Julio-Claudian emperors, and was only resurrected in earnest in the time of Domitian. This view is incorrect and has arisen in part from the view that Tiberius rejected divine honours. Fishwick comments, 'but much has been written that rightly cautions against taking Julio-Claudian "refusals" too literally'.[4] Tiberius' cult thrived during his lifetime, as an inscription from Cyzicus concerning a distinguished benefactress illustrates: '. . . displaying piety in all matters to the eternal house of Tiberius Sebastos Caesar the greatest of the gods and to his immortal rule, dedicated to Polias Athena a cult statue of his mother Sebaste Victorious (Livia) and, receiving her priesthood from the city, she herself at the recent festival of the Panathenaea for the emperors satisfied everything related to piety towards the gods'.[5]

There was also a priest for Tiberius' cult in Iconium,[6] for 'The diffusion of the cult of Augustus and of other members of his family in Asia Minor and throughout the Greek East from the beginning of the empire was rapid, indeed almost instantaneous'.[7] The fact is that the imperial cult grew more spectacularly throughout the empire during the Julio-Claudian

---

3. For a discussion of the petition to the governor of Achaea see A. J. S. Spawforth, 'Corinth, Argos and the Imperial Cult: *Pseudo-Julian, Letters 198*,' *Hesperia* 63/2 (1994): 211-32, and a shorter version, 'The Achaean Federal Imperial Cult I: *Pseudo-Julian, Letters 198*,' *TynB* 46.1 (1995): 151-68.

4. D. Fishwick, *The Imperial Cult in the Latin West: Studies in the Ruler Cult of the Western Provinces of the Roman Empire* (Leiden: E. J. Brill, 1993), 1.2, p. 198. See L. R. Taylor, 'Tiberius' Refusal of Divine Honours,' *TAPA* 60 (1929): 87-101; M. P. Charlesworth, 'The Refusal of Divine Honours: An Augustan Formula,' *PBSR* 15 (1939): 1-10; Chr. Habicht, 'Die augusteische Seit und das erste Jahrundert nach Christi Geburt,' in W. den Boer, *Le Culte des Souverains dans l'empire romain*, 163 (Geneva: Vandoeuvres, 1972): 76-78; and Price, *Rituals and Power*, pp. 72-73.

5. *IGR* 4, no. 144, cited in Price, *The Imperial Cult and Asia Minor*, pp. 63-64.

6. S. Mitchell, *Anatolia: Land, Men, and Gods in Asia Minor* (Oxford: Clarendon, 1993), I, 104.

7. Mitchell, *Anatolia*, I, 100.

and Flavian periods than the early Christian movement ever did, and the establishment of a federal cult in Corinth was a matter of great political, social, and financial importance for the colony.

The other event that seems to have occurred soon after Paul left was the shifting of the site of the Games from Corinth to nearby Isthmia. These ancient games had finally returned to their original site some two centuries after the sacking of Greek Corinth. They had been moved to Sicyon for a century and transferred to the newly established Roman colony c. 40 B.C. for another. The restoration of the Isthmian site and the provision of accommodation were not undertaken until some time in the A.D. 50s.

The imperial cult and the Isthmian Games were not unconnected, because the latter operated under the aegis of the cult every four years, with the 'lesser' Isthmian Games being held biennially. In addition, the federal imperial cult in Corinth was an annual event celebrating the reigning emperor's birthday.

This chapter seeks to explore the impact upon the Christian community of the new province-wide imperial cult established after Paul left Corinth and the restoration of the Isthmian Games to their original site around the same time. It will discuss (I) the newly formed Federal Imperial Cult and the Isthmian Games in Corinth; (II) how the Corinthian Christians handled the Imperial Cult while Paul was in Corinth; (III) the reason why Christians dined in the temple after he left; and (IV) the attitude which some Christians took towards the Federal Imperial Cult and the Isthmian Games.

I. The Federal Imperial Cult and the Games in Corinth

a. The Federal Imperial Cult of Achaea

This cult was an extremely important expression of *Romanitas*:

> This was one reason why the cult became central in the minds of its citizens. Emperor worship was not a political subterfuge, designed to elicit the loyalty of untutored provincials, but was one of the ways in which Romans themselves and provincials alongside them defined their own relationship with a new political phenomenon, an emperor whose pow-

ers and charisma were so transcendent that he appeared to them as both man and god.[8]

In the Province of Asia, for example, the imperial cult and temple in the Roman colony of Aphrodisias were established from the time of the formal deification of Augustus in A.D. 14, having been preceded by the cult of *Thea Rhoma* from the second half of the first century B.C.[9] The provincial imperial cult for Augustus and Rome was founded in the Roman province of Galatia as early as 25 B.C., some seventy years before the arrival of Christianity.[10] Its growth had been nothing short of phenomenal. 'Much of the most detailed evidence for the spread of emperor worship in the central Anatolian provinces comes from Galatia.'[11] Of the centres of early Christian activity which have been excavated in Galatia, the major Julio-Claudian imperial temple in the Roman colony of Pisidian Antioch dating from the middle to late Augustan period has been uncovered. The cult also flourished at Iconium.[12]

In the province of Achaea generally, and in Corinth in particular, there is also evidence of its presence and growth. At the beginning of the first century a Roman official, P. Cornelius Scipio, sought to promote the cult in Messene and other provincial cities.[13] In Corinth, the deified Julius Caesar, who had authorised the establishing of Corinth as a Roman colony, was so venerated soon after his death.[14] A statue, possibly of the deified Julius Caesar, has been excavated.[15] The temple of Octavia, which was the

8. Mitchell, *Anatolia*, I, 103.

9. J. M. Reynolds, 'The Origins and Beginnings of the Imperial Cult in Aphrodisias,' *Proceedings of the Philological Society* 206 (1980): 70-82; 'New Evidence for the Imperial Cult in Julio-Claudian Aphrodisias,' *ZPE* 43 (1981): 317-27; and 'Further Information on Imperial Cult at Aphrodisias,' *St. Cl.* 24 (1986): 109-17.

10. S. J. Friesen, *Twice Neokoros: Ephesus, Asia and the Cult of the Flavian Imperial Family* (Leiden: E. J. Brill, 1993), p. 27.

11. See Mitchell, 'The Imperial Cult,' *Anatolia*, 1, ch. 8, esp. pp. 100, 102.

12. Mitchell, *Anatolia*, I, 104.

13. *SEG* 23, no. 206, cited in Fishwick, *The Imperial Cult in the Latin West*, I, 514.

14. J. B. Rives, *Religion and Authority in Roman Carthage from Augustus to Constantine* (Oxford: Clarendon Press, 1995), p. 61, has demonstrated that it was so for the promotion of that cult in the sister colony of Carthage, which had been founded at the same time as Corinth.

15. This is in the Museum of the American School of Archaeology in Corinth. Fishwick, *The Imperial Cult in the Latin West*, 1.2, ch. 6, traces the deification of Julius Caesar in his lifetime.

site of the imperial cult in Corinth, was dedicated to the sister of Augustus. She was the second imperial woman on whom divine honours had been bestowed.[16] This temple occupied a strategic position overlooking the forum and was built on a raised area so that it was higher than all the other temples, including the recently renovated one dedicated to Apollos.

Not only a deceased emperor but also the reigning one, and even living members of the imperial family, were venerated in the Julio-Claudian era. 'Some eleven figures, including such relatively minor characters as Agrippa Postumus (an adopted son of Augustus) and Antonia the daughter of Claudius, received priesthoods up until the mid-first century A.D.'[17] Gaius' and Claudius' grandmother, the powerful Antonia Augusta (36 B.C.–A.D. 37), was deified while she was alive.[18] She was designated 'goddess Antonia' (θεὰ Ἀντωνία) on a coin struck possibly as early as A.D. 18 during the reign of Tiberius. Her cult was established in her lifetime at Ilium (c. A.D. 18) and at Athens, the place of her conception (A.D. 18-37). The latter shrine possessed a priestess and later a high priest. Other shrines to her have also been located.[19] The relationship of her cult to the wider imperial one is recorded c. A.D. 18 in 'a group portrait inscription' to Rome and Augustus, Tiberius, Julia Augusta, Antonia, and Agrippina.[20] After Antonia's demise Claudius supposedly built a temple in Rome. She was seen to personify various goddesses, and was specifically linked to *Venus Genetrix*. This reflected the popular perception of her as 'the mother of the Imperial *gens*', and 'presumably metaphorically [as] "the mother of Rome"'.[21] In the Principate of Claudius there was renewed interest in Aphrodite, and a marble statue of Antonia in the form

---

16. Pausanias 2.3.1 suggests that it was built when she became the fourth wife of Mark Antony. The first one to be deified was to Fulvia, his previous wife; J. M. C. Toynbee, *Death and Burial in the Roman World* (London: Thames and Hudson, 1971), pp. 46-48. For Octavia's deification in Athens see A. E. Raubitschek, 'Octavia's Deification at Athens,' *TAPA* 77 (1946): 146-50. The question of the use of the 'Octavian' temple for the imperial cult has been reopened for discussion; see M. Walbank, 'Pausanias, Octavia, Temple E,' *Annual of the British School at Athens* 84 (1989): 361-94.

17. S. R. F. Price, *Rituals and Power*, p. 57.

18. E.g., Gaius was addressed as τελικοῦτος θεός (*IGR* 3.145), and his living grandmother, Antonia Augusta, as Ἀντωνία θεά (*IK* 3, no. 88).

19. N. Kokkinos, *Antonia Augusta: A Portrait of a Great Lady* (London: Routledge, 1992), p. 98.

20. Kokkinos, *Antonia*, pp. 45, 110.

21. Kokkinos, *Antonia*, p. 162.

of Venus (Aphrodite) has been located;[22] given that Venus was the patroness of Roman Corinth, Antonia would have been included in the imperial veneration there.[23]

The forerunner to the provincial or federal imperial cult in Achaea was the celebration of imperial festivals on the accession of Gaius and Claudius by the Panachaean assembly.[24] Important evidence in the form of an official petition from the people of Argos to the governor of the province as well as epigraphic evidence shows that it was after Paul had left Corinth that a new provincial imperial cult was established for cities of the Achaean league in Corinth c. A.D. 54.[25]

The official petition from the city of Argos to the governor of the province did not complain about the new federal imperial cult but rather about the large financial contribution they were compelled to make towards what they saw as unnecessary extravagance not central to the cult:[26]

'But now the Corinthians, since Argos has been assigned to their territory — for this the less invidious way of expressing it — by the sovereign city, have grown insolent in ill-doing and are compelling the Argives to pay them tribute. . . . For it is not to furnish gymnastic or musical contests that the Corinthians need so much money, but they buy bears and panthers for the hunting shows which they often exhibit in their theatres. And they themselves by reason of their wealth are naturally able to support these great expenses. . . . (408ff.)

An inscription records the name of the first high priest of the federal cult, Gaius Iulius Spartiaticus. He was a major benefactor and patron of Corinth, and held this priesthood for life.

22. Kokkinos, *Antonia*, pp. 115-21.
23. See the discussion of D. Engels, *Roman Corinth: An Alternative Model for the Classical City* (Chicago: University of Chicago Press, 1990), pp. 97-99. On Aphrodite as the mythical mother of Julius Caesar and the cult of Venus Genetrix see S. Weinstock, *Divus Julius* (Oxford: Clarendon Press, 1971), pp. 15-18.
24. Spawforth, 'The Achaean Federal Imperial Cult I,' 161.
25. Spawforth, 'The Achaean Federal Imperial Cult I,' 161-63. G. Iulius Spartiaticus, '"First of the Achaeans", A Correction,' *Hesperia* 64.2 (1995): 225, suggests that the date could be on the accession of Nero in 54 or earlier. On provincial imperial cults see Fishwick, *The Imperial Cult in the Latin West*, 1.2, chs. 3-12.
26. See Price, *Rituals and Power*, p. 129, for the levy of costs on cities great and small.

> The tribesmen of the Calpurnian tribe (set up this statue), on account of his excellence and unsparing and most lavish generosity both to the divine family and our colony, for their patron Gaius Iulius Spartiaticus . . . flamen of the deified Julius, twice quinquennial duovir, president of the Isthmian and Caesarean Sebastean games, high priest for life of the Augustan house, the first of the Achaeans to hold this office.[27]

With customary praise this inscription records not only the liturgies of Spartiaticus but, in particular, his role as Achaea's first priest of the imperial cult. For this highly coveted liturgy the priest of a federal or provincial cult could be granted permission by the emperor to wear a crown and 'the purple' in procession.[28]

A decree of the Asian assembly shows that the inhabitants of Pergamum had expectations concerning the annual celebration of the provincial imperial cult:

> Since one should each year make clear display of one's piety and of all holy, fitting intentions towards the imperial house, the choir of all Asia, gathering at Pergamum on the most holy birthday of Sebastos Tiberius Caesar god, performs a task that contributes greatly to the glory of Sebastos in hymning the imperial house and performing sacrifices to the Sebastan gods and conducting festivals and feasts.[29]

At Messene in Achaea, a Roman official 'instructed all to wear crowns and to sacrifice [before the statue of the emperor], keeping themselves free from work'.[30] There is evidence of householders sacrificing on altars outside their homes as the procession celebrating the cult passed by.[31] Imperial altars have been found in Achaea, Athens, and Sparta, as well as in Asia Minor.[32] In A.D. 54 a proclamation announcing the accession of Nero invited all 'to wear wreaths and sacrifice oxen'.[33] In a much later pe-

27. West, *Corinth*, 8.2, no. 68.

28. Price, *Rituals and Power*, p. 129. For a description of the procession with the high priest see Dio Chrysostom, *Or.* 35.10.

29. *IGR* 4.1608c = *IEphesos* 7.2, 3801.

30. *SEG* 33.206, ll. 14-15, cited in Price, *Rituals and Power*, p. 112.

31. On these processions see Fishwick, *The Imperial Cult in the Latin West*, II.1, 550-66.

32. Price, *Rituals and Power*, p. 112.

33. *P.Oxy.* 1021.

riod, Tertullian indicated that it was assumed that everyone would take part and that festive attire, including crowns, should be worn and laurels and lamps should be hung on the doors of their homes.[34] There were also expectations that each person would offer up his own libation with wine and incense before images of imperial gods, which were normally distributed by public benefactors, usually the priests connected with the cult.[35] While aspects of the celebration of the cult differed from city to city, it is certain that everyone was under obligation, Provincials or Roman citizens alike, to participate.

b. The Re-siting of the Isthmian Games

After the sacking of Corinth these famous games were held in Sicyon for the following century. They were moved back to Corinth c. 40 B.C. They consisted of the biennial Games, which were designated 'the Lesser Isthmia'; and, when combined with the Caesarean Games and the Imperial Contests, they were designated 'the Greater Isthmia'. The latter were instituted by Tiberius to honour the imperial family.[36]

A Corinthian inscription records the restoration of the Games to the Isthmian site, including the name of its first President. '[Cn. Publicus Regulus . . .], who was [the first] to preside over the Isthmian games at the Isthmus under the sponsorship of *Colonia Laus Julia Corinthiensis* . . . and after the buildings of Caesarea were renovated . . . gave a banquet for all the colonists *(epulumo omnibus colonis)*. His son, [Lucius] Castricius Regulus, (erected this monument) to his father in accordance with a decree of the city council'.[37]

Like Corinth, Isthmia had been plundered at the time of its sacking by the Romans. There is epigraphic evidence recording the building of accommodation for athletes on the Isthmian site and the restoration of buildings there, but this may well refer to a second-century renovation.[38] It has recently been argued that the Games were held in the precincts of Cor-

---

34. *De Corona* 13; cf. 1.1; *Apol.* 35; *De Idolol.* 15; *Ad uxorem* 2.6.

35. Fishwick, *The Imperial Cult*, p. 530.

36. D. Engels, *Roman Corinth*, 52.

37. Kent, *Corinth*, 8.3, no. 153. 'Citizens' is the correct rendering of the term, *colonis*, although Kent does not so translate it thus in no. 153, although he does so in no. 151.

38. See Kent, *Corinth*, 8.3, no. 306 and pp. 120-21 for discussion of dating.

inth for over a century and that it was possibly not until the A.D. fifties that they were finally returned to the nearby Isthmian site. It had originally been surmised that they had been transferred some twenty years before that date.[39] As Regulus was a magistrate *(duovir)* in A.D. 50-51 his presidency of the games, which was the highest public office or liturgy in Corinth, would have been subsequent to that date.[40]

The Games had become so famous by the fifties that they attracted even larger numbers of participants and dignitaries. They became increasingly costly to stage and were privately financed by one person, the President of the Games. In other cities this was a liturgy attached to the role of the *aedile*, but it was separated in Corinth, becoming the most senior and prestigious of all liturgies in the city. The person elected to this office had to possess great wealth, and this liturgy naturally brought great honours to its holders. At a later date Nero himself visited these famous Games and actually participated in the contests.[41]

This inscription of Regulus also reveals that, with the restoration of the Games to Isthmia, a convention was established whereby the President entertained a special segment of Corinthian society at a feast during the games. The privileged élite of Corinth were invited to dine at Isthmia, and Roman citizens *(colonis)* were the invited guests. A distinction has to be drawn between non-Roman inhabitants *(incolae)* residing in Corinth and its Roman citizens.[42] Plutarch subsequently confirms that this custom of entertaining continued and the frequency of the dinners increased, because Sospis, the President of the Games, 'several times entertained all the citizens'.[43] So then, a custom or 'right' to attend was established for the Roman citizens of Corinth.[44] Corinth was not the only city where the impe-

---

39. For the discussion see E. R. Gebhard, 'The Isthmian Games and the Sanctuary of Poseidon in the Early Empire,' in T. E. Gregory, ed., *The* Corinthia *in the Roman Period,* Journal of Roman Archaeology Supp. 8 (Ann Arbor: University of Michigan Press, 1994), pp. 78-94.

40. For the list of magistrates see Kent, *Corinth,* 8.3, p. 30, and for a discussion of dating see M. Amandry, *Le monnayage des duovirs corinthiens,* BCH Supplement 15 (Paris and Athens: École Francaise d'Athènes, 1988), pp. 73-74.

41. D. Engels, *Roman Corinth,* p. 20. He naturally won. It was in fact on that occasion that he granted freedom to Achaea, which involved tax exemptions.

42. D. Engels, *Roman Corinth,* pp. 68, 70.

43. Plutarch, *Quaes. conviv.* 723A.

44. Dio Chrysostom, *Or.* 76.1, 3 defines a custom as 'an unwritten law of a tribe [citizens belonged to different tribes in a city] or a city', and he notes that 'it is impossible to destroy'.

rial cult and games were celebrated with banquets.[45] Fishwick notes that 'games and banquets were a staple appurtenance of major festivals of the imperial cult throughout the empire'.[46]

'The Isthmian Games were linked to the imperial cult through the Caesarean Games and the Imperial Contests.'[47] The coming of the Federal Imperial Cult at this particular moment in Corinth's history would have greatly increased the prestige of these already famous 'lesser' and 'greater' Isthmian Games with their imperial cult connection. It would have been all the more so at this significant moment in the history of these ancient games, viz., their return to the traditional site after an absence of two centuries.

II. The Corinthian Christians and the Imperial Cult

How then did Gentile Christians cope with the obligations to worship the imperial gods while Paul was in Corinth? How did the Christians respond to the imperial cult?[48] Almost thirty years ago Professor F. Millar posed the question, 'But when Gentiles began to convert to Christianity, might we not expect that the pagan communities in which they lived would begin to use against them the accusation of not observing the Imperial cult?'[49]

An unexpected answer may well be found in the outcome of the case of Paul versus the Jews, which is summarised in Acts 18:12-17. Their charge was that Paul was 'deceptively misleading others to the worship of God contrary to the law' (18:13). The term ἀναπείθω does not simply mean 'persuade' — the term (πείθω) was used in Acts 18:4 to describe Paul's activities in the Corinthian synagogue. The former term is used in

45. For evidence see Fishwick, *The Imperial Cult in the Latin West*, II.1, 574-87, who discusses both under the general heading 'entertainment'.

46. Fishwick, *The Imperial Cult in the Latin West*, II.1, 588.

47. Engels, *Roman Corinth*, p. 102.

48. Christianity's confrontation with the cult has been recorded in apocalyptic language at the time of the writing of the Book of Revelation, presumably in the Principate of Domitian. See Price, *Rituals and Power*, pp. 196-98, for a succinct discussion of the cult and its clash with Christianity in Rev. 13. For an important refutation of any wholesale persecution of Christians in that period based on the evidence see the biography of Domitian by B. W. Jones, *The Emperor Domitian* (London: Routledge, 1992), pp. 114-17.

49. F. Millar, 'The Imperial Cult and the Persecutions,' in W. den Boer, *Le Culte des Souverains dans l'empire romain* (Geneva: Vandoeuvres, 1972), p. 163.

legal settings to indicate that a person has operated out of deceit in order to mislead or seduce others.[50] In fact, Liddell and Scott cite Acts 18:13 under their classification 'seduce', 'mislead'. After hearing the Jewish submission Gallio first ruled that under Roman law Paul was not guilty of a 'felony' (ἀδίκημα) or 'a political misdemeanour' (ῥᾳδιούργημα) (Acts 18:14), so he had committed no criminal offence. Among the issues in contention in the case, Gallio observed there were three (περὶ λόγος καὶ ὀνομάτων καὶ νόμου τοῦ καθ' ὑμᾶς).[51] The first term, λόγος, carries a wide range of meanings when used in the semantic field of law — it can refer to 'a debate', 'an argument', 'a law', 'a rule of conduct', or 'a declaration of legal immunity'.[52] If the last meaning was the essence of one of the charges, then it suggests that the Jews had contested any application of their immunity from participating in the imperial cult to the Christian community. Whether that is the case cannot be known with any certainty.

What is certain is that Gallio's judgement declared that as it was a matter of 'law, your own law (νόμου τοῦ καθ' ὑμᾶς), then you have to see to these matters yourselves; I myself refuse to be a judge of these things' (Acts 18:15). This brother of Seneca the philosopher was himself a leading jurist, and therefore his ruling was of importance.[53] The status of Christianity in relation to the cult was thereby declared, not for the whole empire, but for the province of Achaea where Gallio exercised his *imperium* as governor. As Sherwin-White notes, 'the governor's actions are only subject to cancellation by the Princeps [emperor], if he chooses to intervene from above in virtue of his *imperium maius*, or overriding power.'[54] It was only if the

50. For forensic examples see *P.Magd.* 18, where a father protests against the actions of a courtesan who induced his son to sign a bill for 1,000 drachmas in her favour, and *P.Ryl.* 114, where a widow petitions the prefect of Egypt on the grounds that her deceased husband was persuaded to pasture his flocks on the defendant's land and he then stole sixty of them.

51. For a discussion of the meaning of the first term see my 'Gallio's Ruling on the Legal Status of Early Christianity (Acts 18:14-15),' *TynB* 50.2 (Nov. 1999): 218-21.

52. See Liddell and Scott, λόγος III.b. See this additional classification added in the *Revised Supplement* to Liddell and Scott (1996) citing Justinian, *Nov.* 17.6, Edict 2 pr.

53. Paul would argue that Christianity was a Jewish issue in his subsequent appearances in the Roman court of Caesarea Maritima (Acts 24–26). See my 'Official Proceedings and Forensic Speeches in Acts 24–26,' in A. D. Clarke and B. W. Winter, eds., *The Book of Acts in Its Ancient Literary Setting* (Grand Rapids: Eerdmans; Carlisle: Paternoster, 1993), ch. 11, for discussion.

54. A. N. Sherwin-White, *The Roman Citizenship*, 2nd ed. (Oxford: Clarendon Press, 1973), p. 9.

prosecuting Jews possessed some special privilege such as Roman citizenship that they would have the right of appeal to the emperor against Gallio's decision. Given the fact that Claudius had evicted the Jews from Rome, such an appeal would hardly succeed at this stage of Jewish/imperial relations. Gallio's decision meant that the imperial cult at this stage would create no problems for Christians as provincials, for Gentile converts would not have to participate in it and Jewish Christians were already exempt by reason of their ancient religious traditions *(mos maiorum)*.[55]

III. Christians Dining in the Temple after Paul Left

a. 'Rights'

Paul noted that some Christians had reclined in the idol temple at a feast and did so on the grounds of what he emphatically described as '*this* right of yours' (ἡ ἐξουσία ὑμῶν αὕτη).[56] They also encouraged 'weak' Christians who had reservations about reclining at dinner in the temple to do the same as they did (8:10).

The confident Christians exercised their 'right' (ἐξουσία) to do so — it was not their 'liberty', as some translations suggest, for the term does not mean that but rather refers to some right they possessed in Corinth.[57] In contrast to the 'confident' Christians Paul explains that he chooses not to exercise certain rights he has (9:4-6) and that he is keen to make his gospel without charge, so as not to use to the full his right (ἐξουσία) in the gospel (9:18). There were some Christians who decided that they would exercise a particular right that they possessed to eat in the idol temple.

Ordinarily worshippers at temples in Corinth did not worship on the grounds of some 'right' they possessed, for temples were open to everyone. Those at the temple of Asclepius were there for healing, and some attended the temple of Demeter and Kore, not for the purpose of dining as in Greek Corinth, but for delivering curses against adversaries. Paul did not say that

55. See my 'Gallio's Ruling on the Legal Status of Early Christianity,' 221-23.
56. He does this by placing the demonstrative pronoun at the end of the phrase.
57. Paul uses 'right' (ἐξουσία) again five times just a few verses later in his discussion (9:4, 5, 6, 12, 18), not to describe his freedom but his 'rights' as an apostle. A cognate of the term for 'liberty' (ἐλευθερία) (which incidentally he actually uses for his own liberty later in 10:29) is also used by Paul to indicate that he is free (ἐλεύθερος, 9:1).

the Corinthian Christians were simply attending some form of worship in the temple, but that they were there by 'right'. Some Christians had participated in feasts, reclining in the traditional way at dinner in the temple (8:10), and later Paul recounted that they had drunk from 'the cup of demons' and were 'partaking at the table of demons' (10:21). Paul also issued a strong warning against those who sat down to eat and drink and enjoyed the subsequent activities, including immorality (10:7-8) — peripatetic brothel keepers supplied prostitutes for grand occasions,[58] and they may have done so for the 'after-dinners' entertainment for those attending the banquets in the temple of Poseidon at Isthmia.[59] Plutarch warned against 'the need to guard against excess in eating and drinking and against all self-indulgence especially when festivals . . . are at hand'.[60] By a process of elimination based on the extant evidence it is suggested that the dining rights to which Paul refers were connected with entertainment at the Isthmian Games.

b. Justification

If the right to attend the banquet was based on social status, on what grounds did some Christians defend their participation in a meal in a pagan temple? Their justification appears to have been theological.

> We know that 'an idol is nothing in the world', and that 'there is no God but one'. For even though (γὰρ εἴπερ) there are the so-called gods, whether in heaven or on earth; as (ὥσπερ) there are many gods and many lords; but (ἀλλά) for us there is one God, the Father, and one Lord, Jesus Christ. (1 Cor. 8:4-6)

They knew that an idol was only a carving, even though many of their compatriots believed that when they stood before a statue of Athena some said, 'Athena is visible in her statue'.[61] The Christians also knew that 'there is no

---

58. Dio Chrysostom, *Or.* 77/78.4, refers to them as those 'dragging their stock about to the congress . . . of other great festive gatherings'.

59. For a discussion of the activities called 'after dinners' at private banquets see pp. 83-85.

60. 'Advice about Keeping Well' (123E).

61. R. Lane Fox, 'Seeing the Gods', *Pagans and Christians* (London: Penguin; New York: Knopf, 1987), ch. 4, cited on p. 115.

THE INFLUENCE OF SOCIAL CHANGE

God but one'. Paul's description of the 'so-called gods and lords' indicated that they were popularly but erroneously so designated in the minds of Corinthian Christians.[62] The old English term 'commonly' meaning 'normally but incorrectly' serves as a comparable example for this Greek conventional phrase.[63] The Hermetic Writings reflect the argument 'neither other so-called gods . . . only God',[64] and Tertullian later wrote, 'The so-called gods are of course mere names'.[65] In the clause, 'For even though (γὰρ εἴπερ) there are the so-called gods', εἴπερ can be used to imply that the statement is contrary to fact,[66] while the use of 'as' in 'as (ὥσπερ) there are many gods and many lords' can be translated 'just as indeed', which indicates the presence of the images of many gods and many lords in Corinth, a fact verified by Pausanias' description of temples on his visit to this city.[67]

The deified living emperor and members of the imperial family would have been identified among those divinities 'upon the earth' in contrast to the deceased imperial ones, i.e., 'those in heaven'.[68] The lack of gender references did not invalidate the title for female members of the imperial family, for Aphrodite was sometimes addressed as 'lady' or 'goddess' and likewise as 'god' or 'lord'.[69] Therefore deified emperors and living members of the imperial family were judged to be among the 'so-called gods' (λεγόμενοι θεοί), i.e., popularly but erroneously called gods.

---

62. The participial construction 'the so-called' (οἱ λεγόμενοι) was used of kings, philosophers, and sophists who, some thought, made false claims. Others had inappropriately designated the religious phenomena as gods and lords; see, e.g., Epictetus 4.1.51 and synonymous 'so-called' statements in Dio Chrysostom, Or. 31.11, 77/78.34. On the discussion of the construction in first-century writers see J. L. Moles, 'The Career and Conversion of Dio Chrysostom,' JHS 97 (1978): 91.

63. The term 'so-called' cannot be taken to mean 'a concession of the existence of many gods and lords, [which] was not necessarily incompatible with Jewish monotheism' (P. A. Rainbow, 'Monotheism and Christology in 1 Corinthians 8:4-6' [Oxford University D.Phil., 1987], p. 132), or as 'emphatic a qualification of the monotheism of [v. 4] as Paul could have made as a Christian' (J. C. Hurd Jr., The Origins of 1 Corinthians [Macon, Ga.: Mercer University Press, 1983], p. 122).

64. The Hermetic Writings, 2.14.

65. Tertullian, De Idolol. 15.

66. Liddell and Scott.

67. Pausanias, the second-century traveller of religious sites who visited Corinth, records the proliferation of statues and temples (2.3.1).

68. For discussion of this point see pp. 272-74.

69. See my 'Theological and Ethical Responses to Religious Pluralism: 1 Corinthians 8–10,' TynB 41 (1990): 214 for evidence.

IV. The Christians, the Cult, and the Games

From the above discussion we can conclude that, by reason of Gallio's judgement, Christians were exempt from participating in pagan festivals and 'quasi-civic' events in temples. As has been shown, after Paul left Corinth the imperial cult had assumed even greater importance in the capital of Achaea. The Federal cult, coupled with the celebration of the newly re-sited and prestigious Isthmian Games, brought even greater prestige to Corinth. Personal invitations from the President of the famous Games to attend the gala feasts in the temple and to rub shoulders with the good and the great from Greece and those across the Aegean Sea meant that this was now the most prestigious event in Corinth's, indeed Achaea's, calendar. In the light of these important developments in Corinth's religious-cum-cultural life, some socially privileged Christians felt that they could justify theologically the exercising of their rights to attend such festivals, in particular the ones held in the vast complex of the temple of Poseidon at Isthmia, which was under the aegis of one of 'the gods on the earth'. After all, they argued, the Christian doctrine of God implied that an idol was nothing, for there was only one God and one Lord, and there were no problems reclining in the temple to enjoy the dinner (8:4).

How did other groups react to this world of religious pluralism which had become so closely tied to loyalty towards the emperor? Some Stoic and Epicurean philosophers in the Claudian period whose teaching opposed idolatry and participation in such worship in *De natura deorum* permitted their adherents to participate in popular cultic activities as a compromise, while warning them not to treat such activities seriously.[70]

Herod the Great, king of the Jews, had built a temple to Augustus and Rome in a conspicuous site on the harbour of the capital of the Province of Judaea, Caesarea Maritima, and Philip appears to have built one at Bethsaida in A.D. 30 when its name was changed to Julia, after Julius Caesar's daughter.[71] However, Palestinian Jews did not endorse this

70. *P.Oxy.* 215. For evidence of this opposition see my 'In Public and in Private: Early Christianity and Religious Pluralism,' in A. D. Clarke and B. W. Winter, eds., *One God and One Lord: In a World of Religious Pluralism*, 2nd ed. (Grand Rapids: Baker; Carlisle: Paternoster, 1992), ch. 6, esp. pp. 138-39.

71. Josephus, *AJ* 15.339; 18.26; and discussion in K. C. Holum and R. Hohlfelder, *King Herod's Dream: Caesarea on the Sea* (New York and London: Norton, 1988), pp. 142-43.

method, which their rulers used to demonstrate their loyalty to Rome. Re-actions to a slightly later proposal by the emperor Gaius to set up a statue of himself in the Jerusalem temple were such[72] that, however much the cult was promoted by the Julio-Claudian emperors, the Jews of Palestine and the Diaspora never participated in the cult. Jews were able to support *Romanitas,* demonstrating their loyalty to Rome insofar as they offered up a sacrifice for, but not to, the emperor in the temple in Jerusalem.[73]

Professor S. Mitchell recently concluded his discussion of the impe-rial cult in Anatolia with this interesting observation:

> One cannot avoid the impression that the obstacle which stood in the way of the progress of Christianity, and the force which would have drawn new adherents back to conformity with the prevailing paganism, was the public worship of the emperors . . . it was not a change of heart that might win a Christian convert back to paganism, but the over-whelming pressure to conform imposed by the institutions of his city and the activities of his neighbours.[74]

For Paul the question of conscience was a critical factor in deter-mining behaviour. It was out of respect for the conscience of the person that he indicated to the Christian at a private dinner that the food had been offered to idols (10:25). It also ought to have stopped the persons seeking to cajole Christians with weak consciences to join the theologi-cally nimble at the feast in the temple (8:7). Paul was deeply concerned that if the latter did so, then they would commit apostasy and perish — those 'for whom Christ died' (8:10-11). It is interesting to compare this with evidence of apostasy in the next generation, in which Pliny exam-ined those anonymously accused of being Christians. He discovered how a number no longer confessed the faith, and their willingness to sacrifice incense to a statue of the living emperor confirmed this. He used the im-perial cult against the accused to determine whether they were Christians

---

72. This slightly earlier move had been made at Pilate's provocation; H. K. Bond, 'The Coins of Pontius Pilate: Part of an Attempt to Provoke the People or to Integrate Them into Empire,' *JSJ* 27.3 (Aug. 1996): 241-62.

73. For a discussion see M. Pucci Ben Zeev, *Jewish Rights in the Roman World: The Greek and Roman Documents Quoted by Josephus Flavius,* Texts and Studies in Ancient Juda-ism 74 (Tübingen: J. C. B. Mohr [Paul Siebeck], 1999), pp. 471-81, although she does seek to minimise the cult itself.

74. Mitchell, *Anatolia,* II, 10.

or apostates from that faith, and he recorded that those in the latter bracket willingly worshipped the emperor.[75]

Religious pluralism in general and the central place of the imperial cult in *politeia* must have created enormous social pressures for early Christians. In the second century A.D. Epistle to Diognetus it was affirmed that Christians '. . . take part in everything as citizens'.[76] This was also true of the first century,[77] but should it have applied to civic rights and also obligation towards the imperial cult? Tertullian agreed that while Christians participated in civic life, they did not worship gods or 'offer sacrifices for the emperors', only prayers (cf. 1 Tim. 2:1-2), even though this resulted in accusations of sacrilege and treason.[78] He records that the Christians as loyal citizens prayed for the peace and stability of the empire in accordance with 1 Timothy 2:1, and referred to the emperor as 'Lord' but not Lord in God's place. However, they were counted as 'public enemies':

> that they pay no vain, nor false, nor foolish honours to the emperor: that as men believing in the true religion, they prefer to celebrate the Emperors' festivals with a good conscience, instead of riotous behaviour. It is, obviously, a splendid mark of respect to bring fires and couches out into the open air, to have feasting from street to street, to turn the city into one great tavern, to make mud with wine, to rush about in groups to acts of violence, to deeds of shamelessness, to the incitement of lust. . . . For why do we keep the votive days and high rejoicing in honour of the Caesars with chastity, sobriety, and virtue . . . [we] neither cover our door posts with laurels, nor intrude upon the day with lamps nor dress our house up like some new brothel.[79]

Tertullian and his generation of Christians observed the birthday of the emperor and his predecessors with 'a good conscience . . . with chastity, sobriety and virtue'. Not all in the first-century Christian community in Corinth could affirm the same, given what is known of their conduct (8:1–11:1).

---

75. *Letters of Pliny* 96.

76. *The Epistle to Diognetus* 5.4-5.

77. For a survey of the role of Christians in *politeia* see my *Seek the Welfare of the City: Early Christians as Benefactors and Citizens* (Carlisle: Paternoster; Grand Rapids: Eerdmans, 1994), esp. ch. 2.

78. Tertullian, *Apology* 10.1.

79. Tertullian, *Apology* 31, 34-35.

As we have seen, throughout the Julio-Claudian period the imperial cult was of great importance in the empire in promoting *Romanitas*. After Paul left Corinth it assumed even greater importance in the capital with the new federal cult centred there.[80] Coupled with the celebration of the newly sited Isthmian games, it brought even greater prestige to Corinth. Personal invitations from the President of the Games to attend the gala feasts in the temple with the good and the great to celebrate this major event in Corinth's history, indeed Achaea's public life, explains why some Christians sought a theological justification for attending — they argued that 'an idol has no existence' and 'there is no God but one' (8:4). The changed circumstances and the theological knowledge some Christians possessed permitted them to participate in the festivities in the temple, although their exemption from joining in the imperial cult was *ipso facto* given through Gallio's ruling. Paul was concerned that 'weak' Christians would be drawn back into the world of paganism and finally become apostate. The 'strong' were also in far greater danger of falling. Paul concluded part of his response with the warning, 'Therefore let any one who thinks that he stands take heed lest he fall', and 'I imply that what pagans sacrifice they offer to demons and not to God. I do not want you to be in partnership with demons' (10:12), whom they perceived not least of all of being in confrontation with God.

Ancient evidence uncovered to date provides important material confirming the transfer of the Games and the introduction of the Federal Imperial Cult to Corinth. Like the time of the writing of 1 Corinthians there is no date recorded as to when the Games were transferred from Corinth to Isthmia or when the Federal Imperial Cult actually began — Spawforth has suggested the accession of Nero in A.D. 54, or earlier for the latter.[81] The particular problem for New Testament scholars is how to account for the changed circumstances lying behind Paul's long argument on this critical issue, for which no apostolic tradition could be cited, even though he commended them for being diligent in observing them in the following verses (8:1–11:1, 2). These two aspects which are explored here together constituted a major development in the combined religious and cultural spheres of life in Corinth after Paul left.

---

80. See Sherwin-White, *The Roman Citizenship*, pp. 403-8 on the importance the cult of Augustus and Roma assumed in this period.

81. Spawforth, 'The Achaean Federal Imperial Cult I,' 161-63.

CHAPTER 13

Kosher Food and Idol Meat
(1 Corinthians 10:25-28)

'Eat Whatever Is Sold in the Meat Market' (10:25)

Certainly one of the most enigmatic issues in 1 Corinthians concerns Paul's ruling on meat bought in the market — 'whatever is sold in the meat market eat, asking no questions for conscience' sake' (10:25). Why did he not deal with this matter while he was in Corinth? In no part of his discussion does he provide any hint of an apostolic tradition having been delivered to them on this specific matter while he was in Corinth.[1] What changed after Paul left Corinth? In seeking an answer to this question, which has been asked in all the chapters of Part II of this book, it is proposed to examine (I) the importance of concessions made by local civic authorities to Diaspora Jews, especially the provision of 'suitable' slaughtered meat for sale in the market; (II) evidence for, and the inscription on, the daily meat market of Roman Corinth; (III) what happened while Paul was in Corinth which might provide some clues for official actions subsequently; and (IV) what might have changed after he left that could explain his totally unexpected command to buy and eat without question meat bought in the 'market' (μάκελλον) (10:25).

---

1. Some would argue for a 'hymn' or confessional statement in 8:4b-6 introduced by 'we know', but Paul does not specially make reference to this as a formal 'paradosis' as he does in 11:23-25 and 15:3-4.

287

I. Official Food Concessions for Diaspora Jews

Josephus records an official decree which involved provision of kosher food and which was issued on the resolution of the magistrates from the city of Sardis in Asia Minor and passed by the Council and the People. It was dated after October, 47 B.C., not long before the founding of the colony of Corinth in 44 B.C. (*Ant.* 14.259-61).[2] This was not the first discussion of Jewish rights in Sardis, for Lucius Antonius, the *proquaestor* who deputised for Minucius Thermus, the Proconsul of Asia on his recall to Rome, wrote an official letter to the magistrates, the council, and the people of Sardis indicating that the ancient customs of the Jews in that city were to be respected. These included their own 'association', 'a place of their own' — presumably a synagogue — and the right to decide their own 'affairs and controversies with one another' (*Ant.* 14.235). This letter, written earlier than the decree of Sardis in 47 B.C., appears to have been the catalyst for securing recognition of their ancient customs.

The preamble of this decree began with the customary 'whereas' (ἐπεί) in order to explain the context of the official resolution of the Council and the People:

> Whereas the Jewish citizens living in our city have continually received many great privileges from the people and have now come before the Council and the People and have pleaded that as their laws and freedom have been restored to them by the Roman Senate and People, they may, in accordance with their accepted customs, come together and have a communal life and adjudicate suits among themselves, and that a place be given them in which they may gather together with their wives and children and offer their ancestral prayers and sacrifices to God. . . .[3]

The official resolution then declared, 'it has therefore been decreed by the Council and the People (δεδόχθαι τῇ βουλῇ καὶ τῷ δήμῳ) that permission shall be given to them to assemble on sacred days, to do things in accordance with their laws, and also that a place shall be set apart by the magistrates for them to build and inhabit'. The decree concluded, 'so that the market-officials of the city (ὅπως τε τοῖς τῆς πόλεως ἀγορανόμοις

---

2. A. M. Rabello, 'The Legal Condition of the Jews in the Roman Empire,' *ANRW* 2.13 (1980): 684.

3. *Ant.* 14.259-60.

ἐπιμελὲς)[4] shall be charged with the duty of having suitable food for them [the Jews] brought in' (ἢ καὶ τὰ ἐκείνοις πρὸς τροφὴν ἐπιτήδεια ποιεῖν εἰσάγεσθαι, *Ant.* 14.261) for sale in the marketplace, over which they had control.

What credence can be given to the authenticity of this copy of an official decree or any other decrees cited by Josephus? He devoted a section of his work to official decrees either from Rome or cities in which Jews lived and which described their rights (*Ant.* 14.185-264). Rabello has concluded that 'there is no reason to doubt upon the accuracy of any document which deals with the Jews'.[5] Others have not been so optimistic. Recently a thorough examination of the copies of the rights in these decrees was conducted on both the contents and arguments for and against, and it supports their authenticity.[6] In collating the decrees in chapter 10 of book 14 of *The Antiquities of the Jews,* Josephus commenced by contrasting the lack of extant documentary evidence by the Persians and Macedonians on the Jews with the decrees of the Romans. He explained why that was so: 'for they are laid up in the public places of the cities and are extant still in the capitol, and engraved upon pillars of brass' (*Ant.* 14.188). This is in keeping with what we know elsewhere of extant inscriptions and decrees on bronze.[7] Josephus included decrees of those who held the *imperium,* the Proconsul of Asia, and those cities which acted in concert with Roman restoration of Jewish rights, e.g., Sardis. Recent discussion has failed to note two important, but not unconnected, points. First is the special status Josephus enjoyed with the early Flavian emperors, who 'permitted him to live in Vespasian's private residence, granted him prized Roman citizen-

4. ἐπιτήδεια = 'suitable', i.e., kosher.

5. Rabello, 'The Legal Condition of the Jews in the Roman Empire,' 682.

6. M. Pucci Ben Zeev, *Jewish Rights in the Roman World: The Greek and Roman Documents Quoted by Josephus Flavius,* Texts and Studies in Ancient Judaism 74 (Tübingen: J. C. B. Mohr [Paul Siebeck], 1999), pp. 381-408, where she produces evidence of bronze tablets used for decrees and looks at the literary sources and archives. The constitutions of cities existed in bronze in the forum of cities which in the case of *Colonia Genetiva Julia* stretched from the time of Julius Caesar until Trajan's reign, a period similar to those cited by Josephus. See n. 7.

7. See, most recently, J. González, 'The *Lex Irnitana:* A New Flavian Municipal Law,' *JRS* 76 (1986): 147-243; and on the preservation of a constitution from the Republic to the Flavian period, see E. G. Hardy, *Three Spanish Charters and Other Documents* (Oxford: Clarendon Press, 1912), pp. 7-60, where an extant Roman constitution dated from Flavian times preserves many of the original regulations of 45 B.C.

ship, gave him large tracts of land in Judeae, and ultimately exempted him from taxation.' Adopting the name 'Flavius' 'suggests they also brought him under the protection of their family and became his literary patron'.[8] Second, the alteration of decrees of cities was treated as a serious criminal offence. Roman authorities dealt very severely with those who forged or altered official documents, threatening such offenders with the death penalty, as the decree in the time of Claudius by Quintus Veranius indicates.[9] Why would Josephus put himself at such a risk by forging this particular decree and others, and for what purpose?

This decree of Sardis was passed in the wake of the restoration of rights to the Jews by the Roman Senate and People; a parallel can be drawn with the decree of the city of Halicarnassus inasmuch as the reason for affirming Jewish rights in that city is based on Rome's 'friendship and alliance with the Jews' (*Ant.* 14.256-58).

This copy of the decree reflects the legal conventions and literary *genre* of a civic resolution.[10] The final ἵνα or ὅπως clause of such resolutions had a special function in the legal formulation of civic resolutions.[11] It recorded for those who read the inscription that the city had acted appropriately by meeting its obligations. For example, in the case of resolutions honouring civic benefactors, it was customary to declare in the final ἵνα or ὅπως clause 'that all may see that the city of X knows how to bestow appropriate honours on those who are its benefactors'.[12]

---

8. S. Mason, *Josephus and the New Testament* (Peabody, Mass.: Hendrickson, 1992), pp. 50-51.

9. This governor's decree from Myra of A.D. 43-48 prescribes the whipping of any person who altered a legal document. This would include producing a false document allegedly coming from the archives. The death penalty was threatened for any further misdemeanours. See R. K. Sherk, *The Roman Empire: Augustus to Hadrian*, Translated Documents of Greece and Rome (Cambridge: Cambridge University Press, 1988), VI, no. 48. The preservation of archival material was of great significance for the Roman authorities, and this reflects in part the legal bent of Romans generally; Pucci Ben Zeev, *Jewish Rights in the Roman World*, pp. 395-405. See also the official inquiry into not keeping official records properly and in good storage and the steps taken to penalise the officials and arrange to repair official documents in an archive; *P.Fam.Tebt.* 15 (c. A.D. 114-15).

10. For a discussion of this convention see my 'Civic Honours for Christian Benefactors,' *Seek the Welfare of the City: Early Christians as Benefactors and Citizens* (Grand Rapids and Carlisle: Eerdmans and Paternoster, 1994), ch. 2.

11. Winter, 'Civic Honours for Christian Benefactors,' pp. 26-28.

12. Winter, 'Civic Honours for Christian Benefactors,' p. 28, nn. 7-11, for examples.

That the Council and the People of Sardis had followed Rome's restoration of Jewish laws and privileges was seen specifically in the action on the part of the officials who regulated the market, including the sale of meat. This responsibility rested with the persons elected to oversee the commercial affairs of the city and adjudicate on commercial disputes. The decree of Sardis rightly designated the annually elected official as ἀγορανόμος, for which the Latin term is *aedile*. 'They are to have the right and power of managing the corn-supply . . . the drains, the baths and the market and of checking weights and measures.'[13] A later source which traced the history of the office stated, 'they were granted the supervision of the public market, when they came to be called *agoranomoi* [officials of the market] by those who put their names into Greek.'[14] The Sardis decree confirmed their jurisdiction over the meat market, for they were charged with the responsibility for 'bringing in' what was called 'suitable meat' (ἐπιτήδεια), i.e., 'kosher' meat for Jews.

In the same way that the erection of a statue, the gift of a crown of gold, and the allocation of a special seat in the theatre were visible signs that a city had, on its part, acted appropriately, so too the special provision for Jews of a suitable market bore witness to all who read the decree, including the proconsul on his annual assize, that Sardis had responded in concert with Rome to the restoration of full rights for Jews living in that city by the provision of suitable food in a market, which would have included the meat market.[15]

This was not an isolated incident. There is evidence elsewhere that the Romans took cognisance of the Jews' religious scruples and that the action of Sardis was not an isolated, nor a fictitious one. In Rome itself Jews were exempted from the ban against the right to assemble more than once a month;[16] those entitled to it could collect the corn dole on a day other than

13. *Lex Irnitana*, ch. 19.

14. Zoranas, *Ann.* 7.15.i.f.

15. In places with a large Jewish population, later laws permitted them to hold a special market for which they themselves were responsible. However, this was a very much later provision, as is seen from *Codex Theodosianus* 16.8.10 (A.D. 396); cf. *Corpus Juris Civilis Codex* 1.9.9.

16. W. Cotter, 'The *Collegia* and Roman Law: State Restrictions on Voluntary Associations 64 BCE–200 CE,' in J. S. Kloppenborg and S. G. Wilson, eds., *Voluntary Associations in the Graeco-Roman World* (London: Routledge, 1996), ch. 5, esp. pp. 76-78; Pucci Ben Zeev, *Jewish Rights in the Roman World*, pp. 459-60.

the Sabbath,[17] or they could appear in court on the Sabbath day.[18] Dolabella, the Proconsul of Asia, exempted Jews from military service because the Roman army could not issue them rations according to their laws and customs; a number of other decrees mention a similar exemption (*Ant.* 14.223-25). When rations were distributed free of charge, if the food provided was forbidden to Jews, the Roman army would pay Jewish soldiers the value of their rations. Extant sources cited by Josephus refer to similar exemptions in Ephesus and Delos (*Ant.* 14.225-34). Issues relating to litigation between Jews — 'controversies with one another', 'adjudicate suits among themselves' — could be decided in their own courts (*Ant.* 14.235, 259-61) in much the same way that private arbitration could be resorted to by Roman citizens in conflict.[19] Publius Servilius Galba, also a proconsul of Asia, listened to the arguments of the representatives of Miletus and the Jews of that city, and made the judgement in favour of the Jews. It included 'managing their own produce in accordance with their custom' (καὶ τοὺς καρποὺς μεταχειρίζεσθαι, καθὼς ἔθος ἐστὶν αὐτοῖς), i.e., revenues destined for transmission to Jerusalem (*Ant.* 14.244-46).[20] Among the special privileges accorded Diaspora Jews as early as the end of the fourth century B.C. was 'a fixed sum of money from the gymnasiarchs in cities in the East to pay for their own kind of oil' for the use on the body; this was continued under the Romans (*Ant.* 12.119-20).

Pucci Ben Zeev has concluded in her monumental study on Jewish rights that Rome's action 'may not be regarded as proof of a special consideration for Jewish needs, but rather an application of common principles of Roman policy' which were 'yielding and elastic enough to accommodate the most different situations, and most peoples enjoyed, *de facto* or *de iure*, the right to live according to their laws and customs'.[21] It is impor-

17. '. . . in the monthly doles in his own city (Rome), he (Augustus) never put the Jews at a disadvantage in sharing the bounty, but even if the distributions happened to come during the Sabbath when no one (Jew) is permitted to receive or give anything or transact any part of the business of ordinary life, particularly of a lucrative kind, he ordered the dispensers to reserve for the Jews until the morrow the charity which fell to all' (Philo, *Leg.* 158).

18. Josephus, *Ant.* 16.162-65, 167-68.

19. For discussion see Ch. 4, esp. pp. 67-68.

20. This must not be construed to be a reference to managing their own market in Miletus, which in all cities was the responsibility of the market officials, but 'to administer their fruits', i.e., revenues destined for transmission to Jerusalem. See Pucci Ben Zeev, *Jewish Rights in the Roman World*, pp. 201-3, for a history of the discussion of this issue and the arguments for this conclusion.

21. Pucci Ben Zeev, *Jewish Rights in the Roman World*, p. 482.

tant to note that kosher meat was one such Jewish need, indeed a Jewish law, a custom derived from the Torah and a critical factor in what it meant to be a Jew in the Diaspora.

In its preamble the Sardis inscription also reflected another important aspect of Roman policy. One of the ways in which Rome and its governors penalised cities or sectional interests whose activities displeased them was to withdraw privileges it had granted.[22] The giving, the cancellation, and the restoration of concessions were among the most effective means of controlling individual cities and sectional interest in them in the empire — Rome had not created an enormous bureaucracy to rule all the cities of the provinces. The governor and his small entourage used 'the stick and carrot' method to maintain control of a province apart, of course, from the exercise of the *imperium* in criminal actions.[23] The Sardis inscription showed that Jewish rights had been terminated, preventing them for observing their 'ancient traditions' *(mos maiorum)*. It also showed that 'their laws and freedom have been restored to them by the Roman Senate and People' and was provision for the securing of suitable food in the official marketplaces of cities in which they dwelt.

II. The Corinthian Meat Market

According to the orator Aristides, who visited Corinth in A.D. 156, it was 'a kind of marketplace (ἀγορά), a common courtyard of the Greeks, and a religious gathering (πανήγυρις) not like this present one (the Isthmian Games), which is crowded by the Greek race every two years, but one which is crowded with them every year and daily' (ἀλλ᾽ ἦν διὰ παντὸς ἔτους καὶ καθ᾽ ἡμέραν ἑκάστην).[24] 'High-frequency markets are said to have existed in every town, and to have joined shops and the market hall in supplying the "necessities of local life"'. They were to be distinguished from what have been called 'low-frequency' fairs, which were held in con-

---

22. D. Braund, ed., *The Administration of the Roman Empire 241 BC–AD 193* (Exeter: University of Exeter, 1988).

23. See p. 45.

24. *Or.* 46.23. This oration is a panegyric on Corinth and not Poseidon, in whom he did not believe; C. A. Behr, *P. Aelius Aristides: The Complete Works* (Leiden: E. J. Brill, 1981), II, 422. The annual festival would have been the Federal Imperial Cult celebrations; see pp. 271-76.

junction with major activities such as assizes, religious festivals, and games.[25] The latter events, including the famous Isthmian Games, attracted all manner of commercial activities, including travelling brothels,[26] but the daily market was critical for a city the population of which has been estimated to be 80,000 in the time of Paul.[27]

The market, which included both the meat and fish markets, was controlled by civic authorities[28] and was an important source of revenue for them — 'the imperial (and urban) authorities retained a firm grip on all indirect taxes that were levied at markets'.[29] The offering of meat as a sacrifice before using it for consumption was a long-standing convention in the Graeco-Roman world,[30] and therefore concerns of the Jews about meat which had not been offered to idols was critical to their religion.

The meat market in Corinth was built in the time of Augustus along the Lechaion Road and next to a basilica, possibly the court where the *aedile* presided over commercial disputes. The inscription records this substantial family benefaction:[31]

> Quintus Cornelius Secundus, son of [————], of the tribe Aemilia, and his wife Maecia, daughter of [Quintus], his son [____-Cornelius Secundus] Maecianus, his son Quintus Cornelius Secundus, his [daughter] Cornelia [Secunda, who is the wife of Quintus] Maecius Cleogenes the freedman of Quintus (Maecius), [built (?)] the meat market [————] along with [————] and the fish market[————]'.[32]

25. L. de Ligt, *Fairs and Markets in the Roman Empire: Economic and Social Aspects of Periodic Trade in a Pre-industrial Society* (Amsterdam: J. C. Gieben, 1993), p. 28.

26. Dio Chrysostom, *Or.* 77/78.4, records the activities of brothel keepers who were 'dragging their stock about to the congress . . . of other great festive gatherings.'

27. D. Engels, 'Agriculture and Manufactures,' *Roman Corinth: An Alternative for the Classical City* (Chicago: University of Chicago Press, 1990), ch. 2, esp. pp. 22-33.

28. Engels, *Roman Corinth*, p. 18.

29. de Ligt, *Fairs and Markets in the Roman Empire: Economic and Social Aspects of Periodic Trade in a Pre-industrial Society*, p. 169.

30. J.-L. Durand, 'Greek Animals: Towards a Topology of Edible Bodies,' in M. Detienne and J.-P. Vernant, eds., *The Cuisine of Sacrifice among the Greeks* (E.T. Chicago: University of Chicago Press, 1989), pp. 104-5.

31. On the gifts of *macella* by wealthy benefactors see D. W. J. Gill, 'The Meat Market at Corinth (1 Corinthians 10:25),' *TynB* 43.2 (1992): 391, citing D. Perring, 'Spatial Organisation and Social Change in Roman Towns,' in J. Rich and A. Wallace-Hadrill, eds., *City and Country in the Ancient World* (London: Routledge, 1991), p. 281.

32. Kent, *Corinth*, 8.3, no. 321.

We know that the meat *(macellum)* and fish markets *(macellum piscarum)* were a substantial enterprise in Corinth. A cluster of 'shops' surrounded the *tholos*, i.e., the pool, and all of this constituted the meat-market, *macellum* (μάκελλον).[33]

The letter of Lucius Antonius, the *proquaestor*, imposed on the officials of Sardis the recognition of Jewish rights as part of official policy in the Roman East. The Sardis official inscription also bears witness to the agitation of Jews for their rights and privileges based on ancient traditions in the city. The presence of a considerable number of Jews in Corinth was not unknown in Paul's day, and a later inscription bears witness to their synagogue (Philo, *Leg.* 281; Acts 18:4-5).[34] Access to the provincial court for a criminal action was another of their rights (Acts 18:12-17).[35] The above justifies the conclusion that in this Roman colony official provision would also have to be made in the market complex for the Jewish community to secure kosher meat and other foods.

III. When Paul Was in Corinth

Acts 18 records what happened while Paul was in Corinth. The first converts were immediately separated from the Jewish synagogue meeting after one gospel presentation — the opposition was intense as 'they opposed themselves and railed so much that Paul shook out his clothes and said, "Your blood be upon your own heads, I am clean: from henceforth I will go to the Gentiles"' (Acts 18:6). The house of the God-fearer Titius Justus, which adjoined the synagogue, became the place of worship; and Crispus, the ruler of the synagogue, with all his household believed' (Acts 18:1-8). The loss of a potential convert from the synagogue to a rival meeting next door would have been resented.

33. For a discussion of the market see C. K. Williams II, 'Roman Corinth as a Commercial Center,' in T. E. Gregory, ed., *The* Corinthia *in the Roman Period,* Journal of Roman Archaeology Supp. Series 8 (1993), pp. 39-40; and for the inscription see Gill, 'The Meat Market at Corinth (1 Corinthians 10:25),' 389-93.

34. Merritt, *Corinth,* 8.1, no. 111; and for the most recent discussion of the inscription and its dating see I. Levinskaya, *The Book of Acts in Its Diaspora Setting,* in B. Winter, ed., The Book of Acts in Its First Century Setting (Carlisle: Paternoster; Grand Rapids: Eerdmans, 1996), pp. 162-66.

35. Pucci Ben Zeev, *Jewish Rights in the Roman World,* p. 433.

In an important essay T. Rajak has argued that the role of *archi-synagogos* was not a cultic one but 'had far more to do with patronage and philanthropy',[36] for this 'office' had been much influenced by secular categories in *politeia* in the early empire.[37] If she is correct, then the term normally translated 'ruler of the synagogue' could well refer to the role of patron and philanthropist. She gives the example of inscriptions from Asia Minor which recorded gifts to the synagogue of benefactors and a benefactress, none of whom were Jews.[38] If Crispus had fulfilled this role for Corinth's Jewish community,[39] the intensity of their feelings as a result of their loss of a benefactor is explicable. Luke records that the Jews 'with one accord' rose up and brought a criminal case against Paul to Gallio, the governor of the province (18:12). This highly competent jurist refused to proceed after hearing the Jews' preliminary arguments and provided his reasons even before Paul could plead his defence (18:14).[40]

The same passage also recounts the aftermath of the failure of the Jews to secure a case against Paul. Gallio 'dismissed' them (ἀπήλασεν) from the judgement seat, and some of the Corinthians laid into Sosthenes, the subsequent ruler of the synagogue, 'beating him before the judgement seat'. Luke informs us that Gallio turned a blind eye, for he 'cared for none of these things' (18:16-17). This action was one way that loyal Corinthians demonstrated their solidarity with the Roman governor. Roman citizens also saw it as a highly effective weapon, for this was a public humiliation for the head of the Jews in Corinth and a hostile signal to that community.[41]

The Christian Jews, on the basis of Gallio's ruling, were entitled to purchase meat that had not been offered to idols in the marketplace. Even

36. T. Rajak, 'The Jewish Community and Its Boundaries,' in J. Lieu, J. North, and T. Rajak, eds., *The Jews among the Pagans and Christians in the Roman Empire* (London: Routledge, 1992), pp. 9-28.

37. T. Rajak and D. Noy, '*Archisynagogos*: Office, Social Status in the Graeco-Roman World,' *JRS* 83 (1993): 75-93.

38. T. Rajak, 'The Synagogue within the Greco-Roman City,' in S. Fine, ed., *Jews, Christians and Polytheists in the Ancient Synagogue: Cultural Interaction in the Greco-Roman Period* (London: Routledge, 1999), ch. 9.

39. On patronage see pp. 186ff.

40. For discussion of this see my 'Gallio's Ruling on the Legal Status of Early Christianity (Acts 18:14-15),' *TynB* 50.2 (Nov. 1999): 213-24.

41. On humiliation in Roman society see R. A. Kaster, 'The Shame of the Romans,' *TAPA* 127 (1997): 1-19; and on the loss of *dignitas*, D. F. Epstein, *Personal Enmity in Roman Politics 218-43 B.C.* (London: Routledge, 1989), pp. 90-91.

if the Jews were unhappy with that arrangement, they could not move against the sale of 'suitable meat' to Christians. Gallio's ruling was that the Jews' case against Paul was about an internal religious dispute, 'questions about words, and names and your own law' and not some criminal offence (18:14-15).[42] Therefore the officials who governed the meat market might have been involved. Christians were entitled to purchase kosher meat there, and this may have been the reason that Paul needed to provide no tradition on the purchasing of idol meat for the Christian community in Corinth while he was there. If this was the case, then Corinthian Christians had been able to follow the Jerusalem Council's decision concerning food offered to idols (Acts 15:23-29) — a decision that could only be implemented in Gentile cities where kosher meat was available in the official market.

IV. After Paul Left Corinth

After Paul left Corinth we have to speculate as to what may have happened. A case can be argued on the basis of Roman policy and the example from Sardis. It is suggested that, as a move against the Jews, the provision of 'suitable food' was officially withdrawn from the Corinthian meat market. This, at the same time, deprived Christians of access to meat not offered to idols.

Acts refers to the ejection of the Jews from Rome and the arrival of some, including Aquila and Priscilla, in Corinth (18:2). The emperor Claudius expelled the Jews from Rome, punishing them with exile and thereby depriving them of any benefits and privileges which they enjoyed while living at the heart of the empire, including the corn dole for those who were eligible.[43] As a result, the official meat markets would no longer need to make special slaughtering arrangements for Jews in Rome.[44]

---

42. For a discussion of these terms see my 'Gallio's Ruling on the Legal Status of Early Christianity (Acts 18:14-15),' 219.

43. On the distribution to Jews in Rome and the special arrangement so as not to offend their Sabbath, see Philo, *Leg.* 159, and discussion by Pucci Ben Zeev, *Jewish Rights in the Roman World*, p. 439.

44. This may well account for one of the problems in Romans 14, where the issues of the day on which to worship and the eating of meat were in dispute, especially if a meat market was no longer provided for Jews in Rome.

As we have seen, the Sardis inscription indicated the importance attached by the city fathers to the civic provision of the meat market for Jews. Its restoration signalled to all who read that it was more than simply the right of a *politeuma* for the Jews,[45] the right to bring matters to their own courts for resolution, the gift of land for the building of a synagogue, the right to observe the Sabbath, and possibly the provision of 'a ghetto', as important as all these were. Sardis provided evidence of the restoration of Jewish rights following Rome's move with the provision of a place in the meat market where Jews could secure 'suitable food', i.e., meat. What they were required to do for all the citizens of that city with the provision of a meat market, they did for the Jews; this was also a sign to the wider community of the full restoration of rights to this racial minority.[46]

The Jews, whose anger against Paul in the early days of the Christian community spilt over into a precipitous criminal action (Acts 18:12), must have found Gallio's ruling galling indeed. Their case resulted in the worst possible outcome for them, for their hated enemy was given the protection and privileges of Jews. The expression of anti-Semitism in the presence of Gallio in Corinth was further proof of loyal identification with Rome in all things and may have precipitated action subsequently on the part of Corinth's Council (βουλή). It is therefore not impossible that, subsequent to Paul's departure, 'the Council and the People' of Corinth officially discriminated further against Jews by withdrawing some privilege.

Recording that the Jews' laws and privileges were 'restored' in Sardis, the decree implies that these had been withdrawn by that city when the Jews incurred the displeasure of Rome. Sardis had simply acted in concert with the capital of the empire. The situation is paralleled in the time of Claudius when his displeasure against Rome's Jews resulted in their eviction (Acts 18:2). According to Suetonius, Chrestus was the 'instigator of it' (*impulsore Chresto*).[47] It is difficult to determine to whom he was referring, for epigraphic evidence shows that well over thirty persons in Rome were known to have borne this name. Whether he was a 'once well-known slave

---

45. G. Lüderitz, 'What Is the Politeuma?' in J. W. van Henten and P. W. Van der Horst, eds., *Studies in Early Jewish Epigraphy* (Leiden: E. J. Brill, 1994), pp. 183-225.

46. It was only much later that the Jews themselves ran their own markets, especially in Palestine after A.D. 70.

47. 'Life of Claudius' 24.4.

or freedman of Claudius',[48] a Jewish Messianic megastar,[49] or Jesus as the Christ is not critical to this argument. It is important that there appears to be a connection between Rome's policy of a Jewish exodus from Rome and the Corinthian action in beating up the leader of the Jewish synagogue when the case was dismissed by Gallio — Luke particularly recorded that the governor was not motivated to prevent others venting their anti-Jewish feelings on Sosthenes after the case was dismissed (Acts 18:17). It was during his governorship of Achaea that Claudius designated him in the Delphi inscription as 'my friend and proconsul' (ὁ φ[ίλος] μου κα[ὶ ἀνθύ]-πατος),[50] and Gallio would have been keen to show that he was worthy of that imperial accolade.

Could any legitimate actions be taken by the civic authorities to show their loyalty to Rome's policy on the Jews? If they acted against them at an official level, they would have created enormous difficulties had they proscribed assemblies in their synagogue on the Sabbath. Those weekly meetings had been specifically provided for by Augustus at the time of his legislation — it had banned gatherings of associations from meeting more than once a month because they had become hotbeds of political intrigue.[51] Corinth's officialdom could not easily inhibit the Jewish private arbitrators resolving disagreements among their members.[52] The only aspect of Jewish life that the local authorities moved against was the provision of suitable meat at the meat market.

An interesting first-century parallel also exists with respect to the use of oil. An extant reference in that era refers to 'those Jews who did not want

48. H. D. Slingerland, 'Here a Chrestus, There a Chrestus,' *Claudian Policymaking and the Early Imperial Repression of Judaism at Rome,* Studies in the History of Judaism (Atlanta: Scholars Press, 1997), ch. 9, cited on p. 245.

49. E. A. Judge and G. S. R. Thomas, 'The Origins of the Church at Rome: A New Solution,' *RTR* 25 (1966): 81-94. They argue that it is not a reference to Jesus as the Christ, partly on the basis of Suetonius' convention of introducing new topics. He introduces the Christian movement only as a new phenomenon at a later stage in his work in the reign of Nero ('Life of Nero,' 16.2).

50. See A. Plassart, 'L'inscription de Delphes mentionnant le proconsul Gallion,' *REG* 80 (1967): 372-78, for the full text of the composite epigraphic evidence.

51. W. Cotter, 'The *Collegia* and Roman Law: State Restrictions on Voluntary Associations 64 BCE–200 CE,' in J. S. Kloppenberg and S. G. Wilson, eds., *Voluntary Associations in the Graeco-Roman World,* pp. 76-78; O. F. Robinson, *The Criminal Law of Ancient Rome* (London: Duckworth, 1995), p. 80.

52. See p. 288.

to use foreign oil'. In the late sixties A.D. during the first Jewish revolt, the governor of Syria, Mucianus, specifically noted that the Jews were allowed to continue to have this made available to them.[53] Josephus, in recording the Jews' reaction, notes that there was an expectation that this special provision would be withdrawn because of the rebellion in Jerusalem, a city which was under the jurisdiction of the governor of Syria[54] — 'the production and supply of oil was an imperial monopoly'.[55]

It is clear from what Paul wrote that all meat in Corinth was sold in the *macellum*. His subsequent discussion implied that it had been offered in the idol temple, and his ruling suggested that this was so. He commanded Christians to purchase and to eat it (ἐσθίετε). If they were invited to a private dinner and were disposed to go,[56] they were also told to ask no questions because there was none to ask, i.e., there was nothing wrong with a Christian eating meat, if provided by the host. There was definitely one exception — when a companion at a private dinner drew attention to the fact that it had been offered to idols because he thought that it was inappropriate for a Christian to eat it (10:25-29a). It was for the sake of the conscience of the latter who had kindly drawn attention to this fact, and not conscience of the Christian, that Paul requires them to desist from eating.

Paul's justification for this injunction was even more extraordinary. He cited Psalm 24:1, which states who owned the meat — 'the earth is the Lord's, and everything in it'. Paul's choice of this verse was a significant one. The Jews were known to have recited this very text as a blessing over their meals, with the exception perhaps of the Passover.[57] Those who had such a prohibition against eating food offered to idols used the traditional grace which allowed Christians to buy and eat that meat.

Did the Christian community raise the question about buying meat from the marketplace, or did Paul himself rule on this matter on his own

---

53. *Ant.* 12.119-20.

54. M. Goodman, 'Kosher Olive Oil in Antiquity,' in P. R. Davies and R. T. White, eds., *A Tribute to Geza Vermes* (Sheffield: Sheffield Academic Press, 1990), pp. 227-44.

55. A. Kasher, 'The Rights of the Jews of Antioch on the Orontes,' *Proceedings of the American Academy of Jewish Research* 49 (1982): 78-79.

56. The reasons for not going may have had to do with a host who provided sexual pleasures afterwards or may have related to what Plutarch called 'secondary' or 'shadow' guests, i.e., those not invited by the host but brought by an invited guest. For some of the social difficulties of the latter, see Plutarch, *Moralia* 707-10A.

57. *T. Ber.* 4.1.

volition, as he did on marriage matters (7:8-16)? They wrote about 'things offered to idols' and 'eating things sacrificed to idols' (8:1, 4). They did so because some members of the community were unsure what was appropriate Christian conduct. Eating at a feast in an idol temple was one thing, although some were determined to exercise their inalienable rights to do so as citizens of Corinth — in the previous chapter we have explored the new *Sitz im Leben* that gave rise to that activity. Whether to buy meat from the market for personal consumption, as the rest of Corinth did, seems to have been a 'new' issue.[58]

We possess information on the eviction of Jews from Rome by Claudius, the public humiliation of the Corinthian Jews immediately after the dismissal of the case against Paul, and Gallio's quiet acquiescence of the action of other Corinthians out of loyalty to the anti-Semitism of Claudius (Acts 18:17). It has been suggested that after Paul left Corinth the magistrates and the Council moved against the Jewish community by withdrawing kosher meat from the market. Even if we had no evidence from Sardis or archaeological or epigraphic material, it would not be mistaken to postulate the existence of an official meat market in Corinth, part of which made provision for the special situation of Diaspora Jews with 'suitable' food, for all markets provided an official source of revenue in the Roman Empire. Given that the meat market was regulated by the city authorities, we can draw the conclusion that the difficulties addressed in 1 Corinthians 10:25-29, 'to eat *all* (πᾶν) that was sold in the market', may well have arisen because of the withdrawal of special provisions on kosher meat by officials in Corinth. This presented Christians there with a new situation on which Paul, having left Corinth, needed to give an urgent apostolic ruling.

---

58. Paul gives a ruling on what to do at a private dinner party which was a corollary to his declaration on buying food in the marketplace — a ruling which arose out of his own experience and for which he himself had apparently attracted criticism (9:3; 10:27-30).

Bibliography

Adams, J. N. *The Latin Sexual Vocabulary.* London: Duckworth, 1982.

Alcock, S. E. *Graecia Capta: The Landscapes of Roman Greece.* Cambridge: Cambridge University Press, 1993.

Aletti, J.-N., Barrett, C. K., Carrez, M., Montagnini, F., Müller, K., and Schrage, W. *Résurrection du Christ et des Chrétiens (1 Co 15).* Rome: Abbaye de S. Paul, 1985.

Alford, H. *The Greek Testament.* Cambridge: Cambridge University Press, 1877, vol. II.

Allo, E.-B. *Saint Paul: Première Epître aux Corinthiens,* 2nd ed. Paris: LeCoffre, 1956.

Amandry, M. *Le monnayage des duovirs corinthiens.* BCH Supplement 15. Paris and Athens: École Francaise d'Athènes, 1988.

Amunsen, D. W., and Diers, C. J. "The Age of Menopause in Classical Greece and Rome," *Human Biology* 42 (1970): 79-88.

Anderson Jr., J. C. *Roman Architecture and Society.* Baltimore: Johns Hopkins University Press, 1997.

Anderson, G. *Philostratus: Biography and Belles Lettres in the Third Century* AD. London: Croom Helm, 1986.

Anderson, G. *The Second Sophistic: A Cultural Phenomenon in the Roman Empire.* London: Routledge, 1993.

Arafat, K. W. *Pausanias' Greece: Ancient Artists and Roman Rulers.* Cambridge: Cambridge University Press, 1996.

Audollent, A. *Defixionum Tabellae.* Paris, 1904.

Badian, E. *Publicans and Sinners: Private Enterprise in the Service of the Roman Republic.* Oxford: Blackwells, 1972.

Bagdikian, A. "The Civic Officials of Roman Corinth." M.A. thesis, University of Vermont, 1953.

Banks, R., Conrad, E. W., and Newing, E. G., eds., "'Walking' as a Metaphor of the

Christian Life: The Origins of a Significant Pauline Usage," in *Perspectives on Language and Text: Essays and Poems in Honour of Francis I. Andersen on His Sixtieth Birthday, July 28, 1985*, pp. 303-13. Winona Lake: Eisenbrauns, 1987.

Barrett, C. K. *The First Epistle to the Corinthians*, 2nd ed. London: A & C Black, 1971.

Barton, S., and Horsley, G. H. R. "A Hellenistic Cult Group and the New Testament Churches," *JbAC* 24 (1981): 7-41.

Bash, A. *Ambassadors for Christ*. Tübingen: J. C. B. Mohr (Paul Siebeck), 1997.

Bauman, R. A. *Women and Politics in Ancient Rome*. London: Routledge, 1992.

BeDuhn, J. D. "'Because of the angels': Unveiling Paul's Anthropology in 1 Corinthians 11," *JBL* (1999): 295-320.

Bell, H. I. "The Economic Crisis in Egypt under Nero," *JRS* 28 (1938): 5-6.

Blattenberger, D. E. *Rethinking 1 Corintians 11:2-16 through Archeological and Moral-Rhetorical Analysis*, Studies in the Bible and Early Christianity 36. Lewiston: Edwin Mellen Press, 1997.

Boissevain, J. "Patronage in Sicily," *Mana* n.s. 1 (1966): 18-33.

Bond, H. K. "The Coins of Pontius Pilate: Part of an Attempt to Provoke the People or to Integrate Them into Empire," *JSJ* 27.3 (Aug. 1996): 241-62.

Bookidis, N. "The Sanctuary of Demeter and Kore on Acrocorinth: Preliminary Report IV," *Hesperia* 41 (1972): 283-331.

Bookidis, N., and Stroud, R. S. *Demeter and Persephone in Ancient Corinth*, American Excavations in Old Corinth, Corinth Notes no. 2. Meriden, Conn.: The Meriden-Stinehour Press, 1987.

Booth, A. "The Age for Reclining and Its Attendant Perils," in W. J. Slater, ed., *Dining in a Classical Context*, pp. 105-20. Ann Arbor: University of Michigan Press, 1991.

Borg, M. "A New Context for Romans XIII," *NTS* 19 (1973): 205-18.

Boswell, J. *Christianity, Social Tolerance and Homosexuality*. Chicago: The University of Chicago Press, 1980.

Bowersock, G. W. *Greek Sophists in the Roman Empire*. Oxford: Clarendon Press, 1969.

Bowersock, G. W. "A New Inscription of Arrian," *GRBS* 8 (1967): 279-80.

Bowie, E. L. "Greeks and Their Past in the Second Sophistic," *Past and Present* 46 (1970): 3-41.

Bowie, E. L. "The Importance of the Sophists," *Yale Classical Review* 27 (1982): 29-59.

Bradley, K. R. "Loyalty and Obedience," in *Slaves and Masters in the Roman Empire: A Study of Social Control*, ch. 1. Oxford: Oxford University Press, 1987.

Brandt, P.-Y., and Lukinovich, A. "οἶκος and οἰκία chez Marc comparé Matthew at Luc," *Biblica* 78.4 (1997): 525-33.

Braund, D. "*Cohores*: The Governor and His Entourage," in R. Lawrence and

J. Berry, eds., *Cultural Identity in the Roman Empire,* ch. 2. London: Routledge, 1998.

Braund, D., ed., *The Administration of the Roman Empire 241 BC–AD 193.* Exeter: University of Exeter, 1988.

Broneer, O. *"Colonia Laus Iulia Corinthiensis,"* Hesperia 10 (1941): 388-90.

Broneer, O. *Isthmia.* Princeton: American School of Classical Studies in Athens, 1973, vol. 2.

Broughton, T. R. S. *The Magistrates of the Roman Republic.* Atlanta: Scholars Press, 1986, vol. 1.

Browne, G. M. *Documentary Papyri from the Michigan Collection,* 10. American Studies in Papyriology 6 (1970).

Bruce, F. F. *The Acts of the Apostles.* London: Tyndale Press, 1952.

Bruce, F. F. *1 and 2 Corinthians.* London: Oliphants, 1971.

Brunt, P. A. "The Romanization of the Local Ruling Classes in the Roman Empire," in D. M. Pippidi, ed., *Assimilation et résistance à la culture gréco-romaine dans la monde ancien. Travaux du VIe Congrés International d'Etudes Classique,* pp. 124-47. Paris: 'Belles Lettres', 1976.

Buckland, W. W. *The Roman Law of Slavery: The Condition of the Slave in Private Law from Augustus to Justinian.* Cambridge: Cambridge University Press, 1908.

Buckland, W. W., revised P. Stein, *A Text-book of Roman Law from the Time of Cicero to the Time of Ulpian.* Oxford: Clarendon Press, 1991.

Burton, E. *Syntax of the Moods and Tenses in New Testament Greek,* 3rd ed. Edinburgh: T & T Clark, 1889.

Callow, J. C. "To What Do *touto* and *tauta* Refer in Paul's Letters," *Notes on Translation* 70 (1978): 2-8.

Callow, K. "The Disappearing δέ in 1 Corinthians," in D. A. Black ed., *Linguistic and New Testament Interpretations: Essays on Discourse Analysis,* ch. 9. Nashville: Broadman Press, 1992.

Carson, D. A. *Showing the Spirit: A Theological Exposition of 1 Corinthians 12–14.* Grand Rapids: Baker, 1987.

Cartledge, P., and Spawforth, A. *Hellenistic and Roman Sparta: A Tale of Two Cities.* London: Routledge, 1989.

Chadwick, J. *Lexicographica Graeca: Contributions to the Lexicography of Ancient Greek.* Oxford: Clarendon Press, 1996.

Chapple, A. "Local Leadership in the Pauline Churches: Theological and Social Factors in its Development: A Study of 1 Thessalonians, 1 Corinthians and Philippians." Ph.D. dissertation, University of Durham, 1984.

Charlesworth, M. P. "The Refusal of Divine Honours: An Augustan Formula," *PBSR* 15 (1939): 1-10.

Chow, J. K. *Patronage and Power: A Study of Social Networks in Corinth,* SNT Supp. 75. Sheffield: Sheffield Academic Press, 1992.

Clarke, A. D. "'Refresh the hearts of the saints': A Unique Pauline Context," *TynB* 47.2 (1996): 275-300.

Clarke, A. D. "Secular Practices of Christian Leadership, II: Beyond Reproach," *Secular and Christian Leadership in Corinth: A Socio-historical and Exegetical Study of 1 Corinthians 1–6*, ch. 6. Leiden: E. J. Brill, 1993.

Clarke, A. D. *Serve the Community of the Church, First Century Christians in the Graeco-Roman World.* Grand Rapids and Carlisle: Eerdmans and Paternoster, 2000.

Colin, J. "Juvénal, les baladins et les rétiaires d'après le MS d'Oxford," *Atti delle Accademia delle Scienze di Torino* 87 (1952-53): 329-35.

Collins, J. N. *Diakonia: Re-interpreting the Ancient Sources.* Oxford: Oxford University Press, 1990.

Conzelmann, H. *I Corinthians.* E.T. Philadelphia: Fortress, 1975.

Corbeill, A. "Moral Appearance in Action: Effeminacy," *Controlling Laughter: Political Humor in the Late Roman Republic*, ch. 3. Princeton: Princeton University Press, 1996.

Corbett, P. E. *The Roman Law of Marriage.* Oxford: Clarendon Press, 1969.

Cotter, W. "The *Collegia* and Roman Law: State Restrictions on Voluntary Associations 64 BCE–200 CE," in J. S. Kloppenborg and S. G. Wilson, eds., *Voluntary Associations in the Graeco-Roman World*, ch. 5. London: Routledge, 1996.

Crook, J. A. *Legal Advocacy in the Roman World.* London: Duckworth, 1995.

Crook, J. A. *Roman Life and Law, 90 B.C.–A.D. 212.* New York: Cornell University Press, 1967.

D'Ambra, E. "Virgins and Adulterers," *Private Lives, Imperial Virtues: The Freeze of the Forum Transitorium in Rome*, ch. 3. Princeton: Princeton University Press, 1993.

De Vos, C. S. "Stepmothers, Concubines and the Case of PORNEIA in 1 Corinthians 5," *NTS* 44 (1998): 104-14.

de Ligt, L. *Fairs and Markets in the Roman Empire: Economic and Social Aspects of Periodic Trade in a Pre-industrial Society.* Amsterdam: J. C. Gieben, 1993.

Delcor, M. "The Courts of the Church in Corinth and the Courts of Qumran," in J. Murphy-O'Connor, ed., *Paul and Qumran: Studies in New Testament Exegesis*, ch. 4. London: Geoffrey Chapman, 1968.

DeMaris, R. E. "Corinthian Religion and Baptism for the Dead (1 Corinthians 15:29): Insights from Archaeology and Anthropology," *JBL* 114.4 (1995): 661-82.

Deming, W. *Paul on Marriage and Celibacy: The Hellenistic Background of 1 Corinthians 7*, SNTSMS 83. Cambridge: Cambridge University Press, 1995.

Denniston, J. D. *The Greek Particles*, 2nd ed. Oxford: Clarendon Press, 1950.

Desideri, P. *Dione di Prusa: un intellettuale greco nell' Impero Romano.* Messina: Casa Editrice G. d'Anna, 1978.

Detienne, M. "Culinary Practices and the Spirit of Sacrifice," in M. Detienne and

J.-P. Vernant, eds., *The Cuisine of Sacrifice among the Greeks,* ch. 1. Chicago: University of Chicago Press, 1989.

Dewing, H. B. "A *Dialysis* of the Fifth Century A.D. in the Princeton Collection of Papyri," *AJP* 53 (1922): 113-27.

Dickey, E. *Greek Forms of Address: From Herodotus to Lucian.* Oxford: Clarendon Press, 1996.

Dodd, B. J. "Paul's Paradigmatic 'I' and 1 Corinthians 6:12," *JSNT* 59 (1995): 39-58.

Doughty, D. J. "The Presence and Future of Salvation in Corinth," *ZNW* 66 (1975): 61-90.

Dowden, K. "The Roman Audience of the Golden Ass," in J. Tatum, ed., *The Search for the Ancient Novel,* ch. 23. Baltimore: Johns Hopkins University Press, 1994.

Dunbabin, K. M. D., and Dickie, M. W. "*Invidia rumpantur pactora:* Iconography of *Phthonos/Invidia* in Graeco-Roman Art," *JbAC* 26 (1983): 7-37.

Duncan-Jones, R. P. "Patronage and City Privileges — The Case of Guifi," *Epigraphische Studien* 9 (1972): 12-16.

Durand, J.-L. "Greek Animals: Towards a Topology of Edible Bodies," in M. Detienne and J.-P. Vernant, eds., *The Cuisine of Sacrifice among the Greeks,* ch. 3. E.T. Chicago: The University of Chicago Press, 1989.

Edwards, T. C. *Commentary on the First Epistle to the Corinthians.* London: Hodder & Stoughton, 1897.

Eidelstein, E. J., and J. *Aesclepius: Collection and Interpretation of the Testimonies.* Baltimore: Johns Hopkins University Press, 1998.

Engels, D. F. *Roman Corinth: An Alternative for the Classical City.* Chicago: University of Chicago, 1990.

Epstein, D. F. *Personal Enmity in Roman Politics 218-43 BC.* London: Routledge, 1989.

Eriksson, A. "Traditions as Corinthian *Premises,*" in *Traditions as Rhetorical Proofs: Pauline Argumentation in 1 Corinthians.* Stockholm: Almqvist and Wiksell International, 1998.

Eyben, E. *Restless Youth in Ancient Rome.* E.T. London: Routledge, 1993.

Fagan, G. G. *Bathing in Public in the Roman World.* Ann Arbor: University of Michigan Press, 1999.

Fantham, E., et al. "The 'New Woman': Representation and Reality," in *Women in the Classical World,* ch. 10. Oxford: Oxford University Press, 1994.

Faraone, C. A. "The Agonistic Context of Early Greek Binding Spells," in C. A. Faraone and D. Obbink, eds., *Magika Hiera: Ancient Greek Magic and Religion,* ch. 1. Oxford: Oxford University Press, 1991.

Faw, C. E. "On the Writing of First Thessalonians," *JBL* 71 (1952): 217-225.

Fee, G. D. "1 Corinthians 7:1 in the NIV," *JETS* 23/24 (1980): 307-14.

Fee, G. D. *The First Epistle to the Corinthians.* Grand Rapids: Eerdmans, 1987.

Bibliography

Findlay, G. G. *St. Paul's First Epistle to the Corinthians*. Grand Rapids: Eerdmans, 1961.

Fiori, B. "'Covert Allusion' in 1 Corinthians 1–4," *CBQ* 47 (1985): 85-102.

Fishwick, D. *The Imperial Cult in the Latin West: Studies in the Ruler Cult of the Western Provinces of the Roman Empire*. Leiden: E. J. Brill, 1987-1993, vols. I.1–II.

Fisk, B. N. "PORNEUEIN as Body Violation: The Unique Nature of Sexual Sin in 1 Corinthians 6.18," *NTS* 42.4 (Oct. 1996): 540-58.

Forbes, C. *Prophecy and Inspired Speech in Early Christianity and Its Hellenistic Environment*. WUNT 2.75. Tübingen: J. C. B. Mohr (Paul Siebeck), 1995.

Foster, S. "A Note on the 'Note' of J. Schwartz," *SP* 4 (1976-7): 25-32.

Friesen, S. J. *Twice Neokoros: Ephesus, Asia, and the Cult of the Flavian Imperial Family*. Leiden: E. J. Brill, 1993.

Fuller, R. H. "First Corinthians 6:1-11 — An Exegetical Paper," *Ex Auditu* 2 (1986): 96-104.

Furnish, V. P. "Corinth in Paul's Time: What Can Archaeology Tell Us?" *Biblical Archaeology Review* 15 (1988): 14-27.

Gardner, J., and Wiedemann, T. *The Roman Household: A Sourcebook*. London: Routledge, 1991.

Gardner, J. F. *Women in Roman Law and Society*. London: Croom Helm, 1986.

Garland, D. E. "The Christian's Posture towards Marriage and Celibacy: 1 Corinthians 7," *RevExp* 80 (1983): 351-62.

Garnsey, P. *Social Status and Legal Privilege in the Roman Empire*. Oxford: Clarendon Press, 1970.

Garnsey, P. *Famine and Food Supply in the Graeco-Roman World: Responses to Risk and Crisis*. Cambridge: Cambridge University Press, 1988.

Gebhard, E. R. "The Isthmian Games and the Sanctuary of Poseidon in the Early Empire," in T. E. Gregory, ed., *The Corinthia in the Roman Period*, pp. 78-94. Journal of Roman Archaeology Supp. 8. Ann Arbor: University of Michigan Press, 1994.

Gill, D. W. J. "Behind the Classical Facade: Local Religions of the Roman Empire," in A. D. Clarke and B. W. Winter, eds., *One God, One Lord: Christianity in a World of Religious Pluralism*, 2nd ed., ch. 4. Carlisle and Grand Rapids: Paternoster and Baker, 1993.

Gill, D. W. J. "Corinth: A Roman Colony of Achaea," *BZ* 37 (1993): 259-64.

Gill, D. W. J. "The Importance of Roman Portraiture for Head-coverings in 1 Corinthians 11:2-16," *TynB* 41.2 (1990): 245-60.

Gill, D. W. J. "In Search of the Social Elite in the Corinthian Church," *TynB* 44.2 (1993): 323-37.

Gill, D. W. J. "The Meat Market at Corinth (1 Corinthians 10:25)," *TynB* 43.2 (1992): 389-93.

Glancy, J. A. "'Obstacles to Slaves' Participation in the Corinthian Church," *JBL* 117.3 (1998): 481-501.

307

Gleason, M. W. "Favorinus and His Statue," *Making Men: Sophists and Self-Presentation in Ancient Rome*, ch. 1. Princeton: Princeton University Press, 1995.

Glucker, J. *Antiochus and the Late Academy.* Göttingen: Vandenhoeck & Ruprecht, 1978.

Godet, F. *Commentary on the First Epistle to the Corinthians*, vol. I. Edinburgh: T & T Clark, 1898.

González, J. "The *Lex Irnitana:* A New Flavian Municipal Law," *JRS* 76 (1986): 147-243.

Goodman, M. "Kosher Olive Oil in Antiquity," in P. R. Davies and R. T. White, eds., *A Tribute to Geza Vermes*, pp. 227-45. Sheffield: Sheffield Academic Press, 1990.

Gordon, R. "The Veil of Power: Emperors, Sacrifices and Benefactors," in M. Beard and J. North, eds., *Pagan Priests: Religion and Power in the Ancient World*, ch. 8. London: Duckworth, 1990.

Gowers, E. *The Loaded Table: Representations of Food in Roman Literature.* Oxford: Clarendon Press, 1993.

Greene, E. "Sexual Politics in Ovid's *Amores*," *The Erotics of Domination: Male Desire and the Mistress in Latin Love Poetry*, ch. 5. Baltimore: Johns Hopkins University Press, 1998.

Grenfell, B. P., Hunt, A. S., and Hogarth, D. G. *Fayum Towns and Their Papyri.* London, 1900.

Grenfell, B. P., Hunt, A. S., and Smyly, J. G. *The Tebtunis Papyri.* London, 1902.

Griffin, M. T. *Nero: The End of a Dynasty.* London: Batsford, 1984.

Grubbs, J. E. "'Pagan' and 'Christian' Marriage: The State of the Question," *Journal of Early Christian Studies* (1994): 361-412.

Habicht, Chr. "Die augusteische Seit und das erste Jahrundert nach Christi Geburt," in W. den Boer, ed., *Le Culte des Souverains dans l'empire romain*, pp. 76-78. Geneva: Vandoeuvres, 1972.

Hardy, E. G. *Three Spanish Charters and Other Documents.* Oxford: Clarendon Press, 1912.

Harris, W. V. "The Roman Father's Power of Life and Death," in R. S. Bagnall and W. V. Harris, eds., *Studies in Roman Law in Memory of A. Arthur Schiller*, pp. 81-95. Leiden: E. J. Brill, 1986.

Hemer, C. J. *The Book of Acts in the Setting of Hellenistic History.* Tübingen: J. C. B. Mohr (Paul Siebeck), 1989.

Hemer, C. J. "Observations on Pauline Chronology," *Pauline Studies: Essays Presented to Professor F. F. Bruce on His Seventieth Birthday*, ch. 1. Exeter and Grand Rapids: Paternoster and Eerdmans, 1980.

Hengel, M. *The Zealots: Investigations into the Jewish Freedom Movement in the Period from Herod I until 70 A.D.* Edinburgh: T & T Clark, 1989.

Hewitt, J. W. "The Development of Political Gratitude," *TAPA* 55 (1924): 35-51.

Bibliography

Hoff, M. C., and Rotroff, S. I. *The Romanization of Athens: Proceedings of an International Conference.* Oxbow Monograph 94. Oxford: Oxbow Books, 1997.

Holleman, J. *Resurrection and Parousia: A Traditio-Historical Study of Paul's Eschatology in 1 Corinthians 15.* Leiden: E. J. Brill, 1996.

Holum, K. C., and Hohlfelder, R. *King Herod's Dream: Caesarea on the Sea.* New York: Norton, 1988.

Hurd Jr., J. C. *The Origin of 1 Corinthians.* Macon, Ga.: Mercer University Press, 1983.

Jacoby, F. *Die Fragmente der griechischen Historica.* Berlin, 1926.

Jaekel, S. *Menandri sententiae.* Leipzig: Teubner, 1964.

Jameson, M. "Famine in the Greek World," in P. Garnsey and C. R. Whittaker, eds., *Trade and Famine in Classical Antiquity.* CPS Supp. 8, ch. 2. Cambridge: Cambridge Philological Society, 1983.

Jeremias, J. *The Eucharistic Words of Jesus.* E.T. London: S.C.M., 1966.

Jobling, D. "'And Have Dominion . . . ': The Interpretation of Genesis 1:28 in 'Philo Judaeus," *JSJ* 8 (1970): 50-82.

Johnson, E. "The Table of Demons," *ET,* 2nd ser. 8 (1884): 241-49.

Johnson, F. P. *Corinth: Sculpture 1896-1923.* Princeton: American School of Classical Studies in Athens, 1931, vol. 9.

Johnson, G. J. *Early Christian Epithaphs from Anatolia.* Atlanta: Scholars Press, 1995.

Jones, A. H. M. *The Criminal Courts of the Roman Republic and the Principate.* Oxford: Blackwells, 1972.

Jones, B. W. *The Emperor Domitian.* London: Routledge, 1992.

Jones, C. P. *Plutarch and Rome.* Oxford: Clarendon Press, 1971.

Jones, C. P. *The Roman World of Dio Chrysostom.* Cambridge, Mass. and London: Harvard University Press, 1978.

Jones, J. W. *The Law and Legal Theory of the Greeks.* Oxford: Oxford University Press, 1956.

Jordan, D. R. "*Defixiones* from a Well near the Southwest Corner of the Athenian Agora," *Hesperia* 54 (1985): 205-50.

Jordan, D. R. "Inscribed Lead Tablets from the Games in the Sanctuary of Poseidon," *Hesperia* 63 (1994): 111-26.

Jordan, D. R. "A Survey of Greek *Defixiones* Not Included in the Special *Corpora,*" *GRBS* 26 (1985): 151-197.

Jordan, D. R. "Two Inscribed Lead Tablets from a Well in the Athenian Kerameikos," *Ath. Mitt.* 95 (1980): 225-39.

Judge, E. A. "Ancient Beginnings of the Modern World," *Ancient History Resources for Teachers* 23.3 (1993): 125-48.

Judge, E. A. "Ancient Beginnings of the Modern World," in T. W. Hillard et al., eds., *Ancient History in a Modern University,* vol. II, pp. 468-82. Grand Rapids: Eerdmans, 1998.

Judge, E. A. "'*Antike und Christentum*': Some Recent Work from Cologne," *Prudentia* 5.1 (1973): 3-7.

Judge, E. A. "Cultural Conformity and Innovations," *TynB* 35 (1984): 20-21.

Judge, E. A. "Greek Names of Latin Origin," *New Docs.* 2 (1982): 106-8.

Judge, E. A. "Judaism and the Rise of Christianity: A Roman Perspective," *TynB* 45.2 (1993): 355-68.

Judge, E. A. "παύτης," *New Documents Illustrating Early Christianity* 4 (1987): no. 80.

Judge, E. A. *Rank and Status in the World of the Caesars and St. Paul.* Christchurch: University of Canterbury Publications, 1982.

Judge, E. A. "St. Paul and Classical Society," *JAC* 15 (1972): 19-36.

Judge, E. A., and Thomas, G. S. R. "The Origins of the Church at Rome: A New Solution," *RTR* 25 (1966): 81-94.

Kasher, A. "The Rights of the Jews of Antioch on the Orontes," *Proceedings of the American Academy of Jewish Research* 49 (1982): 69-85.

Kaster, R. A. "The Shame of the Romans," *TAPA* 127 (1997): 1-19.

Kearsley, R. "Women in Public Life in the Roman East: Iunia Theodora, Claudia Metrodora and Phoebe, Benefactress of Paul," *TynB* 50.2 (1999): 189-211.

Kelly, J. M. *Roman Litigation.* Oxford: Clarendon Press, 1966.

Kelly, J. M. *Studies in the Civil Judicature of the Roman Republic.* Oxford: Clarendon Press, 1976.

Kent, J. H. *The Inscriptions, 1926-50.* Princeton: American School of Classical Studies in Athens, 1966, vol. 8.3.

Kerferd, G. B. *The Sophistic Movement.* Cambridge: Cambridge University Press, 1981.

Kistemaker, S. J. *Exposition of the First Epistle to the Corinthians.* Grand Rapids: Baker, 1993.

Klauck, H.-J. "Die Hausgemeinde als Lebensform im Urchristentum," *Münchener Theologische Zeitschrift* 32 (1981): 1-15.

Kloppenborg, J. S., and Wilson, S. G., eds., *Voluntary Associations in the Graeco-Roman World.* London: Routledge, 1996.

Knox, M. O, "'House' and 'Palace' in Homer," *JHS* 90 (1970): 117-20.

Kokkinos, N. *Antonia Augusta: A Portrait of a Great Lady.* London: Routledge, 1992.

Körte, A., and Thierfelder, A. *Menandri quae supersunt,* 2nd ed. Leipzig: Teubner, 1959.

Kümmel, W. G. "Verlobung und Heirat bei Paulus (1 Kor 7:36-38)," in W. Eltester, ed., *Neutestamentliche Studien für Rudolf Bultmann,* pp. 275-95. Berlin: Töpelmann, 1957.

Kunkel, W. *An Introduction to Roman Legal and Constitutional History,* 2nd ed. Oxford: Clarendon Press, 1973.

Lampe, G. W. H. *A Patristic Greek Lexicon.* Oxford: Clarendon Press, 1968.

310

Bibliography

Lane Fox, R. *Pagans and Christians.* London and New York: Penguin and Knopf, 1987.

Lassen, E. M. "The Use of the Father Image in Imperial Propaganda and 1 Corinthians 4:14-21," *TynB* 42.1 (1991): 127-36.

Laurence, R. *Roman Pompeii: Space and Society.* London: Routledge, 1994.

Laurence, R. "Territory, Ethnonyms and Geography: The Construction of Identity in Roman Italy," in R. Lawrence and J. Berry, eds., *Cultural Identity in the Roman Empire,* ch. 7. London: Routledge, 1998.

Lee, J. A. L. *A Lexical Study of the Septuagint Version of the Pentateuch,* Septuagint and Cognate Studies 14. Chico: Scholars Press, 1983.

Levick, B. 'Tiberius and the Law: The Development of *maiestas*,' in *Tiberius the Politician,* ch. 11. London: Thames and Hudson, 1976.

Levinskaya, I. *The Book of Acts in Its Diaspora Setting,* in The Book of Acts in Its First Century Setting. Grand Rapids and Carlisle: Eerdmans and Paternoster, 1996, vol. V.

Liddell, H. G., and Scott, R. *A Greek-English Lexicon,* 9th ed. Oxford: Clarendon Press, 1996.

Liebeschuetz, J. H. W. G. *Continuity and Change in Roman Religion.* Oxford: Clarendon Press, 1979.

Lightfoot, J. B. *Notes on the Epistles of Paul from Unpublished Commentaries.* London: Macmillan, 1895.

Lilja, S. *Homosexuality in Republican and Augustan Rome.* Helsinki: Societas Scientiarum Fennica, 1982.

Lintott, A. W. *Imperium Romanum: Politics and Administration.* London: Routledge, 1993.

Lüderitz, G. "What Is the Politeuma?" in J. W. van Henten and P. W. Van der Horst, eds., *Studies in Early Jewish Epigraphy,* pp. 183-225. Leiden: E. J. Brill, 1994.

Malherbe, A. J. "The Beasts at Ephesus," *JBL* 87 (1968): 71-80.

Malherbe, A. J. *Social Aspects of Early Christianity.* Baton Rouge: Louisiana State University Press, 1977.

Mare, W. H. *1 Corinthians.* Grand Rapids: Zondervan, 1976.

Marshall, P. *Enmity in Corinth: Social Conventions in Paul's Relations with the Corinthians.* Tübingen: J. C. B. Mohr (Paul Siebeck), 1987.

Martin, W. J. "I Corinthians 11:2-16: An Interpretation," in W. Ward Gasque and R. P. Martin, eds., *Apostolic History and the Gospel: Biblical and Historical Essays Presented to F. F. Bruce,* pp. 183-225. Exeter: Paternoster, 1970.

Mason, S. *Josephus and the New Testament.* Peabody, Mass.: Hendrickson, 1992.

Mastin, B. A. "Jesus Said Grace," *SJT* 24.4 (Nov. 1971): 449-55.

McGinn, T. A. J. *Prostitution, Sexuality, and the Law in Ancient Rome.* Oxford: Oxford University Press, 1998.

McKay, A. G. *Houses, Villas and Palaces in the Roman World.* London: Thames and Hudson, 1975.

311

BIBLIOGRAPHY

McLean, B. "A Christian Epitaph: The Curse of Judas Iscariot," *Orientalia Christiana Periodica* 58 (1992): 241-44.

Mee, C., Gill, D., Forbes, H., and Foxhall, L. "Rural Settlement Change in the Methana Peninsula, Greece," in G. Barker and J. Lloyd, eds., *Roman Landscapes: Archaeological Survey in the Mediterranean Region*, pp. 223-32. Archaeological Monographs of the British School at Rome. London: British School at Rome, 1991.

Meeks, W. A. *The First Urban Christians: The Social World of the Apostle Paul*. New Haven: Yale University Press, 1983.

Meeks, W. A. *The Origins of Christian Morality: The First Two Centuries*. New Haven: Yale University Press, 1994.

Meggitt, J. J. *Paul, Poverty and Survival*. Edinburgh: T & T Clark, 1998.

Meinecke, A. *Fragmenta comicorum Graecorum*, 2nd ed. Berlin: de Gruyter, 1970.

Merritt, B. D. *Corinth: Greek Inscriptions 1896-1927*, vol. 8.1. Princeton: American School of Classical Studies in Athens, 1931.

Metzger, B. M. *A Textual Commentary on the Greek New Testament*. London and New York: United Bible Societies, 1971.

Metzger, E. *A New Outline of the Roman Civil Trial*. Oxford: Clarendon Press, 1997.

Metzler, J. Millett, M. Roymans, N., and Slofstra, J., eds., *Integration in the Early Roman West: The Role of Culture and Ideology*. Luxembourg: Musée National d'Histoire et d'Art, 1995.

Millar, F. "The Imperial Cult and the Persecutions," in W. den Boer, ed., *Le Culte des Souverains dans l'empire romain*, pp. 145-65. Geneva: Vandoeuvres, 1972.

Millar, F. "The World of the Golden Ass," *JRS* 71 (1981): 63-75.

Millar, F. *The Emperor in the Roman World (31 b.c.–a.d. 337)*. London: Duckworth, 1977.

Mitchell, A. J. "Rich and Poor in the Courts of Corinth: Litigiousness and Status in 1 Corinthians 6:1-11," *NTS* 39 (1993): 562-68.

Mitchell, M. M. *Paul and the Rhetoric of Reconciliation: An Exegetical Investigation of the Language and Composition of 1 Corinthians*. Louisville: Westminster/ John Knox, 1992.

Mitchell, S. *The Celts and the Impact of Roman Rule*, Anatolia: Land, Men, and Gods in Asia Minor, vol. I. Oxford: Clarendon Press, 1993.

Mitchell, S. *The Rise of the Church*, Anatolia: Land, Men, and Gods in Asia Minor, vol. II. Oxford: Clarendon Press, 1993.

Moles, J. L. "The Career and Conversion of Dio Chrysostom," *JRS* 68 (1978): 79-100.

Monserrat, D. *Sex and Society in Graeco-Roman Egypt*. London: Kegan Paul, 1996.

Morley, R. J. "The Past in Clement of Alexandria: A Study of an Attempt to Define Christianity in Socio-Cultural Terms," in E. P. Sanders, ed., *The Shaping of Christianity in the Second and Third Centuries: Jewish and Christian Self-Definition*, vol. 1, ch. 12. Philadelphia: Fortress Press, 1980.

Mott, S. C. "The Power of Giving and Receiving: Reciprocity in Hellenistic Benevolence," in G. F. Hawthorne, ed., *Current Issues in Biblical and Patristic Interpretation: Studies in Honor of Merrill C. Tenney,* pp. 60-72. Grand Rapids: Eerdmans, 1975.

Moule, C. F. D. *Worship in the New Testament.* London: S.C.M., 1961.

Moule, C. F. D. *An Idiom Book of New Testament Greek.* Cambridge: Cambridge University Press, 1959.

Moulton, J. H. *A Grammar of New Testament Greek,* vol. I, 3rd ed. Edinburgh: T & T Clark, 1908.

Müller, C., ed. *Fragmenta Historicum Graecorum.* Paris: Didot, 1867.

Murphy-O'Connor, J. *St. Paul's Corinth: Texts and Archaeology.* Wilmington, Del.: Glazier, 1983.

Musonius Rufus, "On Sexual Indulgence," translated by C. E. Lutz, "Musonius Rufus: The Roman Socrates," *YCS* 10 (1947): 3-147.

Myres, S. J. *Homer and His Critics.* London: Routledge and Kegan Paul, 1958.

Nauck, C. A. *Tragicorum Graecorum fragmenta.* Hildesheim: Olms, 1964.

Naveh, J., and Shaked, S. *Magic Spells and Formulae Aramaic Incantations in Late Antiquity.* Jerusalem: Magnes Press, 1993.

Nicols, J. "*Tabulae patronatus:* A Study of the Agreement between Patron and Client-community," *ANRW* 2.13 (1980): 535-59.

North, H. F. "Canons and Hierarchies of the Classical Virtues in Greek and Latin Literature," in L. Wallach, ed., *The Classical Tradition: Literary and Historical Studies in Honor of Harry Caplan,* pp. 165-83. New York: Cornell University Press, 1966.

Oates, J. F. "Fugitives from Philadelphia," *Essays in Honour of C. Bradford Welles,* pp. 165-83. American Studies in Papyrology 1. New Haven, 1966.

Oliver, J. H. "Epaminondas of Acraephia," *GRBS* 12 (1971): 233-36.

Orr, W. F. "Paul's Treatment of Marriage in 1 Corinthians 7," *Pittsburgh Perspective* 8 (1967): 5-22.

Owens, E. J. *The City in the Greek and Roman World.* London: Routledge, 1991.

Owens, E. J. "Roman Town Planning," in I. M. Barton ed., *Roman Public Buildings,* ch. 1. Exeter Studies in History 20. Exeter: University of Exeter, 1989.

Paige, T. "1 Corinthians 12.2: A Pagan *Pompe,*" *JSNT* 44 (1991): 57-65.

Paige, T. "The Spirit at Corinth." Ph.D. dissertation, University of Sheffield, 1993.

Perring, D. "Spatial Organisation and Social Change in Roman Towns," in J. Rich and A. Wallace-Hadrill, eds., *City and Country in the Ancient World,* ch. 11. London: Routledge, 1991.

Peterman, G. *Paul's Gift from Philippi: Conventions of Gift Exchange and Christian Giving.* Cambridge: Cambridge University Press, 1997.

Peters, F. E. *The Harvest of Hellenism: A History of the Near East from Alexander the Great.* New York, Simon and Schuster, 1970.

Plassart, A. "L'inscription de Delphes mentionnant le proconsul Gallion," *REG* 80 (1967): 372-78.

Pogoloff, S. M. *Logos and Sophia: The Rhetorical Situation of 1 Corinthians*. SBL Dissertation Series 134. Atlanta: Scholars Press, 1992.

Poirier, C., and Frankovic, J. "Celibacy and Charism in 1 Cor. 7:5-7," *HTR* 89.1 (1996): 1-18.

Price, S. R. F. *Rituals and Power: The Imperial Cult and Asia Minor*. Cambridge: Cambridge University Press, 1984.

Pucci Ben Zeev, M. *Jewish Rights in the Roman World: The Greek and Roman Documents Quoted by Josephus Flavius*, Texts and Studies in Ancient Judaism 74. Tübingen: J. C. B. Mohr (Paul Siebeck), 1999.

Rabello, A. M. "The Legal Condition of the Jews in the Roman Empire," *ANRW* 2.13 (1980): 662-762.

Raditsa, L. F. "'Augustus' Legislation concerning Marriage, Procreation, Love Affairs and Adultery," *ANRW* 2.13 (1980): 278-339.

Rainbow, P. A. "Monotheism and Christology in 1 Corinthians 8:4-6." D.Phil. dissertation, Oxford University Press, 1987.

Rajak, T., and Noy, D. "*Archisynagogos:* Office, Social Status in the Graeco-Roman World," *JRS* 83 (1993): 75-93.

Rajak, T. "The Jewish Community and Its Boundaries," in J. Lieu, J. North, and T. Rajak, eds., *The Jews among the Pagans and Christians in the Roman Empire*, pp. 9-28. London: Routledge, 1992.

Rajak, T. "The Synagogue within the Greco-Roman City," in S. Fine, ed., *Jews, Christians and Polytheists in the Ancient Synagogue: Cultural Interaction in the Greco-Roman Period*, ch. 9. London: Routledge, 1999.

Raubitschek, A. E. "Octavia's Deification at Athens," *TAPA* 77 (1946): 146-50.

Rawson, B. *The Politics of Friendship: Pompey and Cicero*. Sydney: Sydney University Press, 1978.

Rawson, B. "The Roman Family," in B. Rawson, ed., *The Family in Ancient Rome: New Perspectives*, ch. 1. London: Croom Helm, 1986.

Reader, W. W. *The Severed Hand and the Upright Corpse: The Declamations of Marcus Antonius Polemo*. Atlanta: Scholars Press, 1996.

Reynolds, J. M. "New Evidence for the Imperial Cult in Julio-Claudian Aphrodisias," *ZPE* 43 (1981): 317-27.

Reynolds, J. M. "The Origins and Beginnings of the Imperial Cult in Aphrodisias," *Proceedings of the Philological Society* 206 (1980): 70-82.

Rhodes, P. J. "Political Activity in Classical Athens," *JHS* 106 (1986): 132-44.

Rickman, G. "The Corn Distribution," in *The Corn Supply of Ancient Rome*. Oxford: Clarendon Press, 1980.

Ritner, R. K. "Curses," in M. Meyer and R. Smith, eds., *Ancient Christian Magic: Coptic Texts of Ritual Power*, ch. 7. San Francisco: Harper, 1994.

Ritner, R. K. *The Mechanics of Ancient Magical Practice*, Studies in Ancient Oriental Civilization 54. Chicago: Oriental Institute of the University of Chicago, 1993.

Rives, J. B. *Religion and Authority in Roman Carthage from Augustus to Constantine.* Oxford: Clarendon Press, 1995.

Robert, L. "Inscriptions Lyciennes Trouvées à Solómos," *BCH* 83 (1959): 498-503.

Roberts, C. H. "Nomina Sacra: Origins and Significance," *Manuscript, Society and Belief in Early Christian Egypt,* Lecture 2. London: The British Academy, 1979.

Robertson, A., and Plummer, A. *1 Corinthians,* 2nd ed. Edinburgh: T & T Clark, 1914.

Robertson, A. T. *A Grammar of the Greek New Testament in the Light of Historical Research.* New York: Hodder and Stoughton, 1914.

Robinson, D. W. B. "To Submit to the Judgement of the Saints," *TynB* 10 (1962): 1-8.

Robinson, O. F. *The Criminal Law of Ancient Rome.* London: Duckworth, 1995.

Rogers, G. M. "The Procession of Statues," *The Sacred Identity of Ephesos: Foundation Myths of a Roman City,* ch. 3. London: Routledge, 1991.

Romano, D. G. "Post–146 BC Land Use in Corinth and Planning of the Roman Colony," in T. E. Gregory, ed., *The* Corinthia *in the Roman Period,* pp. 9-30. Journal of Roman Archaeology Supp. Series 8. Ann Arbor: University of Michigan Press, 1994.

Rosivach, V. J. *When a Young Man Falls in Love: Sexual Exploitation of Women in New Comedy.* London: Routledge, 1998.

Rosner, B. S. "Joseph and Paul Fleeing Immorality," *Paul, Scripture and Ethics: A Study of 1 Corinthians 5–7,* ch. 5. Leiden: E. J. Brill, 1994.

Rosner, B. S. "'No Other Gods': The Jealousy of God and Religious Pluralism," in A. D. Clarke and B. W. Winter, eds., *One God, One Lord: Christianity in a World of Religious Pluralism,* ch. 7, 2nd ed. Grand Rapids and Carlisle: Baker and Paternoster, 1993.

Rosner, B. S., ed., *Understanding Paul's Ethics: Twentieth Century Approaches.* Grand Rapids and Carlisle: Eerdmans and Paternoster, 1995.

Rostyovtzeff, M. *The Social and Economic History of the Roman Empire,* vol. II. Oxford: Clarendon Press, 1957.

Rothaus, R. M. *Corinth: The First City of Greece, An Urban History of Late Antique Cult and Religion.* Leiden: E. J. Brill, 2000.

Roueché, C. "Gladiators and Wild-Beast Fighters," *Performers and Partisans at Aphrodisias in the Roman and Late Roman Periods,* Part I, ch. 5. Journal of Roman Studies Monograph 6, 1993.

Rowe, J. C. *Plato.* Brighton: Harvester, 1984.

Runia, D. T. "Philo's *De aeternitate mundi:* The Problem of Its Interpretation," *Vigiliae Christianae* 35 (1981): 105-151.

Runia, D. T. *Philo of Alexandria and the* Timaeus *of Plato.* Leiden: E. J. Brill, 1986.

Russell, D. A. *Greek Declamations.* Cambridge: Cambridge University Press, 1983.

Russell, D. A. "On Reading Plutarch's Lives," *Greece and Rome* 13 (1966): 139-54.

Russell, D. A., and Wilson, N. G. *Menander Rhetor.* Oxford: Clarendon, 1981.

Saller, R. P. "Corporal Punishment, Authority, Obedience in the Roman Household," in B. Rawson, ed., *Marriage, Divorce and Children in Ancient Rome,* ch. 7. Oxford: Clarendon Press, 1991.

Saller, R. P. *Personal Patronage under the Early Empire.* Cambridge: Cambridge University Press, 1982.

Salmon, E. T. *Roman Colonisation under the Republic.* London: Thames and Hudson, 1969.

Salmon, J. B. *Wealthy Corinth: A History of the City to 338 BC.* Oxford: Clarendon Press, 1984.

Sandback, F. H. *The Comic Theatre of Greece and Rome.* London: Chatto and Windus, 1977.

Schaps, D. M. *Economic Rights of Women in Ancient Greece.* Edinburgh: Edinburgh University Press, 1979.

Schmithals, W. "Die Korintherbriefe als Briefsammlung," *ZNW* 64 (1972): 263-88.

Schmithals, W. *Gnosticism in Corinth.* E.T. Nashville: Abingdon, 1971.

Schnaling, G., ed. *The Novel in the Ancient World.* Leiden: E. J. Brill, 1996.

Schreiber, A. *Die Germeinde in Korinth: Versuch einer gruppendynamischen Betrachtung der Entwicklung der Gemeinde von Korinth auf der Basis des ersten Korinthbriefes* Münster: Aschendorff, 1977.

Schwartz, J. "Note sur la famille de Philon d'Alexandrie," *Mélanges Isidore Lévy. Annuaire de l'Institut de philologie et d'histoire orientales et slaves,* Université libre de Bruxelles 13 (1953): 591-602.

Sherk, R. K. *The Roman Empire: Augustus to Hadrian,* Translated Documents of Greece and Rome. Cambridge: Cambridge University Press, 1988.

Sherwin-White, A. N. "The Claudian Problem and *Viritane* Grants," *The Roman Citizenship,* 2nd ed. Oxford: Clarendon Press, 1973.

Sherwin-White, A. N. *Roman Society and Roman Law in the New Testament.* Oxford: Clarendon Press, 1963.

Shoe, L. "The Roman Ionic Base at Corinth," in L. Freeman Sandler, ed., *Essays in Honor of Karl Lehmann,* pp. 300-303. New York: J. J. Augustin, 1964.

Skidmore, C. *Practical Ethics for Roman Gentlemen: The Works of Valerius Maximus.* Exeter: University of Exeter Press, 1996.

Slater, W. J. *Dining in a Classical Context.* Ann Arbor: University of Michigan Press, 1991.

Slingerland, H. D. "Here a Chrestus, There a Chrestus," *Claudian Policymaking and the Early Imperial Repression of Judaism at Rome,* Studies in the History of Judaism, ch. 9. Atlanta: Scholars Press, 1997.

Spawforth, A. J. S. "Corinth, Argos and the Imperial Cult: *Pseudo-Julian, Letters 198," Hesperia* 63.2 (1994): 211-32.

Spawforth, A. J. S. "Roman Corinth: The Formation of a Colonial Elite," in A. D. Rizaki, ed., *Roman Onomastics in the Greek East Social and Political Aspects.* Μελετήματα 21, Athens, 1996, 167-82.

Spawforth, A. J. S. "The Achaean Federal Imperial Cult I, Part I: *Pseudo-Julian, Letters 198," TynB* 46.1 (1995): 151-68.

Staveley, E. S. *Greek and Roman Voting and Elections.* London: Thames and Hudson, 1972.

Stein, P. *Roman Law in European History.* Cambridge: Cambridge University Press, 1999.

Stroud, R. S. "Curses from Corinth," *AJA* 77 (1973): 228.

Stroud, R. S. "The Sanctuary of Demeter on Acrocorinth in the Roman Period," in T. E. Gregory ed., *The* Corinthia *in the Roman Period,* pp. 65-77. Journal of Roman Archaeology Supp. No. 8. Ann Arbor: University of Michigan, 1995.

Strubbe, J. H. M. "Cursed be he that moves my bones," in *Magika Hiera: Ancient Greek Magic and Religion,* ch. 2. Oxford: Oxford University Press, 1991.

Strubbe, J. H. M. "Curses against Violation of the Grave in Jewish Epitaphs of Asia Minor," in J. W. van Henten and P. W. van der Horst, eds., *Studies in Early Jewish Epigraphy,* pp. 70-128. Leiden: E. J. Brill, 1994.

Syme, R. "C. Vibius Maximus, Prefect of Egypt," *Historia* 6 (1957): 480-87.

Tatum, J., ed. *The Search for the Ancient Novel.* Baltimore: Johns Hopkins University Press, 1994.

Taylor, L. R. "Tiberius' Refusal of Divine Honours," *TAPA* 60 (1929): 87-101.

Temkin, O. *Soranus' Gynaecology.* Baltimore: Johns Hopkins University Press, 1956.

Theissen, G. *Essays on Corinth: The Social Setting of Pauline Christianity.* Philadelphia: Fortress Press, 1982.

Thiselton, A. C. "Realized Eschatology at Corinth," *NTS* 24 (1977-78): 510-26.

Thompson, C. L. "Hairstyles, Head-covering, and St. Paul: Portraits from Roman Corinth," *Biblical Archaeologist* 51.2 (1989): 99-115.

Thrall, M. *Greek Particles in the New Testament.* Leiden: E. J. Brill, 1962.

Toynbee, M. C. *Death and Burial in the Roman World.* London: Thames and Hudson, 1971.

Trebilco, P. R. *Jewish Communities in Asia Minor.* SNTSMS 69. Cambridge: Cambridge University Press, 1991.

Treggiari, S. *Roman Marriage: Iusti Coniuges from the Time of Cicero to the Time of Ulpian.* Oxford: Clarendon Press, 1991.

Trench, R. C. *Synonyms of the New Testament,* 8th ed. London: James Clarke, 1876.

Turton, R. "Greek Racism? Observations on the Character and Limits of Greek Ethnic Prejudice," in G. Tsetskhladze, ed., *Ancient Greeks East and West,* ch. 2. Leiden: E. J. Brill, 1999.

van der Horst, P. W. "A Note on the Judas Curse in Early Christian Inscriptions," in *Hellenism–Judaism–Christianity: Essays on Their Interaction,* pp. 146-50. Kampen: Kok, 1994.

Versnel, H. S. "Beyond Cursing: The Appeal to Justice in Judicial Prayers," in *Magika Hiera: Ancient Greek Magic and Religion,* ch. 3. Oxford: Oxford University Press, 1991.

Veyne, P. "The Roman Empire," in P. Veyne, ed., *A History of Private Life,* ch. 1. E.T. Cambridge, Mass.: Harvard University Press, 1987.

Walbank, M. E. H. "Pausanias, Octavia, and Temple E at Corinth," *Annual of the British School at Athens* 84 (1989): 361-94.

Wallace-Hadrill, A. "*Civilis princeps*: Between Citizen and King," *JRS* 72 (1982): 32-48.

Wallace-Hadrill, A. "Family and Inheritance in the Augustan Marriage Laws," *Proceedings of the Cambridge Philological Society* n.s. 27 (1981): 58-80.

Ward-Perkins, J. B. *Cities of Ancient Greece and Italy: Planning in Classical Antiquity*. London: Sidgwick and Jackson, 1974.

Watson, A. *The Law of Obligations in the Later Roman Republic*. Oxford: Clarendon Press, 1965.

Watson, A. *Roman Slave Law*. Baltimore: Johns Hopkins University Press, 1987.

Weaver, P. R. C. *Familia Caesaris: A Social Study of the Emperor's Freedmen and Slaves*. Cambridge: Cambridge University Press, 1972.

Webster, T. B. L. *An Introduction to Menander*. Manchester: Manchester University Press, 1974.

Weinstock, S. *Divus Julius*. Oxford: Clarendon Press, 1971.

Welbourn, L. L. "On the Discord in Corinth: 1 Corinthians 1–4 and Ancient Politics," *JBL* 106 (1987): 85-111.

Welles, C. B. *Royal Correspondence in the Hellenistic Period: A Study in Greek Epigraphy*. New Haven: Yale University Press, 1934.

Wenham, D. *Paul: Follower of Jesus or Founder of Christianity?* Grand Rapids and Cambridge: Eerdmans, 1995.

Wenham, D. "Whatever Went Wrong in Corinth?" *ET* 108.5 (Feb. 1997): 137-41.

West, A. B. *Corinth: Latin Inscriptions, 1896-1926*. Princeton: American School of Classical Studies in Athens, 1931, vol. 8.2.

Wetstein, J. J. *Η ΚΑΙΝΗ ΔΙΑΘΗΚΗ* (1752), II, 131.

White, J. R. "'Baptism on account of the Dead': The Meaning of 1 Cor. 15:29 in Its Context," *JBL* 116.3 (1997): 487-99.

Wiedemann, T. *Adults and Children in the Roman Empire*. London: Routledge, 1989.

Wifstrand, A. "A Problem concerning the Word Order of the New Testament," *Studia Theologica* 3 (1951): 172-84.

Wilkinson, L. P. *Classical Attitudes to Modern Issues: Population and Family Planning; Women's Liberation; Nudism in Deed and Word; Homosexuality*. London: Willima Kimber, 1979.

Williams, C. A. *Roman Homosexuality: Ideologies of Masculinity in Classical Antiquity*. Oxford: Oxford University Press, 1999.

Williams II, C. K. "A Re-evaluation of Temple E and the West End of the Forum of Corinth," in S. Walker and A. Cameron, eds., *The Greek Renaissance in the Roman Empire*, pp. 156-62. BICS Supp. 55 (1989).

Williams II, C. K. "The Refounding of Corinth: Some Roman Religious Attitudes," in S. Macready and F. S. Thompson, eds., *Roman Architecture in the Greek World*, pp. 26-37. London: The Society of Antiquaries, 1987.

Williams II, C. K. "Roman Corinth as a Commercial Center," in T. E. Gregory, ed., *The* Corinthia *in the Roman Period*, pp. 31-46. Journal of Roman Archaeology Supp. Series 8. Ann Arbor: University of Michigan Press, 1993.

Williams, F. *The Panarion of Epiphanius of Salamis, Books II and III*, Nag Hammadi and Manichaean Studies, vol. XXXVI. Leiden: E. J. Brill, 1994.

Willis, W. "Corinthusne deletus est?" *BZ* 35 (1991): 233-41.

Wimbush, V. L. *Paul the Worldly Ascetic: Response to the World and Self-understanding according to 1 Corinthians 7*. Macon, Ga.: Mercer University Press, 1987.

Winer, G. B. *A Treatise on the Grammar of the Greek New Testament*. Edinburgh: T & T Clark, 1870.

Winkler, J. J. "The Constraints of Eros," in C. A. Faraone and D. Obbink, eds., *Magika Hiera: Ancient Greek Magic and Religion*, pp. 214-43. Oxford: Oxford University Press, 1991.

Winter, B. W. "The Lord's Supper at Corinth: An Alternative Reconstruction," *RTR* 37 (1978): 73-82.

Winter, B. W. "Secular and Christian Responses to Corinthian Famines," *TynB* 40.1 (1989): 86-106.

Winter, B. W. "Theological and Ethical Responses to Religious Pluralism, I Corinthians 8-10," *TynB* 41.2 (1990): 207-226.

Winter, B. W. "The Role of the *captatio benevolentia* in the Speeches of Tertullus and Paul in Acts 24," *JTS* n.s. 42.2 (1991): 505-31.

Winter, B. W. "The Messiah as the Tutor: The Meaning of καθηγητής in Matthew 23:10," *TynB* 42.1 (1991): 152-57.

Winter, B. W. "The Problem with 'Church' for the Early Church," in D. Peterson and J. Pryor, eds., *In the Fullness of Time: Biblical Studies in Honour of Archbishop Robinson*, ch. 13. Sydney: Lancer, 1992.

Winter, B. W. "In Public and in Private: Early Christianity and Religious Pluralism," in A. D. Clarke and B. W. Winter, eds., *One God and One Lord: In a World of Religious Pluralism*, ch. 6, 2nd ed. Grand Rapids and Carlisle: Baker and Paternoster, 1992.

Winter, B. W. "Official Proceedings and Forensic Speeches in Acts 24-26," in A. D. Clarke and B. W. Winter, eds., *The Book of Acts in Its Ancient Literary Setting*, The Book of Acts in Its First Century Setting, vol. I, ch. 11. Carlisle and Grand Rapids: Paternoster and Eerdmans, 1993.

Winter, B. W. "Acts and Food Shortages," in D. W. J. Gill and C. Gempf, eds., *The Book of Acts in Its Graeco-Roman Setting*, The Book of Acts in Its First Century Setting, vol. II, ch. 3. Carlisle and Grand Rapids: Paternoster and Eerdmans, 1994.

Winter, B. W. "'The Imperial Cult' in 'Acts and Roman Religion'," in D. W. J. Gill and C. Gempf, eds., *The Book of Acts in Its Graeco-Roman Setting*, The Book of Acts in Its First Century Setting, vol. II, ch. 4B. Carlisle and Grand Rapids: Paternoster and Eerdmans, 1994.

319

BIBLIOGRAPHY

Winter, B. W. *Seek the Welfare of the City: Early Christians as Benefactors and Citizens.* Grand Rapids and Carlisle: Eerdmans and Paternoster, 1994.

Winter, B. W. "The Achaean Federal Imperial Cult, Part II: The Corinthian Church," *TynB* 46.1 (1995): 169-78.

Winter, B. W. "Civil Litigation in Secular Corinth and the Church," in B. S. Rosner, ed., *Understanding Paul's Ethics: Twentieth Century Approaches*, ch. 4. Grand Rapids and Carlisle: Eerdmans and Paternoster, 1995.

Winter, B. W. *Philo and Paul among the Sophists*, SNTSMS 96. Cambridge: Cambridge University Press, 1997.

Winter, B. W. "The Seasons of This Life and Eschatology in 1 Corinthians 7:29-31," in K. E. Brower and M. W. Elliott, eds., *'The Reader Must Understand': Eschatology in Bible and Theology*, ch. 16. Leicester: Apollos, 1997.

Winter, B. W. "St. Paul as a Critic of Roman Slavery in 1 Corinthians 7:21-23," Proceedings of the International Conference on St. Paul and European Civilization, Παύλεια 3 (Varia, 1998): 339-54.

Winter, B. W. "Gallio's Ruling on the Legal Status of Early Christianity (Acts 18:14-15)," *TynB* 50.2 (Nov. 1999): 213-24.

Winter, B. W. "The Imperial Cult and the Early Christians in Pisidian Antioch (Acts 13 and Galatians 6)," in T. Drew-Bear, M. Tashalan, and C. M. Thomas, eds., *First International Conference on Antioch in Pisidia*, pp. 60-68. Ismit: Kocaeli Press, 2000.

Winter, B. W. "Philodemus and Paul on Rhetorical Delivery (ὑπόκρισις)," in J. T. Fitzgerald, G. Holland, and D. Obbink, eds., *Philodemus and the New Testament World.* Leiden: E. J. Brill, forthcoming.

Wiseman, J. "The Gymnasium Area of Corinth, 1967-68," *Hesperia* 38 (1969): 64-106.

Wiseman, J. "The Gymnasium Area of Corinth, 1969-70," *Hesperia* 41 (1972): 1-42.

Wiseman, J. "Rome and Corinth 1," *ANRW* 2.7.1 (1979): 438-548.

Witherington III, B. *Conflict and Community in Corinth: A Socio-Rhetorical Commentary on 1 and 2 Corinthians.* Grand Rapids and Carlisle: Eerdmans and Paternoster, 1995.

Witherington III, B. "Transcending Imminence: The Gordian Knot of Pauline Eschatology," in K. E. Brower and M. W. Elliott, eds., *'The Reader Must Understand': Eschatology in Bible and Theology*, ch. 7. Leicester: Apollos, 1997.

Woolf, A. *Becoming Roman: The Origins of Provincial Civilization in Gaul.* Cambridge: Cambridge University Press, 1998.

Woolf, A. "Romancing the Celts: A Segmentary Approach to Acculturation," in R. Laurence and J. Berry, eds., *Cultural Identity in the Roman Empire*, ch. 8. London: Routledge, 1998.

Wright, D. "Homosexuals or Prostitutes? The Meaning of ARSENOKOITAI (1 Cor. 6:9; 1 Tim. 1:10)," *Vigiliae Christianae* 38 (1984): 125-53.

Yamauchi, E. M. *Pre-Christian Gnosticism: A Survey of the Proposed Evidence,* 2nd ed. Grand Rapids: Baker, 1983.

Zanker, P. *The Power of Images in the Age of Augustus.* Ann Arbor: University of Michigan Press, 1988.

Zimmerman, R. *The Law of Obligations: Roman Foundations of the Civilian Tradition.* Cape Town: Juta, 1990.

Abbreviations

AJA	*American Journal of Archaeology*
AJP	*American Journal of Philology*
ANRW	*Aufstieg und Niedergang der römischen Welt*
Ath. Mitt.	*Mitteilungen des deutschen archäologischen Instituts, Athenische Abteilung, 1876-*
BAGD	Baur, Arndt, Gingrich and Danker, *A Greek-English Lexicon of the New Testament* (1979)
BCH	*Bulletin de Correspondance Hellenique*
BDF	Blass, Debrunner Funk, *A Greek New Testament* (1961)
BGU	*Ägyptische Urkunden aus den königlichen* (later *Staatlichen*) *Museen zu Berlin, Griechische Urkunden.* Berlin, 1895-
BICS	*Bulletin of the Institute of Classical Studies of the University of London*
BZ	*Biblische Zeitschrift*
CBQ	*Catholic Biblical Quarterly*
CIG	*Corpus Inscriptionum Graecarum*
CIL	*Corpus Inscriptionum Latinarum*
Corinth 8.1	B. D. Merritt, *Greek Inscriptions, 1896-1927* (1931)
Corinth 8.2	A. B. West, *Latin Inscriptions, 1896-1927* (1931)
Corinth 8.3	J. H. Kent, *The Inscriptions, 1926-1950* (1966)
CPS	*Cambridge Philological Society*
Curses	R. K. Ritner, 'Curses,' in M. Meyer and R. Smith, eds., *Ancient Christian Magic: Coptic Texts of Ritual Power* (1994), ch. 7

Abbreviations

Defixionum Tabellae	A. Audollent, *Defixionum Tabellae* (Paris, 1904)
ET	*Expository Times*
GRBS	*Greek, Roman and Byzantine Studies*
HTR	*Harvard Theological Review*
IEph	*Inschriften Griechischer Städte aus Kleinasien XI-XVII. Die Inschriften von Ephesos I-VIII*
IG	*Inscriptiones Graecae* (Berlin, 1873ff.)
IK	*Inschriften Griechischer Städte aus Kleinasien 3: Die Inscriften von Ilion* (ed. P. Frisch), 1975
ILS	*Inscriptiones Latinae Selectae*
JbAC	*Jahrbuch für Antike und Christentum*
LCL	Loeb Classical Library
JBL	*Journal of Biblical Literature*
JETS	*Journal of the Evangelical Theological Society*
JHS	*Journal of Hellenic Studies*
JRS	*Journal of Roman Studies*
JSJ	*Journal for the Study of Judaism in the Persian, Hellenistic and Roman Period*
JSNT	*Journal for the Study of the New Testament*
Liddell and Scott	H. G. Liddell, Robert Scott, and H. Stuart Jones, *Greek-English Lexicon*, 9th ed., 1995
MM	J. H. Moulton and G. Milligan, *The Vocabulary of the Greek Testament Illustrated from the Papyri and Other Literary Sources*, 1930
New Docs.	*New Documents Illustrating Early Christianity*
NTS	*New Testament Studies*
P. Fouad	*Les Papyri Fouad* I, ed. A. Bataille, O. Gueraud, P. Jouguet, N. Lewis, H. Marrou, J. Scherer, and W. G. Waddell, 1939.
P.Cairo.Zen.	*Zenon papyri, Catalogue général des antiquités égyptiennes du Musée du Caire*, ed. C. C. Edgar, 1925-1940
P.Cornell	*Greek Papyri in the Library of Cornell University*, ed. W. L. Westermann and C. J. Kraemer, Jr., 1926.
P.Fam.Tebt.	*A Family Archive from Tebtunis*, ed. B. A. van Groningen, 1950
P.Fay.	*Fayum Towns and Their Papyri*, ed. B. P. Grenfell, A. S. Hunt, and D. G. Hogarth, 1900

ABBREVIATIONS

P.Flor.	*Papiri greco-egizii, Papiri Fiorentini* (Supplementi Filologico-Storici ai Monumenti Antichi)
P.Lond.	*Greek Papyri in the British Museum,* 1893-1974
P.Magd.	*Papyrus de Magdola,* Fascs. I-IV
P.Mich.	*Michigan Papyri,* 1931-
P.Oxy.	*The Oxyrhynchus Papyri,* 1898-
P.Ryl.	*Catalogue of the Greek and Latin Papyri in the John Rylands Library,* 1911-1952
P.Tebt.	*The Tebtunis Papyri,* 1902-1976
P.Zen.	*Greek and Demotic Texts from the Zenon Archive,* 1980
PSI	*Papiri greci e latini* (Pubblicazioni della Società Italiana per la ricerca dei papiri greci e latini in Egitto), 1912-1979.
REG	*Revue des études grecques*
RevExp	*Review and Expositor*
RTR	*Reformed Theological Review*
SEG	*Supplementum Epigraphicum Graecum*
SIG	*Sylloge inscriptionum Graecarum,* ed. Wilhelm Dittenberger
SJT	*Scottish Journal of Theology*
SNT	*Studien zum Neuen Testament*
SNTSMS	Society for New Testament Studies Monograph Series
SP	*Studia Philonica*
TAPA	*Transactions of the American Philological Association*
TDNT	*Theological Dictionary of the New Testament*
TynB	*Tyndale Bulletin*
WUNT	*Wissenschaftliche Untersuchungen zum Neuen Testament*
YCS	*Yale Classical Studies*
ZNW	*Zeitschrift für die neutestamentliche Wissenschaft*
ZPE	*Zeitschrift für Papyrologie und Epigraphik*

Index of Biblical References

Index of Ancient Sources

Index of Modern Authors

Index of Subjects

abortion, 225
adultery, 47-50, 127-29, 133, 228-30
anathema, 174-79. *See also* curses
Apollos, 2, 192
Argos, 4-5, 20; petition against Corinth, 19-20, 110, 274
angels (messengers), 136-37
associations, 74-75, 133-35, 137, 190, 288

baptism, 103-4
body. *See* senses
'brothers', 70-71, 158, 205

Cenchreae, 16, 201-2
Civil litigation, ch. 4. *See also* Roman civil law
Claudius, 38, 59, 218-21, 224, 273-74, 295-99, 307
clients, 88, 130, 135, 139, 185, 188-89, 192-93, 199, 203-4
Corinthian coins, 11
Corinthians' letter, 2
courtship, 245, 251-52. *See also* sexual impropriety
Criminal law, ch. 3. *See also* Roman criminal law
curses, xvi, 164; Anatolian, 172; Christian, 168-69; Coptic, 170-72; Corin-

thian, 164-65, 168-69, 173. *See also* anathema
divisions, 2-3, 68, 86, 159, 181, 183, 192-93, 198
divorce, 51
drunkenness, 82-83, 86, 92, 97-98, 100-101, 143, 150, 158, 228, 244

education, 33, 35; competition, 36-38, 40; disciples, 31-36, 40-43; elite, 81-82, 85, 106-8; fees, 36; oratory, 17-18; permissiveness, 81-82; pupils, 31, 34, 38-40; sophists, 32-33, 35-38, 77; teachers, 31; zealousness, 38-39
engagement. *See* courtship
enmity. *See* strife
eschatology (including overrealised), 25, 28, 96, 104-9, 225, 253, 257-60, 262-63, 268
eternity of the world, 253-55
ethics, ch. 5, 3-4, 20, 28, 76-77, 85, 105-9, 205; popular *(Vulgärethik)*, 76, 271
excommunication, 49, 55, 57
exile, 46, 49-50, 57

famines, xi, 6, 157, 196, 198, 216, 220-25, 232

Printed in the United States
82157LV00008B/49

9 780802 848987